ORACLE®

Oracle Press™

OCA Java® SE 8 Programmer I Exam Guide

(Exam 1Z0-808)

ORACLE®

Oracle Press™

OCA Java® SE 8 Programmer I Exam Guide

(Exam 1Z0-808)

Kathy Sierra
Bert Bates

Mc Graw Hill Education

New York Chicago San Francisco
Athens London Madrid Mexico City
Milan New Delhi Singapore Sydney Toronto

Cataloging-in-Publication Data is on file with the Library of Congress

OCA Java® SE 8 Programmer I Exam Guide (Exam 1Z0-808)

1 2 3 4 5 6 7 8 9 LCR 21 20 19 18 17

ISBN: Book p/n 978-1-260-01136-4 and CD p/n 978-1-260-01137-1
of set 978-1-260-01139-5

MHID: Book p/n 1-260-01136-4 and CD p/n 1-260-01137-2
of set 1-260-01139-9

Sponsoring Editor
Lisa McClain

Editorial Supervisor
Jody McKenzie

Project Editor
LeeAnn Pickrell

Acquisitions Coordinator
Claire Yee

Copy Editor
LeeAnn Pickrell

Proofreader
Lisa McCoy

Indexer
Ted Laux

Production Supervisor
James Kussow

Composition
Cenveo® Publisher Services

Illustration
Cenveo Publisher Services

Art Director, Cover
Jeff Weeks

CONTRIBUTORS

About the Authors

Kathy Sierra was a lead developer for the SCJP exam for Java 5 and Java 6. Kathy worked as a Sun "master trainer," and in 1997, founded JavaRanch.com (now named Coderanch.com), the world's largest Java community website. Her bestselling Java books have won multiple *Software Development Magazine* awards, and she is a founding member of Oracle's Java Champions program.

These days, Kathy is developing advanced training programs in a variety of domains (from horsemanship to computer programming), but the thread that ties all her projects together is helping learners reduce cognitive load.

Bert Bates was a lead developer for many of Sun's Java certification exams, including the SCJP for Java 5 and Java 6. Bert was also one of the lead developers for Oracle's OCA 7 and OCP 7 exams and a contributor on Oracle's OCA 8 and OCP 8 exams. He is a forum moderator on Coderanch.com (formerly JavaRanch.com) and has been developing software for more than 30 years (argh!). Bert is the co-author of several bestselling Java books, and he's a founding member of Oracle's Java Champions program. Now that the book is done, Bert plans to go whack a few tennis balls around and once again start riding his beautiful Icelandic horse, Eyrraros fra Gufudal-Fremri.

About the Technical Review Team

This is the fifth edition of the book that we've cooked up. The first version we worked on was for Java 2. Then we updated the book for the SCJP 5, again for the SCJP 6, again for the OCA 7 and OCP 7 exams, and now for the OCA 8. Every step of the way, we were unbelievably fortunate to have fantastic, JavaRanch.com-centric technical review teams at our sides. Over the course of the last 14 years, we've been "evolving" the book more than rewriting it. Many sections from our original work on the Java 2 book are still intact. On the following pages, we'd like to acknowledge the members of the various technical review teams who have saved our bacon over the years.

About the Java 2 Technical Review Team

Johannes de Jong has been the leader of our technical review teams forever and ever. (He has more patience than any three people we know.) For the Java 2 book, he led our biggest team ever. Our sincere thanks go out to the following volunteers who were knowledgeable, diligent, patient, and picky, picky, picky!

Rob Ross, Nicholas Cheung, Jane Griscti, Ilja Preuss, Vincent Brabant, Kudret Serin, Bill Seipel, Jing Yi, Ginu Jacob George, Radiya, LuAnn Mazza, Anshu Mishra, Anandhi Navaneethakrishnan, Didier Varon, Mary McCartney, Harsha Pherwani, Abhishek Misra, and Suman Das.

About the SCJP 5 Technical Review Team

Andrew

Bill M.

Burk

Devender

Gian

Jef

Jeoren

Jim

Johannes

Kristin

Marcelo

Marilyn

Mark

Mikalai

Seema

Valentin

We don't know who burned the most midnight oil, but we can (and did) count everybody's edits—so in order of most edits made, we proudly present our Superstars.

Our top honors go to **Kristin Stromberg**—every time you see a semicolon used correctly, tip your hat to Kristin. Next up is **Burk Hufnagel** who fixed more code than we care to admit. **Bill Mietelski** and **Gian Franco Casula** caught every kind of error we threw at them—awesome job, guys! **Devender Thareja** made sure we didn't use too much slang, and **Mark Spritzler** kept the humor coming. **Mikalai Zaikin** and **Seema Manivannan** made great catches every step of the way, and **Marilyn de Queiroz** and **Valentin Crettaz** both put in another stellar performance (saving our butts yet again).

Marcelo Ortega, **Jef Cumps** (another veteran), **Andrew Monkhouse**, and **Jeroen Sterken** rounded out our crew of Superstars—thanks to you all. **Jim Yingst** was a member of the Sun exam creation team, and he helped us write and review some of the twistier questions in the book (bwa-ha-ha-ha).

As always, every time you read a clean page, thank our reviewers, and if you do catch an error, it's most certainly because your authors messed up. And oh, one last thanks to **Johannes**. You rule, dude!

About the SCJP 6 Technical Review Team

Fred

Marc P.

Marc W.

Since the upgrade to the Java 6 exam was like a small surgical strike we decided that the technical review team for this update to the book needed to be similarly fashioned. To that end we hand-picked an elite crew of JavaRanch's top gurus to perform the review for the Java 6 exam.

Mikalai

Christophe

Our endless gratitude goes to **Mikalai Zaikin**. Mikalai played a huge role in the Java 5 book, and he returned to help us out again for this Java 6 edition. We need to thank Volha, Anastasia, and Daria for letting us borrow Mikalai. His comments and edits helped us make huge improvements to the book. Thanks, Mikalai!

Marc Peabody gets special kudos for helping us out on a double header! In addition to helping us with Sun's new SCWCD exam, Marc pitched in with a great set of edits for this book—you saved our bacon this winter, Marc! (BTW, we didn't learn until late in the game that Marc, Bryan Basham, and Bert all share a passion for ultimate Frisbee!)

Like several of our reviewers, not only does **Fred Rosenberger** volunteer copious amounts of his time moderating at JavaRanch, he also found time to help us out with this book. Stacey and Olivia, you have our thanks for loaning us Fred for a while.

Marc Weber moderates at some of JavaRanch's busiest forums. Marc knows his stuff and uncovered some really sneaky problems that were buried in the book. While we really appreciate Marc's help, we need to warn you all to watch out—he's got a Phaser!

Finally, we send our thanks to **Christophe Verre**—if we can find him. It appears that Christophe performs his JavaRanch moderation duties from various locations around the globe, including France, Wales, and most recently Tokyo. On more than one occasion Christophe protected us from our own lack of organization. Thanks for your patience, Christophe! It's important to know that these guys all donated their reviewer honorariums to JavaRanch! The JavaRanch community is in your debt.

The OCA 7 and OCP 7 Team

Contributing Authors

Tom

Jeanne

The OCA 7 exam is primarily a useful repackaging of some of the objectives from the SCJP 6 exam. On the other hand, the OCP 7 exam introduced a vast array of brand-new topics. We enlisted several talented Java gurus to help us cover some of the new topics on the OCP 7 exam. Thanks and kudos to **Tom McGinn** for his fantastic work in creating the massive JDBC chapter. Several reviewers told us that Tom did an amazing job channeling the informal tone we use throughout the book. Next, thanks to **Jeanne Boyarsky**. Jeanne was truly a renaissance woman on this project. She contributed to several OCP chapters; she wrote some questions for the master exams; she performed some project management activities; and as if that wasn't enough, she was one of our most energetic technical reviewers. Jeanne, we can't thank you enough. Our thanks go to **Matt Heimer** for his excellent work on the Concurrent chapter. A really tough topic nicely handled! Finally, **Roel De Nijs** and **Roberto Perillo** made some nice contributions to the book *and* helped out on the technical review team—thanks, guys!

Technical Review Team

Roel

Mikalai

Vijitha

Roberto

Roel, what can we say? Your work as a technical reviewer is unparalleled. Roel caught so many technical errors, it made our heads spin. Between the printed book and all the material on the CD, we estimate that there are over 1,500 pages of "stuff" here. It's huge! Roel grinded through page after page, never lost his focus, and made this book better in countless ways. Thank you, Roel!

In addition to her other contributions, **Jeanne** provided one of the most thorough technical reviews we received. (We think she enlisted her team of killer robots to help her!)

It seems like no K&B book would be complete without help from our old friend **Mikalai Zaikin**. Somehow, between earning 812 different Java certifications, being a husband and father (thanks to **Volha**, **Anastasia**, **Daria**, and **Ivan**), and being a "theoretical fisherman" [sic], Mikalai made substantial contributions to the quality of the book; we're honored that you helped us again, Mikalai.

Next up, we'd like to thank **Vijitha Kumara**, JavaRanch moderator and tech reviewer extraordinaire. We had many reviewers help out during the long course of writing this book, but Vijitha was one of the few who stuck with us from Chapter 1 all the way through the master exams and on to Chapter 15. Vijitha, thank you for your help and persistence!

Finally, thanks to the rest of our review team: **Roberto Perillo** (who also wrote some killer exam questions), **Jim Yingst** (was this your fourth time?), other repeat offenders: **Fred Rosenberger**, **Christophe Verre**, **Devaka Cooray**, **Marc Peabody**, and newcomer **Amit Ghorpade**—thanks, guys!

About the OCA 8 Technical Review Team

Campbell

Fritz

Paweł

Vijitha

Tim

Roberto

Due to "pilot error" on your authors' part, the members of the review team for this book were asked to work under a tighter-than-ideal schedule. We owe a huge thanks to our six reviewers for this book, who leapt to action on short notice and once again made numerous fine contributions to the quality of the book. As has become "the norm," all our reviewers are moderators at the finest Java community website in the whole universe, Coderanch.com.

Our first mention goes to **Campbell Ritchie**, long-time Coderanch moderator, hiker of steep hills, and, by our count, most prolific reviewer for this edition. In other words, Campbell found the most errors. Among other pursuits, Campbell is an expert in both pathology and programming, because...why not? Every time you read an error-free page, think of Campbell and thank him.

In a virtual tie for second place in the "errors found" competition, we present **Paweł Baczyński** and **Fritz Walraven**. Paweł calls Poland his home and is most proud of his wife, Ania, and kids, Szymek and Gabrysia. He is almost as proud of the fact that we have to use a special keyboard to spell his name correctly!

Fritz hails from the Netherlands, and if we understand correctly, cheers his kids as they demonstrate their athletic prowess in various sports venues around Amersfoort. Fritz has also volunteered at an orphanage in Uganda (we hope he teaches those kids Java!). Fritz, if we ever meet in person, Bert hereby challenges you to a table tennis match.

We'd like to give a special shout out to Fritz and Pawel for sticking with us from Chapter 1 all the way through to the second practice exam. It was a marathon, and we thank you both.

Next, we'd like to thank returning reviewer **Vijitha Kumara**. That's right, he's helped us before and yet he volunteered again—wow! When Vijitha isn't traveling or hiking, he enjoys what he refers to as "crazy experiments." We love you, Vijitha—don't blow yourself up!

Tim Cooke was there when we needed him, at the beginning of the process and again to help us wrap things up. We like Tim even though he's been known to spend time with nefarious "functional programmers." (We suspect that's where he was when he went missing for a few of the middle-of-the-book chapters.) Tim lives in Ireland and started programming at an early age on an Amstrad CPC 464. Nice!

Finally, a special thanks to another veteran of the technical review team, **Roberto Perillo**. Thanks for coming back to help us again Roberto. Roberto is a family man who loves spending time with his son, Lorenzo. Once Lorenzo has gone to bed, Roberto is known to play a bit of guitar or cheer for the Sao Paulo "Futebol Clube" (we think this is a soccer team).

You guys are all awesome. Thanks for your wonderful assistance.

For Andi

For Bob

CONTENTS AT A GLANCE

CONTENTS

ACKNOWLEDGMENTS

Kathy and Bert would like to thank the following people:

- All the incredibly hard-working folks at McGraw-Hill Education: Tim Green (who's been putting up with us for 14 years now), Lisa McClain, and LeeAnn Pickrell. Thanks for all your help and for being so responsive, patient, flexible, and professional, and the nicest group of people we could hope to work with.
- All our friends at Kraftur (and our other horse-related friends) and, most especially, to Sherry, Steinar, Stina and the girls, Kacie, DJ, Jec, Leslie and David, Annette and Bruce, Lucy, Cait, and Jennifer, Gabrielle, and Mary. Thanks to Pedro and Ely.
- Some of the software professionals and friends who helped us in the early days: Tom Bender, Peter Loerincs, Craig Matthews, Leonard Coyne, Morgan Porter, and Mike Kavenaugh.
- Dave Gustafson for his continued support, insights, and coaching.
- Our wonderful contact and friend at Oracle, Yvonne Prefontaine.
- Our great friends and gurus: Simon Roberts, Bryan Basham, and Kathy Collina.
- Stu, Steve, Burt, and Marc Hedlund for injecting some fun into the process.
- To Eden and Skyler, for being horrified that adults—out of school—would study this hard for an exam.
- To the Coderanch Trail Boss, Paul Wheaton, for running the best Java community site on the Web, and to all the generous and patient JavaRanch, er, Coderanch moderators.

- To all the past and present Java instructors for helping to make learning Java a fun experience, including (to name only a few) Alan Petersen, Jean Tordella, Georgianna Meagher, Anthony Orapallo, Jacqueline Jones, James Cubeta, Teri Cubeta, Rob Weingruber, John Nyquist, Asok Perumainar, Steve Stelting, Kimberly Bobrow, Keith Ratliff, and the most caring and inspiring Java guy on the planet, Jari Paukku.
- Our furry and feathered friends: Eyra, Kara, Draumur, Vafi, Boi, Niki, and Bokeh.
- Finally, to Eric Freeman and Beth Robson for your continued inspiration.

PREFACE

This book's primary objective is to help you prepare for and pass Oracle's OCA Java SE 8 Programmer I certification exam.

This book follows closely both the breadth and the depth of the real exams. For instance, after reading this book, you probably won't emerge as an OO guru, but if you study the material and do well on the Self Tests, you'll have a basic understanding of OO, and you'll do well on the exam. After completing this book, you should feel confident that you have thoroughly reviewed all the objectives that Oracle has established for these exams.

In This Book

This book is organized into six chapters to optimize your learning of the topics covered by the OCA 8 exam. Whenever possible, we've organized the chapters to parallel the Oracle objectives, but sometimes we'll mix up objectives or partially repeat them to present topics in an order better suited to learning the material.

In Every Chapter

We've created a set of chapter components that call your attention to important items, reinforce important points, and provide helpful exam-taking hints. Take a look at what you'll find in every chapter:

- Every chapter begins with the **Certification Objectives**—what you need to know in order to pass the section on the exam dealing with the chapter topic. The Certification Objective headings identify the objectives within the chapter, so you'll always know an objective when you see it!

exam watch

***Exam Watch** notes call attention to information about, and potential pitfalls in, the exam. Because we were on the team that created these exams, we know what you're about to go through!*

- **On the Job** callouts discuss practical aspects of certification topics that might not occur on the exam, but that will be useful in the real world.
- **Exercises** are interspersed throughout the chapters. They help you master skills that are likely to be an area of focus on the exam. Don't just read through the exercises; they are hands-on practice that you should be comfortable completing. Learning by doing is an effective way to increase your competency with a product.
- **From the Classroom** sidebars describe the issues that come up most often in the training classroom setting. These sidebars give you a valuable perspective into certification- and product-related topics. They point out common mistakes and address questions that have arisen from classroom discussions.
- The **Certification Summary** is a succinct review of the chapter and a restatement of salient points regarding the exam.
- The **Two-Minute Drill** at the end of every chapter is a checklist of the main points of the chapter. It can be used for last-minute review.
- The **Self Test** offers questions similar to those found on the certification exam, including multiple choice and pseudo drag-and-drop questions. The answers to these questions, as well as explanations of the answers, can be found at the end of every chapter. By taking the Self Test after completing each chapter, you'll reinforce what you've learned from that chapter, while becoming familiar with the structure of the exam questions.

INTRODUCTION

Organization

This book is organized in such a way as to serve as an in-depth review for the OCA 8 exam, for both experienced Java professionals and those in the early stages of experience with Java technologies. Each chapter covers at least one major aspect of the exam, with an emphasis on the "why" as well as the "how to" of programming in the Java language.

The CD-ROM contains practice exam software with two 80-question exams and a secured PDF version of the book.

What This Book Is Not

You will not find a beginner's guide to learning Java in this book. All 500+ pages of this book are dedicated solely to helping you pass the exam. If you are brand new to Java, we suggest you spend a little time learning the basics. You should not start with this book until you know how to write, compile, and run simple Java programs. We do not, however, assume any level of prior knowledge of the individual topics covered. In other words, for any given topic (driven exclusively by the actual exam objectives), we start with the assumption that you are new to that topic. So we assume you're new to the individual topics, but we assume that you are not new to Java.

We also do not pretend to be both preparing you for the exam and simultaneously making you a complete Java being. This is a certification exam study guide, and it's very clear about its mission. That's not to say that preparing for the exam won't help you become a better Java programmer! On the contrary, even the most experienced Java developers often claim that having to prepare for the certification exam made them far more knowledgeable and well-rounded programmers than they would have been without the exam-driven studying.

On the CD-ROM

For more information on the CD-ROM, please see the Appendix.

Some Pointers

Once you've finished reading this book, set aside some time to do a thorough review. You might want to return to the book several times and make use of all the methods it offers for reviewing the material:

1. *Re-read all the Two-Minute Drills, or have someone quiz you.* You also can use the drills as a way to do a quick cram before the exam. You might want to make some flash cards out of 3 × 5 index cards that have the Two-Minute Drill material on them.
2. *Re-read all the Exam Watch notes.* Remember that these notes are written by authors who helped create the exam. They know what you should expect—and what you should be on the lookout for.
3. *Re-take the Self Tests.* Taking the tests right after you've read the chapter is a good idea because the questions help reinforce what you've just learned. However, it's an even better idea to go back later and do all the questions in the book in one sitting. Pretend that you're taking the live exam. (Whenever you take the Self Tests, mark your answers on a separate piece of paper. That way, you can run through the questions as many times as you need to until you feel comfortable with the material.)
4. *Complete the exercises.* The exercises are designed to cover exam topics, and there's no better way to get to know this material than by practicing. Be sure you understand why you are performing each step in each exercise. If there is something you are not clear on, re-read that section in the chapter.
5. *Write lots of Java code.* We'll repeat this advice several times. When we wrote this book, we wrote hundreds of small Java programs to help us do our research. We have heard from hundreds of candidates who have passed the exam, and in almost every case, the candidates who scored extremely well on the exam wrote lots of code during their studies. Experiment with the code samples in the book, create horrendous lists of compiler errors—put away your IDE, crank up the command line, and write code!

Introduction to the Material in the Book

The OCA 8 exam is considered one of the hardest in the IT industry, and we can tell you from experience that a large chunk of exam candidates goes in to the test unprepared. As programmers, we tend to learn only what we need to complete our current project, given the insane deadlines we're usually under.

But this exam attempts to prove your complete understanding of the Java language, not just the parts of it you've become familiar with in your work.

Experience alone will rarely get you through this exam with a passing mark, because even the things you think you know might work just a little differently than you imagined. It isn't enough to be able to get your code to work correctly; you must understand the core fundamentals in a deep way, and with enough breadth to cover virtually anything that could crop up in the course of using the language.

Who Cares About Certification?

Employers do. Headhunters do. Programmers do. Passing this exam proves three important things to a current or prospective employer: you're smart; you know how to study and prepare for a challenging test; and, most of all, you know the Java language. If an employer has a choice between a candidate who has passed the exam and one who hasn't, the employer knows that the certified programmer does not have to take time to learn the Java language.

But does it mean that you can actually develop software in Java? Not necessarily, but it's a good head start. To really demonstrate your ability to develop (as opposed to just your knowledge of the language), you should consider pursuing the Java Developer Exam, where you're given an assignment to build a program, start to finish, and submit it for an assessor to evaluate and score.

Taking the Programmer's Exam

In a perfect world, you would be assessed for your true knowledge of a subject, not simply how you respond to a series of test questions. But life isn't perfect, and it just isn't practical to evaluate everyone's knowledge on a one-to-one basis.

For most of its certifications, Oracle evaluates candidates using a computer-based testing service operated by Pearson VUE. To discourage simple memorization, Oracle exams present a potentially different set of questions to different candidates. In the development of the exam, hundreds of questions are compiled and refined using beta testers. From this large collection, questions are pulled together from each objective and assembled into many different versions of the exam.

Each Oracle exam has a specific number of questions, and the test's duration is designed to be generous. The time remaining is always displayed in the corner of the testing screen. If time expires during an exam, the test terminates, and incomplete answers are counted as incorrect.

exam watch

Many experienced test-takers do not go back and change answers unless they have a good reason to do so. Only change an answer when you feel you may have misread or misinterpreted the question the first time. Nervousness may make you second-guess every answer and talk yourself out of a correct one.

After completing the exam, you will receive an e-mail from Oracle telling you that your results are available on the Web. As of winter 2017, your results can be found at certview.oracle.com. If you want a printed copy of your certificate, you must make a specific request.

Question Format

Oracle's Java exams pose questions in multiple-choice format.

Multiple-Choice Questions

In earlier versions of the exam, when you encountered a multiple-choice question, you were not told how many answers were correct; but with each version of the exam, the questions have become more difficult, so today, each multiple-choice question tells you how many answers to choose. The Self Test questions at the end of each chapter closely match the format, wording, and difficulty of the real exam questions, with two exceptions:

- Whenever we can, our questions will *not* tell you how many correct answers exist (we will say "Choose all that apply"). We do this to help you master the material. Some savvy test-takers can eliminate wrong answers when the number of correct answers is known. It's also possible, if you know how many answers are correct, to choose the most plausible answers. Our job is to toughen you up for the real exam!
- The real exam typically numbers lines of code in a question. Sometimes we do not number lines of code—mostly so that we have the space to add comments at key places. On the real exam, when a code listing starts with line 1, it means that you're looking at an entire source file. If a code listing starts at a line number greater than 1, that means you're looking at a partial source file. When looking at a partial source file, assume the code you can't see is correct. (For instance, unless explicitly stated, you can assume that a partial source file will have the correct import and package statements.)

exam watch

When you find yourself stumped answering multiple-choice questions, use your scratch paper (or whiteboard) to write down the two or three answers you consider the strongest, then underline the answer you feel is most likely correct. Here is an example of what your scratch paper might look like when you've gone through the test once:

- 21. <u>B</u> or C
- 33. A or <u>C</u>

This is extremely helpful when you mark the question and continue on. You can then return to the question and immediately pick up your thought process where you left off. Use this technique to avoid having to re-read and rethink questions. You will also need to use your scratch paper during complex, text-based scenario questions to create visual images to better understand the question. This technique is especially helpful if you are a visual learner.

Tips on Taking the Exam

The number of questions and passing percentages for every exam are subject to change. Always check with Oracle before taking the exam, at www.Oracle.com.

You are allowed to answer questions in any order, and you can go back and check your answers after you've gone through the test. There are no penalties for wrong answers, so it's better to at least attempt an answer than to not give one at all.

A good strategy for taking the exam is to go through once and answer all the questions that come to you quickly. You can then go back and do the others. Answering one question might jog your memory for how to answer a previous one.

Be very careful on the code examples. Check for syntax errors first: count curly braces, semicolons, and parentheses, and then make sure there are as many left ones as right ones. Look for capitalization errors and other such syntax problems before trying to figure out what the code does.

Many of the questions on the exam will hinge on subtleties of syntax. You will need to have a thorough knowledge of the Java language in order to succeed.

This brings us to another issue that some candidates have reported. The testing center is supposed to provide you with sufficient writing implements so you can work problems out "on paper." In some cases, the centers have provided inadequate markers and dry-erase boards that are too small and cumbersome to use effectively. We recommend that you call ahead and verify that you will be supplied with a sufficiently large whiteboard, sufficiently fine-tipped markers, and a good eraser. What we'd really like to encourage is for everyone to complain to Oracle and Pearson VUE and have them provide actual pencils and at least several sheets of blank paper.

Tips on Studying for the Exam

First and foremost, give yourself plenty of time to study. Java is a complex programming language, and you can't expect to cram what you need to know into a single study session. It is a field best learned over time, by studying a subject and then applying your knowledge. Build yourself a study schedule and stick to it, but be reasonable about the pressure you put on yourself, especially if you're studying in addition to your regular duties at work.

One easy technique to use in studying for certification exams is the 15-minutes-per-day effort. Simply study for a minimum of 15 minutes every day. It is a small but significant commitment. If you have a day where you just can't focus, then give up at 15 minutes. If you have a day where it flows completely for you, study longer. As long as you have more of the "flow days," your chances of succeeding are excellent.

We strongly recommend you use flash cards when preparing for the programmer's exams. A flash card is simply a 3 × 5 or 4 × 6 index card with a question on the front and the answer on the back. You construct these cards yourself as you go through a chapter, capturing any topic you think might need more memorization or practice time. You can drill yourself with them by reading the question, thinking through the answer, and then turning the card over to see if you're correct. Or you can get another person to help you by holding up the card with the question facing you and then verifying your answer. Most of our students have found these to be tremendously helpful, especially because they're so portable that while you're in study mode, you can take them everywhere. Best not to use them while driving, though, except at red lights. We've taken ours everywhere—the doctor's office, restaurants, theaters, you name it.

Certification study groups are another excellent resource, and you won't find a larger or more willing community than on the Coderanch.com Big Moose Saloon certification forums. If you have a question from this book, or any other mock exam question you may have stumbled upon, posting a question in a certification forum will get you an answer in nearly all cases within a day—usually, within a few hours.

Finally, we recommend that you write a lot of little Java programs! During the course of writing this book, we wrote hundreds of small programs, and if you listen to what the most successful candidates say (you know, those guys who got 98 percent), they almost always report that they wrote a lot of code.

Scheduling Your Exam

You can purchase your exam voucher from either Oracle or Pearson VUE. Visit Oracle.com (follow the training/certification links) or visit PearsonVue.com for exam scheduling details and locations of test centers.

Arriving at the Exam

As with any test, you'll be tempted to cram the night before. Resist that temptation. You should know the material by this point, and if you're groggy in the morning, you won't remember what you studied anyway. Get a good night's sleep.

Arrive early for your exam; it gives you time to relax and review key facts. Take the opportunity to review your notes. If you get burned out on studying, you can usually start your exam a few minutes early. We don't recommend arriving late. Your test could be cancelled, or you might not have enough time to complete the exam.

When you arrive at the testing center, you'll need to provide current, valid photo identification. Visit PearsonVue.com for details on the ID requirements. They just want to be sure that you don't send your brilliant Java guru next-door neighbor who you've paid to take the exam for you.

Aside from a brain full of facts, you don't need to bring anything else to the exam room. In fact, your brain is about all you're allowed to take into the exam!

All the tests are closed book, meaning you don't get to bring any reference materials with you. You're also not allowed to take any notes out of the exam room. The test administrator will provide you with a small marker board. If you're allowed to, we do recommend that you bring a water bottle or a juice bottle (call ahead for details of what's allowed). These exams are long and hard, and your brain functions much better when it's well hydrated. In terms of hydration, the ideal approach is to take frequent, small sips. You should also verify how many "bio-breaks" you'll be allowed to take during the exam!

Leave your phone in the car. It will only add stress to the situation, since they are not allowed in the exam room, and can sometimes still be heard if they ring outside of the room. Purses, books, and other materials must be left with the administrator before entering the exam.

Once in the testing room, you'll be briefed on the exam software. You might be asked to complete a survey. The time you spend on the survey is *not* deducted from your actual test time—nor do you get more time if you fill out the survey quickly. Also, remember the questions you get on the exam will *not* change depending on how you answer the survey questions. Once you're done with the survey, the real clock starts ticking and the fun begins.

The testing software allows you to move forward and backward between questions. Most important, there is a Mark check box on the screen—this will prove to be a critical tool, as explained in the next section.

Test-Taking Techniques

Without a plan of attack, candidates can become overwhelmed by the exam or become sidetracked and run out of time. For the most part, if you are comfortable with the material, the allotted time is more than enough to complete the exam. The trick is to keep the time from slipping away during any one particular problem.

Your obvious goal is to answer the questions correctly and quickly, but other factors can distract you. Here are some tips for taking the exam more efficiently.

Size Up the Challenge

First, take a quick pass through all the questions in the exam. "Cherry-pick" the easy questions, answering them on the spot. Briefly read each question, noticing the type of question and the subject. As a guideline, try to spend less than 25 percent of your testing time in this pass.

This step lets you assess the scope and complexity of the exam, and it helps you determine how to pace your time. It also gives you an idea of where to find potential answers to some of the questions. Sometimes the wording of one question might lend clues or jog your thoughts for another question.

If you're not entirely confident in your answer to a question, answer it anyway, but check the Mark box to flag it for later review. In the event you run out of time, at least you've provided a "first guess" answer, rather than leaving it blank.

Second, go back through the entire test, using the insight you gained from the first go-through. For example, if the entire test looks difficult, you'll know better than to spend more than a minute or two on each question. Create a pacing with small milestones—for example, "I need to answer 10 questions every 15 minutes."

At this stage, it's probably a good idea to skip past the time-consuming questions, marking them for the next pass. Try to finish this phase before you're 50 to 60 percent through the testing time.

Third, go back through all the questions you marked for review, using the Review Marked button in the question review screen. This step includes taking a second look at all the questions you were unsure of in previous passes, as well as tackling the time-consuming ones you deferred until now. Chisel away at this group of questions until you've answered them all.

If you're more comfortable with a previously marked question, unmark the Review Marked button now. Otherwise, leave it marked. Work your way through the time-consuming questions now, especially those requiring manual calculations. Unmark them when you're satisfied with the answer.

By the end of this step, you've answered every question in the test, despite having reservations about some of your answers. If you run out of time in the next step, at least you won't lose points for lack of an answer. You're in great shape if you still have 10 to 20 percent of your time remaining.

Review Your Answers

Now you're cruising! You've answered all the questions, and you're ready to do a quality check. Take yet another pass (yes, one more) through the entire test, briefly re-reading each question and your answer.

Carefully look over the questions again to check for "trick" questions. Be particularly wary of those that include a choice of "Does not compile." Be alert for last-minute clues. You're pretty familiar with nearly every question at this point, and you may find a few clues that you missed before.

The Grand Finale

When you're confident with all your answers, finish the exam by submitting it for grading. After you finish your exam, you'll receive an e-mail from Oracle giving you a link to a page where your exam results will be available. As of this writing, you must ask for a hard copy certificate specifically or one will not be sent to you.

Retesting

If you don't pass the exam, don't be discouraged. Try to have a good attitude about the experience, and get ready to try again. Consider yourself a little more educated. You'll know the format of the test a little better, and you'll have a good idea of the difficulty level of the questions you'll get next time around.

If you bounce back quickly, you'll probably remember several of the questions you might have missed. This will help you focus your study efforts in the right area.

Ultimately, remember that Oracle certifications are valuable because they're hard to get. After all, if anyone could get one, what value would it have? In the end, it takes a good attitude and a lot of studying, but you can do it!

Objectives Map

The following table describes the exam objectives and where you will find coverage for them in the book. (Note: We have summarized some of the descriptions you will find on the Oracle.com website.)

Oracle Certified Associate Java SE 8 Programmer (Exam 1Z0-808)

Exam Objective	Study Guide Coverage
Java Basics	
Define the scope of variables (1.1)	Chapter 3
Define the structure of a Java class (1.2)	Chapters 1 and 2
Create executable Java applications with a main method (1.3)	Chapter 1
Import other Java packages to make them accessible in your code (1.4)	Chapter 1
Compare and contrast features of Java (1.5)	Chapter 1
Working with Java Data Types	
Declare and initialize variables (2.1)	Chapters 1 and 3
Differentiate between object reference variables and primitive variables (2.2)	Chapters 1, 2, and 3
Know how to read or write to object fields (2.3)	Whole book
Explain an object's lifecycle (creation, "dereference," and garbage collection) (2.4)	Chapter 3
Use wrapper classes such as Boolean, Double, Integer (2.5)	Chapter 6
Using Operators and Decision Constructs	
Use Java operators (3.1)	Chapters 1 and 4
Test equality between Strings and other objects using == and equals() (3.2)	Chapters 1 and 4
Create if and if/else and ternary constructs (3.4)	Chapters 4 and 5
Use a switch statement (3.5)	Chapter 5
Creating and Using Arrays	
Declare, instantiate, initialize and use a one-dimensional array (4.1)	Chapters 3 and 6
Declare, instantiate, initialize and use multi-dimensional arrays (4.2)	Chapters 3 and 6
Using Loop Constructs	
Create and use while loops (5.1)	Chapter 5
Create and use for loops including the enhanced for loop (5.2)	Chapter 5
Create and use do/while loops (5.3)	Chapter 5
Compare loop constructs (5.4)	Chapter 5
Use break and continue (5.5)	Chapter 5

Exam Objective	Study Guide Coverage
Working with Methods and Encapsulation	
Create methods with arguments and return values (6.1)	Chapter 2
Apply the static keyword to methods and fields (6.2)	Chapters 1 and 2
Create and overload constructors (6.3)	Chapters 1 and 2
Apply access modifiers (6.4)	Chapter 1
Apply encapsulation principles to a class (6.5)	Chapters 2 and 6
Determine the effect upon object references and primitive values when they are passed into methods that change the values (6.6)	Chapter 3
Working with Inheritance	
Describe inheritance and its benefits (7.1)	Chapter 2
Develop code that demonstrates the use of polymorphism (7.2)	Chapter 2
Determine when casting is necessary (7.3)	Chapter 2
Use super and this to access objects and constructors (7.4)	Chapter 2
Use abstract classes and interfaces (7.5)	Chapters 1 and 2
Handling Exceptions	
Differentiate among checked exceptions, RuntimeExceptions, and Errors (8.1)	Chapter 5
Create a try-catch block and determine how exceptions alter normal program flow (8.2)	Chapter 5
Describe the advantages of Exception handling (8.3)	Chapter 5
Create and invoke a method that throws an exception (8.4)	Chapter 5
Recognize common exception classes (8.5)	Chapter 5
Working with Selected Classes from the Java API	
Manipulate data using the StringBuilder class (9.1)	Chapter 6
Create and manipulate Strings (9.2)	Chapter 6
Create and manipulate calendar data (9.3)	Chapter 6
Declare and use an ArrayList (9.4)	Chapter 6
Write a simple Lambda expression that consumes a Lambda Predicate expression (9.5)	Chapter 6

1 Declarations and Access Control

CERTIFICATION OBJECTIVES

- Java Features and Benefits
- Identifiers and Keywords
- javac, java, main(), and Imports
- Declare Classes and Interfaces
- Declare Class Members
- Declare Constructors and Arrays
- Create static Class Members
- Use enums

✓ Two-Minute Drill

Q&A Self Test

We assume that because you're planning on becoming certified, you already know the basics of Java. If you're completely new to the language, this chapter—and the rest of the book—will be confusing; so be sure you know at least the basics of the language before diving into this book. That said, we're starting with a brief, high-level refresher to put you back in the Java mood, in case you've been away for a while.

Java Refresher

A Java program is mostly a collection of *objects* talking to other objects by invoking each other's *methods*. Every object is of a certain *type*, and that type is defined by a *class* or an *interface*. Most Java programs use a collection of objects of many different types. Following is a list of a few useful terms for this object-oriented (OO) language:

- **Class** A template that describes the kinds of state and behavior that objects of its type support.
- **Object** At runtime, when the Java Virtual Machine (JVM) encounters the `new` keyword, it will use the appropriate class to make an object that is an instance of that class. That object will have its own *state* and access to all of the behaviors defined by its class.
- **State (instance variables)** Each object (instance of a class) will have its own unique set of instance variables as defined in the class. Collectively, the values assigned to an object's instance variables make up the object's *state.*
- **Behavior (methods)** When a programmer creates a class, she creates methods for that class. Methods are where the class's logic is stored and where the real work gets done. They are where algorithms get executed and data gets manipulated.

Identifiers and Keywords

All the Java components we just talked about—classes, variables, and methods—need names. In Java, these names are called *identifiers*, and, as you might expect, there are rules for what constitutes a legal Java identifier. Beyond what's *legal*, though, Java (and Oracle) programmers have created *conventions* for naming methods, variables, and classes.

Like all programming languages, Java has a set of built-in *keywords.* These keywords must *not* be used as identifiers. Later in this chapter we'll review the details of these naming rules, conventions, and the Java keywords.

Inheritance

Central to Java and other OO languages is the concept of *inheritance*, which allows code defined in one class or interface to be reused in other classes. In Java, you can define a general (more abstract) *superclass* and then extend it with more specific *subclasses*. The superclass knows nothing of the classes that inherit from it, but all of the subclasses that inherit from the superclass must explicitly declare the inheritance relationship. A subclass that inherits from a superclass is automatically given accessible instance variables and methods defined by the superclass, but the subclass is also free to *override* superclass methods to define more specific behavior. For example, a `Car` *super*class could define general methods common to all automobiles, but a `Ferrari` *sub*class could override the `accelerate()` method that was already defined in the `Car` class.

Interfaces

A powerful companion to inheritance is the use of interfaces. Interfaces are *usually* like a 100 percent abstract superclass that defines the methods a subclass must support, but not *how* they must be supported. In other words, for example, an `Animal` interface might declare that all `Animal` implementation classes have an `eat()` method, but the `Animal` interface doesn't supply any logic for the `eat()` method. That means it's up to the classes that implement the `Animal` interface to define the actual code for how that particular `Animal` type behaves when its `eat()` method is invoked. Note: As of Java 8, interfaces can now include concrete, inheritable methods. We will talk much more about this when we dive into OO in the next chapter.

CERTIFICATION OBJECTIVE

Features and Benefits of Java (OCA Objective 1.5)

1.5 Compare and contrast the features and components of Java such as: platform independence, object orientation, encapsulation, etc.

Perhaps a great topic to start with, on our official coverage of the OCA 8, is to discuss the various benefits that Java provides to programmers. Java is now over 20 years old (wow!) and remains one of the most in-demand programming languages in the world. Somewhat confusingly there is a similarly named language, "JavaScript" (an implementation of the ECMA standard), which is also a very popular language. Java and JavaScript have some aspects in common, but they are not to be confused; they are quite distinct. Let's look at some of the benefits that Java provides to programmers and compare them (when appropriate) to some of Java's competitors. A caveat here, many of these benefits are based on extremely complex topics. These descriptions are by no means definitive, but they're sufficient for the exam:

- **Object oriented** As software systems get larger, they get more difficult to test and enhance. For the last several decades, object-oriented (OO) programming has been the dominant software design approach for large systems, because well-designed OO systems remain testable and enhanceable, even as they grow into huge applications with millions of lines of code. OO design also offers a natural way to think about how the components in a system should be constructed and how they should interact. The classes, objects, system state, and behaviors in well-designed OO systems are easy to map conceptually to their counterparts in the real world.
- **Encapsulation** Encapsulation is a key concept in OO programming. Encapsulation allows a software component to hide its data from other components, protecting the data from being updated without the component's approval or knowledge. Java makes encapsulation far easier to achieve than in non-OO languages.
- **Memory management** Unlike some of its competitors (C and C++), Java provides automatic memory management. In languages that don't provide automatic memory management, keeping track of memory through pointers is quite complex. Further, tracking down bugs related to memory management (often called *memory leaks*) is a common, error-prone, and time-consuming process.
- **Huge library** Java has an enormous library of prewritten, well-tested, and well-supported code. This code is easy to include in your Java applications and is well documented via the Java API. Throughout this book we will explore some of the most used (and most useful) members of Java's standard core library.

- **Secure by design** When compiled Java code is executed, it runs inside the Java Virtual Machine (JVM). The JVM provides a secure "sandbox" for your Java code to run in, and the JVM makes sure that nefarious programmers cannot write Java code that will cause trouble on other people's machines when it runs.
- **Write once, run anywhere (cross-platform execution)** One of the goals (largely, but not perfectly achieved) of Java is that much of the Java code you write can run on many platforms, ranging from tiny Internet-of-Things (IoT) devices, to phones, to laptop computers, to large servers. Another common phrase for this ability to run on many devices is *cross-platform*.
- **Strongly typed** A strongly typed language usually requires the programmer to explicitly declare the types of the data and objects being used in the program. Strong typing allows the Java compiler to catch many potential programming errors before your code even compiles. At the other end of the spectrum are dynamically typed languages. Dynamically typed languages can be less verbose, faster to code initially, and are often preferred in environments where small teams and rapid prototyping are the norm. But strongly typed languages like Java come into their own in large software shops with many teams of programmers and the need for more reliable, testable, production-quality code.
- **Multithreaded** Java provides built-in language features and APIs that allow programs to use many operating-system processes (hence, many "cores") at the same time. As systems grow to handle more computationally intensive problems and larger data sets, the ability to use all of a computer's core processors becomes essential. Multithreaded programming is never simple, but Java provides a rich toolkit to make it as easy as possible.
- **Distributed computing** Another way to tackle big programming problems is to distribute the workload across many machines. The Java API provides several ways to simplify tasks related to distributed computing. One such example is *serialization*, a process in which a Java object is converted to a portable form. Serialized objects can be sent to other machines, deserialized, and then used as a normal Java object.

Again, we've just scratched the surface of these complex topics, but if you understand these brief descriptions, you should be prepared to handle any questions for this objective. So much for the theory, let's get into details...

CERTIFICATION OBJECTIVE

Identifiers and Keywords (OCA Objectives 1.2 and 2.1)

1.2 Define the structure of a Java class.
2.1 Declare and initialize variables (including casting of primitive data types).

Remember that when we list one or more Certification Objectives in the book, as we just did, it means that the following section covers at least some part of that objective. Some objectives will be covered in several different chapters, so you'll see the same objective in more than one place in the book. For example, this section covers declarations and identifiers, but *using* the things you declare is covered primarily in later chapters.

So, we'll start with Java identifiers. The two aspects of Java identifiers that we cover here are

- **Legal identifiers** The rules the compiler uses to determine whether a name is legal.
- **Oracle's Java Code Conventions** Oracle's recommendations for naming classes, variables, and methods. We typically adhere to these standards throughout the book, except when we're trying to show you how a tricky exam question might be coded. You won't be asked questions about the Java Code Conventions, but we strongly recommend you use them.

Legal Identifiers

Technically, legal identifiers must be composed of only Unicode characters, numbers, currency symbols, and connecting characters (such as underscores). The exam doesn't dive into the details of which ranges of the Unicode character set qualify as letters and digits. So, for example, you won't need to know that Tibetan digits range from `\u0420` to `\u0f29`. Here are the rules you *do* need to know:

- Identifiers must start with a letter, a currency character (`$`), or a connecting character such as the underscore (_). Identifiers cannot start with a digit!
- After the first character, identifiers can contain any combination of letters, currency characters, connecting characters, or numbers.

- In practice, there is no limit to the number of characters an identifier can contain.
- You can't use a Java keyword as an identifier. Table 1-1 lists all the Java keywords.
- Identifiers in Java are case sensitive; `foo` and `FOO` are two different identifiers.

Examples of legal and illegal identifiers follow. First some legal identifiers:

```
int _a;
int $c;
int ______2_w;
int _$;
int this_is_a_very_detailed_name_for_an_identifier;
```

The following are illegal (it's your job to recognize why):

```
int :b;
int -d;
int e#;
int .f;
int 7g;
```

TABLE 1-1 Complete List of Java Keywords (`assert` added in 1.4, `enum` added in 1.5)

abstract	boolean	break	byte	case	catch
char	class	const	continue	default	do
double	else	extends	final	finally	float
for	goto	if	implements	import	instanceof
int	interface	long	native	new	package
private	protected	public	return	short	static
strictfp	super	switch	synchronized	this	throw
throws	transient	try	void	volatile	while
assert	enum				

Oracle's Java Code Conventions

Oracle estimates that over the lifetime of a standard piece of code, 20 percent of the effort will go into the original creation and testing of the code, and 80 percent of the effort will go into the subsequent maintenance and enhancement of the code. Agreeing on, and coding to, a set of code standards helps to reduce the effort involved in testing, maintaining, and enhancing any piece of code. Oracle has created a set of coding standards for Java and published those standards in a document cleverly titled "Java Code Conventions," which you can find if you start at `java.oracle.com`. It's a great document, short, and easy to read, and we recommend it highly.

That said, you'll find that many of the questions in the exam don't follow the code conventions because of the limitations in the test engine that is used to deliver the exam internationally. One of the great things about the Oracle certifications is that the exams are administered uniformly throughout the world. To achieve that, the code listings that you'll see in the real exam are often quite cramped and do not follow Oracle's code standards. To toughen you up for the exam, we'll often present code listings that have a similarly cramped look and feel, often indenting our code only two spaces as opposed to the Oracle standard of four.

We'll also jam our curly braces together unnaturally, and we'll sometimes put several statements on the same line...ouch! For example:

```
class Wombat implements Runnable {
  private int i;
  public synchronized void run() {
    if (i%5 != 0) { i++; }
    for(int x=0; x<5; x++, i++)
      { if (x > 1) Thread.yield(); }
    System.out.print(i + " ");
  }
  public static void main(String[] args) {
    Wombat n = new Wombat();
    for(int x=100; x>0; --x) { new Thread(n).start(); }
} }
```

Consider yourself forewarned—you'll see lots of code listings, mock questions, and real exam questions that are this sick and twisted. Nobody wants you to write your code like this—not your employer, not your coworkers, not us, not Oracle, and not the exam creation team! Code like this was created only so that complex concepts could be tested within a universal testing tool. The only standards that *are* followed as much as possible in the real exam are the naming standards. Here are the naming standards that Oracle recommends and that we use in the exam and in most of the book:

- **Classes and interfaces** The first letter should be capitalized, and if several words are linked together to form the name, the first letter of the inner words should be uppercase (a format that's sometimes called "CamelCase"). For classes, the names should typically be nouns. Here are some examples:

  ```
  Dog
  Account
  PrintWriter
  ```

For interfaces, the names should typically be adjectives, like these:

```
Runnable
Serializable
```

- **Methods** The first letter should be lowercase, and then normal CamelCase rules should be used. In addition, the names should typically be verb-noun pairs. For example:

```
getBalance
doCalculation
setCustomerName
```

- **Variables** Like methods, the CamelCase format should be used, but starting with a lowercase letter. Oracle recommends short, meaningful names, which sounds good to us. Some examples:

```
buttonWidth
accountBalance
myString
```

- **Constants** Java constants are created by marking variables `static` and `final`. They should be named using uppercase letters with underscore characters as separators:

```
MIN_HEIGHT
```

CERTIFICATION OBJECTIVE

Define Classes (OCA Objectives 1.2, 1.3, 1.4, 6.4, and 7.5)

1.2 Define the structure of a Java class.
1.3 Create executable Java applications with a main method; run a Java program from the command line; including console output. (sic)
1.4 Import other Java packages to make them accessible in your code.
6.4 Apply access modifiers.
7.5 Use abstract classes and interfaces.

When you write code in Java, you're writing classes or interfaces. Within those classes, as you know, are variables and methods (plus a few other things). How you declare your classes, methods, and variables dramatically affects your code's behavior. For example, a `public` method can be accessed from code running anywhere in your application. Mark that method `private`, though, and it vanishes from everyone's radar (except the class in which it was declared).

For this objective, we'll study the ways in which you can declare and modify (or not) a class. You'll find that we cover modifiers in an extreme level of detail, and although we know you're already familiar with them, we're starting from the very beginning. Most Java programmers think they know how all the modifiers work, but on closer study they often find out that they don't (at least not to the degree needed for the exam). Subtle distinctions are everywhere, so you need to be absolutely certain you're completely solid on everything in this section's objectives before taking the exam.

Source File Declaration Rules

Before we dig into class declarations, let's do a quick review of the rules associated with declaring classes, `import` statements, and `package` statements in a source file:

- There can be only one `public` class per source code file.
- Comments can appear at the beginning or end of any line in the source code file; they are independent of any of the positioning rules discussed here.
- If there *is* a `public` class in a file, the name of the file must match the name of the `public` class. For example, a class declared as `public class Dog { }` must be in a source code file named `Dog.java`.
- If the class is part of a package, the `package` statement must be the first line in the source code file, before any `import` statements that may be present.
- If there are `import` statements, they must go *between* the `package` statement (if there is one) and the class declaration. If there isn't a `package` statement, then the `import` statement(s) must be the first line(s) in the source code file. If there are no `package` or `import` statements, the class declaration must be the first line in the source code file.
- `import` and `package` statements apply to *all* classes within a source code file. In other words, there's no way to declare multiple classes in a file and have them in different packages or use different imports.
- A file can have more than one non-`public` class.
- Files with no `public` classes can have a name that does not match any of the classes in the file.

Using the javac and java Commands

In this book, we're going to talk about invoking the `javac` and `java` commands about 1000 times. Although in the **real world** you'll probably use an integrated development environment (IDE) most of the time, you could see a few questions on the exam that use the command line instead, so we're going to review the basics. (By the way, we did NOT use an IDE while writing this book. We still have a slight preference for the command line while studying for the exam; all IDEs do their best to be "helpful," and sometimes they'll fix your problems without telling you. That's nice on the job, but maybe not so great when you're studying for a certification exam!)

Compiling with javac

The `javac` command is used to invoke Java's compiler. You can specify many options when running `javac`. For example, there are options to generate debugging information or compiler warnings. Here's the structural overview for `javac`:

```
javac [options] [source files]
```

There are additional command-line options called `@argfiles`, but they're rarely used, and you won't need to study them for the exam. Both the `[options]` and the `[source files]` are optional parts of the command, and both allow multiple entries. The following are legal `javac` commands:

```
javac -help
javac -version Foo.java Bar.java
```

The first invocation doesn't compile any files, but prints a summary of valid options. The second invocation passes the compiler an option (`-version`, which prints the version of the compiler you're using) and passes the compiler two `.java` files to compile (`Foo.java` and `Bar.java`). Whenever you specify multiple options and/or files, they should be separated by spaces.

Launching Applications with java

The `java` command is used to invoke the Java Virtual Machine (JVM). Here's the basic structure of the command:

```
java [options] class [args]
```

The `[options]` and `[args]` parts of the `java` command are optional, and they can both have multiple values. You must specify exactly one class file to execute, and the `java` command assumes you're talking about a `.class` file, so you don't specify the `.class` extension on the command line. Here's an example:

```
java -showversion MyClass x 1
```

This command can be interpreted as "Show me the version of the JVM being used, and then launch the file named `MyClass.class` and send it two String *arguments* whose values are `x` and `1`." Let's look at the following code:

```
public class MyClass {
  public static void main(String[] args) {
    System.out.println(args[0] + " " + args[1]);
  }
}
```

It's compiled and then invoked as follows:

```
java MyClass x 1
```

The output will be

```
x 1
```

We'll be getting into arrays in depth later, but for now it's enough to know that args—like all arrays—use a zero-based index. In other words, the first command-line argument is assigned to `args[0]`, the second argument is assigned to `args[1]`, and so on.

Using public static void main(String[] args)

The use of the `main()` method is implied in most of the questions on the exam, and on the OCA exam it is specifically covered. For the .0001 percent of you who don't know, `main()` is the method that the JVM uses to start execution of a Java program.

First off, it's important for you to know that naming a method `main()` doesn't give it the superpowers we normally associate with `main()`. As far as the compiler and the JVM are concerned, the **only** version of `main()` with superpowers is the `main()` with this signature:

```
public static void main(String[] args)
```

Other versions of `main()` with other signatures are perfectly legal, but they're treated as normal methods. There is some flexibility in the declaration of the "special" `main()` method (the one used to start a Java application): the order of its modifiers can be altered a little; the `String` array doesn't have to be named `args`;

and it can be declared using var-args syntax. The following are all legal declarations for the "special" `main()`:

```
static public void main(String[] args)
public static void main(String... x)
static public void main(String bang_a_gong[])
```

For the OCA 8 exam, the only other thing that's important for you to know is that `main()` **can be overloaded**. We'll cover overloading in detail in the next chapter.

Import Statements and the Java API

There are a gazillion Java classes in the world. The Java API has thousands of classes, and the Java community has written the rest. We'll go out on a limb and contend that all Java programmers everywhere use a combination of classes they wrote and classes that other programmers wrote. Suppose we created the following:

```
public class ArrayList {
  public static void main(String[] args) {
    System.out.println("fake ArrayList class");
  }
}
```

This is a perfectly legal class, but as it turns out, one of the most commonly used classes in the Java API is also named `ArrayList`, or so it seems.... The API version's actual name is `java.util.ArrayList`. That's its *fully qualified name.* The use of fully qualified names is what helps Java developers make sure that two versions of a class like `ArrayList` don't get confused. So now let's say that I want to use the `ArrayList` class from the API:

```
public class MyClass {
  public static void main(String[] args) {
    java.util.ArrayList<String> a =
      new java.util.ArrayList<String>();
  }
}
```

(First off, trust us on the `<String>` syntax; we'll get to that later.) Although this is legal, it's also a LOT of keystrokes. Since we programmers are basically lazy (there, we said it), we like to use other people's classes a LOT, AND we hate to type. If we had a large program, we might end up using `ArrayLists` many times.

`import` statements to the rescue! Instead of the preceding code, our class could look like this:

```
import java.util.ArrayList;
public class MyClass {
  public static void main(String[] args) {
    ArrayList<String> a = new ArrayList<String>();
}}
```

We can interpret the `import` statement as saying, "In the Java API there is a package called `'util'`, and in that package is a class called '`ArrayList`'. Whenever you see the word '`ArrayList`' in this class, it's just shorthand for: `'java.util.ArrayList'`." (Note: Lots more on packages to come!) If you're a C programmer, you might think that the `import` statement is similar to an `#include`. Not really. All a Java `import` statement does is save you some typing. That's it.

As we just implied, a package typically has many classes. The `import` statement offers yet another keystroke-saving capability. Let's say you wanted to use a few different classes from the `java.util` package: `ArrayList` and `TreeSet`. You can add a wildcard character (`*`) to your `import` statement that means, "If you see a reference to a class you're not sure of, you can look through the entire package for that class," like so:

```
import java.util.*;
public class MyClass {
  public static void main(String[] args) {
    ArrayList<String> a = new ArrayList<String>();
    TreeSet<String> t = new TreeSet<String>();
  }
}
```

When the compiler and the JVM see this code, they'll know to look through `java.util` for `ArrayList` and `TreeSet`. For the exam, the last thing you'll need to remember about using `import` statements in your classes is that you're free to mix and match. It's okay to say this:

```
ArrayList<String> a = new ArrayList<String>();
java.util.ArrayList<String> a2 = new java.util.ArrayList<String>();
```

Static Import Statements

Dear Reader, We really struggled with where to include this discussion of static imports. From a learning perspective, this is probably not the ideal location, but from a reference perspective, we thought it made sense. As you're learning the material for the first time, you might be confused by some of the ideas in this section. If that's the case, we apologize. Put a sticky note on this page and circle back around after you're finished with Chapter 3. On the other hand, once you're past the learning stage and you're using this book as a reference, we think putting this section here will be quite useful. Now, on to static imports.

Sometimes classes will contain *static members*. (We'll talk more about static class members later, but since we're on the topic of imports we thought we'd toss in static imports now.) Static class members can exist in the classes you write and in a lot of the classes in the Java API.

As we said earlier, ultimately the only value `import` statements have is that they save typing and they can make your code easier to read. In Java 5 (a long time ago), the `import` statement was enhanced to provide even greater keystroke-reduction capabilities, although some would argue that this comes at the expense of readability. This feature is known as *static imports.* Static imports can be used when you want to "save typing" while using a class's static members. (You can use this feature on classes in the API and on your own classes.) Here's a "before and after" example using a few static class members provided by a commonly used class in the Java API, `java.lang.Integer`. This example also uses a static member that you've used a thousand times, probably without ever giving it much thought; the `out` field in the `System` class.

Before static imports:

```
public class TestStatic {
  public static void main(String[] args) {
    System.out.println(Integer.MAX_VALUE);
    System.out.println(Integer.toHexString(42));
  }
}
```

After static imports:

```
import static java.lang.System.out;              // 1
import static java.lang.Integer.*;               // 2
public class TestStaticImport {
  public static void main(String[] args)  {
    out.println(MAX_VALUE);                      // 3
    out.println(toHexString(42));                // 4
  }
}
```

Both classes produce the same output:

```
2147483647
2a
```

Let's look at what's happening in the code that's using the static import feature:

1. Even though the feature is commonly called "static import," the syntax MUST be `import static` followed by the fully qualified name of the `static` member you want to import, or a wildcard. In this case, we're doing a static import on the `System` class `out` object.
2. In this case, we might want to use several of the `static` members of the `java.lang.Integer` class. This static import statement uses the wildcard to say, "I want to do static imports of ALL the `static` members in this class."

3. Now we're finally seeing the *benefit* of the static import feature! We didn't have to type the `System` in `System.out.println`! Wow! Second, we didn't have to type the `Integer` in `Integer.MAX_VALUE`. So in this line of code we were able to use a shortcut for a `static` method AND a constant.
4. Finally, we do one more shortcut, this time for a method in the `Integer` class.

We've been a little sarcastic about this feature, but we're not the only ones. We're not convinced that saving a few keystrokes is worth possibly making the code a little harder to read, but enough developers requested it that it was added to the language.

Here are a couple of rules for using static imports:

- You must say `import static`; you can't say `static import`.
- Watch out for ambiguously named `static` members. For instance, if you do a static import for both the `Integer` class and the `Long` class, referring to `MAX_VALUE` will cause a compiler error, because both `Integer` and `Long` have a `MAX_VALUE` constant and Java won't know which `MAX_VALUE` you're referring to.
- You can do a static import on `static` object references, constants (remember they're `static` and `final`), and `static` methods.

exam watch

As you've seen, when using `import` and `import static` statements, sometimes you can use the wildcard character * to do some simple searching for you. (You can search within a package or within a class.) As you saw earlier, if you want to "search through the `java.util` package for class names," you can say this:

```
import java.util.*;                    // ok to search the java.util package
```

In a similar vein, if you want to "search through the `java.lang.Integer` class for static members," you can say this:

```
import static java.lang.Integer.*;    // ok to search the
                                       // java.lang.Integer class
```

But you can't create broader searches. For instance, you CANNOT use an `import` to search through the entire Java API:

```
import java.*;    // Legal, but this WILL NOT search across packages.
```

Class Declarations and Modifiers

The class declarations we'll discuss in this section are limited to top-level classes. In addition to top-level classes, Java provides for another category of class known as *nested classes* or *inner classes*. Inner classes are included on the OCP exam, but not the OCA exam. When you become an OCP candidate, you're going to love learning about inner classes. No, really. Seriously.

The following code is a bare-bones class declaration:

```
class MyClass { }
```

This code compiles just fine, but you can also add modifiers before the class declaration. In general, modifiers fall into two categories:

- Access modifiers (`public`, `protected`, `private`)
- Nonaccess modifiers (including `strictfp`, `final`, and `abstract`)

We'll look at access modifiers first, so you'll learn how to restrict or allow access to a class you create. Access control in Java is a little tricky because there are four access *controls* (levels of access) but only three access *modifiers*. The fourth access control level (called *default* or *package* access) is what you get when you don't use any of the three access modifiers. In other words, *every* class, method, and instance variable you declare has an access *control*, whether you explicitly type one or not. Although all four access *controls* (which means all three *modifiers*) work for most method and variable declarations, a class can be declared with only `public` or *default* access; the other two access control levels don't make sense for a class, as you'll see.

on the job

Java is a package-centric language; the developers assumed that for good organization and name scoping, you would put all your classes into packages. They were right, and you should. Imagine this nightmare: Three different programmers, in the same company but working on different parts of a project, write a class named `Utilities`. If those three `Utilities` classes have not been declared in any explicit package and are in the classpath, you won't have any way to tell the compiler or JVM which of the three you're trying to reference. Oracle recommends that developers use reverse domain names, appended with division and/or project names. For example, if your domain name is `geeksanonymous.com` and you're working on the client code for the TwelvePointOSteps program, you would name your package something like `com.geeksanonymous.steps.client`. That would essentially change the name of your class to `com.geeksanonymous.steps.client.Utilities`.

You might still have name collisions within your company if you don't come up with your own naming schemes, but you're guaranteed not to collide with classes developed outside your company (assuming they follow Oracle's naming convention, and if they don't, well, Really Bad Things could happen).

Class Access

What does it mean to access a class? When we say code from one class (class A) has access to another class (class B), it means class A can do one of three things:

- Create an *instance* of class B.
- *Extend* class B (in other words, become a subclass of class B).
- *Access* certain methods and variables within class B, depending on the access control of those methods and variables.

In effect, access means *visibility*. If class A can't *see* class B, the access level of the methods and variables within class B won't matter; class A won't have any way to access those methods and variables.

Default Access A class with default access has *no* modifier preceding it in the declaration! It's the access control you get when you don't type a modifier in the class declaration. Think of *default* access as *package*-level access, because a class with default access can be seen only by classes within the same package. For example, if class A and class B are in different packages, and class A has default access, class B won't be able to create an instance of class A or even declare a variable or return type of class A. In fact, class B has to pretend that class A doesn't even exist or the compiler will complain. Look at the following source file:

```
package cert;
class Beverage { }
```

Now look at the second source file:

```
package exam.stuff;
import cert.Beverage;
class Tea extends Beverage { }
```

As you can see, the superclass (`Beverage`) is in a different package from the subclass (`Tea`). The `import` statement at the top of the `Tea` file is trying (fingers crossed) to import the `Beverage` class. The `Beverage` file compiles fine, but when we try to compile the `Tea` file, we get *something like* this:

```
Can't access class cert.Beverage. Class or interface must be public, in same
package, or an accessible member class.
import cert.Beverage;
```

(Note: For various reasons, the error messages we show throughout this book might not match the error messages you get. Don't worry, the real point is to understand when you're apt to get an error of some sort.)

`Tea` won't compile because its superclass, `Beverage`, has default access and is in a different package. You can do one of two things to make this work. You could put both classes in the same package, or you could declare `Beverage` as `public`, as the next section describes.

When you see a question with complex logic, be sure to look at the access modifiers first. That way, if you spot an access violation (for example, a class in package A trying to access a default class in package B), you'll know the code won't compile so you don't have to bother working through the logic. It's not as if you don't have anything better to do with your time while taking the exam. Just choose the "Compilation fails" answer and zoom on to the next question.

Public Access

A class declaration with the `public` keyword gives all classes from all packages access to the `public` class. In other words, *all* classes in the Java Universe (JU) have access to a `public` class. Don't forget, though, that if a `public` class you're trying to use is in a different package from the class you're writing, you'll still need to import the `public` class.

In the example from the preceding section, we may not want to place the subclass in the same package as the superclass. To make the code work, we need to add the keyword `public` in front of the superclass (`Beverage`) declaration, as follows:

```
package cert;
public class Beverage { }
```

This changes the `Beverage` class so it will be visible to all classes in all packages. The class can now be instantiated from all other classes, and any class is now free to subclass (extend from) it—unless, that is, the class is also marked with the nonaccess modifier `final`. Read on.

Other (Nonaccess) Class Modifiers

You can modify a class declaration using the keyword `final`, `abstract`, or `strictfp`. These modifiers are in addition to whatever access control is on the class, so you could, for example, declare a class as both `public` and `final`. But you can't always mix nonaccess modifiers. You're free to use `strictfp` in combination with `final`, for example, but you must never, ever, ever mark a class as both `final` *and* `abstract`. You'll see why in the next two sections.

You won't need to know how `strictfp` works, so we're focusing only on modifying a class as `final` or `abstract`. For the exam, you need to know only that strictfp is a keyword and can be used to modify a class or a method, but never a variable. Marking a class as strictfp means that any method code in the class will conform strictly to the IEEE 754 standard rules for floating points. Without that modifier, floating points used in the methods might behave in a platform-dependent way. If you don't declare a class as strictfp, you can still get strictfp behavior on a method-by-method basis by declaring a method as strictfp. If you don't know the IEEE 754 standard, now's not the time to learn it. You have, as they say, bigger fish to fry.

Final Classes

When used in a class declaration, the final keyword means the class can't be subclassed. In other words, no other class can ever extend (inherit from) a final class, and any attempts to do so will result in a compiler error.

So why would you ever mark a class final? After all, doesn't that violate the whole OO notion of inheritance? You should make a final class only if you need an absolute guarantee that none of the methods in that class will ever be overridden. If you're deeply dependent on the implementations of certain methods, then using final gives you the security that nobody can change the implementation out from under you.

You'll notice many classes in the Java core libraries are final. For example, the String class cannot be subclassed. Imagine the havoc if you couldn't guarantee how a String object would work on any given system your application is running on! If programmers were free to extend the String class (and thus substitute their new String subclass instances where java.lang.String instances are expected), civilization—as we know it—could collapse. So use final for safety, but only when you're certain that your final class has indeed said all that ever needs to be said in its methods. Marking a class final means, in essence, your class can't ever be improved upon, or even specialized, by another programmer.

There's a benefit to having nonfinal classes in this scenario: Imagine that you find a problem with a method in a class you're using, but you don't have the source code. So you can't modify the source to improve the method, but you can extend the class and override the method in your new subclass and substitute the subclass everywhere the original superclass is expected. If the class is final, though, you're stuck.

Let's modify our Beverage example by placing the keyword final in the declaration:

```
package cert;
public final class Beverage {
  public void importantMethod() { }
}
```

Now let's try to compile the `Tea` subclass:

```
package exam.stuff;
import cert.Beverage;
class Tea extends Beverage { }
```

We get an error—something like this:

```
Can't subclass final classes: class
cert.Beverage class Tea extends Beverage{
1 error
```

In practice, you'll almost never make a final class. A final class obliterates a key benefit of OO—extensibility. Unless you have a serious safety or security issue, assume that someday another programmer will need to extend your class. If you don't, the next programmer forced to maintain your code will hunt you down and <insert really scary thing>.

Abstract Classes An `abstract` class can never be instantiated. Its sole purpose, mission in life, raison d'être, is to be extended (subclassed). (Note, however, that you can compile and execute an `abstract` class, as long as you don't try to make an instance of it.) Why make a class if you can't make objects out of it? Because the class might be just too, well, *abstract*. For example, imagine you have a class `Car` that has generic methods common to all vehicles. But you don't want anyone actually creating a generic abstract `Car` object. How would they initialize its state? What color would it be? How many seats? Horsepower? All-wheel drive? Or more importantly, how would it behave? In other words, how would the methods be implemented?

No, you need programmers to instantiate actual car types such as `BMWBoxster` and `SubaruOutback`. We'll bet the Boxster owner will tell you his car does things the Subaru can do "only in its dreams." Take a look at the following `abstract` class:

```
abstract class Car {
   private double price;
   private String model;
   private String year;
   public abstract void goFast();
   public abstract void goUpHill();
   public abstract void impressNeighbors();
   // Additional, important, and serious code goes here
}
```

The preceding code will compile fine. However, if you try to instantiate a `Car` in another body of code, you'll get a compiler error something like this:

```
AnotherClass.java:7: class Car is an abstract
class. It can't be instantiated.
      Car x = new Car();
1 error
```

Notice that the methods marked `abstract` end in a semicolon rather than curly braces.

Look for questions with a method declaration that ends with a semicolon, rather than curly braces. If the method is in a class—as opposed to an interface—then both the method and the class must be marked `abstract`. You might get a question that asks how you could fix a code sample that includes a method ending in a semicolon but without an `abstract` modifier on the class or method. In that case, you could either mark the method and class `abstract` or change the semicolon to code (like a curly brace pair). Remember that if you change a method from `abstract` to nonabstract, don't forget to change the semicolon at the end of the method declaration into a curly brace pair!

We'll look at `abstract` methods in more detail later in this objective, but always remember that if even a single method is `abstract`, the whole class must be declared `abstract`. One `abstract` method spoils the whole bunch. You can, however, put nonabstract methods in an `abstract` class. For example, you might have methods with implementations that shouldn't change from Car type to Car type, such as `getColor()` or `setPrice()`. By putting nonabstract methods in an `abstract` class, you give all concrete subclasses (concrete just means not abstract) inherited method implementations. The good news there is that concrete subclasses get to inherit functionality and need to implement only the methods that define subclass-specific behavior.

(By the way, if you think we misused *raison d'être* earlier, don't send an e-mail. We'd like to see *you* work it into a programmer certification book.)

Coding with `abstract` class types (including interfaces, discussed later in this chapter) lets you take advantage of *polymorphism* and gives you the greatest degree of flexibility and extensibility. You'll learn more about polymorphism in Chapter 2.

You can't mark a class as both `abstract` and `final`. They have nearly opposite meanings. An `abstract` class must be subclassed, whereas a `final` class must not be subclassed. If you see this combination of `abstract` and `final` modifiers used for a class or method declaration, the code will not compile.

EXERCISE 1-1

Creating an Abstract Superclass and Concrete Subclass

The following exercise will test your knowledge of `public`, default, `final`, and `abstract` classes. Create an `abstract` superclass named `Fruit` and a concrete subclass named `Apple`. The superclass should belong to a package called `food` and the subclass can belong to the default package (meaning it isn't put into a package explicitly). Make the superclass `public` and give the subclass default access.

1. Create the superclass as follows:

```
package food;
public abstract class Fruit{ /* any code you want */}
```

2. Create the subclass in a separate file as follows:

```
import food.Fruit;
class Apple extends Fruit{ /* any code you want */}
```

3. Create a directory called `food` off the directory in your class path setting.
4. Attempt to compile the two files. If you want to use the `Apple` class, make sure you place the `Fruit.class` file in the `food` subdirectory.

CERTIFICATION OBJECTIVE

Use Interfaces (OCA Objective 7.5)

7.6 *Use abstract classes and interfaces.*

Declaring an Interface

In general, when you create an interface, you're defining a contract for *what* a class can do, without saying anything about *how* the class will do it.

Note: As of Java 8, you can now also describe the *how*, but you usually won't. Until we get to the new interface-related features of Java 8—`default` and `static` methods—we will discuss interfaces from a traditional perspective, which is again, defining a contract for *what* a class can do.

An interface is a contract. You could write an interface `Bounceable`, for example, that says in effect, "This is the `Bounceable` interface. Any concrete class type that implements this interface must agree to write the code for the `bounce()` and `setBounceFactor()` methods."

By defining an interface for `Bounceable`, any class that wants to be treated as a `Bounceable` thing can simply implement the `Bounceable` interface and provide code for the interface's two methods.

Interfaces can be implemented by any class, from any inheritance tree. This lets you take radically different classes and give them a common characteristic. For example, you might want both a `Ball` and a `Tire` to have bounce behavior, but `Ball` and `Tire` don't share any inheritance relationship; `Ball` extends `Toy` while `Tire` extends only `java.lang.Object`. But by making both `Ball` and `Tire` implement `Bounceable`, you're saying that `Ball` and `Tire` can be treated as "Things that can bounce," which in Java translates to, "Things on which you can invoke the `bounce()` and `setBounceFactor()` methods." Figure 1-1 illustrates the relationship between interfaces and classes.

FIGURE 1-1

The relationship between interfaces and classes

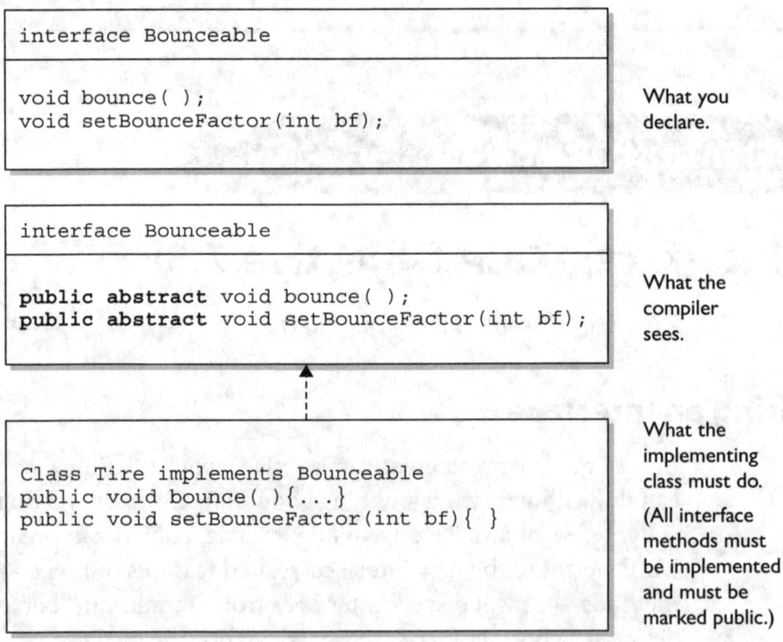

Think of a traditional interface as a 100 percent `abstract` class. Like an `abstract` class, an interface defines abstract methods that take the following form:

```
abstract void bounce();  // Ends with a semicolon rather than
                         // curly braces
```

But although an `abstract` class can define both `abstract` and nonabstract methods, an interface *generally* has only `abstract` methods. Another way interfaces differ from `abstract` classes is that interfaces have very little flexibility in how the methods and variables defined in the interface are declared. These rules are strict:

- Interface methods are implicitly `public` and `abstract`, unless declared as `default` or `static`. In other words, you do not need to actually type the `public` or `abstract` modifiers in the method declaration, but the method is still always `public` and `abstract`.
- All variables defined in an interface must be `public`, `static`, and `final`—in other words, interfaces can declare only constants, not instance variables.
- Interface methods cannot be marked `final`, `strictfp`, or `native`. (More on these modifiers later in the chapter.)
- An interface can *extend* one or more other interfaces.
- An interface cannot extend anything but another interface.
- An interface cannot implement another interface or class.
- An interface must be declared with the keyword `interface`.
- Interface types can be used polymorphically (see Chapter 2 for more details).

The following is a legal interface declaration:

```
public abstract interface Rollable { }
```

Typing in the `abstract` modifier is considered redundant; interfaces are implicitly abstract whether you type `abstract` or not. You just need to know that both of these declarations are legal and functionally identical:

```
public abstract interface Rollable { }
public interface Rollable { }
```

The `public` modifier is required if you want the interface to have `public` rather than default access.

We've looked at the interface declaration, but now we'll look closely at the methods within an interface:

```
public interface Bounceable {
    public abstract void bounce();
    public abstract void setBounceFactor(int bf);
}
```

Typing in the `public` and `abstract` modifiers on the methods is redundant, though, since all interface methods are implicitly `public` and `abstract`. Given that rule, you can see that the following code is exactly equivalent to the preceding interface:

```
public interface Bounceable {
      void bounce();                 // No modifiers
      void setBounceFactor(int bf);  // No modifiers
}
```

You must remember that all interface methods not declared `default` or `static` are `public` and `abstract` regardless of what you see in the interface definition.

Look for interface methods declared with any combination of `public`, `abstract`, or no modifiers. For example, the following five method declarations, if declared within their own interfaces, are legal and identical!

```
void bounce();
public void bounce();
abstract void bounce();
public abstract void bounce();
abstract public void bounce();
```

The following interface method declarations won't compile:

```
final void bounce();          // final and abstract can never be used
                              // together, and abstract is implied
private void bounce();        // interface methods are always public
protected void bounce();      // (same as above)
```

Declaring Interface Constants

You're allowed to put constants in an interface. By doing so, you guarantee that any class implementing the interface will have access to the same constant. By placing the constants right in the interface, any class that implements the interface has direct access to the constants, just as if the class had inherited them.

You need to remember one key rule for interface constants. They must always be

```
public static final
```

So that sounds simple, right? After all, interface constants are no different from any other publicly accessible constants, so they obviously must be declared `public`, `static`, and `final`. But before you breeze past the rest of this discussion, think about the implications: **Because interface constants are defined in an interface, they don't have to be *declared* as `public`, `static`, or `final`. They must be `public`, `static`, and `final`, but you don't actually have to declare them that way.** Just as interface methods are always `public` and `abstract` whether you say so in the code or not, any variable defined in an interface must be—and implicitly is—a `public` constant. See if you can spot the problem with the following code (assume two separate files):

```
interface Foo {
  int BAR = 42;
  void go();
}

class Zap implements Foo {
  public void go() {
     BAR = 27;
  }
}
```

You can't change the value of a constant! Once the value has been assigned, the value can never be modified. The assignment happens in the interface itself (where the constant is declared), so the implementing class can access it and use it, but as a read-only value. So the `BAR = 27` assignment will not compile.

exam watch

Look for interface definitions that define constants, but without explicitly using the required modifiers. For example, the following are all identical:

```
public int x = 1;                  // Looks non-static and non-final,
                                   // but isn't!
int x = 1;                         // Looks default, non-final,
                                   // non-static, but isn't!
static int x = 1;                  // Doesn't show final or public
final int x = 1;                   // Doesn't show static or public
public static int x = 1;           // Doesn't show final
public final int x = 1;            // Doesn't show static
static final int x = 1;            // Doesn't show public
public static final int x = 1;     // what you get implicitly
```

Any combination of the required (but implicit) modifiers is legal, as is using no modifiers at all! On the exam, you can expect to see questions you won't be able to answer correctly unless you know, for example, that an interface variable is `final` and can never be given a value by the implementing (or any other) class.

Declaring `default` Interface Methods

As of Java 8, interfaces can include inheritable* methods with concrete implementations. (*The strict definition of "inheritance" has gotten a little fuzzy with Java 8; we'll talk more about inheritance in Chapter 2.) These concrete methods are called `default` methods. In the next chapter we'll talk a lot about the various OO-related rules that are impacted because of `default` methods. For now we'll just cover the simple declaration rules:

- `default` methods are declared by using the `default` keyword. The `default` keyword can be used only with interface method signatures, not class method signatures.
- `default` methods are `public` by definition, and the `public` modifier is optional.
- `default` methods **cannot** be marked as `private`, `protected`, `static`, `final`, or `abstract`.
- `default` methods must have a concrete method body.

Here are some examples of legal and illegal `default` methods:

```
interface TestDefault {
  default int m1(){return 1;} // legal
  public default void m2(){;} // legal
  static default void m3(){;} // illegal: default cannot be marked static
  default void m4();          // illegal: default must have a method body
}
```

Declaring `static` Interface Methods

As of Java 8, interfaces can include `static` methods with concrete implementations. As with interface `default` methods, there are OO implications that we'll discuss in Chapter 2. For now, we'll focus on the basics of declaring and using `static` interface methods:

- `static` interface methods are declared by using the `static` keyword.
- `static` interface methods are public by default, and the `public` modifier is optional.
- `static` interface methods cannot be marked as `private`, `protected`, `final`, or `abstract`.

- `static` interface methods must have a concrete method body.
- When invoking a `static` interface method, the method's type (interface name) MUST be included in the invocation.

Here are some examples of legal and illegal static interface methods and their use:

```
interface StaticIface {
  static int m1(){ return 42; }          // legal
  public static void m2(){ ; }           // legal
  // final static void m3(){ ; }         // illegal: final not allowed
  // abstract static void m4(){ ; }      // illegal: abstract not allowed
  // static void m5();                   // illegal: needs a method body
}

public class TestSIF implements StaticIface {
  public static void main(String[] args) {
    System.out.println(StaticIface.m1());    // legal: m1()'s type
                                             // must be included
    new TestSIF().go();
    // System.out.println(m1());         // illegal: reference to interface
                                         // is  required
  }
  void go() {
    System.out.println(StaticIface.m1());  // also legal from an instance
  }
}
```

which produces this output:

```
42
42
```

As we said earlier, we'll return to our discussion of `default` methods and `static` methods for interfaces in Chapter 2.

CERTIFICATION OBJECTIVE

Declare Class Members (OCA Objectives 2.1, 2.2, 2.3, 4.1, 4.2, 6.2, 6.3, and 6.4)

2.1 *Declare and initialize variables (including casting of primitive data types).*
2.2 *Differentiate between object reference variables and primitive variables.*
2.3 *Know how to read or write to object fields.*

4.1 Declare, instantiate, initialize, and use a one-dimensional array.
4.2 Declare, instantiate, initialize, and use multidimensional array. (sic)
6.2 Apply the static keyword to methods and fields.
6.3 Create and overload constructors; including impact on default constructors. (sic)
6.4 Apply access modifiers.

We've looked at what it means to use a modifier in a class declaration, and now we'll look at what it means to modify a method or variable declaration.

Methods and instance (nonlocal) variables are collectively known as *members*. You can modify a member with both access and nonaccess modifiers, and you have more modifiers to choose from (and combine) than when you're declaring a class.

Access Modifiers

Because method and variable members are usually given access control in exactly the same way, we'll cover both in this section.

Whereas a *class* can use just two of the four access control levels (default or `public`), members can use all four:

- `public`
- `protected`
- default
- `private`

Default protection is what you get when you don't type an access modifier in the member declaration. The default and `protected` access control types have almost identical behavior, except for one difference that we will mention later.

Note: As of Java 8, the word `default` can ALSO be used to declare certain methods in interfaces. When used in an interface's method declaration, `default` has a different meaning than what we are describing for the rest of this chapter.

It's crucial that you know access control inside and outside for the exam. There will be quite a few questions where access control plays a role. Some questions test several concepts of access control at the same time, so not knowing one small part of access control could mean you blow an entire question.

What does it mean for code in one class to have access to a member of another class? For now, ignore any differences between methods and variables. If class A has access to a member of class B, it means that class B's member is visible to class A. When a class does not have access to another member, the compiler will slap you for trying to access something that you're not even supposed to know exists!

You need to understand two different access issues:

- Whether method code in one class can *access* a member of another class
- Whether a subclass can *inherit* a member of its superclass

The first type of access occurs when a method in one class tries to access a method or a variable of another class, using the dot operator (.) to invoke a method or retrieve a variable. For example:

```
class Zoo {
  public String coolMethod() {
    return "Wow  baby";
  }
}
class Moo {
  public void useAZoo() {
    Zoo z = new Zoo();
    // If the preceding line compiles Moo has access
    // to the Zoo class
    // But... does it have access to the coolMethod()?
    System.out.println("A Zoo says, " + z.coolMethod());
    // The preceding line works because Moo can access the
    // public method
  }
}
```

The second type of access revolves around which, if any, members of a superclass a subclass can access through inheritance. We're not looking at whether the subclass can, say, invoke a method on an instance of the superclass (which would just be an example of the first type of access). Instead, we're looking at whether the subclass *inherits* a member of its superclass. Remember, if a subclass *inherits* a member, it's exactly as if the subclass actually declared the member itself. In other words, if a subclass *inherits* a member, the subclass *has* the member. Here's an example:

```
class Zoo {
  public String coolMethod() {
    return "Wow  baby";
  }
}
class Moo extends Zoo {
  public void useMyCoolMethod() {
    // Does an instance of Moo inherit the coolMethod()?
    System.out.println("Moo says, " + this.coolMethod());
    // The preceding line works because Moo can inherit the
    // public method
    // Can an instance of Moo invoke coolMethod() on an
    // instance of Zoo?
```

```
            Zoo z = new Zoo();
            System.out.println("Zoo says, " + z.coolMethod());
            // coolMethod() is public, so Moo can invoke it on a Zoo
            // reference
        }
    }
```

Figure 1-2 compares a class inheriting a member of another class and accessing a member of another class using a reference of an instance of that class.

FIGURE 1-2

Comparison of inheritance vs. dot operator for member access

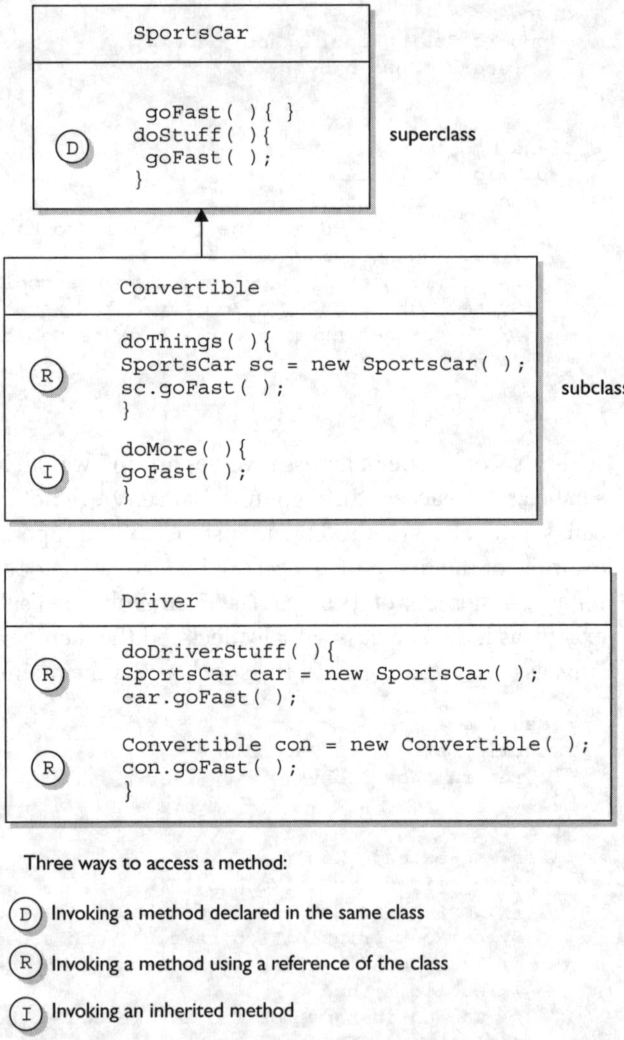

Much of access control (both types) centers on whether the two classes involved are in the same or different packages. Don't forget, though, that if class A *itself* can't be accessed by class B, then no members within class A can be accessed by class B.

You need to know the effect of different combinations of class and member access (such as a default class with a `public` variable). To figure this out, first look at the access level of the class. If the class itself will not be visible to another class, then none of the members will be visible either, even if the member is declared `public`. Once you've confirmed that the class is visible, then it makes sense to look at access levels on individual members.

Public Members

When a method or variable member is declared `public`, it means all other classes, regardless of the package they belong to, can access the member (assuming the class itself is visible).

Look at the following source file:

```
package book;
import cert.*;  // Import all classes in the cert package
class Goo {
  public static void main(String[] args) {
    Sludge o = new Sludge();
    o.testIt();
  }
}
```

Now look at the second file:

```
package cert;
public class Sludge {
  public void testIt() { System.out.println("sludge"); }
}
```

As you can see, `Goo` and `Sludge` are in different packages. However, `Goo` can invoke the method in `Sludge` without problems because both the `Sludge` class and its `testIt()` method are marked `public`.

For a subclass, if a member of its superclass is declared `public`, the subclass inherits that member regardless of whether both classes are in the same package:

```
package cert;
public class Roo {
  public String doRooThings() {
    // imagine the fun code that goes here
    return "fun";
  }
}
```

The Roo class declares the doRooThings() member as public. So if we make a subclass of Roo, any code in that Roo subclass can call its own inherited doRooThings() method.

Notice in the following code that the doRooThings() method is invoked without having to preface it with a reference:

```
package notcert;   // Not the package Roo is in
import cert.Roo;
class Cloo extends Roo {
  public void testCloo() {
    System.out.println(doRooThings());
  }
}
```

Remember, if you see a method invoked (or a variable accessed) without the dot operator (.), it means the method or variable belongs to the class where you see that code. It also means that the method or variable is implicitly being accessed using the this reference. So in the preceding code, the call to doRooThings() in the Cloo class could also have been written as this.doRooThings(). The reference this always refers to the currently executing object—in other words, the object running the code where you see the this reference. Because the this reference is implicit, you don't need to preface your member access code with it, but it won't hurt. Some programmers include it to make the code easier to read for new (or non) Java programmers.

Besides being able to invoke the doRooThings() method on itself, code from some other class can call doRooThings() on a Cloo instance, as in the following:

```
package notcert;
class Toon {
  public static void main(String[] args) {
    Cloo c = new Cloo();
    System.out.println(c.doRooThings()); // No problem; method
                                         //is public
  }
}
```

Private Members

Members marked private can't be accessed by code in any class other than the class in which the private member was declared. Let's make a small change to the Roo class from an earlier example:

```
package cert;
public class Roo {
  private String doRooThings() {
```

```
    // imagine the fun code that goes here, but only the Roo
    // class knows
    return "fun";
  }
}
```

The `doRooThings()` method is now `private`, so no other class can use it. If we try to invoke the method from any other class, we'll run into trouble:

```
package notcert;
import cert.Roo;
class  UseARoo {
  public void testIt() {
    Roo r = new Roo(); //So far so good; class Roo is public
    System.out.println(r.doRooThings()); // Compiler error!
  }
}
```

If we try to compile `UseARoo`, we get a compiler error something like this:

```
cannot find symbol
symbol   : method doRooThings()
```

It's as if the method `doRooThings()` doesn't exist, and as far as any code outside of the `Roo` class is concerned, this is true. A `private` member is invisible to any code outside the member's own class.

What about a subclass that tries to inherit a `private` member of its superclass? When a member is declared `private`, a subclass can't inherit it. For the exam, you need to recognize that a subclass can't see, use, or even think about the `private` members of its superclass. You can, however, declare a matching method in the subclass. But regardless of how it looks, ***it is not an overriding method!*** It is simply a method that happens to have the same name as a `private` method (which you're not supposed to know about) in the superclass. The rules of overriding do not apply, so you can make this newly-declared-but-just-happens-to-match method declare new exceptions, or change the return type, or do anything else you want it to do.

```
package cert;
public class Roo {
   private String doRooThings() {
    // imagine the fun code that goes here, but no other class
    // will know
    return "fun";
   }
}
```

The `doRooThings()` method is now off limits to all subclasses, even those in the same package as the superclass:

```
package cert;                          // Cloo and Roo are in the same package
class  Cloo extends Roo {              // Still OK, superclass Roo is public
  public void testCloo() {
    System.out.println(doRooThings()); // Compiler error!
  }
}
```

If we try to compile the subclass `Cloo`, the compiler is delighted to spit out an error something like this:

```
%javac Cloo.java
Cloo.java:4: Undefined method: doRooThings()
      System.out.println(doRooThings());
1 error
```

Can a `private` method be overridden by a subclass? That's an interesting question, but the answer is no. Because the subclass, as we've seen, cannot inherit a `private` method, it, therefore, cannot override the method—overriding depends on inheritance. We'll cover the implications of this in more detail a little later in this section as well as in Chapter 2, but for now, just remember that a method marked `private` cannot be overridden. Figure 1-3 illustrates the effects of the `public` and `private` modifiers on classes from the same or different packages.

Protected and Default Members

Note: Just a reminder, in the next several sections, when we use the word "default," we're talking about access control. We're NOT talking about the new kind of Java 8 interface method that can be declared `default`.

The `protected` and default access control levels are almost identical, but with one critical difference. A *default* member may be accessed only if the class accessing the member belongs to the same package, whereas a `protected` member can be accessed (through inheritance) by a subclass ***even if the subclass is in a different package.*** Take a look at the following two classes:

```
package certification;
public class OtherClass {
  void testIt() {   // No modifier means method has default
                    // access
    System.out.println("OtherClass");
  }
}
```

FIGURE 1-3

Effects of `public` and `private` access

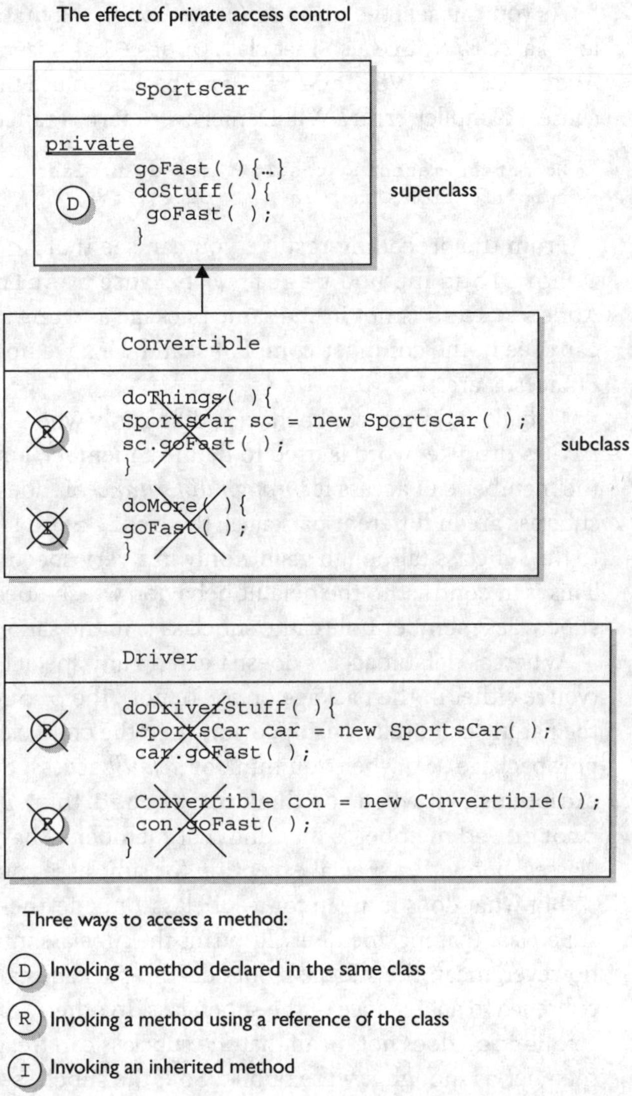

In another source code file you have the following:

```
package somethingElse;
import certification.OtherClass;
class AccessClass {
  static public void main(String[] args) {
    OtherClass o = new OtherClass();
    o.testIt();
  }}
```

As you can see, the `testIt()` method in the first file has *default* (think *package-level*) access. Notice also that class `OtherClass` is in a different package from the `AccessClass`. Will `AccessClass` be able to use the method `testIt()`? Will it cause a compiler error? Will Daniel ever marry Francesca? Stay tuned.

```
No method matching testIt() found in class
certification.OtherClass.    o.testIt();
```

From the preceding results, you can see that `AccessClass` can't use the `OtherClass` method `testIt()` because `testIt()` has default access and `AccessClass` is not in the same package as `OtherClass`. So `AccessClass` can't see it, the compiler complains, and we have no idea who Daniel and Francesca are.

Default and protected behavior differ only when we talk about subclasses. If the `protected` keyword is used to define a member, any subclass of the class declaring the member can access it *through inheritance*. It doesn't matter if the superclass and subclass are in different packages; the `protected` superclass member is still visible to the subclass (although visible only in a very specific way, as we'll see a little later). This is in contrast to the default behavior, which doesn't allow a subclass to access a superclass member unless the subclass is in the same package as the superclass.

Whereas default access doesn't extend any special consideration to subclasses (you're either in the package or you're not), the `protected` modifier respects the parent-child relationship, even when the child class moves away (and joins a new package). So when you think of *default* access, think *package* restriction. No exceptions. But when you think `protected`, think *package + kids*. A class with a `protected` member is marking that member as having package-level access for all classes, but with a special exception for subclasses outside the package.

But what does it mean for a subclass-outside-the-package to have access to a superclass (parent) member? It means the subclass inherits the member. It does not, however, mean the subclass-outside-the-package can access the member using a reference to an instance of the superclass. In other words, `protected` = inheritance. `Protected` does not mean that the subclass can treat the `protected` superclass member as though it were public. So if the subclass-outside-the-package gets a reference to the superclass (by, for example, creating an instance of the superclass somewhere in the subclass's code), the subclass cannot use the dot operator on the superclass reference to access the `protected` member. To a subclass-outside-the-package, a `protected` member might as well be default (or even `private`), when the subclass is using a reference to the superclass. **The subclass can see the `protected` member only through inheritance.**

Are you confused? Hang in there and it will all become clearer with the next batch of code examples.

Protected Details

Let's take a look at a `protected` instance variable (remember, an instance variable is a member) of a superclass.

```
package certification;
public class Parent {
   protected int x = 9; // protected access
}
```

The preceding code declares the variable x as `protected`. This makes the variable *accessible* to all other classes *inside* the certification package, as well as *inheritable* by any subclasses *outside* the package.

Now let's create a subclass in a different package and attempt to use the variable `x` (that the subclass inherits):

```
package other;                          // Different package
import certification.Parent;
class Child extends Parent {
   public void testIt() {
      System.out.println("x is " + x); // No problem; Child
                                        // inherits x
   }
}
```

The preceding code compiles fine. Notice, though, that the `Child` class is accessing the `protected` variable through inheritance. Remember that any time we talk about a subclass having access to a superclass member, we could be talking about the subclass inheriting the member, not simply accessing the member through a reference to an instance of the superclass (the way any other nonsubclass would access it). Watch what happens if the subclass `Child` (outside the superclass's package) tries to access a `protected` variable using a `Parent` class reference:

```
package other;
import certification.Parent;
class Child extends Parent {
   public void testIt() {
      System.out.println("x is " + x);             // No problem; Child
                                                   // inherits x
      Parent p = new Parent();                     // Can we access x using
                                                   // the p reference?
      System.out.println("X in parent is " + p.x); // Compiler error!
   }
}
```

The compiler is more than happy to show us the problem:

```
%javac -d . other/Child.java
other/Child.java:9: x has protected access in certification.Parent
System.out.println("X in parent is " + p.x);
                                        ^
1 error
```

So far, we've established that a `protected` member has essentially package-level or default access to all classes except for subclasses. We've seen that subclasses outside the package can inherit a `protected` member. Finally, we've seen that subclasses outside the package can't use a superclass reference to access a protected member. ***For a subclass outside the package, the protected member can be accessed only through inheritance.***

But there's still one more issue we haven't looked at: What does a `protected` member look like to other classes trying to use the subclass-outside-the-package to get to the subclass's inherited `protected` superclass member? For example, using our previous `Parent`/`Child` classes, what happens if some other class—`Neighbor`, say—in the same package as the `Child` (subclass) has a reference to a `Child` instance and wants to access the member variable `x`? In other words, how does that `protected` member behave once the subclass has inherited it? Does it maintain its `protected` status such that classes in the `Child`'s package can see it?

No! Once the subclass-outside-the-package inherits the `protected` member, that member (as inherited by the subclass) becomes private to any code outside the subclass, with the exception of subclasses of the subclass. So if class `Neighbor` instantiates a `Child` object, then even if class `Neighbor` is in the same package as class `Child`, class `Neighbor` won't have access to the `Child`'s inherited (but `protected`) variable `x`. Figure 1-4 illustrates the effect of `protected` access on classes and subclasses in the same or different packages.

Whew! That wraps up `protected`, the most misunderstood modifier in Java. Again, it's used only in very special cases, but you can count on it showing up on the exam. Now that we've covered the `protected` modifier, we'll switch to default member access, a piece of cake compared to `protected`.

Default Details

Let's start with the default behavior of a member in a superclass. We'll modify the `Parent`'s member `x` to make it default.

```
package certification;
public class Parent {
  int x = 9; // No access modifier, means default
             // (package) access
}
```

FIGURE 1-4 Effects of `protected` access

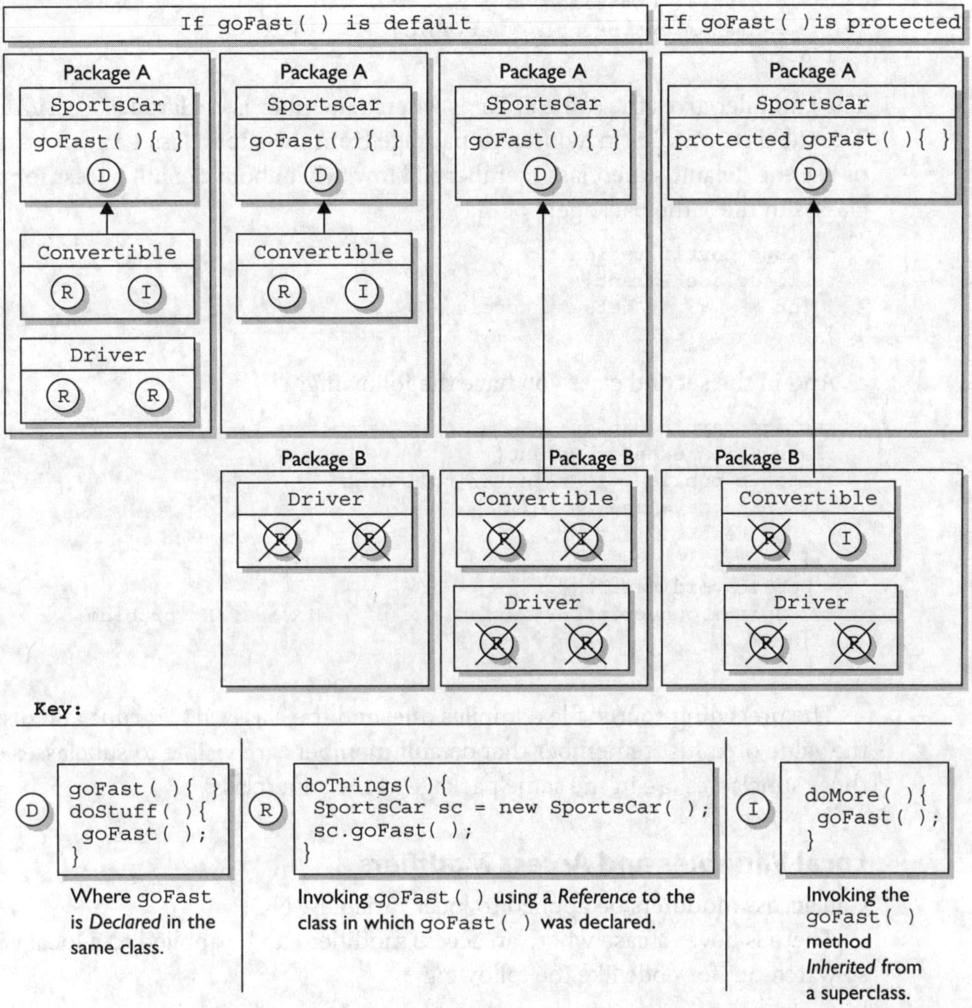

Notice we didn't place an access modifier in front of the variable `x`. Remember that if you don't type an access modifier before a class or member declaration, the access control is default, which means package level. We'll now attempt to access the default member from the `Child` class that we saw earlier.

When we try to compile the `Child.java` file, we get an error like this:

```
Child.java:4: Undefined variable: x
      System.out.println("Variable x is " + x);
1 error
```

The compiler gives the same error as when a member is declared as `private`. The subclass `Child` (in a different package from the superclass `Parent`) can't see or use the default superclass member `x`! Now, what about default access for two classes in the same package?

```
package certification;
public class Parent{
  int x = 9; // default access
}
```

And in the second class you have the following:

```
package certification;
class Child extends Parent{
  static public void main(String[] args) {
    Child sc = new Child();
    sc.testIt();
  }
  public void testIt() {
    System.out.println("Variable x is " + x); // No problem;
  }
}
```

The preceding source file compiles fine, and the class `Child` runs and displays the value of `x`. Just remember that default members are visible to subclasses only if those subclasses are in the same package as the superclass.

Local Variables and Access Modifiers

Can access modifiers be applied to local variables? NO!

There is never a case where an access modifier can be applied to a local variable, so watch out for code like the following:

```
class Foo {
  void doStuff() {
    private int x = 7;
    this.doMore(x);
  }
}
```

You can be certain that any local variable declared with an access modifier will not compile. In fact, there is only one modifier that can ever be applied to local variables—`final`.

That about does it for our discussion on member access modifiers. Table 1-2 shows all the combinations of access and visibility; you really should spend some time with it. Next, we're going to dig into the other (nonaccess) modifiers that you can apply to member declarations.

TABLE 1-2 Determining Access to Class Members

Visibility	Public	Protected	*Default*	Private
From the same class	Yes	Yes	Yes	Yes
From any class in the same package	Yes	Yes	Yes	No
From a subclass in the same package	Yes	Yes	Yes	No
From a subclass outside the same package	Yes	Yes, *through inheritance*	No	No
From any nonsubclass class outside the package	Yes	No	No	No

Nonaccess Member Modifiers

We've discussed member access, which refers to whether code from one class can invoke a method (or access an instance variable) from another class. That still leaves a boatload of other modifiers you can use on member declarations. Two you're already familiar with—`final` and `abstract`—because we applied them to class declarations earlier in this chapter. But we still have to take a quick look at `transient`, `synchronized`, `native`, `strictfp`, and then a long look at the Big One, `static`, much later in the chapter.

We'll look first at modifiers applied to methods, followed by a look at modifiers applied to instance variables. We'll wrap up this section with a look at how `static` works when applied to variables and methods.

Final Methods

The `final` keyword prevents a method from being overridden in a subclass and is often used to enforce the API functionality of a method. For example, the `Thread` class has a method called `isAlive()` that checks whether a thread is still active. If you extend the `Thread` class, though, there is really no way that you can correctly implement this method yourself (it uses native code, for one thing), so the designers have made it `final`. Just as you can't subclass the `String` class (because we need to be able to trust in the behavior of a String object), you can't override many of the methods in the core class libraries. This can't-be-overridden restriction provides for safety and security, but you should use it with great caution. Preventing a subclass from overriding a method stifles many of the benefits of OO, including extensibility through polymorphism. A typical `final` method declaration looks like this:

```
class SuperClass{
  public final void showSample() {
    System.out.println("One thing.");
  }
}
```

It's legal to extend `SuperClass`, since the *class* isn't marked `final`, but we can't override the `final` *method* `showSample()`, as the following code attempts to do:

```
class SubClass extends SuperClass{
  public void showSample() { // Try to override the final
                             // superclass method
    System.out.println("Another thing.");
  }
}
```

Attempting to compile the preceding code gives us something like this:

```
%javac FinalTest.java
FinalTest.java:5: The method void showSample() declared in class
SubClass cannot override the final method of the same signature
declared in class SuperClass.
Final methods cannot be overridden.
     public void showSample() { }
1 error
```

Final Arguments

Method arguments are the variable declarations that appear in between the parentheses in a method declaration. A typical method declaration with multiple arguments looks like this:

```
public Record getRecord(int fileNumber, int recNumber) {}
```

Method arguments are essentially the same as local variables. In the preceding example, the variables `fileNumber` and `recNumber` will both follow all the rules applied to local variables. This means they can also have the modifier `final`:

```
public Record getRecord(int fileNumber, final int recNumber) {}
```

In this example, the variable `recNumber` is declared as `final`, which, of course, means it can't be modified within the method. In this case, "modified" means reassigning a new value to the variable. In other words, a `final` parameter must keep the same value as the argument had when it was passed into the method.

Abstract Methods

An `abstract` method is a method that's been *declared* (as `abstract`) but not *implemented*. In other words, the method contains no functional code. And if you recall from the earlier section "Abstract Classes," an `abstract` method declaration doesn't even have curly braces for where the implementation code goes, but instead closes with a semicolon. In other words, *it has no method body*. You mark a method `abstract` when you want to force subclasses to provide the implementation. For example, if you write an `abstract` class `Car` with a method `goUpHill()`, you might want to force each subtype of `Car` to define its own `goUpHill()` behavior, specific to that particular type of car.

```
public abstract void showSample();
```

Notice that the `abstract` method ends with a semicolon instead of curly braces. **It is illegal to have even a single `abstract` method in a class that is not explicitly declared `abstract`!** Look at the following illegal class:

```
public class IllegalClass{
  public abstract void doIt();
}
```

The preceding class will produce the following error if you try to compile it:

```
IllegalClass.java:1: class IllegalClass must be declared
abstract.
It does not define void doIt() from class IllegalClass.
public class IllegalClass{
1 error
```

You can, however, have an `abstract` class with no `abstract` methods. The following example will compile fine:

```
public abstract class LegalClass{
   void goodMethod() {
      // lots of real implementation code here
   }
}
```

In the preceding example, `goodMethod()` is not `abstract`. Three different clues tell you it's not an `abstract` method:

- The method is not marked `abstract`.
- The method declaration includes curly braces, as opposed to ending in a semicolon. In other words, the method has a method body.
- The method **might** provide actual implementation code inside the curly braces.

Any class that extends an `abstract` class must implement all `abstract` methods of the superclass, unless the subclass is *also* `abstract`. The rule is this: **The first concrete subclass of an `abstract` class must implement *all* `abstract` methods of the superclass.**

Concrete just means nonabstract, so if you have an `abstract` class extending another `abstract` class, the `abstract` subclass doesn't need to provide implementations for the inherited `abstract` methods. Sooner or later, though, somebody's going to make a nonabstract subclass (in other words, a class that can be instantiated), and that subclass will have to implement all the `abstract` methods from up the inheritance tree. The following example demonstrates an inheritance tree with two `abstract` classes and one concrete class:

```
public abstract class Vehicle {
  private String type;
  public abstract void goUpHill();  // Abstract method
  public String getType() {         // Non-abstract method
    return type;
  }
}

public abstract class Car extends Vehicle {
  public abstract void goUpHill();  // Still abstract
  public void doCarThings() {
    // special car code goes here
  }
}

public class Mini extends Car {
  public void goUpHill() {
    // Mini-specific going uphill code
  }
}
```

So how many methods does class `Mini` have? Three. It inherits both the `getType()` and `doCarThings()` methods because they're `public` and concrete (nonabstract). But because `goUpHill()` is `abstract` in the superclass `Vehicle` and is never implemented in the `Car` class (so it remains `abstract`), it means class `Mini`—as the first concrete class below `Vehicle`—must implement the `goUpHill()` method. In other words, class `Mini` can't pass the buck (of `abstract` method implementation) to the next class down the inheritance tree, but class `Car` can, since `Car`, like `Vehicle`, is `abstract`. Figure 1-5 illustrates the effects of the `abstract` modifier on concrete and `abstract` subclasses.

Look for concrete classes that don't provide method implementations for `abstract` methods of the superclass. The following code won't compile:

```
public abstract class A {
  abstract void foo();
}
class B extends A {
  void foo(int I) { }
}
```

FIGURE 1-5

The effects of the `abstract` modifier on concrete and `abstract` subclasses

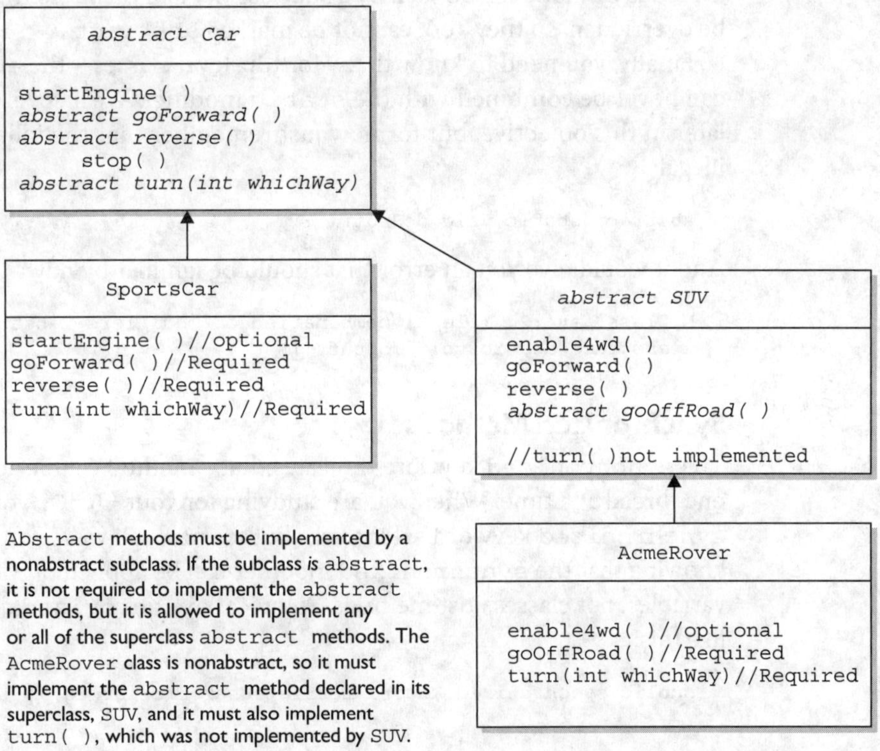

Class B won't compile because it doesn't implement the inherited `abstract` method `foo()`. Although the `foo(int I)` method in class B might appear to be an implementation of the superclass's `abstract` method, it is simply an overloaded method (a method using the same identifier, but different arguments), so it doesn't fulfill the requirements for implementing the superclass's `abstract` method. We'll look at the differences between overloading and overriding in detail in Chapter 2.

A method can never, ever, ever be marked as both `abstract` and `final`, or both `abstract` and `private`. Think about it—`abstract` methods must be implemented (which essentially means overridden by a subclass), whereas `final` and `private` methods cannot ever be overridden by a subclass. Or to phrase it another way, an `abstract` designation means the superclass doesn't know anything about how the subclasses should behave in that method, whereas a `final` designation means the superclass knows everything about how all subclasses (however far down the inheritance tree they may be) should behave in that method. The `abstract` and `final` modifiers are virtually opposites. Because `private` methods cannot even be seen by a subclass (let alone inherited), they, too, cannot be overridden, so they, too, cannot be marked `abstract`.

Finally, you need to know that—for top-level classes—the `abstract` modifier can never be combined with the `static` modifier. We'll cover `static` methods later in this objective, but for now just remember that the following would be illegal:

```
abstract static void doStuff();
```

And it would give you an error that should be familiar by now:

```
MyClass.java:2: illegal combination of modifiers: abstract and static
  abstract static void doStuff();
```

Synchronized Methods

The `synchronized` keyword indicates that a method can be accessed by only one thread at a time. When you are studying for your OCP 8, you'll study the `synchronized` keyword extensively, but for now...all we're concerned with is knowing that the `synchronized` modifier can be applied only to methods—not variables, not classes, just methods. A typical `synchronized` declaration looks like this:

```
public synchronized Record retrieveUserInfo(int id) { }
```

You should also know that the `synchronized` modifier can be matched with any of the four access control levels (which means it can be paired with any of the three access modifier keywords).

Native Methods

The `native` modifier indicates that a method is implemented in platform-dependent code, often in C. You don't need to know how to use `native` methods for the exam, other than knowing that `native` is a modifier (thus a reserved keyword) and that `native` can be applied only to *methods*—not classes, not variables, just methods. Note that a `native` method's body must be a semicolon (`;`) (like `abstract` methods), indicating that the implementation is omitted.

Strictfp Methods

We looked earlier at using `strictfp` as a class modifier, but even if you don't declare a class as `strictfp`, you can still declare an individual method as `strictfp`. Remember, `strictfp` forces floating points (and any floating-point operations) to adhere to the IEEE 754 standard. With `strictfp`, you can predict how your floating points will behave regardless of the underlying platform the JVM is running on. The downside is that if the underlying platform is capable of supporting greater precision, a `strictfp` method won't be able to take advantage of it.

You'll want to study the IEEE 754 if you need something to help you fall asleep. For the exam, however, you don't need to know anything about `strictfp` other than what it's used for—that it can modify a class or method declaration, and that a variable can never be declared `strictfp`.

Methods with Variable Argument Lists (var-args)

Java allows you to create methods that can take a variable number of arguments. Depending on where you look, you might hear this capability referred to as "variable-length argument lists," "variable arguments," "var-args," "varargs," or our personal favorite (from the department of obfuscation), "variable arity parameters." They're all the same thing, and we'll use the term "var-args" from here on out.

As a bit of background, we'd like to clarify how we're going to use the terms "argument" and "parameter" throughout this book:

- **arguments** The things you specify between the parentheses when you're *invoking* a method:

```
doStuff("a", 2);  // invoking doStuff, so "a" & 2 are
                  // arguments
```

- **parameters** The things in the *method's signature* that indicate what the method must receive when it's invoked:

```
void doStuff(String s, int a) { }   // we're expecting two
                                    // parameters:
                                    // String and int
```

Let's review the declaration rules for var-args:

- **Var-arg type** When you declare a var-arg parameter, you must specify the type of the argument(s) this parameter of your method can receive. (This can be a primitive type or an object type.)
- **Basic syntax** To declare a method using a var-arg parameter, you follow the type with an ellipsis (. . .), a space, and then the name of the array that will hold the parameters received.
- **Other parameters** It's legal to have other parameters in a method that uses a var-arg.
- **Var-arg limits** **The var-arg must be the last parameter in the method's signature, and you can have only one var-arg in a method.**
- Let's look at some legal and illegal var-arg declarations:

Legal:

```
void doStuff(int... x) { }                 // expects from 0 to many ints
                                           // as parameters
void doStuff2(char c, int... x)  { }       // expects first a char,
                                           // then 0 to many ints
void doStuff3(Animal... animal) { }        // 0 to many Animals
```

Illegal:

```
void doStuff4(int x...) { }                // bad syntax
void doStuff5(int... x, char... y) { }     // too many var-args
void doStuff6(String... s, byte b) { }     // var-arg must be last
```

Constructor Declarations

In Java, objects are constructed. Every time you make a new object, at least one constructor is invoked. Every class has a constructor, although if you don't create one explicitly, the compiler will build one for you. There are tons of rules concerning constructors, and we're saving our detailed discussion for Chapter 2. For now, let's focus on the basic declaration rules. Here's a simple example:

```
class Foo {
  protected Foo() { }          // this is Foo's constructor
  protected void Foo() { }  // this is a badly named, but legal, method
}
```

The first thing to notice is that constructors look an awful lot like methods. A key difference is that a constructor can't ever, ever, ever, have a return type…ever! Constructor declarations can, however, have all of the normal access modifiers, and they can take arguments (including var-args), just like methods. The other BIG RULE to understand about constructors is that they must have the same name as the class in which they are declared. Constructors can't be marked `static` (they are, after all, associated with object instantiation), and they can't be marked `final` or `abstract` (because they can't be overridden). Here are some legal and illegal constructor declarations:

```
class Foo2 {
  // legal constructors
  Foo2() { }
  private Foo2(byte b) { }
  Foo2(int x) { }
  Foo2(int x, int... y) { }
  // illegal constructors
  void Foo2() { }              // it's a method, not a constructor
  Foo() { }                    // not a method or a constructor
  Foo2(short s);               // looks like an abstract method
  static Foo2(float f) { }     // can't be static
  final Foo2(long x) { }       // can't be final
  abstract Foo2(char c) { }    // can't be abstract
  Foo2(int... x, int t) { }    // bad var-arg syntax
}
```

Variable Declarations

There are two types of variables in Java:

- **Primitives** A primitive can be one of eight types: `char`, `boolean`, `byte`, `short`, `int`, `long`, `double`, or `float`. Once a primitive has been declared, its primitive type can never change, although in most cases its value can change.

- **Reference variables** A reference variable is used to refer to (or access) an object. A reference variable is declared to be of a specific type, and that type can never be changed. A reference variable can be used to refer to any object of the declared type or of a *subtype* of the declared type (a compatible type). We'll talk a lot more about using a reference variable to refer to a subtype in Chapter 2, when we discuss polymorphism.

Declaring Primitives and Primitive Ranges

Primitive variables can be declared as class variables (statics), instance variables, method parameters, or local variables. You can declare one or more primitives, of the same primitive type, in a single line. In Chapter 3 we will discuss the various ways in which they can be initialized, but for now we'll leave you with a few examples of primitive variable declarations:

```
byte b;
boolean myBooleanPrimitive;
int x, y, z;                    // declare three int primitives
```

On previous versions of the exam you needed to know how to calculate ranges for all the Java primitives. For the current exam, you can skip some of that detail, but it's still important to understand that for the integer types the sequence from small to big is `byte`, `short`, `int`, and `long`, and that `doubles` are bigger than `floats`.

You will also need to know that the number types (both integer and floating-point types) are all signed and how that affects their ranges. First, let's review the concepts.

All six number types in Java are made up of a certain number of 8-bit bytes and are *signed*, meaning they can be negative or positive. The leftmost bit (the most significant digit) is used to represent the sign, where a 1 means negative and 0 means positive, as shown in Figure 1-6. The rest of the bits represent the value, using two's complement notation.

FIGURE 1-6

The sign bit for a byte

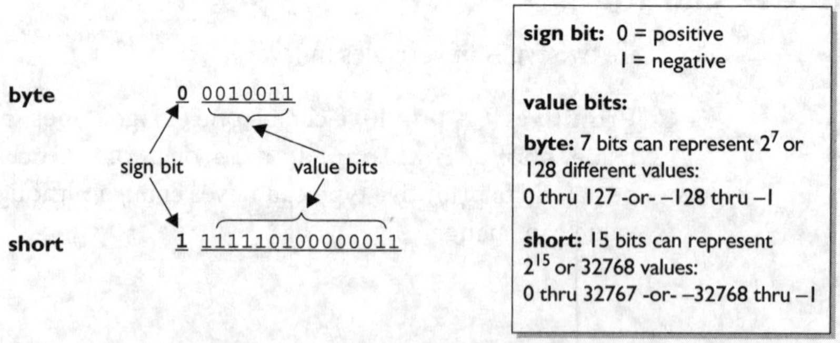

TABLE 1-3 Ranges of Numeric Primitives

Type	Bits	Bytes	Minimum Range	Maximum Range
byte	8	1	-2^{7}	$2^{7} - 1$
short	16	2	-2^{15}	$2^{15} - 1$
int	32	4	-2^{31}	$2^{31} - 1$
long	64	8	-2^{63}	$2^{63} - 1$
float	32	4	n/a	n/a
double	64	8	n/a	n/a

Table 1-3 shows the primitive types with their sizes and ranges. Figure 1-6 shows that with a byte, for example, there are 256 possible numbers (or 2^{8}). Half of these are negative, and half – 1 are positive. The positive range is one less than the negative range because the number 0 is stored as a positive binary number. We use the formula $-2^{(\text{bits}-1)}$ to calculate the negative range, and we use $2^{(\text{bits}-1)} - 1$ for the positive range. Again, if you know the first two columns of this table, you'll be in good shape for the exam.

The range for floating-point numbers is complicated to determine, but luckily you don't need to know these for the exam (although you are expected to know that a double holds 64 bits and a float 32).

There is not a range of `boolean` values; a `boolean` can be only `true` or `false`. If someone asks you for the bit depth of a `boolean`, look them straight in the eye and say, "That's virtual-machine dependent." They'll be impressed.

The `char` type (a character) contains a single, 16-bit Unicode character. Although the extended ASCII set known as ISO Latin-1 needs only 8 bits (256 different characters), a larger range is needed to represent characters found in languages other than English. Unicode characters are actually represented by unsigned 16-bit integers, which means 2^{16} possible values, ranging from 0 to 65535 ($2^{16} - 1$). You'll learn in Chapter 3 that because a `char` is really an integer type, it can be assigned to any number type large enough to hold 65535 (which means anything larger than a `short`; although both `chars` and `shorts` are 16-bit types, remember that a `short` uses 1 bit to represent the sign, so fewer positive numbers are acceptable in a short).

Declaring Reference Variables

Reference variables can be declared as static variables, instance variables, method parameters, or local variables. You can declare one or more reference variables, of the same type, in a single line. In Chapter 3 we will discuss the various ways in which they can be initialized, but for now we'll leave you with a few examples of reference variable declarations:

```
Object o;
Dog myNewDogReferenceVariable;
String s1, s2, s3;              // declare three String vars.
```

Instance Variables

Instance variables are defined inside the class, but outside of any method, and are initialized only when the class is instantiated. Instance variables are the fields that belong to each unique object. For example, the following code defines fields (instance variables) for the name, title, and manager for employee objects:

```
class Employee {
  //  define fields (instance variables) for employee instances
  private String name;
  private String title;
  private String manager;
  // other code goes here including access methods for private
  // fields
}
```

The preceding `Employee` class says that each employee instance will know its own name, title, and manager. In other words, each instance can have its own unique values for those three fields. For the exam, you need to know that instance variables

- Can use any of the four access *levels* (which means they can be marked with any of the three access *modifiers*)
- Can be marked `final`
- Can be marked `transient`
- Cannot be marked `abstract`
- Cannot be marked `synchronized`
- Cannot be marked `strictfp`
- Cannot be marked `native`
- Cannot be marked `static` because then they'd become class variables

We've already covered the effects of applying access control to instance variables (it works the same way as it does for member methods). A little later in this chapter we'll look at what it means to apply the `final` or `transient` modifier to an instance variable. First, though, we'll take a quick look at the difference between instance and local variables. Figure 1-7 compares the way in which modifiers can be applied to methods versus variables.

FIGURE 1-7

Comparison of modifiers on variables vs. methods

Local Variables	Variables (nonlocal)	Methods
final	final public protected private static transient volatile	final public protected private static abstract synchronized strictfp native

Local (Automatic/Stack/Method) Variables

A local variable is a variable declared within a method. That means the variable is not just initialized within the method, but also declared within the method. Just as the local variable starts its life inside the method, it's also destroyed when the method has completed. Local variables are always on the stack, not the heap. (We'll talk more about the stack and the heap in Chapter 3.) Although the value of the variable might be passed into, say, another method that then stores the value in an instance variable, the variable itself lives only within the scope of the method.

Just don't forget that while the local variable is on the stack, if the variable is an object reference, the object itself will still be created on the heap. There is no such thing as a stack object, only a stack variable. You'll often hear programmers use the phrase "local object," but what they really mean is, "locally declared reference variable." So if you hear a programmer use that expression, you'll know that he's just too lazy to phrase it in a technically precise way. You can tell him we said that—unless he knows where we live.

Local variable declarations can't use most of the modifiers that can be applied to instance variables, such as `public` (or the other access modifiers), `transient`, `volatile`, `abstract`, or `static`, but as we saw earlier, local variables can be marked `final`. And as you'll learn in Chapter 3 (but here's a preview), before a local variable can be *used*, it must be *initialized* with a value. For instance:

```
class TestServer {
  public void logIn() {
    int count = 10;
  }
}
```

Typically, you'll initialize a local variable in the same line in which you declare it, although you might still need to reassign it later in the method. The key is to remember that a local variable must be initialized before you try to use it. The compiler will reject any code that tries to use a local variable that hasn't been assigned a value because—unlike instance variables—local variables don't get default values.

A local variable can't be referenced in any code outside the method in which it's declared. In the preceding code example, it would be impossible to refer to the variable `count` anywhere else in the class except within the scope of the method `logIn()`. Again, that's not to say that the value of `count` can't be passed out of the method to take on a new life. But the variable holding that value, `count`, can't be accessed once the method is complete, as the following illegal code demonstrates:

```
class TestServer {
  public void logIn() {
    int count = 10;
  }
  public void doSomething(int i) {
    count = i;   // Won't compile! Can't access count outside
                 // method logIn()
  }
}
```

It is possible to declare a local variable with the same name as an instance variable. It's known as *shadowing*, as the following code demonstrates:

```
class TestServer {
   int count = 9;          // Declare an instance variable named count
   public void logIn() {
      int count = 10;      // Declare a local variable named count
      System.out.println("local variable count is " + count);
   }
   public void count() {
      System.out.println("instance variable count is " + count);
   }
   public static void main(String[] args) {
      new TestServer().logIn();
```

```
        new TestServer().count();
    }
}
```

The preceding code produces the following output:

```
local variable count is 10
instance variable count is 9
```

Why on Earth (or the planet of your choice) would you want to do that? Normally, you won't. But one of the more common reasons is to name a parameter with the same name as the instance variable to which the parameter will be assigned.

The following (wrong) code is trying to set an instance variable's value using a parameter:

```
class Foo {
   int size = 27;
   public void setSize(int size) {
      size = size;  // ??? which size equals which size???
   }
}
```

So you've decided that—for overall readability—you want to give the parameter the same name as the instance variable its value is destined for, but how do you resolve the naming collision? Use the keyword `this`. The keyword `this` always, always, always refers to the object currently running. The following code shows this in action:

```
class Foo {
   int size = 27;
   public void setSize(int size) {
      this.size = size;  // this.size means the current object's
                         // instance variable, size. The size
                         // on the right is the parameter
   }
}
```

Array Declarations

In Java, arrays are objects that store multiple variables of the same type or variables that are all subclasses of the same type. Arrays can hold either primitives or object references, but an array itself will always be an object on the heap, even if the array is declared to hold primitive elements. In other words, there is no such thing as a primitive array, but you can make an array of primitives.

For the exam, you need to know three things:

- How to make an array reference variable (declare)
- How to make an array object (construct)
- How to populate the array with elements (initialize)

For this objective, you only need to know how to declare an array; we'll cover constructing and initializing arrays in Chapter 5.

on the job

Arrays are efficient, but many times you'll want to use one of the Collection types from java.util (including `HashMap`, `ArrayList`, and `TreeSet`). Collection classes offer more flexible ways to access an object (for insertion, deletion, reading, and so on) and, unlike arrays, can expand or contract dynamically as you add or remove elements. There are Collection types for a wide range of needs. Do you need a fast sort? A group of objects with no duplicates? A way to access a name-value pair? Java provides a wide variety of Collection types to address these situations, but the only Collection type on the exam is `ArrayList`, and Chapter 5 discusses `ArrayList` in more detail.

Arrays are declared by stating the type of elements the array will hold (an object or a primitive), followed by square brackets to either side of the identifier.

Declaring an Array of Primitives:

```
int[] key;          // Square brackets before name (recommended)
int key [];         // Square brackets after name (legal but less
                    // readable)
```

Declaring an Array of Object References:

```
Thread[] threads;  // Recommended
Thread threads []; // Legal but less readable
```

on the job

When declaring an array reference, you should always put the array brackets immediately after the declared type, rather than after the identifier (variable name). That way, anyone reading the code can easily tell that, for example, key is a reference to an `int` array object, not an `int` primitive.

We can also declare multidimensional arrays, which are, in fact, arrays of arrays. This can be done in the following manner:

```
String[][][] occupantName;
String[] managerName [];
```

The first example is a three-dimensional array (an array of arrays of arrays), and the second is a two-dimensional array. Notice in the second example, we have one square bracket before the variable name and one after. This is perfectly legal to the compiler, proving once again that just because it's legal doesn't mean it's right.

exam watch

It is never legal to include the size of the array in your declaration. Yes, we know you can do that in some other languages, which is why you might see a question or two that include code similar to the following:

```
int[5] scores;
```

The preceding code won't compile. Remember, the JVM doesn't allocate space until you actually instantiate the array object. That's when size matters.

In Chapter 6, we'll spend a lot of time discussing arrays, how to initialize and use them and how to deal with multidimensional arrays…stay tuned!

Final Variables

Declaring a variable with the `final` keyword makes it impossible to reassign that variable once it has been initialized with an explicit value (notice we said "explicit" rather than "default"). For primitives, this means that once the variable is assigned a value, the value can't be altered. For example, if you assign 10 to the `int` variable `x`, then `x` is going to stay 10, forever. So that's straightforward for primitives, but what does it mean to have a `final` object reference variable? A reference variable marked `final` can never be reassigned to refer to a different object. The data within the object can be modified, but the reference variable cannot be changed. In other words, a `final` reference still allows you to modify the state of the object it refers to, but you can't modify the reference variable to make it refer to a different object. Burn this in: there are no `final` objects, only `final` references. We'll explain this in more detail in Chapter 3.

We've now covered how the `final` modifier can be applied to classes, methods, and variables. Figure 1-8 highlights the key points and differences of the various applications of `final`.

FIGURE 1-8

Effect of `final` on variables, methods, and classes

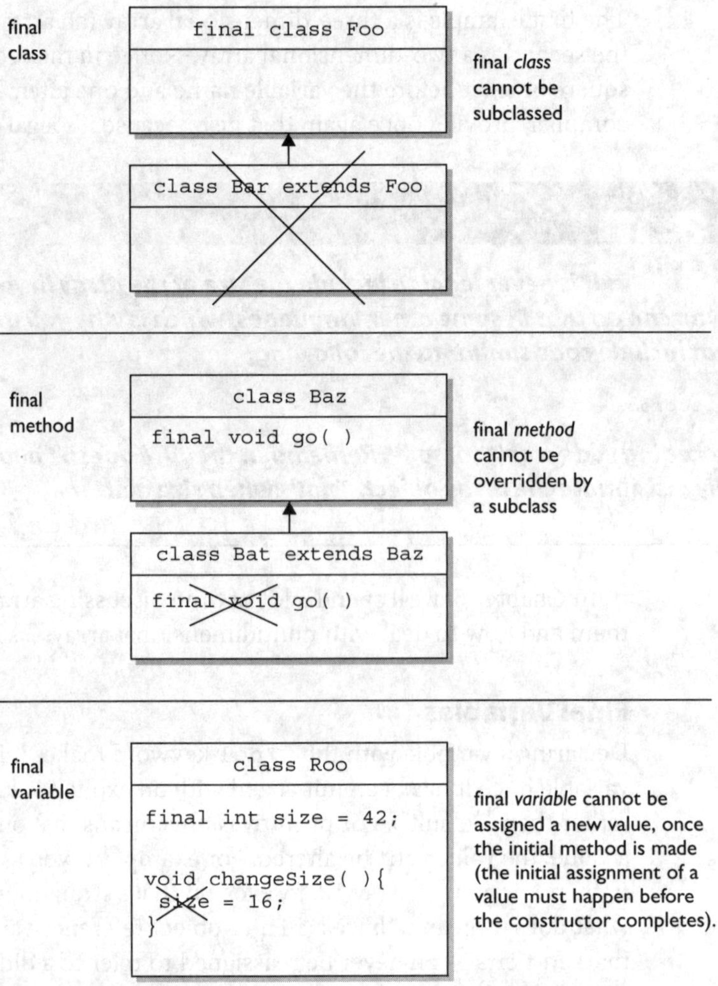

Transient Variables

If you mark an instance variable as `transient`, you're telling the JVM to skip (ignore) this variable when you attempt to serialize the object containing it. Serialization is one of the coolest features of Java; it lets you save (sometimes called "flatten") an object by writing its state (in other words, the value of its instance variables) to a special type of I/O stream. With serialization, you can save an object to a file or even ship it over a wire for reinflating (deserializing) at the other end in another JVM. We were happy when serialization was added to the exam as of Java 5, but we're sad to say that as of Java 7, serialization is no longer on the exam.

Volatile Variables

The `volatile` modifier tells the JVM that a thread accessing the variable must always reconcile its own private copy of the variable with the master copy in memory. Say what? Don't worry about it. For the exam, all you need to know about `volatile` is that it exists.

on the job

The `volatile` modifier may also be applied to project managers!

Static Variables and Methods

Note: The discussion of `static` in this section DOES NOT include the new `static` interface method discussed earlier in this chapter. Don't you just love how the Java 8 folks reused important Java terms?

The `static` modifier is used to create variables and methods that will exist independently of any instances created for the class. All `static` members exist before you ever make a new instance of a class, and there will be only one copy of a `static` member regardless of the number of instances of that class. In other words, all instances of a given class share the same value for any given `static` variable. We'll cover `static` members in great detail in the next chapter.

Things you can mark as `static`:

- Methods
- Variables
- A class nested within another class, but not within a method (not on the OCA 8 exam)
- Initialization blocks

Things you can't mark as `static`:

- Constructors (makes no sense; a constructor is used only to create instances)
- Classes (unless they are nested)
- Interfaces (unless they are nested)
- Method local inner classes (not on the OCA 8 exam)
- Inner class methods and instance variables (not on the OCA 8 exam)
- Local variables

CERTIFICATION OBJECTIVE

Declare and Use enums (OCA Objective 1.2)

1.2 Define the structure of a Java class.

Note: During the creation of this book, Oracle adjusted some of the objectives for the OCA exam. We're not 100 percent sure that the topic of enums is included in the OCA exam, but we've decided that it's better to be safe than sorry, so we recommend that OCA candidates study this section. In any case, you're likely to encounter the use of enums in the Java code you read, so learning about them will pay off regardless.

Declaring enums

Java lets you restrict a variable to having one of only a few predefined values—in other words, one value from an enumerated list. (The items in the enumerated list are called, surprisingly, enums.)

Using enums can help reduce the bugs in your code. For instance, imagine you're creating a commercial-coffee-establishment application, and in your coffee shop application, you might want to restrict your `CoffeeSize` selections to `BIG`, `HUGE`, and `OVERWHELMING`. If you let an order for a LARGE or a GRANDE slip in, it might cause an error. enums to the rescue. With the following simple declaration, you can guarantee that the compiler will stop you from assigning anything to a `CoffeeSize` except `BIG`, `HUGE`, or `OVERWHELMING`:

```
enum CoffeeSize { BIG, HUGE, OVERWHELMING };
```

From then on, the only way to get a `CoffeeSize` will be with a statement something like this:

```
CoffeeSize cs = CoffeeSize.BIG;
```

It's not required that enum constants be in all caps, but borrowing from the Oracle code convention that constants are named in caps, it's a good idea.

The basic components of an enum are its constants (that is, `BIG`, `HUGE`, and `OVERWHELMING`), although in a minute you'll see that there can be a lot more to an enum. enums can be declared as their own separate class or as a class member; however, they must not be declared within a method!

Here's an example declaring an enum *outside* a class:

```
enum CoffeeSize { BIG, HUGE, OVERWHELMING }  // this cannot be
                                             // private or protected
class Coffee {
   CoffeeSize size;
}
public class CoffeeTest1 {
   public static void main(String[] args) {
      Coffee drink = new Coffee();
      drink.size = CoffeeSize.BIG;           // enum outside class
   }
}
```

The preceding code can be part of a single file (or, in general, enum classes can exist in their own file like `CoffeeSize.java`). But remember, in this case the file must be named `CoffeeTest1.java` because that's the name of the `public` class in the file. The key point to remember is that an enum that isn't enclosed in a class can be declared with only the `public` or default modifier, just like a non-inner class. Here's an example of declaring an enum *inside* a class:

```
class Coffee2 {
  enum CoffeeSize {BIG, HUGE, OVERWHELMING }
  CoffeeSize size;
}
public class CoffeeTest2 {
  public static void main(String[] args) {
    Coffee2 drink = new Coffee2();
    drink.size = Coffee2.CoffeeSize.BIG;    // enclosing class
                                            // name required
  }
}
```

The key points to take away from these examples are that enums can be declared as their own class or enclosed in another class, and that the syntax for accessing an enum's members depends on where the enum was declared.

The following is NOT legal:

```
public class CoffeeTest1 {
  public static void main(String[] args) {
    enum CoffeeSize { BIG, HUGE, OVERWHELMING } // WRONG! Cannot
                                                // declare enums
                                                // in methods
    Coffee drink = new Coffee();
    drink.size = CoffeeSize.BIG;
  }
}
```

To make it more confusing for you, the Java language designers made it optional to put a semicolon at the end of the enum declaration (when no other declarations for this enum follow):

```
public class CoffeeTest1 {
  enum CoffeeSize { BIG, HUGE, OVERWHELMING }; // <--semicolon
                                               // is optional here
  public static void main(String[] args) {
    Coffee drink = new Coffee();
    drink.size = CoffeeSize.BIG;
  }
}
```

So what gets created when you make an enum? The most important thing to remember is that enums are not `String`s or `int`s! Each of the enumerated `CoffeeSize` values is actually an instance of `CoffeeSize`. In other words, `BIG` is of type `CoffeeSize`. Think of an enum as a kind of class that looks something (but not exactly) like this:

```
// conceptual example of how you can think
// about enums
class CoffeeSize {
    public static final CoffeeSize BIG =
                              new CoffeeSize("BIG", 0);
    public static final CoffeeSize HUGE =
                              new CoffeeSize("HUGE", 1);
    public static final CoffeeSize OVERWHELMING =
                              new CoffeeSize("OVERWHELMING", 2);

    CoffeeSize(String enumName, int index) {
       // stuff here
    }
   public static void main(String[] args) {
     System.out.println(CoffeeSize.BIG);
   }
}
```

Notice how each of the enumerated values, `BIG`, `HUGE`, and `OVERWHELMING`, is an instance of type `CoffeeSize`. They're represented as `static` and `final`, which, in the Java world, is thought of as a constant. Also notice that each enum value knows its index or position—in other words, the order in which enum values are declared matters. You can think of the `CoffeeSize` enums as existing in an array of type `CoffeeSize`, and as you'll see in a later chapter, you can iterate through the values of an enum by invoking the `values()` method on any enum type. (Don't worry about that in this chapter.)

Declaring Constructors, Methods, and Variables in an enum

Because an enum really is a special kind of class, you can do more than just list the enumerated constant values. You can add constructors, instance variables, methods, and something really strange known as a *constant specific class body*. To understand why you might need more in your enum, think about this scenario: Imagine you want to know the actual size, in ounces, that map to each of the three CoffeeSize constants. For example, you want to know that BIG is 8 ounces, HUGE is 10 ounces, and OVERWHELMING is a whopping 16 ounces.

You could make some kind of a lookup table using some other data structure, but that would be a poor design and hard to maintain. The simplest way is to treat your enum values (BIG, HUGE, and OVERWHELMING) as objects, each of which can have its own instance variables. Then you can assign those values at the time the enums are initialized by passing a value to the enum constructor. This takes a little explaining, but first look at the following code:

```
enum CoffeeSize {
    // 8, 10 & 16 are passed to the constructor
    BIG(8), HUGE(10), OVERWHELMING(16);
    CoffeeSize(int ounces) {     // constructor
      this.ounces = ounces;
    }

    private int ounces;          // an instance variable
    public int getOunces() {
      return ounces;
    }
}

class Coffee {
   CoffeeSize size;              // each instance of Coffee has an enum

   public static void main(String[] args) {
      Coffee drink1 = new Coffee();
      drink1.size = CoffeeSize.BIG;

      Coffee drink2 = new Coffee();
      drink2.size = CoffeeSize.OVERWHELMING;

      System.out.println(drink1.size.getOunces());  // prints 8
      for(CoffeeSize cs: CoffeeSize.values())
         System.out.println(cs + " " + cs.getOunces());
   }
}
```

which produces:

```
8
BIG 8
HUGE 10
OVERWHELMING 16
```

Note: Every enum has a static method, `values()`, that returns an array of the enum's values in the order they're declared.

The key points to remember about enum constructors are

- You can NEVER invoke an enum constructor directly. The enum constructor is invoked automatically, with the arguments you define after the constant value. For example, `BIG(8)` invokes the `CoffeeSize` constructor that takes an `int`, passing the `int` literal 8 to the constructor. (Behind the scenes, of course, you can imagine that `BIG` is also passed to the constructor, but we don't have to know—or care—about the details.)
- You can define more than one argument to the constructor, and you can overload the enum constructors, just as you can overload a normal class constructor. We discuss constructors in much more detail in Chapter 2. To initialize a `CoffeeSize` with both the number of ounces and, say, a lid type, you'd pass two arguments to the constructor as `BIG(8, "A")`, which means you have a constructor in `CoffeeSize` that takes both an `int` and a `String`.

And, finally, you can define something really strange in an enum that looks like an anonymous inner class. It's known as a *constant specific class body*, and you use it when you need a particular constant to override a method defined in the enum.

Imagine this scenario: You want enums to have two methods—one for ounces and one for lid code (a `String`). Now imagine that most coffee sizes use the same lid code, `"B"`, but the OVERWHELMING size uses type `"A"`. You can define a `getLidCode()` method in the `CoffeeSize` enum that returns `"B"`, but then you need a way to override it for OVERWHELMING. You don't want to do some hard-to-maintain `if/then` code in the `getLidCode()` method, so the best approach might be to somehow have the OVERWHELMING constant override the `getLidCode()` method.

This looks strange, but you need to understand the basic declaration rules:

```
enum CoffeeSize {
     BIG(8),
     HUGE(10),
```

```
    OVERWHELMING(16) {            // start a code block that defines
                                  // the "body" for this constant

      public String getLidCode() {   // override the method
                                     // defined in CoffeeSize
        return "A";
      }
    };    // the semicolon is REQUIRED when more code follows

    CoffeeSize(int ounces) {
      this.ounces = ounces;
    }

   private int ounces;

   public int getOunces() {
     return ounces;
   }
   public String getLidCode() {     // this method is overridden
                                    // by the OVERWHELMING constant

     return "B";                    // the default value we want to
                                    // return for CoffeeSize constants
   }
 }
```

CERTIFICATION SUMMARY

After absorbing the material in this chapter, you should be familiar with some of the nuances of the Java language. You may also be experiencing confusion around why you ever wanted to take this exam in the first place. That's normal at this point. If you hear yourself asking, "What was I thinking?" just lie down until it passes. We would like to tell you that it gets easier…that this was the toughest chapter and it's all downhill from here.

Let's briefly review what you'll need to know for the exam:

There will be many questions dealing with keywords indirectly, so be sure you can identify which are keywords and which aren't.

You need to understand the rules associated with creating legal identifiers and the rules associated with source code declarations, including the use of `package` and `import` statements.

You learned the basic syntax for the `java` and `javac` command-line programs.

You learned about when `main()` has superpowers and when it doesn't.

We covered the basics of `import` and `import static` statements. It's tempting to think that there's more to them than saving a bit of typing, but there isn't.

You now have a good understanding of access control as it relates to classes, methods, and variables. You've looked at how access modifiers (`public`, `protected`, and `private`) define the access control of a class or member.

You learned that `abstract` classes can contain both `abstract` and nonabstract methods, but that if even a single method is marked `abstract`, the class must be marked `abstract`. Don't forget that a concrete (nonabstract) subclass of an `abstract` class must provide implementations for all the `abstract` methods of the superclass, but that an `abstract` class does not have to implement the `abstract` methods from its superclass. An `abstract` subclass can "pass the buck" to the first concrete subclass.

We covered interface implementation. Remember that interfaces can extend another interface (even multiple interfaces), and that any class that implements an interface must implement all methods from all the interfaces in the inheritance tree of the interface the class is implementing.

You've also looked at the other modifiers, including `static`, `final`, `abstract`, `synchronized`, and so on. You've learned how some modifiers can never be combined in a declaration, such as mixing `abstract` with either `final` or `private`.

Keep in mind that there are no `final` objects in Java. A reference variable marked `final` can never be changed, but the object it refers to can be modified. You've seen that `final` applied to methods means a subclass can't override them, and when applied to a class, the `final` class can't be subclassed.

Methods can be declared with a var-arg parameter (which can take from zero to many arguments of the declared type), but that you can have only one var-arg per method, and it must be the method's last parameter.

Make sure you're familiar with the relative sizes of the numeric primitives. Remember that while the values of nonfinal variables can change, a reference variable's type can never change.

You also learned that arrays are objects that contain many variables of the same type. Arrays can also contain other arrays.

Remember what you've learned about `static` variables and methods, especially that `static` members are per-class as opposed to per-instance. Don't forget that a `static` method can't directly access an instance variable from the class it's in because it doesn't have an explicit reference to any particular instance of the class.

Finally, we covered `enums`. An `enum` is a safe and flexible way to implement constants. Because they are a special kind of class, `enums` can be declared very simply, or they can be quite complex—including such attributes as methods, variables, constructors, and a special type of inner class called a constant specific class body.

Before you hurl yourself at the practice test, spend some time with the following optimistically named "Two-Minute Drill." Come back to this particular drill often as you work through this book and especially when you're doing that last-minute cramming. Because—and here's the advice you wished your mother had given you before you left for college—it's not what you know, it's when you know it.

For the exam, knowing what you can't do with the Java language is just as important as knowing what you can do. Give the sample questions a try! They're very similar to the difficulty and structure of the real exam questions and should be an eye opener for how difficult the exam can be. Don't worry if you get a lot of them wrong. If you find a topic that you are weak in, spend more time reviewing and studying. Many programmers need two or three serious passes through a chapter (or an individual objective) before they can answer the questions confidently.

✓ TWO-MINUTE DRILL

Remember that in this chapter, when we talk about classes, we're referring to non-inner classes, in other words, *top-level* classes.

Java Features and Benefits (OCA Objective 1.5)

- ☐ While Java provides many benefits to programmers, for the exam you should remember that Java supports object-oriented programming in general, encapsulation, automatic memory management, a large API (library), built-in security features, multiplatform compatibility, strong typing, multithreading, and distributed computing.

Identifiers (OCA Objective 2.1)

- ☐ Identifiers can begin with a letter, an underscore, or a currency character.
- ☐ After the first character, identifiers can also include digits.
- ☐ Identifiers can be of any length.

Executable Java Files and main() (OCA Objective 1.3)

- ☐ You can compile and execute Java programs using the command-line programs `javac` and `java`, respectively. Both programs support a variety of command-line options.
- ☐ The only versions of `main()` methods with special powers are those versions with method signatures equivalent to `public static void main(String[] args)`.
- ☐ `main()` can be overloaded.

Imports (OCA Objective 1.4)

- ☐ An `import` statement's only job is to save keystrokes.
- ☐ You can use an asterisk (`*`) to search through the contents of a single package.
- ☐ Although referred to as "static imports," the syntax is `import static`....
- ☐ You can import API classes and/or custom classes.

Source File Declaration Rules (OCA Objective 1.2)

- ☐ A source code file can have only one `public` class.
- ☐ If the source file contains a `public` class, the filename must match the `public` class name.
- ☐ A file can have only one `package` statement, but it can have multiple `imports`.
- ☐ The `package` statement (if any) must be the first (noncomment) line in a source file.
- ☐ The `import` statements (if any) must come after the `package` statement (if any) and before the first class declaration.
- ☐ If there is no `package` statement, `import` statements must be the first (noncomment) statements in the source file.
- ☐ `package` and `import` statements apply to all classes in the file.
- ☐ A file can have more than one nonpublic class.
- ☐ Files with no `public` classes have no naming restrictions.

Class Access Modifiers (OCA Objective 6.4)

- ☐ There are three access modifiers: `public`, `protected`, and `private`.
- ☐ There are four access levels: `public`, `protected`, default, and `private`.
- ☐ Classes can have only `public` or default access.
- ☐ A class with default access can be seen only by classes within the same package.
- ☐ A class with `public` access can be seen by all classes from all packages.
- ☐ Class visibility revolves around whether code in one class can
  - ☐ Create an instance of another class
  - ☐ Extend (or subclass) another class
  - ☐ Access methods and variables of another class

Class Modifiers (Nonaccess) (OCA Objectives 1.2, 7.1, and 7.5)

- ☐ Classes can also be modified with `final`, `abstract`, or `strictfp`.
- ☐ A class cannot be both `final` and `abstract`.
- ☐ A `final` class cannot be subclassed.
- ☐ An `abstract` class cannot be instantiated.

- ☐ A single abstract method in a class means the whole class must be abstract.
- ☐ An abstract class can have both abstract and nonabstract methods.
- ☐ The first concrete class to extend an abstract class must implement all of its abstract methods.

Interface Implementation (OCA Objective 7.5)

- ☐ Usually, interfaces are contracts for what a class can do, but they say nothing about the way in which the class must do it.
- ☐ Interfaces can be implemented by any class from any inheritance tree.
- ☐ Usually, an interface is like a 100 percent abstract class and is implicitly abstract whether or not you type the abstract modifier in the declaration.
- ☐ Usually interfaces have only abstract methods.
- ☐ Interface methods are by default public and usually abstract—explicit declaration of these modifiers is optional.
- ☐ Interfaces can have constants, which are always implicitly public, static, and final.
- ☐ Interface constant declarations of public, static, and final are optional in any combination.
- ☐ As of Java 8, interfaces can have concrete methods declared as either default or static.

Note: This section uses some concepts that we HAVE NOT yet covered. Don't panic: once you've read through all of the book, this section will make sense as a reference.

- ☐ A legal nonabstract implementing class has the following properties:
  - ☐ It provides concrete implementations for the interface's methods.
  - ☐ It must follow all legal override rules for the methods it implements.
  - ☐ It must not declare any new checked exceptions for an implementation method.
  - ☐ It must not declare any checked exceptions that are broader than the exceptions declared in the interface method.
  - ☐ It may declare runtime exceptions on any interface method implementation regardless of the interface declaration.

- ❑ It must maintain the exact signature (allowing for covariant returns) and return type of the methods it implements (but does not have to declare the exceptions of the interface).
- ❑ A class implementing an interface can itself be `abstract`.
- ❑ An `abstract` implementing class does not have to implement the interface methods (but the first concrete subclass must).
- ❑ A class can extend only one class (no multiple inheritance), but it can implement many interfaces.
- ❑ Interfaces can extend one or more other interfaces.
- ❑ Interfaces cannot extend a class or implement a class or interface.
- ❑ When taking the exam, verify that interface and class declarations are legal before verifying other code logic.

Member Access Modifiers (OCA Objective 6.4)

- ❑ Methods and instance (nonlocal) variables are known as "members."
- ❑ Members can use all four access levels: `public`, `protected`, default, and `private`.
- ❑ Member access comes in two forms:
  - ❑ Code in one class can access a member of another class.
  - ❑ A subclass can inherit a member of its superclass.
- ❑ If a class cannot be accessed, its members cannot be accessed.
- ❑ Determine class visibility before determining member visibility.
- ❑ `public` members can be accessed by all other classes, even in other packages.
- ❑ If a superclass member is `public`, the subclass inherits it—regardless of package.
- ❑ Members accessed without the dot operator (`.`) must belong to the same class.
- ❑ `this.` always refers to the currently executing object.
- ❑ `this.aMethod()` is the same as just invoking `aMethod()`.
- ❑ `private` members can be accessed only by code in the same class.
- ❑ `private` members are not visible to subclasses, so `private` members cannot be inherited.

- ☐ Default and `protected` members differ only when subclasses are involved:
  - ☐ Default members can be accessed only by classes in the same package.
  - ☐ `protected` members can be accessed by other classes in the same package, plus subclasses, regardless of package.
  - ☐ `protected` = package + kids (kids meaning subclasses).
  - ☐ For subclasses outside the package, the `protected` member can be accessed only through inheritance; a subclass outside the package cannot access a `protected` member by using a reference to a superclass instance. (In other words, inheritance is the only mechanism for a subclass outside the package to access a `protected` member of its superclass.)
  - ☐ A `protected` member inherited by a subclass from another package is not accessible to any other class in the subclass package, except for the subclass's own subclasses.

Local Variables (OCA Objectives 2.1 and 6.4)

- ☐ Local (method, automatic, or stack) variable declarations cannot have access modifiers.
- ☐ `final` is the only modifier available to local variables.
- ☐ Local variables don't get default values, so they must be initialized before use.

Other Modifiers—Members (OCA Objectives 7.1 and 7.5)

- ☐ `final` methods cannot be overridden in a subclass.
- ☐ `abstract` methods are declared with a signature, a return type, and an optional `throws` clause, but they are not implemented.
- ☐ `abstract` methods end in a semicolon—no curly braces.
- ☐ Three ways to spot a nonabstract method:
  - ☐ The method is not marked `abstract`.
  - ☐ The method has curly braces.
  - ☐ The method **MIGHT** have code between the curly braces.
- ☐ The first nonabstract (concrete) class to extend an `abstract` class must implement all of the `abstract` class's `abstract` methods.
- ☐ The `synchronized` modifier applies only to methods and code blocks.
- ☐ `synchronized` methods can have any access control and can also be marked `final`.

- ☐ `abstract` methods must be implemented by a subclass, so they must be inheritable. For that reason
  - ☐ `abstract` methods cannot be `private`.
  - ☐ `abstract` methods cannot be `final`.
- ☐ The `native` modifier applies only to methods.
- ☐ The `strictfp` modifier applies only to classes and methods.

Methods with var-args (OCA Objective 1.2)

- ☐ Methods can declare a parameter that accepts from zero to many arguments, a so-called var-arg method.
- ☐ A var-arg parameter is declared with the syntax `type... name`; for instance: `doStuff(int... x) { }`.
- ☐ A var-arg method can have only one var-arg parameter.
- ☐ In methods with normal parameters and a var-arg, the var-arg must come last.

Constructors (OCA Objectives 1.2, and 6.3)

- ☐ Constructors must have the same name as the class
- ☐ Constructors can have arguments, but they cannot have a return type.
- ☐ Constructors can use any access modifier (even `private`!).

Variable Declarations (OCA Objective 2.1)

- ☐ Instance variables can
  - ☐ Have any access control
  - ☐ Be marked `final` or `transient`
- ☐ Instance variables can't be `abstract`, `synchronized`, `native`, or `strictfp`.
- ☐ It is legal to declare a local variable with the same name as an instance variable; this is called "shadowing."
- ☐ `final` variables have the following properties:
  - ☐ `final` variables cannot be reassigned once assigned a value.
  - ☐ `final` reference variables cannot refer to a different object once the object has been assigned to the `final` variable.
  - ☐ `final` variables must be initialized before the constructor completes.

- ☐ There is no such thing as a `final` object. An object reference marked `final` does NOT mean the object itself can't change.
- ☐ The `transient` modifier applies only to instance variables.
- ☐ The `volatile` modifier applies only to instance variables.

Array Declarations (OCA Objectives 4.1 and 4.2)

- ☐ Arrays can hold primitives or objects, but the array itself is always an object.
- ☐ When you declare an array, the brackets can be to the left or to the right of the variable name.
- ☐ It is never legal to include the size of an array in the declaration.
- ☐ An array of objects can hold any object that passes the IS-A (or `instanceof`) test for the declared type of the array. For example, if `Horse` extends `Animal`, then a `Horse` object can go into an `Animal` array.

Static Variables and Methods (OCA Objective 6.2)

- ☐ They are not tied to any particular instance of a class.
- ☐ No class instances are needed in order to use `static` members of the class or interface.
- ☐ There is only one copy of a `static` variable/class, and all instances share it.
- ☐ `static` methods do not have direct access to nonstatic members.

enums (OCA Objective 1.2)

- ☐ An `enum` specifies a list of constant values assigned to a type.
- ☐ An `enum` is NOT a `String` or an `int`; an `enum` constant's type is the `enum` type. For example, `SUMMER` and `FALL` are of the `enum` type `Season`.
- ☐ An `enum` can be declared outside or inside a class, but NOT in a method.
- ☐ An `enum` declared outside a class must NOT be marked `static`, `final`, `abstract`, `protected`, or `private`.
- ☐ `enum`s can contain constructors, methods, variables, and constant-specific class bodies.

- ☐ enum constants can send arguments to the enum constructor, using the syntax `BIG(8)`, where the `int` literal 8 is passed to the enum constructor.
- ☐ enum constructors can have arguments and can be overloaded.
- ☐ enum constructors can NEVER be invoked directly in code. They are always called automatically when an enum is initialized.
- ☐ The semicolon at the end of an enum declaration is optional. These are legal:
  - ☐
    ```
    enum Foo { ONE, TWO, THREE}
    enum Foo { ONE, TWO, THREE};
    ```
- ☐ `MyEnum.values()` returns an array of MyEnum's values.

SELF TEST

The following questions will help you measure your understanding of the material presented in this chapter. Read all the choices carefully, as there may be more than one correct answer. Choose all correct answers for each question. Stay focused.

If you have a rough time with these at first, don't beat yourself up. Be positive. Repeat nice affirmations to yourself like, "I am smart enough to understand enums" and "OK, so that other guy knows enums better than I do, but I bet he can't <insert something you *are* good at> like me."

1. Which are true? (Choose all that apply.)

A. "X extends Y" is correct if and only if X is a class and Y is an interface

B. "X extends Y" is correct if and only if X is an interface and Y is a class

C. "X extends Y" is correct if X and Y are either both classes or both interfaces

D. "X extends Y" is correct for all combinations of X and Y being classes and/or interfaces

2. Given:

```
class Rocket {
  private void blastOff() { System.out.print("bang "); }
}
public class Shuttle extends Rocket {
  public static void main(String[] args) {
    new Shuttle().go();
  }
  void go() {
    blastOff();
    // Rocket.blastOff();  // line A
  }
  private void blastOff() { System.out.print("sh-bang "); }
}
```

Which are true? (Choose all that apply.)

A. As the code stands, the output is `bang`

B. As the code stands, the output is `sh-bang`

C. As the code stands, compilation fails

D. If line A is uncommented, the output is `bang bang`

E. If line A is uncommented, the output is `sh-bang bang`

F. If line A is uncommented, compilation fails.

3. Given that the `for` loop's syntax is correct, and given:

```
import static java.lang.System.*;
class _ {
  static public void main(String[] __A_V_) {
    String $ = "";
    for(int x=0; ++x < __A_V_.length; )    // for loop
      $ += __A_V_[x];
    out.println($);
  }
}
```

And the command line:

```
java _ - A .
```

What is the result?

A. `-A`

B. `A.`

C. `-A.`

D. `_A.`

E. `_-A.`

F. Compilation fails

G. An exception is thrown at runtime

4. Given:

```
 1. enum Animals {
 2.   DOG("woof"), CAT("meow"), FISH("burble");
 3.   String sound;
 4.   Animals(String s) { sound = s; }
 5. }
 6. class TestEnum {
 7.   static Animals a;
 8.   public static void main(String[] args) {
 9.     System.out.println(a.DOG.sound + " " + a.FISH.sound);
10.   }
11. }
```

What is the result?

A. `woof burble`

B. Multiple compilation errors

C. Compilation fails due to an error on line 2

D. Compilation fails due to an error on line 3

E. Compilation fails due to an error on line 4

F. Compilation fails due to an error on line 9

5. Given two files:

```
1. package pkgA;
2. public class Foo {
3. int a = 5;
4. protected int b = 6;
5. public int c = 7;
6. }
```

```
3. package pkgB;
4. import pkgA.*;
5. public class Baz {
6.   public static void main(String[] args) {
7.     Foo f = new Foo();
8.     System.out.print(" " + f.a);
9.     System.out.print(" " + f.b);
10.    System.out.println(" " + f.c);
11.  }
12. }
```

What is the result? (Choose all that apply.)

A. 5 6 7

B. 5 followed by an exception

C. Compilation fails with an error on line 7

D. Compilation fails with an error on line 8

E. Compilation fails with an error on line 9

F. Compilation fails with an error on line 10

6. Given:

```
public class Electronic implements Device
  { public void doIt() { } }

abstract class Phone1 extends Electronic { }

abstract class Phone2 extends Electronic
  { public void doIt(int x) { } }

class Phone3 extends Electronic implements Device
  { public void doStuff() { } }

interface Device { public void doIt(); }
```

What is the result? (Choose all that apply.)

A. Compilation succeeds

B. Compilation fails with an error on line 1

C. Compilation fails with an error on line 3

D. Compilation fails with an error on line 5

E. Compilation fails with an error on line 7

F. Compilation fails with an error on line 9

7. Given:

```
 4. class Announce {
 5.   public static void main(String[] args) {
 6.     for(int __x = 0; __x < 3; __x++) ;
 7.     int #lb = 7;
 8.     long [] x [5];
 9.     Boolean []ba[];
10.   }
11. }
```

What is the result? (Choose all that apply.)

A. Compilation succeeds

B. Compilation fails with an error on line 6

C. Compilation fails with an error on line 7

D. Compilation fails with an error on line 8

E. Compilation fails with an error on line 9

8. Given:

```
 3. public class TestDays {
 4.   public enum Days { MON, TUE, WED };
 5.   public static void main(String[] args) {
 6.     for(Days d : Days.values() )
 7.       ;
 8.     Days [] d2 = Days.values();
 9.     System.out.println(d2[2]);
10.   }
11. }
```

What is the result? (Choose all that apply.)

A. `TUE`

B. `WED`

C. The output is unpredictable

D. Compilation fails due to an error on line 4

E. Compilation fails due to an error on line 6

F. Compilation fails due to an error on line 8

G. Compilation fails due to an error on line 9

9. Given:

```
4. public class Frodo extends Hobbit {
5.   public static void main(String[] args) {
6.     int myGold = 7;
7.     System.out.println(countGold(myGold, 6));
8.   }
9. }
10. class Hobbit {
11.   int countGold(int x, int y) { return x + y; }
12. }
```

What is the result?

A. `13`

B. Compilation fails due to multiple errors

C. Compilation fails due to an error on line 6

D. Compilation fails due to an error on line 7

E. Compilation fails due to an error on line 11

10. Given:

```
interface Gadget {
  void doStuff();
}
abstract class Electronic {
  void getPower() { System.out.print("plug in "); }
}
public class Tablet extends Electronic implements Gadget {
  void doStuff() { System.out.print("show book "); }
  public static void main(String[] args) {
    new Tablet().getPower();
    new Tablet().doStuff();
  }
}
```

Which are true? (Choose all that apply.)

A. The class `Tablet` will NOT compile

B. The interface `Gadget` will NOT compile

C. The output will be `plug in show book`

D. The `abstract` class `Electronic` will NOT compile

E. The class `Tablet` CANNOT both extend and implement

11. Given that the Integer class is in the java.lang package and given:

```
1. // insert code here
2. class StatTest {
3.   public static void main(String[] args) {
4.     System.out.println(Integer.MAX_VALUE);
5.   }
6. }
```

Which, inserted independently at line 1, compiles? (Choose all that apply.)

A. `import static java.lang;`

B. `import static java.lang.Integer;`

C. `import static java.lang.Integer.*;`

D. `static import java.lang.Integer.*;`

E. `import static java.lang.Integer.MAX_VALUE;`

F. None of the above statements are valid import syntax

12. Given:

```
interface MyInterface {
  // insert code here
}
```

Which lines of code—inserted independently at `insert code here`—will compile? (Choose all that apply.)

A. `public static m1() {;}`

B. `default void m2() {;}`

C. `abstract int m3();`

D. `final short m4() {return 5;}`

E. `default long m5();`

F. `static void m6() {;}`

13. Which are true? (Choose all that apply.)

A. Java is a dynamically typed programming language

B. Java provides fine-grained control of memory through the use of pointers

C. Java provides programmers the ability to create objects that are well encapsulated

D. Java provides programmers the ability to send Java objects from one machine to another

E. Java is an implementation of the ECMA standard

F. Java's encapsulation capabilities provide its primary security mechanism

SELF TEST ANSWERS

1. ☑ **C** is correct.
☒ **A** is incorrect because classes implement interfaces, they don't extend them. **B** is incorrect because interfaces only "inherit from" other interfaces. **D** is incorrect based on the preceding rules. (OCA Objective 7.5)

2. ☑ **B** and **F** are correct. Since `Rocket.blastOff()` is `private`, it can't be overridden, and it is invisible to class `Shuttle`.
☒ **A, C, D,** and **E** are incorrect based on the above. (OCA Objective 6.4)

3. ☑ **B** is correct. This question is using valid (but inappropriate and weird) identifiers, static imports, `main()`, and pre-incrementing logic. (Note: You might get a compiler warning when compiling this code.)
☒ **A, C, D, E, F,** and **G** are incorrect based on the above. (OCA Objective 1.2)

4. ☑ **A** is correct; `enum`s can have constructors and variables.
☒ **B, C, D, E,** and **F** are incorrect; these lines all use correct syntax. (OCA Objective 1.2)

5. ☑ **D** and **E** are correct. Variable `a` has default access, so it cannot be accessed from outside the package. Variable `b` has protected access in `pkgA`.
☒ **A, B, C,** and **F** are incorrect based on the above information. (OCA Objectives 1.4 and 6.5)

6. ☑ **A** is correct; all of these are legal declarations.
☒ **B, C, D, E,** and **F** are incorrect based on the above information. (OCA Objective 7.5)

7. ☑ **C** and **D** are correct. Variable names cannot begin with a #, and an array declaration can't include a size without an instantiation. The rest of the code is valid.
☒ **A, B,** and **E** are incorrect based on the above. (OCA Objective 2.1)

8. ☑ **B** is correct. Every `enum` comes with a `static values()` method that returns an array of the `enum`'s values in the order in which they are declared in the `enum`.
☒ **A, C, D, E, F,** and **G** are incorrect based on the above information. (OCP Objective 1.2)

9. ☑ **D** is correct. The `countGold()` method cannot be invoked from a static context.
☒ **A, B, C,** and **E** are incorrect based on the above information. (OCA Objective 6.2)

10. ☑ **A** is correct. By default, an interface's methods are `public` so the `Tablet.doStuff` method must be public, too. The rest of the code is valid.
☒ **B, C, D,** and **E** are incorrect based on the above. (OCA Objective 7.5)

11. ☑ **C** and **E** are correct syntax for static imports. Line 4 isn't making use of `static imports`, so the code will also compile with none of the imports.
☒ **A, B, D,** and **F** are incorrect based on the above. (OCA Objective 1.4)

12. ☑ **B, C,** and **F** are correct. As of Java 8, interfaces can have `default` and `static` methods.
☒ **A, D,** and **E** are incorrect. **A** has no return type; **D** cannot have a method body; and **E** needs a method body. (OCA Objective 7.5)

13. ☑ **C** and **D** are correct.
☒ **A** is incorrect because Java is a statically typed language. **B** is incorrect because it does not provide pointers. **E** is incorrect because JavaScript is an implementation of the ECMA standard, not Java. **F** is incorrect because the use of bytecode and the JVM provide Java's primary security mechanisms.

2 Object Orientation

CERTIFICATION OBJECTIVES

- Describe Encapsulation
- Implement Inheritance
- Use IS-A and HAS-A Relationships (OCP)
- Use Polymorphism
- Use Overriding and Overloading
- Understand Casting
- Use Interfaces
- Understand and Use Return Types
- Develop Constructors
- Use static Members
- ✓ Two-Minute Drill
- Q&A Self Test

Being an Oracle Certified Associate (OCA) 8 means you must be at one with the object-oriented aspects of Java. You must dream of inheritance hierarchies; the power of polymorphism must flow through you; and encapsulation must become second nature to you. (Coupling, cohesion, composition, and design patterns will become your bread and butter when you're an Oracle Certified Professional [OCP] 8.) This chapter will prepare you for all the object-oriented objectives and questions you'll encounter on the exam. We have heard of many experienced Java programmers who haven't really become fluent with the object-oriented tools that Java provides, so we'll start at the beginning.

CERTIFICATION OBJECTIVE

Encapsulation (OCA Objectives 6.1 and 6.5)

6.1 Create methods with arguments and return values; including overloaded methods.
6.5 Apply encapsulation principles to a class.

Imagine you wrote the code for a class and another dozen programmers from your company all wrote programs that used your class. Now imagine that later on, you didn't like the way the class behaved, because some of its instance variables were being set (by the other programmers from within their code) to values you hadn't anticipated. *Their* code brought out errors in *your* code. (Relax, this is just hypothetical.) Well, it is a Java program, so you should be able to ship out a newer version of the class, which they could replace in their programs without changing any of their own code.

This scenario highlights two of the promises/benefits of an object-oriented (OO) language: flexibility and maintainability. But those benefits don't come automatically. You have to do something. You have to write your classes and code in a way that supports flexibility and maintainability. So what if Java supports OO? It can't design your code for you. For example, imagine you made your class with `public` instance variables, and those other programmers were setting the instance variables directly, as the following code demonstrates:

```
public class BadOO {
  public int size;
  public int weight;
  ...
```

```
}
public class ExploitBadOO {
  public static void main (String [] args) {
    BadOO b = new BadOO();
    b.size = -5; // Legal but bad!!
  }
}
```

And now you're in trouble. How are you going to change the class in a way that lets you handle the issues that come up when somebody changes the `size` variable to a value that causes problems? Your only choice is to go back in and write method code to adjust `size` (a `setSize(int a)` method, for example) and then insulate the `size` variable with, say, a private access modifier. But as soon as you make that change to your code, you break everyone else's!

The ability to make changes in your implementation code without breaking the code of others who use your code is a key benefit of encapsulation. You want to hide implementation details behind a public programming interface. By *interface*, we mean the set of accessible methods your code makes available for other code to call—in other words, your code's API. By hiding implementation details, you can rework your method code (perhaps also altering the way variables are used by your class) without forcing a change in the code that calls your changed method.

If you want maintainability, flexibility, and extensibility (and, of course, you do), your design must include encapsulation. How do you do that?

- Keep instance variables hidden (with an access modifier, often `private`).
- Make `public` accessor methods, and force calling code to use those methods rather than directly accessing the instance variable. These so-called accessor methods allow users of your class to **set** a variable's value or **get** a variable's value.
- For these accessor methods, use the most common naming convention of `set<SomeProperty>` and `get<SomeProperty>`.

Figure 2-1 illustrates the idea that encapsulation forces callers of our code to go through methods rather than accessing variables directly.

We call the access methods *getters* and *setters*, although some prefer the fancier terms *accessors* and *mutators*. (Personally, we don't like the word "mutate.") Regardless of what you call them, they're methods that other programmers must

FIGURE 2-1 The nature of encapsulation

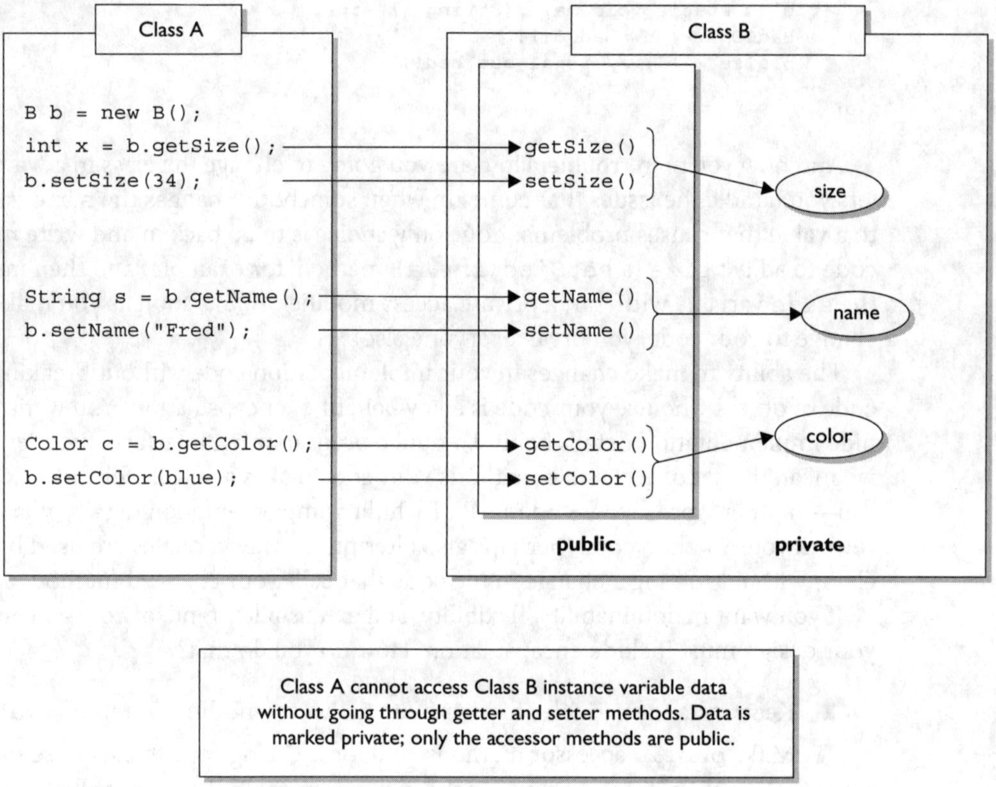

go through in order to access your instance variables. They look simple, and you've probably been using them forever:

```
public class Box {
  // hide the instance variable; only an instance
  // of Box can access it
  private int size;
  // Provide public getters and setters
  public int getSize() {
    return size;
  }
```

```
    public void setSize(int newSize) {
      size = newSize;
    }
  }
```

Wait a minute. How useful is the previous code? It doesn't even do any validation or processing. What benefit can there be from having getters and setters that add no functionality? The point is, you can change your mind later and add more code to your methods without breaking your API. Even if today you don't think you really need validation or processing of the data, good OO design dictates that you plan for the future. To be safe, force calling code to go through your methods rather than going directly to instance variables. *Always.* Then you're free to rework your method implementations later, without risking the wrath of those dozen programmers who know where you live.

Note: In Chapter 6 we'll revisit the topic of encapsulation as it applies to instance variables that are also reference variables. It's trickier than you might think, so stay tuned! (Also, we'll wait until Chapter 6 to challenge you with encapsulation-themed mock questions.)

exam watch

Look out for code that appears to be asking about the behavior of a method, when the problem is actually a lack of encapsulation. Look at the following example, and see if you can figure out what's going on:

```
class Foo {
  public int left = 9;
  public int right = 3;
  public void setLeft(int leftNum) {
    left = leftNum;
    right = leftNum/3;
  }
  // lots of complex test code here
}
```

Now consider this question: Is the value of right always going to be one-third the value of left? It looks like it will, until you realize that users of the `Foo` class don't need to use the `setLeft()` method! They can simply go straight to the instance variables and change them to any arbitrary `int` value.

CERTIFICATION OBJECTIVE

Inheritance and Polymorphism (OCA Objectives 7.1 and 7.2)

7.1 Describe inheritance and its benefits.

7.2 Develop code that demonstrates the use of polymorphism; including overriding and object type versus reference type (sic).

Inheritance is everywhere in Java. It's safe to say that it's almost (almost?) impossible to write even the tiniest Java program without using inheritance. To explore this topic, we're going to use the `instanceof` operator, which we'll discuss in more detail in Chapter 4. For now, just remember that `instanceof` returns `true` if the reference variable being tested is of the type being compared to. This code

```
class Test {
  public static void main(String [] args) {
    Test t1 = new Test();
    Test t2 = new Test();
    if (!t1.equals(t2))
      System.out.println("they're not equal");
    if (t1 instanceof Object)
      System.out.println("t1's an Object");
  }
}
```

produces this output:

```
they're not equal
t1's an Object
```

Where did that `equals` method come from? The reference variable `t1` is of type `Test`, and there's no `equals` method in the `Test` class. Or is there? The second `if` test asks whether `t1` is an instance of class `Object`, and because it *is* (more on that soon), the `if` test succeeds.

Hold on...how can `t1` be an instance of type `Object`, when we just said it was of type `Test`? I'm sure you're way ahead of us here, but it turns out that every class in Java is a subclass of class `Object` (except, of course, class `Object` itself). In other words, every class you'll ever use or ever write will inherit from class `Object`. You'll always have an `equals` method, a `clone` method, `notify`, `wait`, and others available to use. Whenever you create a class, you automatically inherit all of class `Object`'s methods.

Why? Let's look at that `equals` method for instance. Java's creators correctly assumed that it would be very common for Java programmers to want to compare instances of their classes to check for equality. If class `Object` didn't have an `equals` method, you'd have to write one yourself—you and every other Java programmer. That one `equals` method has been inherited billions of times. (To be fair, `equals` has also been *overridden* billions of times, but we're getting ahead of ourselves.)

The Evolution of Inheritance

Up until Java 8, when the topic of inheritance was discussed, it usually revolved around subclasses inheriting methods from their superclasses. While this simplification was never perfectly correct, it became less correct with the new features available in Java 8. As the following table shows, it's now possible to inherit concrete methods from interfaces. This is a big change. For the rest of the chapter, when we talk about inheritance generally, we will tend to use the terms "subtypes" and "supertypes" to acknowledge that both classes and interfaces need to be accounted for. We will tend to use the terms "subclass" and "superclass" when we're discussing a specific example that's under discussion. Inheritance is a key aspect of most of the topics we'll be discussing in this chapter, so be prepared for LOTS of discussion about the interactions between supertypes and subtypes!

As you study the following table, you'll notice that as of Java 8 interfaces can contain two types of concrete methods, `static` and `default`. We'll discuss these important additions later in this chapter.

Table 2-1 summarizes the elements of classes and interfaces relative to inheritance.

TABLE 2-1 Inheritable Elements of Classes and Interfaces

Elements of Types	Classes	Interfaces
Instance variables	Yes	Not applicable
Static variables	Yes	Only constants
Abstract methods	Yes	Yes
Instance methods	Yes	Java 8, default methods
Static methods	Yes	Java 8, inherited no, accessible yes
Constructors	No	Not applicable
Initialization blocks	No	Not applicable

For the exam, you'll need to know that you can create inheritance relationships in Java by *extending* a class or by implementing an interface. It's also important to understand that the two most common reasons to use inheritance are

- To promote code reuse
- To use polymorphism

Let's start with reuse. A common design approach is to create a fairly generic version of a class with the intention of creating more specialized subclasses that inherit from it. For example:

```
class GameShape {
  public void displayShape() {
    System.out.println("displaying shape");
  }
  // more code
}

class PlayerPiece extends GameShape {
  public void movePiece() {
    System.out.println("moving game piece");
  }
  // more code
}

public class TestShapes {
  public static void main (String[] args) {
    PlayerPiece shape = new PlayerPiece();
    shape.displayShape();
    shape.movePiece();
  }
}
```

outputs:

```
displaying shape
moving game piece
```

Notice that the `PlayerPiece` class inherits the generic `displayShape()` method from the less-specialized class `GameShape` and also adds its own method, `movePiece()`. Code reuse through inheritance means that methods with generic functionality—such as `displayShape()`, which could apply to a wide range of different kinds of shapes in a game—don't have to be reimplemented. That means all specialized subclasses of `GameShape` are guaranteed to have the capabilities of the more general superclass. You don't want to have to rewrite the `displayShape()` code in each of your specialized components of an online game.

But you knew that. You've experienced the pain of duplicate code when you make a change in one place and have to track down all the other places where that same (or very similar) code exists.

The second (and related) use of inheritance is to allow your classes to be accessed polymorphically—a capability provided by interfaces as well, but we'll get to that in a minute. Let's say that you have a `GameLauncher` class that wants to loop through a list of different kinds of `GameShape` objects and invoke `displayShape()` on each of them. At the time you write this class, you don't know every possible kind of `GameShape` subclass that anyone else will ever write. And you sure don't want to have to redo *your* code just because somebody decided to build a dice shape six months later.

The beautiful thing about polymorphism ("many forms") is that you can treat any *subclass* of `GameShape` as a `GameShape`. In other words, you can write code in your `GameLauncher` class that says, "I don't care what kind of object you are as long as you inherit from (extend) `GameShape`. And as far as I'm concerned, if you extend `GameShape`, then you've definitely got a `displayShape()` method, so I know I can call it."

Imagine we now have two specialized subclasses that extend the more generic `GameShape` class, `PlayerPiece` and `TilePiece`:

```
class GameShape {
  public void displayShape() {
    System.out.println("displaying shape");
  }
  // more code
}

class PlayerPiece extends GameShape {
  public void movePiece() {
    System.out.println("moving game piece");
  }
  // more code
}

class TilePiece extends GameShape {
  public void getAdjacent() {
    System.out.println("getting adjacent tiles");
  }
  // more code
}
```

Now imagine a test class has a method with a declared argument type of `GameShape`, which means it can take any kind of `GameShape`. In other words, any subclass of `GameShape` can be passed to a method with an argument of type `GameShape`. This code

```
public class TestShapes {
  public static void main (String[] args) {
    PlayerPiece player = new PlayerPiece();
    TilePiece tile = new TilePiece();
    doShapes(player);
    doShapes(tile);
  }

  public static void doShapes(GameShape shape) {
    shape.displayShape();
  }
}
```

outputs:

```
displaying shape
displaying shape
```

The key point is that the `doShapes()` method is declared with a `GameShape` argument but can be passed any subtype (in this example, a subclass) of `GameShape`. The method can then invoke any method of `GameShape`, without any concern for the actual runtime class type of the object passed to the method. There are implications, though. The `doShapes()` method knows only that the objects are a type of `GameShape` since that's how the parameter is declared. And using a reference variable declared as type `GameShape`—regardless of whether the variable is a method parameter, local variable, or instance variable—means that *only* the methods of `GameShape` can be invoked on it. The methods you can call on a reference are totally dependent on the *declared* type of the variable, no matter what the actual object is, that the reference is referring to. That means you can't use a `GameShape` variable to call, say, the `getAdjacent()` method even if the object passed in *is* of type `TilePiece`. (We'll see this again when we look at interfaces.)

IS-A and HAS-A Relationships

Note: As of Winter 2017, the OCA 8 exam won't ask you **directly** about IS-A and HAS-A relationships. But understanding IS-A and HAS-A relationships will help OCA 8 candidates with many of the questions on the exam.

IS-A

In OO, the concept of IS-A is based on inheritance (or interface implementation). IS-A is a way of saying, "This thing is a type of that thing." For example, a Mustang is a type of Horse, so in OO terms we can say, "Mustang IS-A Horse." Subaru IS-A Car. Broccoli IS-A Vegetable (not a very fun one, but it still counts). You express the IS-A relationship in Java through the keywords `extends` (for *class* inheritance) and `implements` (for *interface* implementation).

```
public class Car {
  // Cool Car code goes here
}

public class Subaru extends Car {
  // Important Subaru-specific stuff goes here
  // Don't forget Subaru inherits accessible Car members which
  // can include both methods and variables.
}
```

A Car is a type of Vehicle, so the inheritance tree might start from the `Vehicle` class as follows:

```
public class Vehicle { ... }
public class Car extends Vehicle { ... }
public class Subaru extends Car { ... }
```

In OO terms, you can say the following:

`Vehicle` is the superclass of `Car`.
`Car` is the subclass of `Vehicle`.
`Car` is the superclass of `Subaru`.
`Subaru` is the subclass of `Vehicle`.
`Car` inherits from `Vehicle`.
`Subaru` inherits from both `Vehicle` and `Car`.
`Subaru` is derived from `Car`.
`Car` is derived from `Vehicle`.
`Subaru` is derived from `Vehicle`.
`Subaru` is a subtype of both `Vehicle` and `Car`.

Returning to our IS-A relationship, the following statements are true:

"`Car` extends `Vehicle`" means "`Car` IS-A `Vehicle`."
"`Subaru` extends `Car`" means "`Subaru` IS-A `Car`."

And we can also say:

"Subaru IS-A Vehicle"

because a class is said to be "a type of" anything further up in its inheritance tree. If the expression (`Foo instanceof Bar`) is `true`, then class `Foo` IS-A `Bar`, even if `Foo` doesn't directly extend `Bar`, but instead extends some other class that is a subclass of `Bar`. Figure 2-2 illustrates the inheritance tree for `Vehicle`, `Car`, and `Subaru`. The arrows move from the subclass to the superclass. In other words, a class's arrow points toward the class from which it extends.

FIGURE 2-2

Inheritance tree for `Vehicle`, `Car`, `Subaru`

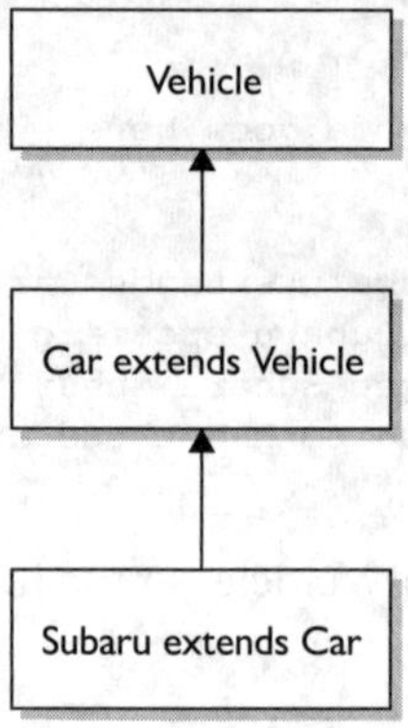

HAS-A

HAS-A relationships are based on use, rather than inheritance. In other words, class A HAS-A B if code in class A has a reference to an instance of class B. For example, you can say the following:

A `Horse` IS-A `Animal`. A `Horse` HAS-A `Halter`.

The code might look like this:

```
public class Animal { }
public class Horse extends Animal {
  private Halter myHalter;
}
```

In this code, the `Horse` class has an instance variable of type `Halter` (a halter is a piece of gear you might have if you have a horse), so you can say that a "`Horse` HAS-A `Halter`." In other words, `Horse` has a reference to a `Halter`. `Horse` code can use that `Halter` reference to invoke methods on the `Halter` and get `Halter` behavior without having `Halter`-related code (methods) in the `Horse` class itself. Figure 2-3 illustrates the HAS-A relationship between `Horse` and `Halter`.

FIGURE 2-3

HAS-A relationship between `Horse` and `Halter`

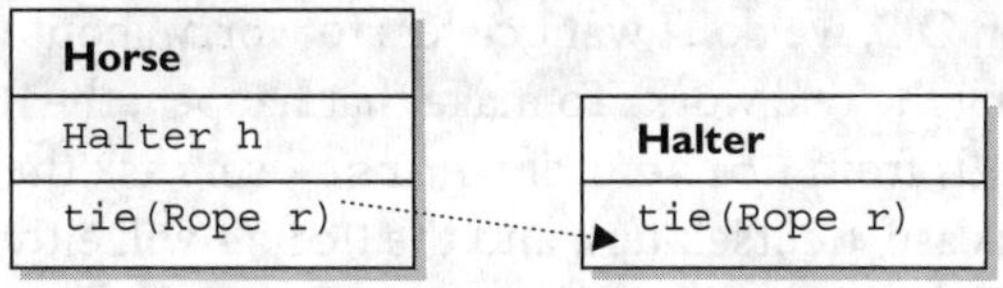

`Horse` class has a `Halter`, because `Horse` declares an instance variable of type `Halter`. When code invokes `tie()` on a `Horse` instance, the `Horse` invokes `tie()` on the `Horse` object's `Halter` instance variable.

HAS-A relationships allow you to design classes that follow good OO practices by not having monolithic classes that do a gazillion different things. Classes (and their resulting objects) should be specialists. As our friend Andrew says, "Specialized classes can actually help reduce bugs." The more specialized the class, the more likely it is that you can reuse the class in other applications. If you put all the `Halter`-related code directly into the `Horse` class, you'll end up duplicating code in the `Cow` class, `UnpaidIntern` class, and any other class that might need `Halter` behavior. By keeping the `Halter` code in a separate, specialized `Halter` class, you have the chance to reuse the `Halter` class in multiple applications.

Users of the `Horse` class (that is, code that calls methods on a `Horse` instance) think that the `Horse` class has `Halter` behavior. The `Horse` class might have a `tie(LeadRope rope)` method, for example. Users of the `Horse` class should never have to know that when they invoke the `tie()` method, the `Horse` object turns around and delegates the call to its `Halter` class by invoking `myHalter.tie(rope)`. The scenario just described might look like this:

```
public class Horse extends Animal {
  private Halter myHalter = new Halter();
  public void tie(LeadRope rope) {
    myHalter.tie(rope);  // Delegate tie behavior to the
                         // Halter object
  }
}
public class Halter {
  public void tie(LeadRope aRope) {
    // Do the actual tie work here
  }
}
```

In OO, we don't want callers to worry about which class or object is actually doing the real work. To make that happen, the `Horse` class hides implementation details from `Horse` users. `Horse` users ask the `Horse` object to do things (in this case, tie itself up), and the `Horse` will either do it or, as in this example, ask something else (like perhaps an inherited `Animal` class method) to do it. To the caller, though, it always appears that the `Horse` object takes care of itself. Users of a `Horse` should not even need to know that there is such a thing as a `Halter` class.

FROM THE CLASSROOM

Object-Oriented Design

IS-A and HAS-A relationships and encapsulation are just the tip of the iceberg when it comes to OO design. Many books and graduate theses have been dedicated to this topic. The reason for the emphasis on proper design is simple: money. The cost to deliver a software application has been estimated to be as much as ten times more expensive for poorly designed programs.

Even the best OO designers (often called "architects") make mistakes. It is difficult to visualize the relationships between hundreds, or even thousands, of classes. When mistakes are discovered during the implementation (code writing) phase of a project, the amount of code that must be rewritten can sometimes mean programming teams have to start over from scratch.

The software industry has evolved to aid the designer. Visual object modeling languages, such as the Unified Modeling Language (UML), allow designers to design and easily modify classes without having to write code first because OO components are represented graphically. This allows designers to create a map of the class relationships and helps them recognize errors before coding begins. Another innovation in OO design is design patterns. Designers noticed that many OO designs apply consistently from project to project and that it was useful to apply the same designs because it reduced the potential to introduce new design errors. OO designers then started to share these designs with each other. Now there are many catalogs of these design patterns both on the Internet and in book form.

Although passing the Java certification exam does not require you to understand OO design this thoroughly, hopefully this background information will help you better appreciate why the test writers chose to include encapsulation and IS-A and HAS-A relationships on the exam.

—Jonathan Meeks,
Sun Certified Java Programmer

CERTIFICATION OBJECTIVE

Polymorphism (OCA Objective 7.2)

7.2 Develop code that demonstrates the use of polymorphism; including overriding and object type versus reference type (sic).

Remember that any Java object that can pass more than one IS-A test can be considered polymorphic. Other than objects of type `Object`, *all* Java objects are polymorphic in that they pass the IS-A test for their own type and for class `Object`.

Remember, too, that the only way to access an object is through a reference variable. There are a few key things you should know about references:

- A reference variable can be of only one type, and once declared, that type can never be changed (although the object it references can change).
- A reference is a variable, so it can be reassigned to other objects (unless the reference is declared `final`).
- A reference variable's type determines the methods that can be invoked on the object the variable is referencing.
- A reference variable can refer to any object of the same type as the declared reference, or—this is the big one—**it can refer to any *subtype* of the declared type!**
- A reference variable can be declared as a class type or an interface type. If the variable is declared as an interface type, it can reference any object of any class that *implements* the interface.

Earlier we created a `GameShape` class that was extended by two other classes, `PlayerPiece` and `TilePiece`. Now imagine you want to animate some of the shapes on the gameboard. But not *all* shapes are able to be animated, so what do you do with class inheritance?

Could we create a class with an `animate()` method and have only *some* of the `GameShape` subclasses inherit from that class? If we can, then we could have `PlayerPiece`, for example, extend *both* the `GameShape` class and `Animatable` class, whereas the `TilePiece` would extend only `GameShape`. But no, this won't work! Java supports only single class inheritance! That means a class can have only one immediate superclass. In other words, if `PlayerPiece` is a class, there is no way to say something like this:

```
class PlayerPiece extends GameShape, Animatable { // NO!
  // more code
}
```

A *class* cannot *extend* more than one class: that means one parent per class. A class *can* have multiple ancestors, however, since class B could extend class A, and class C could extend class B, and so on. So any given class might have multiple classes up its inheritance tree, but that's not the same as saying a class directly extends two classes.

on the job

Some languages (such as C++) allow a class to extend more than one other class. This capability is known as "multiple inheritance." The reason that Java's creators chose not to allow multiple class inheritance is that it can become quite messy. In a nutshell, the problem is that if a class extended two other classes, and both superclasses had, say, a `doStuff()` method, which version of `doStuff()` would the subclass inherit? This issue can lead to a scenario known as the "Deadly Diamond of Death," because of the shape of the class diagram that can be created in a multiple inheritance design. The diamond is formed when classes B and C both extend A, and both B and C inherit a method from A. If class D extends both B and C, and both B and C have overridden the method in A, class D has, in theory, inherited two different implementations of the same method. Drawn as a class diagram, the shape of the four classes looks like a diamond.

exam watch

To reiterate, as of Java 8, interfaces can have concrete methods (called `default` methods). This allows for a form of multiple interhance, which we'll discuss later in the chapter.

So if that doesn't work, what else could you do? You could simply put the `animate()` code in `GameShape`, and then disable the method in classes that can't be animated. But that's a bad design choice for many reasons—it's more error prone; it makes the `GameShape` class less cohesive; and it means the `GameShape` API "advertises" that all shapes can be animated when, in fact, that's not true since only some of the `GameShape` subclasses will be able to run the `animate()` method successfully.

So what *else* could you do? You already know the answer—create an `Animatable` *interface*, and have only the `GameShape` subclasses that can be animated implement that interface. Here's the interface:

```
public interface Animatable {
  public void animate();
}
```

And here's the modified `PlayerPiece` class that implements the interface:

```
class PlayerPiece extends GameShape implements Animatable {
  public void movePiece() {
    System.out.println("moving game piece");
  }
  public void animate() {
    System.out.println("animating...");
  }
  // more code
}
```

So now we have a `PlayerPiece` that passes the IS-A test for both the `GameShape` class and the `Animatable` interface. That means a `PlayerPiece` can be treated polymorphically as one of four things at any given time, depending on the declared type of the reference variable:

- An `Object` (since any object inherits from `Object`)
- A `GameShape` (since `PlayerPiece` extends `GameShape`)
- A `PlayerPiece` (since that's what it really is)
- An `Animatable` (since `PlayerPiece` implements `Animatable`)

The following are all legal declarations. Look closely:

```
PlayerPiece player = new PlayerPiece();
Object o = player;
GameShape shape = player;
Animatable mover = player;
```

There's only one object here—an instance of type `PlayerPiece`—but there are four different types of reference variables, all referring to that one object on the heap. Pop quiz: Which of the preceding reference variables can invoke the `displayShape()` method? Hint: Only two of the four declarations can be used to invoke the `displayShape()` method.

Remember that method invocations allowed by the compiler are based solely on the declared type of the reference, regardless of the object type. So looking at the four reference types again—Object, GameShape, PlayerPiece, and Animatable—which of these four types know about the displayShape() method?

You guessed it—both the GameShape class and the PlayerPiece class are known (by the compiler) to have a displayShape() method, so either of those reference types can be used to invoke displayShape(). Remember that to the compiler, a PlayerPiece IS-A GameShape, so the compiler says, "I see that the declared type is PlayerPiece, and since PlayerPiece extends GameShape, that means PlayerPiece inherited the displayShape() method. Therefore, PlayerPiece can be used to invoke the displayShape() method."

Which methods can be invoked when the PlayerPiece object is being referred to using a reference declared as type Animatable? Only the animate() method. Of course, the cool thing here is that any class from any inheritance tree can also implement Animatable, so that means if you have a method with an argument declared as type Animatable, you can pass in PlayerPiece objects, SpinningLogo objects, and anything else that's an instance of a class that implements Animatable. And you can use that parameter (of type Animatable) to invoke the animate() method, but not the displayShape() method (which it might not even have), or anything other than what is known to the compiler based on the reference type. The compiler always knows, though, that you can invoke the methods of class Object on any object, so those are safe to call regardless of the reference—class or interface—used to refer to the object.

We've left out one big part of all this, which is that even though the compiler only knows about the declared reference type, the Java Virtual Machine (JVM) at runtime knows what the object really is. And that means that even if the PlayerPiece object's displayShape() method is called using a GameShape reference variable, if the PlayerPiece overrides the displayShape() method, the JVM will invoke the PlayerPiece version! The JVM looks at the real object at the other end of the reference, "sees" that it has overridden the method of the declared reference variable type, and invokes the method of the object's actual class. But there is one other thing to keep in mind:

Polymorphic method invocations apply only to *instance methods.* You can always refer to an object with a more general reference variable type (a superclass or interface), but at runtime, the ONLY things that are dynamically selected based on the actual *object* (rather than the *reference* type) are instance methods. Not *static* methods. Not *variables.* Only overridden instance methods are dynamically invoked based on the real object's type.

Because this definition depends on a clear understanding of overriding and the distinction between static methods and instance methods, we'll cover those later in the chapter.

CERTIFICATION OBJECTIVE

Overriding/Overloading (OCA Objectives 6.1 and 7.2)

6.1 Create methods with arguments and return values; including overloaded methods.
7.2 Develop code that demonstrates the use of polymorphism; including overriding and object type versus reference type (sic).

The exam will use overridden and overloaded methods on many, many questions. These two concepts are often confused (perhaps because they have similar names?), but each has its own unique and complex set of rules. It's important to get really clear about which "over" uses which rules!

Overridden Methods

Any time a type inherits a method from a supertype, you have the opportunity to override the method (unless, as you learned earlier, the method is marked `final`). The key benefit of overriding is the ability to define behavior that's specific to a particular subtype. The following example demonstrates a `Horse` subclass of `Animal` overriding the `Animal` version of the `eat()` method:

```
public class Animal {
  public void eat() {
    System.out.println("Generic Animal Eating Generically");
  }
}
class Horse extends Animal {
  public void eat() {
    System.out.println("Horse eating hay, oats, "
                       + "and horse treats");
  }
}
```

For abstract methods you inherit from a supertype, you have no choice: You *must* implement the method in the subtype ***unless the subtype is also abstract.*** Abstract methods must be *implemented* by the first concrete subclass, but this is a lot like saying the concrete subclass *overrides* the abstract methods of the supertype(s). So you could think of abstract methods as methods you're forced to override—eventually.

The `Animal` class creator might have decided that for the purposes of polymorphism, all `Animal` subtypes should have an `eat()` method defined in a unique way. Polymorphically, when an `Animal` reference refers not to an `Animal` instance, but to an `Animal` subclass instance, the caller should be able to invoke `eat()` on the `Animal` reference, but the actual runtime object (say, a `Horse` instance) will run its own specific `eat()` method. Marking the `eat()` method abstract is the `Animal` programmer's way of saying to all subclass developers, "It doesn't make any sense for your new subtype to use a generic `eat()` method, so you have to come up with your *own* `eat()` method implementation!" A (nonabstract) example of using polymorphism looks like this:

```
public class TestAnimals {
  public static void main (String [] args) {
    Animal a = new Animal();
    Animal b = new Horse();  // Animal ref, but a Horse object
    a.eat(); // Runs the Animal version of eat()
    b.eat(); // Runs the Horse version of eat()
  }
}
class Animal {
  public void eat() {
    System.out.println("Generic Animal Eating Generically");
  }
}
class Horse extends Animal {
  public void eat() {
    System.out.println("Horse eating hay, oats, "
                       + "and horse treats");
   }
   public void buck() { }
}
```

In the preceding code, the test class uses an `Animal` reference to invoke a method on a `Horse` object. Remember, the compiler will allow only methods in class `Animal` to be invoked when using a reference to an `Animal`. The following would not be legal given the preceding code:

```
Animal c = new Horse();
c.buck();  // Can't invoke buck();
           // Animal class doesn't have that method
```

To reiterate, the compiler looks only at the reference type, not the instance type. Polymorphism lets you use a more abstract supertype (including an interface) reference to one of its subtypes (including interface implementers).

The overriding method cannot have a more restrictive access modifier than the method being overridden (for example, you can't override a method marked `public` and make it `protected`). Think about it: If the `Animal` class advertises a `public eat()` method and someone has an `Animal` reference (in other words, a reference declared as type `Animal`), that someone will assume it's safe to call `eat()` on the `Animal` reference regardless of the actual instance that the `Animal` reference is referring to. If a subtype were allowed to sneak in and change the access modifier on the overriding method, then suddenly at runtime—when the JVM invokes the true object's (`Horse`) version of the method rather than the reference type's (`Animal`) version—the program would die a horrible death. (Not to mention the emotional distress for the one who was betrayed by the rogue subtype.)

Let's modify the polymorphic example we saw earlier in this section:

```
public class TestAnimals {
  public static void main (String [] args) {
    Animal a = new Animal();
    Animal b = new Horse(); // Animal ref, but a Horse object
    a.eat();                // Runs the Animal version of eat()
    b.eat();                // Runs the Horse version of eat()
  }
}
class Animal {
  public void eat() {
    System.out.println("Generic Animal Eating Generically");
  }
}
class Horse extends Animal {
  private void eat() {     // whoa! - it's private!
    System.out.println("Horse eating hay, oats, "
                       + "and horse treats");
  }
}
```

If this code compiled (which it doesn't), the following would fail at runtime:

```
Animal b = new Horse();  // Animal ref, but a Horse
                         // object, so far so good
b.eat();                 // Meltdown at runtime!
```

The variable `b` is of type `Animal`, which has a `public eat()` method. But remember that at runtime, Java uses virtual method invocation to dynamically select the actual version of the method that will run, based on the actual instance. An `Animal` reference can always refer to a `Horse` instance, because `Horse`

IS-A(n) `Animal`. What makes that supertype reference to a subtype instance possible is that the subtype is guaranteed to be able to do everything the supertype can do. Whether the `Horse` instance overrides the inherited methods of `Animal` or simply inherits them, anyone with an `Animal` reference to a `Horse` instance is free to call all accessible `Animal` methods. For that reason, an overriding method must fulfill the contract of the superclass.

Note: In Chapter 5 we will explore exception handling in detail. Once you've studied Chapter 5, you'll appreciate this single handy list of overriding rules. The rules for overriding a method are as follows:

- The argument list must exactly match that of the overridden method. If they don't match, you can end up with an overloaded method you didn't intend.
- The return type must be the same as, or a subtype of, the return type declared in the original overridden method in the superclass. (More on this in a few pages when we discuss covariant returns.)
- The access level can't be more restrictive than that of the overridden method.
- The access level CAN be less restrictive than that of the overridden method.
- Instance methods can be overridden only if they are inherited by the subtype. A subtype within the same package as the instance's supertype can override any supertype method that is not marked `private` or `final`. A subtype in a different package can override only those non`final` methods marked `public` or `protected` (since `protected` methods are inherited by the subtype).
- The overriding method CAN throw any unchecked (runtime) exception, regardless of whether the overridden method declares the exception. (More in Chapter 5.)
- The overriding method must NOT throw checked exceptions that are new or broader than those declared by the overridden method. For example, a method that declares a `FileNotFoundException` cannot be overridden by a method that declares a `SQLException`, `Exception`, or any other nonruntime exception unless it's a subclass of `FileNotFoundException`.
- The overriding method can throw narrower or fewer exceptions. Just because an overridden method "takes risks" doesn't mean that the overriding subtype's exception takes the same risks. Bottom line: an overriding method doesn't have to declare any exceptions that it will never throw, regardless of what the overridden method declares.
- You cannot override a method marked `final`.

- You cannot override a method marked `static`. We'll look at an example in a few pages when we discuss `static` methods in more detail.
- If a method can't be inherited, you cannot override it. Remember that overriding implies that you're reimplementing a method you inherited! For example, the following code is not legal, and even if you added an `eat()` method to `Horse`, it wouldn't be an override of `Animal`'s `eat()` method:

```
public class TestAnimals {
  public static void main (String [] args) {
    Horse h =  new Horse();
    h.eat(); // Not legal because Horse didn't inherit eat()
  }
}
class Animal {
  private void eat() {
    System.out.println("Generic Animal Eating Generically");
  }
}
class Horse extends Animal { }
```

Invoking a Supertype Version of an Overridden Method

Often, you'll want to take advantage of some of the code in the supertype version of a method, yet still override it to provide some additional specific behavior. It's like saying, "Run the supertype version of the method, and then come back down here and finish with my subtype additional method code." (Note that there's no requirement that the supertype version run before the subtype code.) It's easy to do in code using the keyword `super` as follows:

```
public class Animal {
  public void eat() { }
  public void printYourself() {
    // Useful printing code goes here
  }
}
class Horse extends Animal {
  public void printYourself() {
    // Take advantage of Animal code, then add some more
    super.printYourself();  // Invoke the superclass
                            // (Animal) code
                            // Then do Horse-specific
                            // print work here
  }
}
```

In a similar way, you can access an interface's overridden method with the syntax:

```
InterfaceX.super.doStuff();
```

Note: Using `super` to invoke an overridden method applies only to instance methods. (Remember that `static` methods can't be overridden.) And you can use `super` only to access a method in a type's supertype, not the supertype of the supertype—that is, you **cannot** say `super.super.doStuff()` and you **cannot** say: InterfaceX.`super.super.doStuff()`.

exam watch

If a method is overridden but you use a polymorphic (supertype) reference to refer to the subtype object with the overriding method, the compiler assumes you're calling the supertype version of the method. If the supertype version declares a checked exception, but the overriding subtype method does not, the compiler still thinks you are calling a method that declares an exception (more in Chapter 5). Let's look at an example:

```
class Animal {
  public void eat() throws Exception {
                     // throws an Exception
  }
}
class Dog2 extends Animal {
  public void eat() { /* no Exceptions */}
  public static void main(String [] args) {
    Animal a = new Dog2();
    Dog2 d = new Dog2();
    d.eat();           // ok
    a.eat();           // compiler error -
                       // unreported exception
  }
}
```

This code will not compile because of the exception declared on the `Animal eat()` method. This happens even though, at runtime, the `eat()` method used would be the `Dog` version, which does not declare the exception.

Examples of Illegal Method Overrides

Let's take a look at overriding the `eat()` method of `Animal`:

```
public class Animal {
  public void eat() { }
}
```

Table 2-2 lists examples of illegal overrides of the `Animal eat()` method, given the preceding version of the `Animal` class.

TABLE 2-2 Examples of Illegal Overrides

Illegal Override Code	Problem with the Code
`private void eat() { }`	Access modifier more restrictive
`public void eat() throws IOException { }`	Declares a checked exception not defined by superclass version
`public void eat(String food) { }`	A legal overload, not an override, because the argument list changed
`public String eat() { }`	Not an override because of the return type, and not an overload either because there's no change in the argument list

Overloaded Methods

Over*loaded* methods let you reuse the same method name in a class, but with different arguments (and, optionally, a different return type). Overloading a method often means you're being a little nicer to those who call your methods because your code takes on the burden of coping with different argument types rather than forcing the caller to do conversions prior to invoking your method. The rules aren't too complex:

- Overloaded methods MUST change the argument list.
- Overloaded methods CAN change the return type.
- Overloaded methods CAN change the access modifier.
- Overloaded methods CAN declare new or broader checked exceptions.
- A method can be overloaded in the *same* type or in a *subtype*. In other words, if class A defines a `doStuff(int i)` method, the subclass B could define a `doStuff(String s)` method without overriding the superclass version that takes an `int`. So two methods with the same name but in different types can still be considered overloaded if the subtype inherits one version of the method and then declares another overloaded version in its type definition.

exam watch

Less experienced Java developers are often confused about the subtle differences between overloaded and overridden methods. Be careful to recognize when a method is overloaded rather than overridden. You might see a method that appears to be violating a rule for overriding, but that is actually a legal overload, as follows:

```
public class Foo {
  public void doStuff(int y, String s) { }
  public void moreThings(int x) { }
}
class Bar extends Foo {
  public void doStuff(int y, long s) throws IOException { }
}
```

It's tempting to see the `IOException` as the problem because the overridden `doStuff()` method doesn't declare an exception and `IOException` is checked by the compiler. But the `doStuff()` method is not overridden! Subclass `Bar` overloads the `doStuff()` method by varying the argument list, so the `IOException` is fine.

Legal Overloads

Let's look at a method we want to overload:

```
public void changeSize(int size, String name, float pattern) { }
```

The following methods are legal overloads of the `changeSize()` method:

```
public void changeSize(int size, String name) { }
private int changeSize(int size, float pattern) { }
public void changeSize(float pattern, String name)
                            throws IOException { }
```

Invoking Overloaded Methods

In Chapter 6 we will look at how boxing and var-args impact overloading. (You still have to pay attention to what's covered here, however.)

When a method is invoked, more than one method of the same name might exist for the object type you're invoking a method on. For example, the `Horse` class might have three methods with the same name but with different argument lists, which means the method is overloaded.

Deciding which of the matching methods to invoke is based on the arguments. If you invoke the method with a `String` argument, the overloaded version that takes a `String` is called. If you invoke a method of the same name but pass it a `float`, the overloaded version that takes a `float` will run. If you invoke the method of the same name but pass it a `Foo` object, and there isn't an overloaded version that takes a `Foo`, then the compiler will complain that it can't find a match. The following are examples of invoking overloaded methods:

```
class Adder {
  public int addThem(int x, int y) {
    return x + y;
  }

  // Overload the addThem method to add doubles instead of ints
  public double addThem(double x, double y) {
    return x + y;
  }
}
  // From another class, invoke the addThem() method
public class TestAdder {
  public static void main (String [] args) {
    Adder a = new Adder();
    int b = 27;
    int c = 3;
    int result = a.addThem(b,c);                 // Which addThem is invoked?
    double doubleResult = a.addThem(22.5,9.3); // Which addThem?
   }
}
```

In this `TestAdder` code, the first call to `a.addThem(b,c)` passes two `int`s to the method, so the first version of `addThem()`—the overloaded version that takes two `int` arguments—is called. The second call to `a.addThem(22.5, 9.3)` passes two `double`s to the method, so the second version of `addThem()`—the overloaded version that takes two double arguments—is called.

Invoking overloaded methods that take object references rather than primitives is a little more interesting. Say you have an overloaded method such that one version takes an `Animal` and one takes a `Horse` (subclass of `Animal`). If you pass a `Horse` object in the method invocation, you'll invoke the overloaded version that takes a `Horse`. Or so it looks at first glance:

```
class Animal { }
class Horse extends Animal { }
class UseAnimals {
  public void doStuff(Animal a) {
    System.out.println("In the Animal version");
  }
```

```
    public void doStuff(Horse h) {
      System.out.println("In the Horse version");
    }
    public static void main (String [] args) {
      UseAnimals ua = new UseAnimals();
      Animal animalObj = new Animal();
      Horse horseObj = new Horse();
      ua.doStuff(animalObj);
      ua.doStuff(horseObj);
    }
  }
```

The output is what you expect:

```
In the Animal version
In the Horse version
```

But what if you use an `Animal` reference to a `Horse` object?

```
Animal animalRefToHorse = new Horse();
  ua.doStuff(animalRefToHorse);
```

Which of the overloaded versions is invoked? You might want to answer, "The one that takes a `Horse` since it's a `Horse` object at runtime that's being passed to the method." But that's not how it works. The preceding code would actually print this:

```
in the Animal version
```

Even though the actual object at runtime is a `Horse` and not an `Animal`, the choice of which overloaded method to call (in other words, the signature of the method) is NOT dynamically decided at runtime.

Just remember that the *reference* type (not the object type) determines which overloaded method is invoked!

To summarize, which over*ridden* version of the method to call (in other words, from which class in the inheritance tree) is decided at *runtime* based on *object* type, but which over*loaded* version of the method to call is based on the *reference* type of the argument passed at *compile* time.

If you invoke a method passing it an `Animal` reference to a `Horse` object, the compiler knows only about the `Animal`, so it chooses the overloaded version of the method that takes an `Animal`. It does not matter that, at runtime, a `Horse` is actually being passed.

exam watch

Can `main()` be overloaded?

```
class DuoMain {
  public static void main(String[] args) {
    main(1);
  }
  static void main(int i) {
    System.out.println("overloaded main");
  }
}
```

Absolutely! But the only `main()` with JVM superpowers is the one with the signature you've seen about 100 times already in this book.

Polymorphism in Overloaded and Overridden Methods How does polymorphism work with overloaded methods? From what we just looked at, it doesn't appear that polymorphism matters when a method is overloaded. If you pass an `Animal` reference, the overloaded method that takes an `Animal` will be invoked, even if the actual object passed is a `Horse`. Once the `Horse` masquerading as `Animal` gets in to the method, however, the `Horse` object is still a `Horse` despite being passed into a method expecting an `Animal`. So it's true that polymorphism doesn't determine which overloaded version is called; however, polymorphism does come into play when the decision is about which overridden version of a method is called. But sometimes a method is both overloaded and overridden. Imagine that the `Animal` and `Horse` classes look like this:

```
public class Animal {
  public void eat() {
    System.out.println("Generic Animal Eating Generically");
  }
}
public class Horse extends Animal {
  public void eat() {
    System.out.println("Horse eating hay ");
  }
  public void eat(String s) {
    System.out.println("Horse eating " + s);
  }
}
```

Notice that the `Horse` class has both overloaded and overridden the `eat()` method. Table 2-3 shows which version of the three `eat()` methods will run depending on how they are invoked.

TABLE 2-3 Examples of Legal and Illegal Overrides

Method Invocation Code	Result
`Animal a = new Animal();` `a.eat();`	`Generic Animal Eating Generically`
`Horse h = new Horse();` `h.eat();`	`Horse eating hay`
`Animal ah = new` **`Horse()`**`;` `ah.eat();`	`Horse eating hay` Polymorphism works—the actual object type (`Horse`), not the reference type (`Animal`), is used to determine which `eat()` is called.
`Horse he = new Horse();` `he.eat("Apples");`	`Horse eating Apples` The overloaded `eat(String s)` method is invoked.
`Animal a2 = new Animal();` `a2.eat("treats");`	Compiler error! Compiler sees that the `Animal` class doesn't have an `eat()` method that takes a `String`.
`Animal ah2 = new` **`Horse()`**`;` `ah2.eat("Carrots");`	Compiler error! Compiler still looks only at the reference and sees that `Animal` doesn't have an `eat()` method that takes a `String`. Compiler doesn't care that the actual object might be a `Horse` at runtime.

exam watch

Don't be fooled by a method that's overloaded but not overridden by a subclass. It's perfectly legal to do the following:

```
public class Foo {
  void doStuff() { }
}
class Bar extends Foo {
  void doStuff(String s) { }
}
```

The `Bar` class has two `doStuff()` methods: the no-arg version it inherits from `Foo` (and does not override) and the overloaded `doStuff(String s)` defined in the `Bar` class. Code with a reference to a `Foo` can invoke only the no-arg version, but code with a reference to a `Bar` can invoke either of the overloaded versions.

Table 2-4 summarizes the difference between overloaded and overridden methods.

TABLE 2-4 Differences Between Overloaded and Overridden Methods

	Overloaded Method	Overridden Method
Argument(s)	Must change.	Must not change.
Return type	Can change.	Can't change except for covariant returns. (Covered later this chapter.)
Exceptions	Can change.	Can reduce or eliminate. Must not throw new or broader checked exceptions.
Access	Can change.	Must not make more restrictive (can be less restrictive).
Invocation	*Reference* type determines which overloaded version (based on declared argument types) is selected. Happens at *compile* time. The actual *method* that's invoked is still a virtual method invocation that happens at runtime, but the compiler will already know the *signature* of the method to be invoked. So at runtime, the argument match will already have been nailed down, just not the *class* in which the method lives.	*Object* type (in other words, *the type of the actual instance on the heap*) determines which method is selected. Happens at *runtime.*

We'll cover constructor overloading later in the chapter, where we'll also cover the other constructor-related topics that are on the exam. Figure 2-4 illustrates the way overloaded and overridden methods appear in class relationships.

FIGURE 2-4

Overloaded and overridden methods in class relationships

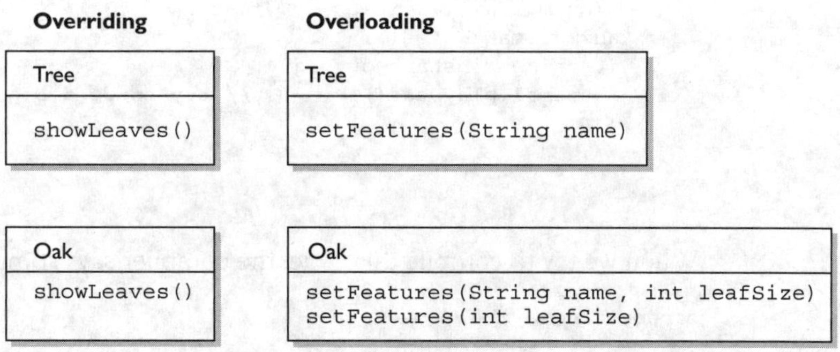

CERTIFICATION OBJECTIVE

Casting (OCA Objectives 2.2 and 7.3)

2.2 *Differentiate between object reference variables and primitive variables.*
7.3 *Determine when casting is necessary.*

You've seen how it's both possible and common to use general reference variable types to refer to more specific object types. It's at the heart of polymorphism. For example, this line of code should be second nature by now:

```
Animal animal = new Dog();
```

But what happens when you want to use that `animal` reference variable to invoke a method that only class `Dog` has? You know it's referring to a `Dog`, and you want to do a `Dog`-specific thing? In the following code, we've got an array of `Animals`, and whenever we find a `Dog` in the array, we want to do a special `Dog` thing. Let's agree for now that all this code is okay, except that we're not sure about the line of code that invokes the `playDead` method.

```
class Animal {
  void makeNoise() {System.out.println("generic noise"); }
}
class Dog extends Animal {
  void makeNoise() {System.out.println("bark"); }
  void playDead() { System.out.println("roll over"); }
}

class CastTest2 {
  public static void main(String [] args) {
    Animal [] a = {new Animal(), new Dog(), new Animal() };
    for(Animal animal : a) {
      animal.makeNoise();
      if(animal instanceof Dog) {
        animal.playDead();          // try to do a Dog behavior?
      }
    }
  }
}
```

When we try to compile this code, the compiler says something like this:

```
cannot find symbol
```

The compiler is saying, "Hey, class `Animal` doesn't have a `playDead()` method." Let's modify the `if` code block:

```
if(animal instanceof Dog) {
  Dog d = (Dog) animal;      // casting the ref. var.
  d.playDead();
}
```

The new and improved code block contains a cast, which in this case is sometimes called a *downcast*, because we're casting down the inheritance tree to a more specific class. Now the compiler is happy. Before we try to invoke `playDead`, we cast the `animal` variable to type `Dog`. What we're saying to the compiler is, "We know it's really referring to a `Dog` object, so it's okay to make a new `Dog` reference variable to refer to that object." In this case we're safe, because before we ever try the cast, we do an `instanceof` test to make sure.

It's important to know that the compiler is forced to trust us when we do a downcast, even when we screw up:

```
class Animal { }
class Dog extends Animal { }
class DogTest {
  public static void main(String [] args) {
    Animal animal = new Animal();
    Dog d = (Dog) animal;          // compiles but fails later
  }
}
```

It can be maddening! This code compiles! But when we try to run it, we'll get an exception, something like this:

```
java.lang.ClassCastException
```

Why can't we trust the compiler to help us out here? Can't it see that `animal` is of type `Animal`? All the compiler can do is verify that the two types are in the same inheritance tree, so that depending on whatever code might have come before the downcast, it's possible that `animal` is of type `Dog`. The compiler must allow things that might possibly work at runtime. However, if the compiler knows with certainty that the cast could not possibly work, compilation will fail. The following replacement code block will NOT compile:

```
Animal animal = new Animal();
Dog d = (Dog) animal;
String s = (String) animal;    // animal can't EVER be a String
```

In this case, you'll get an error like this:

```
inconvertible types
```

Unlike downcasting, *upcasting* (casting *up* the inheritance tree to a more general type) works implicitly (that is, you don't have to type in the cast) because when you upcast you're implicitly restricting the number of methods you can invoke, as opposed to *down*casting, which implies that later on, you might want to invoke a more *specific* method. Here's an example:

```
class Animal { }
class Dog extends Animal { }

class DogTest {
  public static void main(String [] args) {
    Dog d = new Dog();
    Animal a1 = d;              // upcast ok with no explicit cast
    Animal a2 = (Animal) d;     // upcast ok with an explicit cast
  }
}
```

Both of the previous upcasts will compile and run without exception because a Dog IS-A(n) Animal, which means that anything an Animal can do, a Dog can do. A Dog can do more, of course, but the point is that anyone with an Animal reference can safely call Animal methods on a Dog instance. The Animal methods may have been overridden in the Dog class, but all we care about now is that a Dog can always do at least everything an Animal can do. The compiler and JVM know it, too, so the implicit upcast is always legal for assigning an object of a subtype to a reference of one of its supertype classes (or interfaces). If Dog implements Pet and Pet defines beFriendly(), then a Dog can be implicitly cast to a Pet, but the only Dog method you can invoke then is beFriendly(), which Dog was forced to implement because Dog implements the Pet interface.

One more thing...if Dog implements Pet, then, if Beagle extends Dog but Beagle does not *declare* that it implements Pet, Beagle is still a Pet! Beagle is a Pet simply because it extends Dog, and Dog's already taken care of the Pet parts for itself and for all its children. The Beagle class can always override any method it inherits from Dog, including methods that Dog implemented to fulfill its interface contract.

And just one more thing...if Beagle does declare that it implements Pet, just so that others looking at the Beagle class API can easily see that Beagle IS-A

`Pet` without having to look at `Beagle`'s superclasses, `Beagle` still doesn't need to implement the `beFriendly()` method if the `Dog` class (`Beagle`'s superclass) has already taken care of that. In other words, if `Beagle` IS-A `Dog`, and `Dog` IS-A `Pet`, then `Beagle` IS-A `Pet` and has already met its `Pet` obligations for implementing the `beFriendly()` method since it inherits the `beFriendly()` method. The compiler is smart enough to say, "I know `Beagle` already IS a `Dog`, but it's okay to make it more obvious by adding a cast."

So don't be fooled by code that shows a concrete class that declares it implements an interface but doesn't implement the *methods* of the interface. Before you can tell whether the code is legal, you must know what the supertypes of this implementing class have declared. If any supertype in its inheritance tree has already provided concrete (that is, nonabstract) method implementations, then regardless of whether the supertype declares that it implements the interface, the subclass is under no obligation to reimplement (override) those methods.

exam watch

The exam creators will tell you that they're forced to jam tons of code into little spaces "because of the exam engine." Although that's partially true, they ALSO like to obfuscate. The following code

```
Animal a = new Dog();
Dog d = (Dog) a;
d.doDogStuff();
```

can be replaced with this easy-to-read bit of fun:

```
Animal a = new Dog();
((Dog)a).doDogStuff();
```

In this case the compiler needs all those parentheses; otherwise, it thinks it's been handed an incomplete statement.

CERTIFICATION OBJECTIVE

Implementing an Interface (OCA Objective 7.5)

7.5 Use abstract classes and interfaces.

When you implement an interface, you're agreeing to adhere to the contract defined in the interface. That means you're agreeing to provide legal implementations for every abstract method defined in the interface, and that anyone who knows what the interface methods look like (not how they're implemented, but how they can be called and what they return) can rest assured that they can invoke those methods on an instance of your implementing class.

For example, if you create a class that implements the `Runnable` interface (so that your code can be executed by a specific thread), you must provide the `public void run()` method. Otherwise, the poor thread could be told to go execute your `Runnable` object's code and—surprise, surprise—the thread then discovers the object has no `run()` method! (At which point, the thread would blow up and the JVM would crash in a spectacular yet horrible explosion.) Thankfully, Java prevents this meltdown from occurring by running a compiler check on any class that claims to implement an interface. If the class says it's implementing an interface, it darn well better have an implementation for each abstract method in the interface (with a few exceptions that we'll look at in a moment).

Assuming an interface `Bounceable` with two methods, `bounce()` and `setBounceFactor()`, the following class will compile:

```
public class Ball implements Bounceable {  // Keyword
                                           // 'implements'
  public void bounce() { }
  public void setBounceFactor(int bf) { }
}
```

Okay, we know what you're thinking: "This has got to be the worst implementation class in the history of implementation classes." It compiles, though. And it runs. The interface contract guarantees that a class will have the method (in other words, others can call the method subject to access control), but it never guaranteed a good implementation—or even any actual implementation code in the body of the method. (Keep in mind, though, that if the interface declares that a method is NOT void, your class's implementation code has to include a return statement.) The compiler will never say, "Um, excuse me, but did you really mean to put nothing between those curly braces? HELLO. This is a method after all, so shouldn't it do something?"

Implementation classes must adhere to the same rules for method implementation as a class extending an `abstract` class. To be a legal implementation class, a nonabstract implementation class must do the following:

- Provide concrete (nonabstract) implementations for all abstract methods from the declared interface.
- Follow all the rules for legal overrides, such as the following:
  - Declare no checked exceptions on implementation methods other than those declared by the interface method or subclasses of those declared by the interface method.
  - Maintain the signature of the interface method, and maintain the same return type (or a subtype). (But it does not have to declare the exceptions declared in the interface method declaration.)

exam watch

Implementation classes are NOT required to implement an interface's static or default methods. We'll discuss this in more depth later in the chapter.

But wait, there's more! An implementation class can itself be `abstract`! For example, the following is legal for a class `Ball` implementing `Bounceable`:

```
abstract class Ball implements Bounceable { }
```

Notice anything missing? We never provided the implementation methods. And that's okay. If the implementation class is `abstract`, it can simply pass the buck to its first concrete subclass. For example, if class `BeachBall` extends `Ball`, and `BeachBall` is not `abstract`, then `BeachBall` has to provide an implementation for all the abstract methods from `Bounceable`:

```
class BeachBall extends Ball {
  // Even though we don't say it in the class declaration above,
  // BeachBall implements Bounceable, since BeachBall's abstract
  // superclass (Ball) implements Bounceable

  public void bounce() {
  // interesting BeachBall-specific bounce code

  }
  public void setBounceFactor(int bf) {
  // clever BeachBall-specific code for setting
  // a bounce factor

  }
```

```
    // if class Ball defined any abstract methods,
    // they'll have to be
    // implemented here as well.
}
```

Look for classes that claim to implement an interface but don't provide the correct method implementations. Unless the implementing class is abstract, the implementing class must provide implementations for all abstract methods defined in the interface.

You need to know two more rules, and then we can put this topic to sleep (or put you to sleep; we always get those two confused):

1. A class can implement more than one interface. It's perfectly legal to say, for example, the following:

   ```
   public class Ball implements Bounceable, Serializable, Runnable { ... }
   ```

   You can extend only one class, but you can implement many interfaces (which, as of Java 8, means a form of multiple inheritance, which we'll discuss shortly). In other words, subclassing defines who and what you are, whereas implementing defines a role you can play or a hat you can wear, despite how different you might be from some other class implementing the same interface (but from a different inheritance tree). For example, a Person extends HumanBeing (although for some, that's debatable). But a Person may also implement Programmer, Snowboarder, Employee, Parent, or PersonCrazyEnoughToTakeThisExam.

2. An interface can itself extend another interface. The following code is perfectly legal:

   ```
   public interface Bounceable extends Moveable { }   // ok!
   ```

What does that mean? The first concrete (nonabstract) implementation class of `Bounceable` must implement all the abstract methods of `Bounceable`, plus all the abstract methods of `Moveable`! The subinterface, as we call it, simply adds more requirements to the contract of the superinterface. You'll see this concept applied in many areas of Java, especially Java EE, where you'll often have to build your own interface that extends one of the Java EE interfaces.

Hold on, though, because here's where it gets strange. An interface can extend more than one interface! Think about that for a moment. You know that when we're talking about classes, the following is illegal:

```
public class Programmer extends Employee, Geek { } // Illegal!
```

As we mentioned earlier, a class is not allowed to extend multiple classes in Java. An interface, however, is free to extend multiple interfaces:

```
interface Bounceable extends Moveable, Spherical {   // ok!
  void bounce();
  void setBounceFactor(int bf);
}
interface Moveable {
  void moveIt();
}
interface Spherical {
  void doSphericalThing();
}
```

In the next example, `Ball` is required to implement `Bounceable`, plus all abstract methods from the interfaces that `Bounceable` extends (including any interfaces those interfaces extend, and so on, until you reach the top of the stack—or is it the bottom of the stack?). So `Ball` would need to look like the following:

```
class Ball implements Bounceable {

  public void bounce() { }              // Implement Bounceable's methods
  public void setBounceFactor(int bf) { }

  public void moveIt() { }              // Implement Moveable's method

  public void doSphericalThing() { }   // Implement Spherical
}
```

If class `Ball` fails to implement any of the abstract methods from `Bounceable`, `Moveable`, or `Spherical`, the compiler will jump up and down wildly, red in the face, until it does. Unless, that is, class `Ball` is marked `abstract`. In that case, `Ball` could choose to implement any, all, or none of the abstract methods from any of the interfaces, thus leaving the rest of the implementations to a concrete subclass of `Ball`, as follows:

```
abstract class Ball implements Bounceable {
  public void bounce() { ... }   // Define bounce behavior
  public void setBounceFactor(int bf) { ... }
  // Don't implement the rest; leave it for a subclass
}
class SoccerBall extends Ball {  // class SoccerBall must
                                 // implement the interface
                                 // methods that Ball didn't
```

```
    public void moveIt() { ... }
    public void doSphericalThing() { ... }
    // SoccerBall can choose to override the Bounceable methods
    // implemented by Ball
    public void bounce() { ... }
}
```

Figure 2-5 compares concrete and `abstract` examples of extends and implements for both classes and interfaces.

FIGURE 2-5 Comparing concrete and `abstract` examples of extends and implements

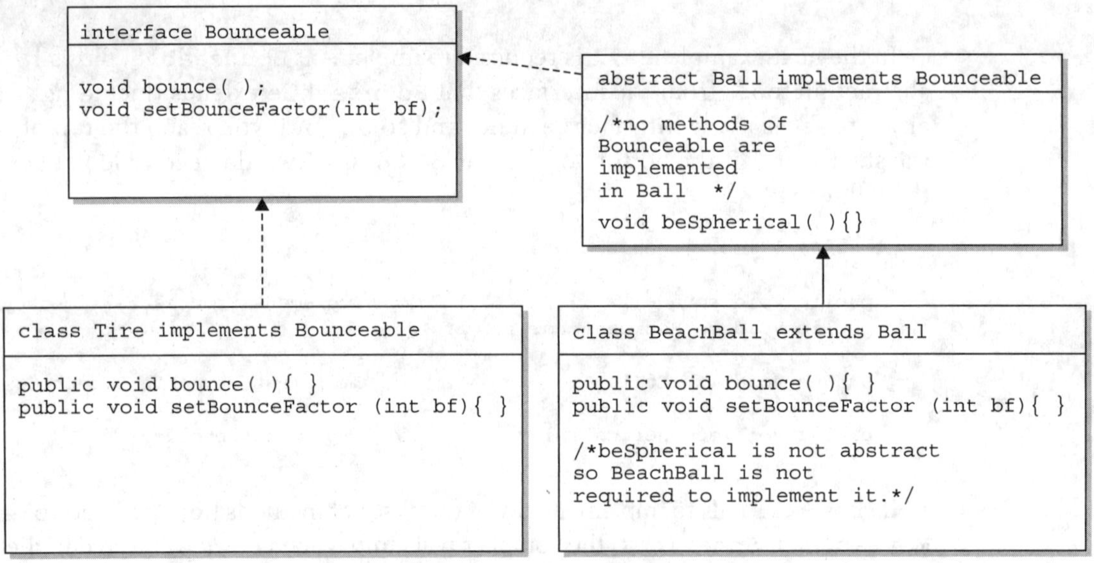

Because `BeachBall` is the first concrete class to implement `Bounceable`, it must provide implementations for all methods of `Bounceable`, except those defined in the abstract class `Ball`. Because `Ball` did not provide implementations of `Bounceable` methods, `BeachBall` was required to implement all of them.

Java 8—Now with Multiple Inheritance!

It might have already occurred to you that since interfaces can now have concrete methods and classes can implement multiple interfaces, the spectre of multiple inheritance and the Deadly Diamond of Death can rear its ugly head! Well, you're partly correct. A class CAN implement interfaces with duplicate, concrete method signatures! But the good news is that the compiler's got your back, and if you DO

exam watch

Look for illegal uses of `extends` and `implements`. The following shows examples of legal and illegal class and interface declarations:

```
class Foo { }                                  // OK
class Bar implements Foo  { }                  // No! Can't implement a class
interface Baz { }                              // OK
interface Fi { }                               // OK
interface Fee implements Baz { }               // No! an interface can't
                                               // implement an interface
interface Zee implements Foo { }               // No! an interface can't
                                               // implement a class
interface Zoo extends Foo { }                  // No! an interface can't
                                               // extend a class
interface Boo extends Fi { }                   // OK. An interface can extend
                                               // an interface
class Toon extends Foo, Button { }             // No! a class can't extend
                                               // multiple classes
class Zoom implements Fi, Baz { }              // OK. A class can implement
                                               // multiple interfaces
interface Vroom extends Fi, Baz { }            // OK. An interface can extend
                                               // multiple interfaces
class Yow extends Foo implements Fi { }        // OK. A class can do both
                                               // (extends must be 1st)
class Yow extends Foo implements Fi, Baz { } // OK. A class can do all three
                                               // (extends must be 1st)
```

Burn these in, and watch for abuses in the questions you get on the exam. Regardless of what the question appears to be testing, the real problem might be the class or interface declaration. Before you get caught up in, say, tracing a complex threading flow, check to see if the code will even compile. (Just that tip alone may be worth your putting us in your will!) (You'll be impressed by the effort the exam developers put into distracting you from the real problem.) (How did people manage to write anything before parentheses were invented?)

want to implement both interfaces, you'll have to provide an overriding method in your class. Let's look at the following code:

```
interface I1 {
  default int doStuff() { return 1; }
}
interface I2 {
  default int doStuff() { return 2; }
}
```

```
public class MultiInt implements I1, I2 {  // needs to override
  public static void main(String[] args) {
    new MultiInt().go();
  }
  void go() {
    System.out.println(doStuff());
}
//  public int doStuff() {
//    return 3;
// }
}
```

As the code stands, it WILL NOT COMPILE because it's not clear which version of `doStuff()` should be used. In order to make the code compile, you need to override `doStuff()` in the class. Uncommenting the class's `doStuff()` method would allow the code to compile and when run produce the following output:

```
3
```

CERTIFICATION OBJECTIVE

Legal Return Types (OCA Objectives 2.2 and 6.1)

2.2 Differentiate between object reference variables and primitive variables.
6.1 Create methods with arguments and return values; including overloaded methods.

This section covers two aspects of return types: what you can declare as a return type, and what you can actually return as a value. What you can and cannot declare is pretty straightforward, but it all depends on whether you're overriding an inherited method or simply declaring a new method (which includes overloaded methods). We'll take just a quick look at the difference between return type rules for overloaded and overriding methods, because we've already covered that in this chapter. We'll cover a small bit of new ground, though, when we look at polymorphic return types and the rules for what is and is not legal to actually return.

Return Type Declarations

This section looks at what you're allowed to declare as a return type, which depends primarily on whether you are overriding, overloading, or declaring a new method.

Return Types on Overloaded Methods

Remember that method overloading is not much more than name reuse. The overloaded method is a completely different method from any other method of the same name. So if you inherit a method but overload it in a subtype, you're not subject to the restrictions of overriding, which means you can declare any return type you like. What you can't do is change *only* the return type. To overload a method, remember, you must change the argument list. The following code shows an overloaded method:

```
public class Foo{
  void go() { }
}
public class Bar extends Foo {
  String go(int x) {
    return null;
  }
}
```

Notice that the `Bar` version of the method uses a different return type. That's perfectly fine. As long as you've changed the argument list, you're overloading the method, so the return type doesn't have to match that of the supertype version. What you're NOT allowed to do is this:

```
public class Foo{
  void go() { }
}
public class Bar extends Foo {
  String go() { // Not legal! Can't change only the return type
    return null;
  }
}
```

Overriding and Return Types and Covariant Returns

When a subtype wants to change the method implementation of an inherited method (an override), the subtype must define a method that matches the inherited version exactly. Or, since Java 5, you're allowed to change the return type in the overriding method as long as the new return type is a *subtype* of the declared return type of the overridden (superclass) method.

Let's look at a covariant return in action:

```
class Alpha {
  Alpha doStuff(char c) {
    return new Alpha();
  }
}
class Beta extends Alpha {
  Beta doStuff(char c) {      // legal override since Java 1.5
    return new Beta();
  }
}
```

Since Java 5, this code compiles. If you were to attempt to compile this code with a 1.4 compiler or with the source flag as follows,

```
javac -source 1.4 Beta.java
```

you would get a compiler error like this:

```
attempting to use incompatible return type
```

Other rules apply to overriding, including those for access modifiers and declared exceptions, but those rules aren't relevant to the return type discussion.

exam watch

For the exam, be sure you know that overloaded methods can change the return type, but overriding methods can do so only within the bounds of covariant returns. Just that knowledge alone will help you through a wide range of exam questions.

Returning a Value

You have to remember only six rules for returning a value:

1. You can return `null` in a method with an object reference return type.

```
public Button doStuff() {
  return null;
}
```

2. An array is a perfectly legal return type.

```
public String[] go() {
  return new String[] {"Fred", "Barney", "Wilma"};
}
```

3. In a method with a primitive return type, you can return any value or variable that can be implicitly converted to the declared return type.

```
public int foo() {
  char c = 'c';
  return c;  // char is compatible with int
}
```

4. In a method with a primitive return type, you can return any value or variable that can be explicitly cast to the declared return type.

```
public int foo() {
  float f = 32.5f;
  return (int) f;
}
```

5. You must *not* return anything from a method with a void return type.

```
public void bar() {
  return "this is it";  // Not legal!!
}
```

(Although you can say `return;`)

6. In a method with an object reference return type, you can return any object type that can be implicitly cast to the declared return type.

```
public Animal getAnimal() {
  return new Horse();  // Assume Horse extends Animal
}

public Object getObject() {
  int[] nums = {1,2,3};
  return nums;         // Return an int array, which is still an object
}

public interface Chewable { }
public class Gum implements Chewable { }

public class TestChewable {
  // Method with an interface return type
  public Chewable getChewable() {
    return new Gum();  // Return interface implementer
  }
}
```

exam watch

Watch for methods that declare an abstract class or interface return type, and know that any object that passes the IS-A test (in other words, would test true using the `instanceof` operator) can be returned from that method. For example:

```
public abstract class Animal { }
public class Bear extends Animal { }
public class Test {
  public Animal go() {
    return new Bear();  // OK, Bear "is-a" Animal
  }
}
```

This code will compile, and the return value is a subtype.

CERTIFICATION OBJECTIVE

Constructors and Instantiation (OCA Objectives 6.3 and 7.4)

6.3 Create and overload constructors; including impact on default constructors (sic)
7.4 Use super and this to access objects and constructors.

Objects are constructed. You CANNOT make a new object without invoking a constructor. In fact, you can't make a new object without invoking not just the constructor of the object's actual class type, but also the constructor of each of its superclasses! Constructors are the code that runs whenever you use the keyword new. (Okay, to be a bit more accurate, there can also be initialization blocks that run when you say `new`, and we're going to cover `init` blocks and their static initialization counterparts after we discuss constructors.) We've got plenty to talk about here—we'll look at how constructors are coded, who codes them, and how they work at runtime. So grab your hardhat and a hammer, and let's do some object building.

Constructor Basics

Every class, *including abstract classes*, MUST have a constructor. Burn that into your brain. But just because a class must have a constructor doesn't mean the programmer has to type it. A constructor looks like this:

```
class Foo {
  Foo() { } // The constructor for the Foo class
}
```

Notice what's missing? There's no return type! Two key points to remember about constructors are that they have no return type, and their names must exactly match the class name. Typically, constructors are used to initialize the instance variable state, as follows:

```
class Foo {
  int size;
  String name;
  Foo(String name, int size) {
    this.name = name;
    this.size = size;
  }
}
```

In the preceding code example, the `Foo` class does not have a no-arg constructor. That means the following will fail to compile:

```
Foo f = new Foo();            // Won't compile, no matching constructor
```

but the following will compile:

```
Foo f = new Foo("Fred", 43);  // No problem. Arguments match
                              // the Foo constructor.
```

So it's very common (and desirable) for a class to have a no-arg constructor, regardless of how many other overloaded constructors are in the class (yes, constructors can be overloaded). You can't always make that work for your classes; occasionally you have a class where it makes no sense to create an instance without supplying information to the constructor. A `java.awt.Color` object, for example, can't be created by calling a no-arg constructor, because that would be like saying to the JVM, "Make me a new Color object, and I really don't care what color it is...you pick." Do you seriously want the JVM making your style decisions?

Constructor Chaining

We know that constructors are invoked at runtime when you say `new` on some class type as follows:

```
Horse h = new Horse();
```

But what *really* happens when you say `new Horse()`? (Assume `Horse` extends `Animal` and `Animal` extends `Object`.)

1. The `Horse` constructor is invoked. Every constructor invokes the constructor of its superclass with an (implicit) call to `super()`, unless the constructor invokes an overloaded constructor of the same class (more on that in a minute).
2. The `Animal` constructor is invoked (`Animal` is the superclass of `Horse`).
3. The `Object` constructor is invoked (`Object` is the ultimate superclass of all classes, so class `Animal` extends `Object` even though you don't actually type "extends Object" into the `Animal` class declaration; it's implicit.) At this point we're on the top of the stack.
4. If class `Object` had any instance variables, then they would be given their explicit values. By *explicit* values, we mean values that are assigned at the time the variables are declared, such as `int x = 27`, where `27` is the explicit value (as opposed to the default value) of the instance variable.
5. The `Object` constructor completes.
6. The `Animal` instance variables are given their explicit values (if any).
7. The `Animal` constructor completes.
8. The `Horse` instance variables are given their explicit values (if any).
9. The `Horse` constructor completes.

Figure 2-6 shows how constructors work on the call stack.

FIGURE 2-6

Constructors on the call stack

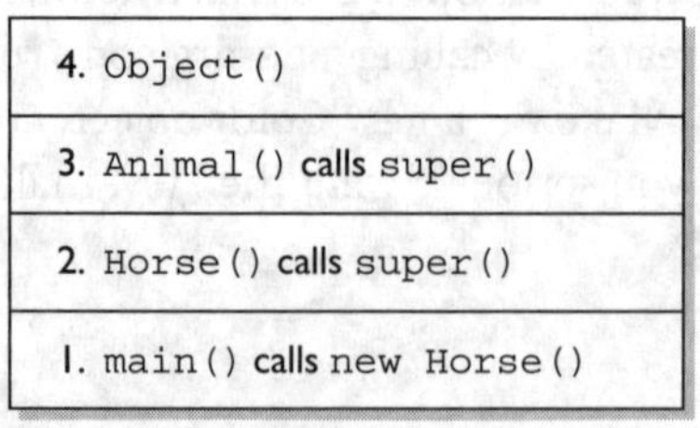

Rules for Constructors

The following list summarizes the rules you'll need to know for the exam (and to understand the rest of this section). You MUST remember these, so be sure to study them more than once.

- Constructors can use any access modifier, including `private`. (A `private` constructor means only code within the class itself can instantiate an object of that type, so if the `private` constructor class wants to allow an instance of the class to be used, the class must provide a static method or variable that allows access to an instance created from within the class.)
- The constructor name must match the name of the class.
- Constructors must not have a return type.
- It's legal (but stupid) to have a method with the same name as the class, but that doesn't make it a constructor. If you see a return type, it's a method rather than a constructor. In fact, you could have both a method and a constructor with the same name—the name of the class—in the same class, and that's not a problem for Java. Be careful not to mistake a method for a constructor—be sure to look for a return type.
- If you don't type a constructor into your class code, a default constructor will be automatically generated by the compiler.
- The default constructor is ALWAYS a no-arg constructor.
- If you want a no-arg constructor and you've typed any other constructor(s) into your class code, the compiler won't provide the no-arg constructor (or any other constructor) for you. In other words, if you've typed in a constructor with arguments, you won't have a no-arg constructor unless you typed it in yourself!
- Every constructor has, as its first statement, either a call to an overloaded constructor (`this()`) or a call to the superclass constructor (`super()`), although remember that this call can be inserted by the compiler.
- If you do type in a constructor (as opposed to relying on the compiler-generated default constructor), and you do not type in the call to `super()` or a call to `this()`, the compiler will insert a no-arg call to `super()` for you as the very first statement in the constructor.
- A call to `super()` can either be a no-arg call or can include arguments passed to the super constructor.

- A no-arg constructor is not necessarily the default (that is, compiler-supplied) constructor, although the default constructor is always a no-arg constructor. The default constructor is the one the compiler provides! Although the default constructor is always a no-arg constructor, you're free to put in your own no-arg constructor.
- You cannot make a call to an instance method or access an instance variable until after the super constructor runs.
- Only static variables and methods can be accessed as part of the call to `super()` or `this()`. (Example: `super(Animal.NAME)` is OK, because `NAME` is declared as a static variable.)
- Abstract classes have constructors, and those constructors are always called when a concrete subclass is instantiated.
- Interfaces do not have constructors. Interfaces are not part of an object's inheritance tree.
- The only way a constructor can be invoked is from within another constructor. In other words, you can't write code that actually calls a constructor as follows:

```
class Horse {
  Horse() { } // constructor
  void doStuff() {
    Horse();  // calling the constructor - illegal!
  }
}
```

Determine Whether a Default Constructor Will Be Created

The following example shows a `Horse` class with two constructors:

```
class Horse {
  Horse() { }
  Horse(String name) { }
}
```

Will the compiler put in a default constructor for this class? No!

How about for the following variation of the class?

```
class Horse {
  Horse(String name) { }
}
```

Now will the compiler insert a default constructor? No!

What about this class?

```
class Horse { }
```

Now we're talking. The compiler will generate a default constructor for this class because the class doesn't have any constructors defined.

Okay, what about this class?

```
class Horse {
  void Horse() { }
}
```

It might look like the compiler won't create a constructor, since one is already in the `Horse` class. Or is it? Take another look at the preceding `Horse` class.

What's wrong with the `Horse()` constructor? It isn't a constructor at all! It's simply a method that happens to have the same name as the class. Remember, the return type is a dead giveaway that we're looking at a method, not a constructor.

How do you know for sure whether a default constructor will be created? Because you didn't write any constructors in your class.

How do you know what the default constructor will look like? Because...

- The default constructor has the same access modifier as the class.
- The default constructor has no arguments.
- The default constructor includes a no-arg call to the super constructor (`super()`).

Table 2-5 shows what the compiler will (or won't) generate for your class.

What happens if the super constructor has arguments? Constructors can have arguments just as methods can, and if you try to invoke a method that takes, say, an `int`, but you don't pass anything to the method, the compiler will complain as follows:

```
class Bar {
  void takeInt(int x) { }
}

class UseBar {
  public static void main (String [] args) {
    Bar b = new Bar();
    b.takeInt();  // Try to invoke a no-arg takeInt() method
  }
}
```

TABLE 2-5 Compiler-Generated Constructor Code

Class Code (What You Type)	Compiler-Generated Constructor Code (in Bold)

class Foo { }	class Foo {
	  Foo() {
	    super();
	  }
	}

class Foo {
  Foo() { }
}
	class Foo {
	  Foo() {
	    super();
	  }
	}

public class Foo { }	public class Foo {
	  public Foo() {
	    super();
	  }
	}

class Foo {
  Foo(String s) { }
}
	class Foo {
	  Foo(String s) {
	    super();
	  }
	}

class Foo {
  Foo(String s) {
    super();
  }
}
	Nothing; compiler doesn't need to insert anything.

class Foo {
  void Foo() { }
}
	class Foo {
	  void Foo() { }
	  Foo() {
	    super();
	  }
	}
	(void Foo() is a method, not a constructor.)

The compiler will complain that you can't invoke `takeInt()` without passing an `int`. Of course, the compiler enjoys the occasional riddle, so the message it spits out on some versions of the JVM (your mileage may vary) is less than obvious:

```
UseBar.java:7: takeInt(int) in Bar cannot be applied to ()
    b.takeInt();
     ^
```

But you get the idea. The bottom line is that there must be a match for the method. And by match, we mean the argument types must be able to accept the values or variables you're passing and in the order you're passing them. Which brings us back to constructors (and here you were thinking we'd never get there), which work exactly the same way.

So if your super constructor (that is, the constructor of your immediate superclass/parent) has arguments, you must type in the call to `super()`, supplying the appropriate arguments. Crucial point: if your superclass does not have a no-arg constructor, you must type a constructor in your class (the subclass) because you need a place to put in the call to `super()` with the appropriate arguments.

The following is an example of the problem:

```
class Animal {
  Animal(String name) { }
}

class Horse extends Animal {
  Horse() {
    super();  // Problem!
  }
}
```

And once again the compiler treats us with stunning lucidity:

```
Horse.java:7: cannot resolve symbol
symbol  : constructor Animal  ()
location: class Animal
  super();  // Problem!
  ^
```

If you're lucky (and it's a full moon), *your* compiler might be a little more explicit. But again, the problem is that there just isn't a match for what we're trying to invoke with `super()`—an `Animal` constructor with no arguments.

Another way to put this is that if your superclass does *not* have a no-arg constructor, then in your subclass you will not be able to use the default constructor supplied by the compiler. It's that simple. Because the compiler can *only* put in a call to a no-arg `super()`, you won't even be able to compile something like this:

```
class Clothing {
  Clothing(String s) { }
}
class TShirt extends Clothing { }
```

Trying to compile this code gives us exactly the same error we got when we put a constructor in the subclass with a call to the no-arg version of `super()`:

```
Clothing.java:4: cannot resolve symbol
symbol  : constructor Clothing  ()
location: class Clothing
class TShirt extends Clothing { }
^
```

In fact, the preceding `Clothing` and `TShirt` code is implicitly the same as the following code, where we've supplied a constructor for `TShirt` that's identical to the default constructor supplied by the compiler:

```
class Clothing {
  Clothing(String s) { }
}
class TShirt extends Clothing {
                // Constructor identical to compiler-supplied
                // default constructor
  TShirt() {
    super();    // Won't work!
  }             // tries to invoke a no-arg Clothing constructor
                // but there isn't one
}
```

One last point on the whole default constructor thing (and it's probably very obvious, but we have to say it or we'll feel guilty for years), ***constructors are never inherited***. They aren't methods. They can't be overridden (because they aren't methods, and only instance methods can be overridden). So the type of constructor(s) your superclass has in no way determines the type of default constructor you'll get. Some folks mistakenly believe that the default constructor somehow matches the super constructor, either by the arguments the default constructor will have (remember, the default constructor is always a no-arg) or by the arguments used in the compiler-supplied call to `super()`.

So although constructors can't be overridden, you've already seen that they can be overloaded, and typically are.

Overloaded Constructors

Overloading a constructor means typing in multiple versions of the constructor, each having a different argument list, like the following examples:

```
class Foo {
  Foo() { }
  Foo(String s) { }
}
```

The preceding Foo class has two overloaded constructors: one that takes a string, and one with no arguments. Because there's no code in the no-arg version, it's actually identical to the default constructor the compiler supplies—but remember, since there's already a constructor in this class (the one that takes a string), the compiler won't supply a default constructor. If you want a no-arg constructor to overload the with-args version you already have, you're going to have to type it yourself, just as in the Foo example.

Overloading a constructor is typically used to provide alternate ways for clients to instantiate objects of your class. For example, if a client knows the animal name, they can pass that to an `Animal` constructor that takes a string. But if they don't know the name, the client can call the no-arg constructor, and that constructor can supply a default name. Here's what it looks like:

```
public class Animal {
  String name;
  Animal(String name) {
    this.name = name;
  }

  Animal() {
    this(makeRandomName());
  }

  static String makeRandomName() {
    int x = (int) (Math.random() * 5);
    String name = new String[] {"Fluffy", "Fido",
                                "Rover", "Spike",
                                "Gigi"}[x];
    return name;
  }

  public static void main (String [] args) {
    Animal a = new Animal();
    System.out.println(a.name);
    Animal b = new Animal("Zeus");
    System.out.println(b.name);
  }
}
```

Running the code four times produces this output:

```
% java Animal
Gigi
Zeus
```

```
% java Animal
Fluffy
Zeus

% java Animal
Rover
Zeus

% java Animal
Fluffy
Zeus
```

There's a lot going on in the preceding code. Figure 2-7 shows the call stack for constructor invocations when a constructor is overloaded.

FIGURE 2-7

Overloaded constructors on the call stack

4. `Object()`
3. `Animal(String s)` calls `super()`
2. `Animal()` calls `this(randomlyChosenNameString)`
1. `main()` calls `new Animal()`

Take a look at the call stack, and then let's walk through the code straight from the top.

- **Line 2** Declare a `String` instance variable name.
- **Lines 3–5** Constructor that takes a `String` and assigns it to instance variable name.
- **Line 7** Here's where it gets fun. Assume every animal needs a name, but the client (calling code) might not always know what the name should be, so the `Animal` class will assign a random name. The no-arg constructor generates a name by invoking the `makeRandomName()` method.
- **Line 8** The no-arg constructor invokes its own overloaded constructor that takes a `String`, in effect calling it the same way it would be called if client code were doing a `new` to instantiate an object, passing it a `String` for the name. The overloaded invocation uses the keyword `this`, but uses it as though it were a method named `this()`. So line 8 is simply calling the constructor on line 3, passing it a randomly selected `String` rather than a client-code chosen name.
- **Line 11** Notice that the `makeRandomName()` method is marked `static`! That's because you cannot invoke an instance (in other words, nonstatic)

method (or access an instance variable) until after the `super` constructor has run. And since the `super` constructor will be invoked from the constructor on line 3, rather than from the one on line 7, line 8 can use only a static method to generate the name. If we wanted all `animals` not specifically named by the caller to have the same default name, say, "Fred," then line 8 could have read `this("Fred");` rather than calling a method that returns a string with the randomly chosen name.

- **Line 12** This doesn't have anything to do with constructors, but since we're all here to learn, it generates a random integer between 0 and 4.
- **Line 13** Weird syntax, we know. We're creating a new `String` object (just a single `String` instance), but we want the string to be selected randomly from a list. Except we don't have the list, so we need to make it. So in that one line of code we
    1. Declare a `String` variable name.
    2. Create a `String` array (anonymously—we don't assign the array itself to a variable).
    3. Retrieve the string at index `[x]` (x being the random number generated on line 12) of the newly created `String` array.
    4. Assign the string retrieved from the array to the declared instance variable name. We could have made it much easier to read if we'd just written

    ```
    String[] nameList = {"Fluffy", "Fido", "Rover", "Spike",
                         "Gigi"};

    String name = nameList[x];
    ```

    But where's the fun in that? Throwing in unusual syntax (especially for code wholly unrelated to the real question) is in the spirit of the exam. Don't be startled! (Okay, be startled, but then just say to yourself, "Whoa!" and get on with it.)
- **Line 18** We're invoking the no-arg version of the constructor (causing a random name from the list to be passed to the other constructor).
- **Line 20** We're invoking the overloaded constructor that takes a string representing the name.

The key point to get from this code example is in line 8. Rather than calling `super()`, we're calling `this()`, and `this()` always means a call to another constructor in the same class. Okay, fine, but what happens after the call to this()? Sooner or later the super() constructor gets called, right? Yes, indeed. A call to this() just means you're delaying the inevitable. Some constructor, somewhere, must make the call to super().

Key Rule: The first line in a constructor must be a call to super() or a call to this().

No exceptions. If you have neither of those calls in your constructor, the compiler will insert the no-arg call to super(). In other words, if constructor A() has a call to this(), the compiler knows that constructor A() will not be the one to invoke super().

The preceding rule means a constructor can never have both a call to super() and a call to this(). Because each of those calls must be the first statement in a constructor, you can't legally use both in the same constructor. That also means the compiler will not put a call to super() in any constructor that has a call to this().

Thought question: What do you think will happen if you try to compile the following code?

```
class A {
  A() {
    this("foo");
  }
  A(String s) {
    this();
  }
}
```

Your compiler may not actually catch the problem (it varies depending on your compiler, but most won't catch the problem). It assumes you know what you're doing. Can you spot the flaw? Given that a super constructor must always be called, where would the call to super() go? Remember, the compiler won't put in a default constructor if you've already got one or more constructors in your class. And when the compiler doesn't put in a default constructor, it still inserts a call to super() in any constructor that doesn't explicitly have a call to the super constructor—unless, that is, the constructor already has a call to this(). So in the preceding code, where can super() go? The only two constructors in the class both have calls to this(), and, in fact, you'll get exactly what you'd get if you typed the following method code:

```
public void go() {
  doStuff();
}
```

```
public void doStuff() {
  go();
}
```

Now can you see the problem? Of course you can. The stack explodes! It gets higher and higher and higher until it just bursts open and method code goes spilling out, oozing out of the JVM right onto the floor. Two overloaded constructors both calling `this()` are two constructors calling each other—over and over and over, resulting in this:

```
% java A
Exception in thread "main" java.lang.StackOverflowError
```

The benefit of having overloaded constructors is that you offer flexible ways to instantiate objects from your class. The benefit of having one constructor invoke another overloaded constructor is to avoid code duplication. In the `Animal` example, there wasn't any code other than setting the name, but imagine if after line 4 there was still more work to be done in the constructor. By putting all the other constructor work in just one constructor, and then having the other constructors invoke it, you don't have to write and maintain multiple versions of that other important constructor code. Basically, each of the other not-the-real-one overloaded constructors will call another overloaded constructor, passing it whatever data it needs (data the client code didn't supply).

Constructors and instantiation become even more exciting (just when you thought it was safe) when you get to inner classes, but we know you can stand to have only so much fun in one chapter, and besides, you don't have to deal with inner classes until you tackle the OCP exam.

CERTIFICATION OBJECTIVE

Initialization Blocks (OCA Objectives 1.2 and 6.3-ish)

1.2 Define the structure of a Java class
6.3 Create and overload constructors; including impact on default constructors

We've talked about two places in a class where you can put code that performs operations: methods and constructors. Initialization blocks are the third place in a Java program where operations can be performed. Static initialization blocks run when the class is first loaded, and instance initialization blocks run whenever an instance is created (a bit similar to a constructor). Let's look at an example:

```
class SmallInit {
static int x;
int y;

static { x = 7 ; }          // static init block
{ y = 8; }                  // instance init block
}
```

As you can see, the syntax for initialization blocks is pretty terse. They don't have names, they can't take arguments, and they don't return anything. A *static* initialization block runs *once* when the class is first loaded. An *instance* initialization block runs once *every time a new instance is created*. Remember when we talked about the order in which constructor code executed? Instance `init` block code runs right after the call to `super()` in a constructor—in other words, after all `super` constructors have run.

You can have many initialization blocks in a class. It is important to note that unlike methods or constructors, *the order in which initialization blocks appear in a class matters*. When it's time for initialization blocks to run, if a class has more than one, they will run in the order in which they appear in the class file—in other words, from the top down. Based on the rules we just discussed, can you determine the output of the following program?

```
class Init {
  Init(int x) { System.out.println("1-arg const"); }
  Init() { System.out.println("no-arg const"); }
  static { System.out.println("1st static init"); }
  { System.out.println("1st instance init"); }
  { System.out.println("2nd instance init"); }
  static { System.out.println("2nd static init"); }

  public static void main(String [] args) {
    new Init();
    new Init(7);
  }
}
```

To figure this out, remember these rules:

- `init` blocks execute in the order in which they appear.
- Static `init` blocks run once, when the class is first loaded.
- Instance `init` blocks run every time a class instance is created.
- Instance `init` blocks run after the constructor's call to `super()`.

With those rules in mind, the following output should make sense:

```
1st static init
2nd static init
1st instance init
2nd instance init
no-arg const
1st instance init
2nd instance init
1-arg const
```

As you can see, the instance `init` blocks each ran twice. Instance `init` blocks are often used as a place to put code that all the constructors in a class should share. That way, the code doesn't have to be duplicated across constructors.

Finally, if you make a mistake in your static `init` block, the JVM can throw an `ExceptionInInitializerError`. Let's look at an example:

```
class InitError {
  static int [] x = new int[4];
  static { x[4] = 5; }              // bad array index!
  public static void main(String [] args) { }
}
```

It produces something like this:

```
Exception in thread "main" java.lang.ExceptionInInitializerError
Caused by: java.lang.ArrayIndexOutOfBoundsException: 4
        at InitError.<clinit>(InitError.java:3)
```

exam watch

By convention, `init` blocks usually appear near the top of the class file, somewhere around the constructors. However, this is the OCA exam we're talking about. Don't be surprised if you find an `init` block tucked in between a couple of methods, looking for all the world like a compiler error waiting to happen!

CERTIFICATION OBJECTIVE

Statics (OCA Objective 6.2)

6.2 *Apply the static keyword to methods and fields.*

Static Variables and Methods

The `static` modifier has such a profound impact on the behavior of a method or variable that we're treating it as a concept entirely separate from the other modifiers. To understand the way a `static` member works, we'll look first at a reason for using one. Imagine you've got a utility class or interface with a method that always runs the same way; its sole function is to return, say, a random number. It wouldn't matter which instance of the class performed the method—it would always behave exactly the same way. In other words, the method's behavior has no dependency on the state (instance variable values) of an object. So why, then, do you need an object when the method will never be instance-specific? Why not just ask the type itself to run the method?

Let's imagine another scenario: Suppose you want to keep a running count of all instances instantiated from a particular class. Where do you actually keep that variable? It won't work to keep it as an instance variable within the class whose instances you're tracking, because the count will just be initialized back to a default value with each new instance. The answer to both the utility-method-always-runs-the-same scenario and the keep-a-running-total-of-instances scenario is to use the `static` modifier. Variables and methods marked `static` belong to the type, rather than to any particular instance. In fact, for classes, you can use a `static` method or variable without having any instances of that class at all. You need only have the type available to be able to invoke a `static` method or access a `static` variable. `static` variables, too, can be accessed without having an instance of a class. But if there are instances, a `static` variable of a class will be shared by all instances of that class; there is only one copy.

The following code declares and uses a `static` counter variable:

```
class Frog {
  static int frogCount = 0;  // Declare and initialize
                             // static variable
  public Frog() {
    frogCount += 1;          // Modify the value in the constructor
  }
```

```
    public static void main (String [] args) {
      new Frog();
      new Frog();
      new Frog();
      System.out.println("Frog count is now " + frogCount);
    }
  }
```

In the preceding code, the static frogCount variable is set to zero when the Frog class is first loaded by the JVM, before any Frog instances are created! (By the way, you don't actually need to initialize a static variable to zero; static variables get the same default values instance variables get.) Whenever a Frog instance is created, the Frog constructor runs and increments the static frogCount variable. When this code executes, three Frog instances are created in main(), and the result is

```
Frog count is now 3
```

Now imagine what would happen if frogCount were an instance variable (in other words, nonstatic):

```
class Frog {
  int frogCount = 0;   // Declare and initialize
                       // instance variable
  public Frog() {
    frogCount += 1;    // Modify the value in the constructor
  }
  public static void main (String [] args) {
    new Frog();
    new Frog();
    new Frog();
    System.out.println("Frog count is now " + frogCount);
  }
}
```

When this code executes, it should still create three Frog instances in main(), but the result is...a compiler error! We can't get this code to compile, let alone run.

```
Frog.java:11: nonstatic variable frogCount cannot be referenced
from a static context
  System.out.println("Frog count is " + frogCount);
                                        ^
  1 error
```

The JVM doesn't know which Frog object's frogCount you're trying to access. The problem is that main() is itself a static method and thus isn't running against any particular instance of the class; instead it's running on the class itself. A static method can't access a nonstatic (instance) variable because there is no instance! That's not to say there aren't instances of the class alive on the heap, but rather that even if there are, the `static` method doesn't know anything about them. The same applies to instance methods; a `static` method can't directly invoke a nonstatic method. Think static = class, nonstatic = instance. Making the method called by the JVM (`main()`) a `static` method means the JVM doesn't have to create an instance of your class just to start running code.

exam watch

One of the mistakes most often made by new Java programmers is attempting to access an instance variable (which means nonstatic variable) from the static `main()` method (which doesn't know anything about any instances, so it can't access the variable). The following code is an example of illegal access of a nonstatic variable from a `static` method:

```
class Foo {
  int x = 3;
    public static void main (String [] args) {
      System.out.println("x is " + x);
  }
}
```

Understand that this code will never compile, because you can't access a nonstatic (instance) variable from a `static` method. Just think of the compiler saying, "Hey, I have no idea which `Foo` object's `x` variable you're trying to print!" Remember, it's the class running the `main()` method, not an instance of the class.

Of course, the tricky part for the exam is that the question won't look as obvious as the preceding code. The problem you're being tested for—accessing a nonstatic variable from a `static` method—will be buried in code that might appear to be testing something else. For example, the preceding code would be more likely to appear as

```
class Foo {
  int x = 3;
  float y = 4.3f;
  public static void main (String [] args) {
     for (int z = x; z < ++x; z--, y = y + z)
     // complicated looping and branching code
  }
}
```

So while you're trying to follow the logic, the real issue is that `x` and `y` can't be used within `main()` because `x` and `y` are instance, not `static`, variables! The same applies for accessing nonstatic methods from a `static` method. The rule is, a `static` method of a class can't access a nonstatic (instance) method or variable of its own class.

Accessing Static Methods and Variables

Since you don't need to have an instance in order to invoke a static method or access a static variable, how do you invoke or use a `static` member? What's the syntax? We know that with a regular old instance method, you use the dot operator on a reference to an instance:

```
class Frog {
  int frogSize = 0;
  public int getFrogSize() {
    return frogSize;
  }
  public Frog(int s) {
    frogSize = s;
  }
  public static void main (String [] args) {
    Frog f = new Frog(25);
    System.out.println(f.getFrogSize()); // Access instance
                                         // method using f
  }
}
```

In the preceding code, we instantiate a `Frog`, assign it to the reference variable `f`, and then use that `f` reference to invoke a method on the `Frog` instance we just created. In other words, the `getFrogSize()` method is being invoked on a specific `Frog` object on the heap.

But this approach (using a reference to an object) isn't appropriate for accessing a `static` method, because there might not be any instances of the class at all! So the way we access a `static` method (or `static` variable) is to use the dot operator on the type name, as opposed to using it on a reference to an instance, as follows:

```
class Frog {
  private static int frogCount = 0;  // static variable
  static int getCount() {            // static getter method
    return frogCount;
  }
  public Frog() {
    frogCount += 1;          // Modify the value in the constructor
  }
}

class TestFrog {
  public static void main (String [] args) {
    new Frog();
    new Frog();
    new Frog();
    System.out.println("from static "+Frog.getCount());  // static context
    new Frog();
```

```
    new TestFrog().go();
    Frog f = new Frog();
    System.out.println("use ref var "+f.getCount());      // use reference var
  }
  void go() {
    System.out.println("from inst "+Frog.getCount());     // instance context
  }
}
```

which produces the output:

```
from static 3
from instance 4
use ref var 5
```

But just to make it really confusing, the Java language also allows you to use an object reference variable to access a `static` member. Did you catch the last line of `main()`? It included this invocation:

```
f.getCount(); // Access a static using an instance variable
```

In the preceding code, we instantiate a `Frog`, assign the new `Frog` object to the reference variable `f`, and then use the `f` reference to invoke a `static` method! But even though we are using a specific `Frog` instance to access the `static` method, the rules haven't changed. This is merely a syntax trick to let you use an object reference variable (but not the object it refers to) to get to a `static` method or variable, but the `static` member is still unaware of the particular instance used to invoke the `static` member. In the `Frog` example, the compiler knows that the reference variable `f` is of type `Frog`, and so the `Frog` class `static` method is run with no awareness or concern for the `Frog` instance at the other end of the `f` reference. In other words, the compiler cares only that reference variable `f` is declared as type `Frog`.

Invoking static methods from interfaces is almost the same as invoking static methods from classes, except the "instance variable syntax trick" just discussed works only for static methods in classes. The following code demonstrates how interface static methods can and cannot be invoked:

```
interface FrogBoilable {
  static int getCtoF(int cTemp) {                  // interface static method
    return (cTemp * 9 / 5) + 32;
  }
  default String hop() { return "hopping"; }     // interface default method
}

public class DontBoilFrogs implements FrogBoilable {
  public static void main(String[] args) {
    new DontBoilFrogs().go();
  }
```

```
  void go() {
    System.out.println(hop());                       // 1 - ok for default m
    // System.out.println(getCtoF(100));             // 2 - cannot find symbol

    System.out.println(FrogBoilable.getCtoF(100));  // 3 - ok for static m
    DontBoilFrogs dbf = new DontBoilFrogs();
    // System.out.println(dbf.getCtoF(100));         // 4 - cannot find symbol
  }
}
```

Let's review the code:

- **Line 1** is a legal invocation of an interface's `default` method.
- **Line 2** is an **illegal** attempt to invoke an interface's `static` method.
- **Line 3** is THE legal way to invoke an interface's `static` method.
- **Line 4** is another **illegal** attempt to invoke an interface's `static` method.

Figure 2-8 illustrates the effects of the `static` modifier on methods and variables.

FIGURE 2-8

The effects of `static` on methods and variables

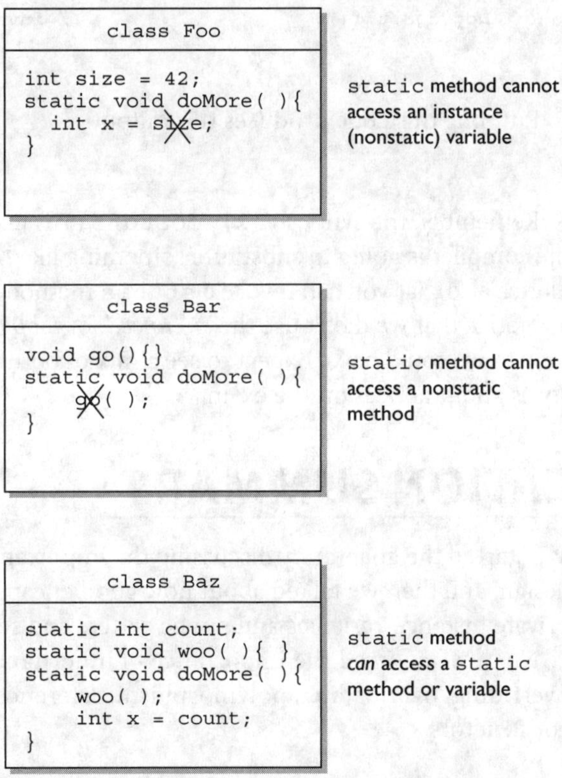

Finally, remember that `static` *methods can't be overridden*! This doesn't mean they can't be redefined in a subclass, but redefining and overriding aren't the same thing. Let's look at an example of a redefined (remember, not overridden) `static` method:

```
class Animal {
  static void doStuff() {
    System.out.print("a ");
  }
}
class Dog extends Animal {
  static void doStuff() {              // it's a redefinition,
                                       // not an override
    System.out.print("d ");
  }
  public static void main(String [] args) {
    Animal [] a = {new Animal(), new Dog(), new Animal()};
    for(int x = 0; x < a.length; x++) {
      a[x].doStuff();                  // invoke the static method
    }
    Dog.doStuff();                     // invoke using the class name
  }
}
```

Running this code produces this output:

```
a a a d
```

Remember, the syntax `a[x].doStuff()` is just a shortcut (the syntax trick)—the compiler is going to substitute something like `Animal.doStuff()` instead. Notice also that you can invoke a `static` method by using the class name.

Notice that we didn't use the *enhanced* for *loop* here (covered in Chapter 5), even though we could have. Expect to see a mix of both Java 1.4 and Java 5–8 coding styles and practices on the exam.

CERTIFICATION SUMMARY

We started the chapter by discussing the importance of encapsulation in good OO design, and then we talked about how good encapsulation is implemented: with private instance variables and public getters and setters.

Next, we covered the importance of inheritance, so that you can grasp overriding, overloading, polymorphism, reference casting, return types, and constructors.

We covered IS-A and HAS-A. IS-A is implemented using inheritance, and HAS-A is implemented by using instance variables that refer to other objects.

Polymorphism was next. Although a reference variable's type can't be changed, it can be used to refer to an object whose type is a subtype of its own. We learned how to determine what methods are invocable for a given reference variable.

We looked at the difference between overridden and overloaded methods, learning that an overridden method occurs when a subtype inherits a method from a supertype and then reimplements the method to add more specialized behavior. We learned that, at runtime, the JVM will invoke the subtype version on an instance of a subtype and the supertype version on an instance of the supertype. `Abstract` methods must be "overridden" (technically, `abstract` methods must be implemented, as opposed to overridden, since there really isn't anything to override).

We saw that overriding methods must declare the same argument list and return type or they can return a subtype of the declared return type of the supertype's overridden method), and that the access modifier can't be more restrictive. The overriding method also can't throw any new or broader checked exceptions that weren't declared in the overridden method. You also learned that the overridden method can be invoked using the syntax `super.doSomething();`.

Overloaded methods let you reuse the same method name in a class, but with different arguments (and, optionally, a different return type). Whereas overriding methods must not change the argument list, overloaded methods must. But unlike overriding methods, overloaded methods are free to vary the return type, access modifier, and declared exceptions any way they like.

We learned the mechanics of casting (mostly downcasting) reference variables and when it's necessary to do so.

Implementing interfaces came next. An interface describes a *contract* that the implementing class must follow. The rules for implementing an interface are similar to those for extending an `abstract` class. As of Java 8, interfaces can have concrete methods, which are labeled `default`. Also, remember that a class can implement more than one interface and that interfaces can extend another interface.

We also looked at method return types and saw that you can declare any return type you like (assuming you have access to a class for an object reference return type), unless you're overriding a method. Barring a covariant return, an overriding method must have the same return type as the overridden method of the superclass. We saw that, although overriding methods must not change the return type, overloaded methods can (as long as they also change the argument list).

Finally, you learned that it is legal to return any value or variable that can be implicitly converted to the declared return type. So, for example, a `short` can be returned when the return type is declared as an `int`. And (assuming `Horse` extends `Animal`), a `Horse` reference can be returned when the return type is declared an `Animal`.

We covered constructors in detail, learning that if you don't provide a constructor for your class, the compiler will insert one. The compiler-generated constructor is called the default constructor, and it is always a no-arg constructor with a no-arg call to `super()`. The default constructor will never be generated if even a single constructor exists in your class (regardless of the arguments of that constructor); so if you need more than one constructor in your class and you want a no-arg constructor, you'll have to write it yourself. We also saw that constructors are not inherited and that you can be confused by a method that has the same name as the class (which is legal). The return type is the giveaway that a method is not a constructor because constructors do not have return types.

We saw how all the constructors in an object's inheritance tree will always be invoked when the object is instantiated using `new`. We also saw that constructors can be overloaded, which means defining constructors with different argument lists. A constructor can invoke another constructor of the same class using the keyword `this()`, as though the constructor were a method named `this()`. We saw that every constructor must have either `this()` or `super()` as the first statement (although the compiler can insert it for you).

After constructors, we discussed the two kinds of initialization blocks and how and when their code runs.

We looked at `static` methods and variables. `static` members are tied to the class or interface, not an instance, so there is only one copy of any `static` member. A common mistake is to attempt to reference an instance variable from a `static` method. Use the respective class or interface name with the dot operator to access `static` members.

And, once again, you learned that the exam includes tricky questions designed largely to test your ability to recognize just how tricky the questions can be.

✓ TWO-MINUTE DRILL

Here are some of the key points from each certification objective in this chapter.

Encapsulation, IS-A, HAS-A* (OCA Objective 6.5)

- ☐ Encapsulation helps hide implementation behind an interface (or API).
- ☐ Encapsulated code has two features:
  - ☐ Instance variables are kept protected (usually with the `private` modifier).
  - ☐ Getter and setter methods provide access to instance variables.
- ☐ IS-A refers to inheritance or implementation.
- ☐ IS-A is expressed with the keyword `extends` or `implements`.
- ☐ IS-A, "inherits from," and "is a subtype of" are all equivalent expressions.
- ☐ HAS-A means an instance of one class "has a" reference to an instance of another class or another instance of the same class. *HAS-A is NOT on the exam, but it's good to know.

Inheritance (OCA Objective 7.1)

- ☐ Inheritance allows a type to be a subtype of a supertype and thereby inherit `public` and `protected` variables and methods of the supertype.
- ☐ Inheritance is a key concept that underlies IS-A, polymorphism, overriding, overloading, and casting.
- ☐ All classes (except class `Object`) are subclasses of type `Object`, and therefore they inherit `Object`'s methods.

Polymorphism (OCA Objective 7.2)

- ☐ Polymorphism means "many forms."
- ☐ A reference variable is always of a single, unchangeable type, but it can refer to a subtype object.
- ☐ A single object can be referred to by reference variables of many different types—as long as they are the same type or a supertype of the object.
- ☐ The reference variable's type (not the object's type) determines which methods can be called!
- ☐ Polymorphic method invocations apply only to overridden *instance* methods.

Overriding and Overloading (OCA Objectives 6.1 and 7.2)

- ☐ Methods can be overridden or overloaded; constructors can be overloaded but not overridden.
- ☐ With respect to the method it overrides, the overriding method
  - ☐ Must have the same argument list
  - ☐ Must have the same return type or a subclass (known as a covariant return)
  - ☐ Must not have a more restrictive access modifier
  - ☐ May have a less restrictive access modifier
  - ☐ Must not throw new or broader checked exceptions
  - ☐ May throw fewer or narrower checked exceptions, or any unchecked exception
- ☐ `final` methods cannot be overridden.
- ☐ Only inherited methods may be overridden, and remember that private methods are not inherited.
- ☐ A subclass uses `super.overriddenMethodName()` to call the superclass version of an overridden method.
- ☐ A subclass uses `MyInterface.super.overriddenMethodName()` to call the super interface version on an overridden method.
- ☐ Overloading means reusing a method name but with different arguments.
- ☐ Overloaded methods
  - ☐ Must have different argument lists
  - ☐ May have different return types, if argument lists are also different
  - ☐ May have different access modifiers
  - ☐ May throw different exceptions
- ☐ Methods from a supertype can be overloaded in a subtype.
- ☐ Polymorphism applies to overriding, not to overloading.
- ☐ Object type (not the reference variable's type) determines which overridden method is used at runtime.
- ☐ Reference type determines which overloaded method will be used at compile time.

Reference Variable Casting (OCA Objective 7.3)

- ☐ There are two types of reference variable casting: downcasting and upcasting.
  - ☐ **Downcasting** If you have a reference variable that refers to a subtype object, you can assign it to a reference variable of the subtype. You must make an explicit cast to do this, and the result is that you can access the subtype's members with this new reference variable.
  - ☐ **Upcasting** You can assign a reference variable to a supertype reference variable explicitly or implicitly. This is an inherently safe operation because the assignment restricts the access capabilities of the new variable.

Implementing an Interface (OCA Objective 7.5)

- ☐ When you implement an interface, you are fulfilling its contract.
- ☐ You implement an interface by properly and concretely implementing all the abstract methods defined by the interface.
- ☐ A single class can implement many interfaces.

Return Types (OCA Objectives 7.2 and 7.5)

- ☐ Overloaded methods can change return types; overridden methods cannot, except in the case of covariant returns.
- ☐ Object reference return types can accept `null` as a return value.
- ☐ An array is a legal return type, both to declare and return as a value.
- ☐ For methods with primitive return types, any value that can be implicitly converted to the return type can be returned.
- ☐ Nothing can be returned from a `void`, but you can return nothing. You're allowed to simply say `return` in any method with a `void` return type to bust out of a method early. But you can't return nothing from a method with a non-`void` return type.
- ☐ Methods with an object reference return type can return a subtype.
- ☐ Methods with an interface return type can return any implementer.

Constructors and Instantiation (OCA Objectives 6.3 and 7.4)

- ☐ A constructor is always invoked when a new object is created.
- ☐ Each superclass in an object's inheritance tree will have a constructor called.
- ☐ Every class, even an abstract class, has at least one constructor.
- ☐ Constructors must have the same name as the class.
- ☐ Constructors don't have a return type. If you see code with a return type, it's a method with the same name as the class; it's not a constructor.
- ☐ Typical constructor execution occurs as follows:
  - ☐ The constructor calls its superclass constructor, which calls its superclass constructor, and so on all the way up to the `Object` constructor.
  - ☐ The `Object` constructor executes and then returns to the calling constructor, which runs to completion and then returns to its calling constructor, and so on back down to the completion of the constructor of the actual instance being created.
- ☐ Constructors can use any access modifier (even `private`!).
- ☐ The compiler will create a default constructor if you don't create any constructors in your class.
- ☐ The default constructor is a no-arg constructor with a no-arg call to `super()`.
- ☐ The first statement of every constructor must be a call either to `this()` (an overloaded constructor) or to `super()`.
- ☐ The compiler will add a call to `super()` unless you have already put in a call to `this()` or `super()`.
- ☐ Instance members are accessible only after the `super` constructor runs.
- ☐ `Abstract` classes have constructors that are called when a concrete subclass is instantiated.
- ☐ Interfaces do not have constructors.
- ☐ If your superclass does not have a no-arg constructor, you must create a constructor and insert a call to `super()` with arguments matching those of the superclass constructor.
- ☐ Constructors are never inherited; thus they cannot be overridden.
- ☐ A constructor can be directly invoked only by another constructor (using a call to `super()` or `this()`).

- ☐ Regarding issues with calls to `this()`:
  - ☐ They may appear only as the first statement in a constructor.
  - ☐ The argument list determines which overloaded constructor is called.
  - ☐ Constructors can call constructors, and so on, but sooner or later one of them better call `super()` or the stack will explode.
  - ☐ Calls to `this()` and `super()` cannot be in the same constructor. You can have one or the other, but never both.

Initialization Blocks (OCA Objective 1.2 and 6.3-ish)

- ☐ Use `static init` blocks—`static { /* code here */ }`—for code you want to have run once, when the class is first loaded. Multiple blocks run from the top down.
- ☐ Use normal `init` blocks—`{ /* code here }`—for code you want to have run for every new instance, right after all the super constructors have run. Again, multiple blocks run from the top of the class down.

Statics (OCA Objective 6.2)

- ☐ Use `static` methods to implement behaviors that are not affected by the state of any instances.
- ☐ Use `static` variables to hold data that is class specific as opposed to instance specific—there will be only one copy of a `static` variable.
- ☐ All `static` members belong to the class, not to any instance.
- ☐ A `static` method can't access an instance variable directly.
- ☐ Use the dot operator to access `static` members, but remember that using a reference variable with the dot operator is really a syntax trick, and the compiler will substitute the class name for the reference variable; for instance:

  ```
  d.doStuff();
  ```

  becomes

  ```
  Dog.doStuff();
  ```

- ☐ To invoke an interface's static method use `MyInterface.doStuff()` syntax.
- ☐ `static` methods can't be overridden, but they can be redefined.

SELF TEST

1. Given:

```
public abstract interface Frobnicate { public void twiddle(String s); }
```

Which is a correct class? (Choose all that apply.)

A.
```
public abstract class Frob implements Frobnicate {
  public abstract void twiddle(String s) { }
}
```
B.
```
public abstract class Frob implements Frobnicate { }
```
C.
```
public class Frob extends Frobnicate {
  public void twiddle(Integer i) { }
}
```
D.
```
public class Frob implements Frobnicate {
  public void twiddle(Integer i) { }
}
```
E.
```
public class Frob implements Frobnicate {
  public void twiddle(String i) { }
  public void twiddle(Integer s) { }
}
```

2. Given:

```
class Top {
  public Top(String s) { System.out.print("B"); }
}
public class Bottom2 extends Top {
  public Bottom2(String s) { System.out.print("D"); }
  public static void main(String [] args) {
    new Bottom2("C");
    System.out.println(" ");
  }
}
```

What is the result?

A. BD

B. DB

C. BDC

D. DBC

E. Compilation fails

3. Given:

```
class Clidder {
  private final void flipper() { System.out.println("Clidder"); }
}
public class Clidlet extends Clidder {
  public final void flipper() { System.out.println("Clidlet");  }
  public static void main(String [] args) {
    new Clidlet().flipper();
  }
}
```

What is the result?

A. `Clidlet`

B. `Clidder`

C. `Clidder`
   `Clidlet`

D. `Clidlet`
   `Clidder`

E. Compilation fails

Special Note: The next question crudely simulates a style of question known as "drag-and-drop." Up through the SCJP 6 exam, drag-and-drop questions were included on the exam. As of spring 2014, Oracle DOES NOT include any drag-and-drop questions on its Java exams, but just in case Oracle's policy changes, we left a few in the book.

4. Using the **fragments** below, complete the following **code** so it compiles. Note that you may not have to fill in all of the slots.

Code:

```
class AgedP {
  __________ __________ __________ __________ __________
  public AgedP(int x) {
    __________ __________ __________ __________ __________
  }
}
public class Kinder extends AgedP {
  __________ __________ __________ __________ ________ __________
  public Kinder(int x) {
    __________ __________ __________ __________ __________ ();
  }
}
```

Fragments: Use the following fragments zero or more times:

`AgedP`	`super`	`this`	
`(`	`)`	`{`	`}`
`;`			

5. Given:

```
class Bird {
  { System.out.print("b1 "); }
  public Bird() { System.out.print("b2 "); }
}
class Raptor extends Bird {
  static { System.out.print("r1 "); }
  public Raptor() { System.out.print("r2 "); }
  { System.out.print("r3 "); }
  static { System.out.print("r4 "); }
}
class Hawk extends Raptor {
  public static void main(String[] args) {
    System.out.print("pre ");
    new Hawk();
    System.out.println("hawk ");
  }
}
```

What is the result?

A. `pre b1 b2 r3 r2 hawk`

B. `pre b2 b1 r2 r3 hawk`

C. `pre b2 b1 r2 r3 hawk r1 r4`

D. `r1 r4 pre b1 b2 r3 r2 hawk`

E. `r1 r4 pre b2 b1 r2 r3 hawk`

F. `pre r1 r4 b1 b2 r3 r2 hawk`

G. `pre r1 r4 b2 b1 r2 r3 hawk`

H. The order of output cannot be predicted

I. Compilation fails

Note: You'll probably never see this many choices on the real exam!

6. Given the following:

```
class X { void do1() { } }
class Y extends X { void do2() { } }

class Chrome {
  public static void main(String [] args) {
    X x1 = new X();
```

```
 7.     X x2 = new Y();
 8.     Y y1 = new Y();
 9.     // insert code here
10. } }
```

Which of the following, inserted at line 9, will compile? (Choose all that apply.)

A. `x2.do2();`

B. `(Y)x2.do2();`

C. `((Y)x2).do2();`

D. None of the above statements will compile

7. Given:

```
public class Locomotive {
  Locomotive() { main("hi"); }

  public static void main(String[] args) {
    System.out.print("2 ");
  }
  public static void main(String args) {
    System.out.print("3 " + args);
  }
}
```

What is the result? (Choose all that apply.)

A. `2` will be included in the output

B. `3` will be included in the output

C. `hi` will be included in the output

D. Compilation fails

E. An exception is thrown at runtime

8. Given:

```
class Dog {
  public void bark() { System.out.print("woof "); }
}
class Hound extends Dog {
  public void sniff() { System.out.print("sniff "); }
  public void bark() { System.out.print("howl "); }
}
public class DogShow {
  public static void main(String[] args) { new DogShow().go(); }
  void go() {
    new Hound().bark();
    ((Dog) new Hound()).bark();
    ((Dog) new Hound()).sniff();
  }
}
```

What is the result? (Choose all that apply.)

A. `howl howl sniff`

B. `howl woof sniff`

C. `howl howl` followed by an exception

D. `howl woof` followed by an exception

E. Compilation fails with an error at line 14

F. Compilation fails with an error at line 15

9. Given:

```
 3. public class Redwood extends Tree {
 4.   public static void main(String[] args) {
 5.     new Redwood().go();
 6.   }
 7.   void go() {
 8.     go2(new Tree(), new Redwood());
 9.     go2((Redwood) new Tree(), new Redwood());
10.   }
11.   void go2(Tree t1, Redwood r1) {
12.      Redwood r2 = (Redwood)t1;
13.      Tree t2 = (Tree)r1;
14.   }
15. }
16. class Tree { }
```

What is the result? (Choose all that apply.)

A. An exception is thrown at runtime

B. The code compiles and runs with no output

C. Compilation fails with an error at line 8

D. Compilation fails with an error at line 9

E. Compilation fails with an error at line 12

F. Compilation fails with an error at line 13

10. Given:

```
public class Tenor extends Singer {
  public static String sing() { return "fa"; }
  public static void main(String[] args) {
    Tenor t = new Tenor();
    Singer s = new Tenor();
    System.out.println(t.sing() + " " + s.sing());
  }
}
class Singer { public static String sing() { return "la"; } }
```

What is the result?

A. `fa fa`

B. `fa la`

C. `la la`

D. Compilation fails

E. An exception is thrown at runtime

11. Given:

```
class Alpha {
  static String s = " ";
  protected Alpha() { s += "alpha "; }
}
class SubAlpha extends Alpha {
  private SubAlpha() { s += "sub "; }
}
public class SubSubAlpha extends Alpha {
  private SubSubAlpha() { s += "subsub "; }
  public static void main(String[] args) {
    new SubSubAlpha();
    System.out.println(s);
  }
}
```

What is the result?

A. `subsub`

B. `sub subsub`

C. `alpha subsub`

D. `alpha sub subsub`

E. Compilation fails

F. An exception is thrown at runtime

12. Given:

```
class Building {
  Building() {  System.out.print("b ");  }
  Building(String name) {
    this();   System.out.print("bn " + name);
  }
}
public class House extends Building {
  House() {  System.out.print("h ");  }
  House(String name) {
    this();   System.out.print("hn " + name);
  }
  public static void main(String[] args) { new House("x "); }
}
```

What is the result?

A. `h hn x`

B. `hn x h`

C. `b h hn x`

D. `b hn x h`

E. `bn x h hn x`

F. `b bn x h hn x`

G. `bn x b h hn x`

H. Compilation fails

13. Given:

```
class Mammal {
  String name = "furry ";
  String makeNoise() { return "generic noise"; }
}
class Zebra extends Mammal {
  String name = "stripes ";
  String makeNoise() { return "bray"; }
}
public class ZooKeeper {
  public static void main(String[] args) { new ZooKeeper().go(); }
  void go() {
    Mammal m = new Zebra();
    System.out.println(m.name + m.makeNoise());
  }
}
```

What is the result?

A. `furry bray`

B. `stripes bray`

C. `furry generic noise`

D. `stripes generic noise`

E. Compilation fails

F. An exception is thrown at runtime

14. Given:

```
interface FrogBoilable {
  static int getCtoF(int cTemp) {
    return (cTemp * 9 / 5) + 32;
  }
  default String hop() { return "hopping "; }
```

```
 6. }
 7. public class DontBoilFrogs implements FrogBoilable {
 8.   public static void main(String[] args) {
 9.     new DontBoilFrogs().go();
10.   }
11.   void go() {
12.     System.out.print(hop());
13.     System.out.println(getCtoF(100));
14.     System.out.println(FrogBoilable.getCtoF(100));
15.     DontBoilFrogs dbf = new DontBoilFrogs();
16.     System.out.println(dbf.getCtoF(100));
17.   }
18. }
```

What is the result? (Choose all that apply.)

A. `hopping 212`

B. Compilation fails due to an error on line 2

C. Compilation fails due to an error on line 5

D. Compilation fails due to an error on line 12

E. Compilation fails due to an error on line 13

F. Compilation fails due to an error on line 14

G. Compilation fails due to an error on line 16

15. Given:

```
interface I1 {
  default int doStuff() { return 1; }
}
interface I2 {
  default int doStuff() { return 2; }
}
public class MultiInt implements I1, I2 {
  public static void main(String[] args) {
    new MultiInt().go();
  }
  void go() {
    System.out.println(doStuff());
  }
  int doStuff() {
    return 3;
  }
}
```

What is the result?

A. `1`

B. `2`

C. `3`

D. The output is unpredictable

E. Compilation fails

F. An exception is thrown at runtime

16. Given:

```
interface MyInterface {
  default int doStuff() {
    return 42;
  }
}
public class IfaceTest implements MyInterface {
  public static void main(String[] args) {
    new IfaceTest().go();
  }
  void go() {
    // INSERT CODE HERE
  }
  public int doStuff() {
    return 43;
  }
}
```

Which line(s) of code, inserted independently at // INSERT CODE HERE, will allow the code to compile? (Choose all that apply.)

A. `System.out.println("class: " + doStuff());`

B. `System.out.println("iface: " + super.doStuff());`

C. `System.out.println("iface: " + MyInterface.super.doStuff());`

D. `System.out.println("iface: " + MyInterface.doStuff());`

E. `System.out.println("iface: " + super.MyInterface.doStuff());`

F. None of the lines, A–E will allow the code to compile

SELF TEST ANSWERS

1. ☑ **B** and **E** are correct. B is correct because an `abstract` class need not implement any or all of an interface's methods. E is correct because the class implements the interface method and additionally overloads the `twiddle()` method.
   ☒ **A, C,** and **D** are incorrect. A is incorrect because `abstract` methods have no body. C is incorrect because classes implement interfaces; they don't extend them. D is incorrect because overloading a method is not implementing it. (OCA Objectives 7.1 and 7.5)

2. ☑ **E** is correct. The implied `super()` call in `Bottom2`'s constructor cannot be satisfied because there is no no-arg constructor in `Top`. A default, no-arg constructor is generated by the compiler only if the class has no constructor defined explicitly.
   ☒ **A, B, C,** and **D** are incorrect based on the above. (OCA Objective 6.3)

3. ☑ **A** is correct. Although a `final` method cannot be overridden, in this case, the method is private and, therefore, hidden. The effect is that a new, accessible, method flipper is created. Therefore, no polymorphism occurs in this example, the method invoked is simply that of the child class, and no error occurs.
   ☒ **B, C, D,** and **E** are incorrect based on the preceding. (OCA Objective 7.2)

Special Note: This next question crudely simulates a style of question known as "drag-and-drop." Up through the SCJP 6 exam, drag-and-drop questions were included on the exam. As of spring 2014, Oracle DOES NOT include any drag-and-drop questions on its Java exams, but just in case Oracle's policy changes, we left a few in the book.

4. Here is the answer:

```
class AgedP {
  AgedP() {}
  public AgedP(int x) {
  }
}
public class Kinder extends AgedP {
  public Kinder(int x) {
    super();
  }
}
```

As there is no droppable tile for the variable `x` and the parentheses (in the `Kinder` constructor) are already in place and empty, there is no way to construct a call to the superclass constructor that takes an argument. Therefore, the only remaining possibility is to create a call to the no-arg superclass constructor. This is done as `super();`. The line cannot be left blank, as the parentheses are already in place. Further, since the superclass constructor called is the no-arg version, this constructor must be created. It will not be created by the compiler because another constructor is already present. (OCA Objectives 6.3 and 7.4)
Note: As you can see, many questions test for OCA Objective 7.1, we're going to stop mentioning objective 7.1.

5. ☑ **D** is correct. Static `init` blocks are executed at class loading time; instance `init` blocks run right after the call to `super()` in a constructor. When multiple `init` blocks of a single type occur in a class, they run in order, from the top down.
☒ **A, B, C, E, F, G, H,** and **I** are incorrect based on the above. Note: You'll probably never see this many choices on the real exam! (OCA Objective 6.3)

6. ☑ **C** is correct. Before you can invoke `Y`'s `do2` method, you have to cast `x2` to be of type `Y`.
☒ **A, B,** and **D** are incorrect based on the preceding. B looks like a proper cast, but without the second set of parentheses, the compiler thinks it's an incomplete statement. (OCA Objective 7.3)

7. ☑ **A** is correct. It's legal to overload `main()`. Since no instances of `Locomotive` are created, the constructor does not run and the overloaded version of `main()` does not run.
☒ **B, C, D,** and **E** are incorrect based on the preceding. (OCA Objectives 1.3 and 6.3)

8. ☑ **F** is correct. Class `Dog` doesn't have a `sniff` method.
☒ **A, B, C, D,** and **E** are incorrect based on the above information. (OCA Objectives 7.2 and 7.3)

9. ☑ **A** is correct. A `ClassCastException` will be thrown when the code attempts to downcast a `Tree` to a `Redwood`.
☒ **B, C, D, E,** and **F** are incorrect based on the above information. (OCA Objective 7.3)

10. ☑ **B** is correct. The code is correct, but polymorphism doesn't apply to `static` methods.
☒ **A, C, D,** and **E** are incorrect based on the above information. (OCA Objectives 6.2 and 7.2)

11. ☑ **C** is correct. Watch out, because `SubSubAlpha` extends `Alpha`! Because the code doesn't attempt to make a `SubAlpha`, the private constructor in `SubAlpha` is okay.
☒ **A, B, D, E,** and **F** are incorrect based on the above information. (OCA Objectives 6.3 and 7.2)

12. ☑ **C** is correct. Remember that constructors call their superclass constructors, which execute first, and that constructors can be overloaded.
☒ **A, B, D, E, F, G,** and **H** are incorrect based on the above information. (OCA Objectives 6.3 and 7.4)

13. ☑ **A** is correct. Polymorphism is only for instance methods, not instance variables.
☒ **B, C, D, E,** and **F** are incorrect based on the above information. (OCA Objective 6.3)

14. ☑ **E** and **G** are correct. Neither of these lines of code uses the correct syntax to invoke an interface's static method.
☒ **A, B, C, D,** and **F** are incorrect based on the above information. (OCP Objectives 6.2 and 7.5)

15. ☑ **E** is correct. This is kind of a trick question; the implementing method must be marked `public`. If it was, all the other code is legal, and the output would be 3. If you understood all the multiple inheritance rules and just missed the access modifier, give yourself half credit.
☒ **A, B, C, D,** and **F** are incorrect based on the above information. (OCP Objective 7.5)

16. ☑ **A** and **C** are correct. A uses correct syntax to invoke the class's method, and C uses the correct syntax to invoke the interface's overloaded `default` method.
☒ **B, D, E,** and **F** are incorrect. (OCP Objective 7.5)

3 Assignments

CERTIFICATION OBJECTIVES

- Use Class Members
- Understand Primitive Casting
- Understand Variable Scope
- Differentiate Between Primitive Variables and Reference Variables
- Determine the Effects of Passing Variables into Methods
- Understand Object Lifecycle and Garbage Collection

✓ Two-Minute Drill

Q&A Self Test

Stack and Heap—Quick Review

For most people, understanding the basics of the stack and the heap makes it far easier to understand topics like argument passing, polymorphism, threads, exceptions, and garbage collection. In this section, we'll stick to an overview, but we'll expand these topics several more times throughout the book.

For the most part, the various pieces (methods, variables, and objects) of Java programs live in one of two places in memory: the stack or the heap. For now, we're concerned about only three types of things—instance variables, local variables, and objects:

- Instance variables and objects live on the heap.
- Local variables live on the stack.

Let's take a look at a Java program and how its various pieces are created and map into the stack and the heap:

```
1. class Collar { }
2.
3. class Dog {
4.   Collar c;                        // instance variable
5.   String name;                     // instance variable
6.
7.   public static void main(String [] args) {
8.
9.     Dog d;                         // local variable: d
10.    d = new Dog();
11.    d.go(d);
12.  }
13.  void go(Dog dog) {               // local variable: dog
14.    c = new Collar();
15.    dog.setName("Aiko");
16.  }
17.  void setName(String dogName) {   // local var: dogName
18.    name = dogName;
19.    // do more stuff
20.  }
21. }
```

Figure 3-1 shows the state of the stack and the heap once the program reaches line 19. Following are some key points:

- Line 7—`main()` is placed on the stack.
- Line 9—Reference variable `d` is created on the stack, but there's no `Dog` object yet.

FIGURE 3-1 Overview of the stack and the heap

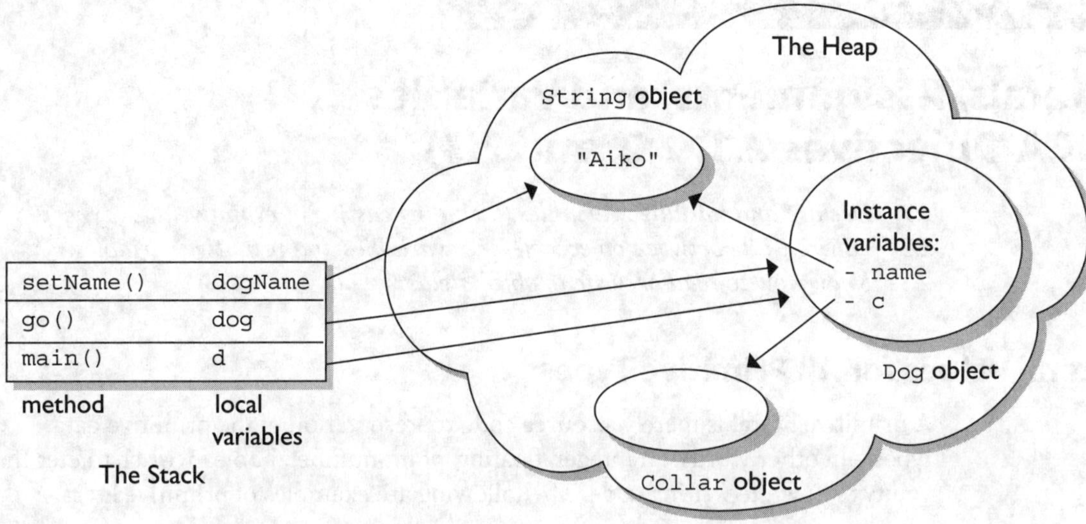

- Line 10—A new Dog object is created on the heap and is assigned to the d reference variable.
- Line 11—A copy of the reference variable d is passed to the go() method.
- Line 13—The go() method is placed on the stack, with the dog parameter as a local variable.
- Line 14—A new Collar object is created on the heap and assigned to Dog's instance variable.
- Line 17—setName() is added to the stack, with the dogName parameter as its local variable.
- Line 18—The name instance variable now also refers to the String object.
- Notice that two *different* local variables refer to the same Dog object.
- Notice that one local variable and one instance variable both refer to the same String Aiko.
- After Line 19 completes, setName() completes and is removed from the stack. At this point the local variable dogName disappears, too, although the String object it referred to is still on the heap.

CERTIFICATION OBJECTIVE

Literals, Assignments, and Variables (OCA Objectives 2.1, 2.2, and 2.3)

2.1 Declare and initialize variables (including casting of primitive data types).
2.2 Differentiate between object reference variables and primitive variables.
2.3 Know how to read or write to object fields.

Literal Values for All Primitive Types

A primitive literal is merely a source code representation of the primitive data types—in other words, an integer, floating-point number, boolean, or character that you type in while writing code. The following are examples of primitive literals:

```
'b'           // char literal
42            // int literal
false         // boolean literal
2546789.343   // double literal
```

Integer Literals

There are four ways to represent integer numbers in the Java language: decimal (base 10), octal (base 8), hexadecimal (base 16), and, as of Java 7, binary (base 2). Most exam questions with integer literals use decimal representations, but the few that use octal, hexadecimal, or binary are worth studying for. Even though the odds that you'll ever actually use octal in the real world are astronomically tiny, they were included in the exam just for fun. Before we look at the four ways to represent integer numbers, let's first discuss a new feature added to Java 7: literals with underscores.

Numeric Literals with Underscores As of Java 7, numeric literals can be declared using underscore characters (_), ostensibly to improve readability. Let's compare a pre-Java 7 declaration to an easier-to-read Java 7 declaration:

```
int pre7  = 1000000;     // pre Java 7 - we hope it's a million
int with7 = 1_000_000;   // much clearer!
```

The main rule you have to keep track of is that you CANNOT use the underscore literal at the beginning or end of the literal. The potential gotcha here is that you're free to use the underscore in "weird" places:

```
int i1  = _1_000_000;    // illegal, can't begin with an "_"
int i2 = 10_0000_0;      // legal, but confusing
```

As a final note, remember that you can use the underscore character for any of the numeric types (including doubles and floats), but for doubles and floats, you CANNOT add an underscore character directly next to the decimal point, or next to the X or B in hex or binary numbers (which are coming up soon).

Decimal Literals Decimal integers need no explanation; you've been using them since grade one or earlier. Chances are you don't keep your checkbook in hex. (If you do, there's a Geeks Anonymous [GA] group ready to help.) In the Java language, they are represented as is, with no prefix of any kind, as follows:

```
int length = 343;
```

Binary Literals Also new to Java 7 is the addition of binary literals. Binary literals can use only the digits 0 and 1. Binary literals must start with either `0B` or `0b`, as shown:

```
int b1 = 0B101010;    // set b1 to binary 101010 (decimal 42)
int b2 = 0b00011;     // set b2 to binary 11 (decimal 3)
```

Octal Literals Octal integers use only the digits 0 to 7. In Java, you represent an integer in octal form by placing a zero in front of the number, as follows:

```
class Octal {
  public static void main(String [] args) {
    int six = 06;       // Equal to decimal 6
    int seven = 07;     // Equal to decimal 7
    int eight = 010;    // Equal to decimal 8
    int nine = 011;     // Equal to decimal 9
    System.out.println("Octal 010 = " + eight);
  }
}
```

You can have up to 21 digits in an octal number, not including the leading 0. If we run the preceding program, it displays the following:

```
Octal 010 = 8
```

Hexadecimal Literals Hexadecimal (hex for short) numbers are constructed using 16 distinct symbols. Because we never invented single-digit symbols for the numbers 10 through 15, we use alphabetic characters to represent these digits. Counting from 0 through 15 in hex looks like this:

```
0 1 2 3 4 5 6 7 8 9 a b c d e f
```

Java will accept uppercase or lowercase letters for the extra digits (one of the few places Java is not case sensitive!). You are allowed up to 16 digits in a hexadecimal number, not including the prefix `0x` (or `0X`) or the optional suffix extension `L`, which will be explained a bit later in the chapter. All of the following hexadecimal assignments are legal:

```
class HexTest {
  public static void main (String [] args) {
    int x = 0X0001;
    int y = 0x7fffffff;
    int z = 0xDeadCafe;
    System.out.println("x = " + x + " y = " + y + " z = " + z);
  }
}
```

Running `HexTest` produces the following output:

```
x = 1 y = 2147483647 z = -559035650
```

Don't be misled by changes in case for a hexadecimal digit or the `x` preceding it. `0XCAFE` and `0xcafe` are both legal *and have the same value.*

All four integer literals (binary, octal, decimal, and hexadecimal) are defined as `int` by default, but they may also be specified as `long` by placing a suffix of `L` or `l` after the number:

```
long jo = 110599L;
long so = 0xFFFFl;  // Note the lowercase 'l'
```

Floating-point Literals

Floating-point numbers are defined as a number, a decimal symbol, and more numbers representing the fraction. In the following example, the number 11301874.9881024 is the literal value:

```
double d = 11301874.9881024;
```

Floating-point literals are defined as `double` (64 bits) by default, so if you want to assign a floating-point literal to a variable of type `float` (32 bits), you must attach the suffix F or f to the number. If you don't do this, the compiler will complain about a possible loss of precision, because you're trying to fit a number into a (potentially) less precise "container." The F suffix gives you a way to tell the compiler, "Hey, I know what I'm doing, and I'll take the risk, thank you very much."

```
float f = 23.467890;          // Compiler error, possible loss
                              // of precision
float g = 49837849.029847F;   // OK; has the suffix "F"
```

You may also optionally attach a D or d to double literals, but it is not necessary because this is the default behavior.

```
double d = 110599.995011D; // Optional, not required
double  g = 987.897;       // No 'D' suffix, but OK because the
                           // literal is a double by default
```

Look for numeric literals that include a comma; here's an example:

```
int x = 25,343;            // Won't compile because of the comma
```

Boolean Literals

Boolean literals are the source code representation for boolean values. A boolean value can be defined only as `true` or `false`. Although in C (and some other languages), it is common to use numbers to represent `true` or `false`, this will not work in Java. Again, repeat after me: "Java is not C."

```
boolean t = true;  // Legal
boolean  f = 0;    // Compiler error!
```

Be on the lookout for questions that use numbers where `booleans` are required. You might see an `if` test that uses a number, as in the following:

```
int x = 1;  if (x) {  } // Compiler error!
```

Character Literals

A `char` literal is represented by a single character in single quotes:

```
char a = 'a';
char b = '@';
```

You can also type in the Unicode value of the character, using the Unicode notation of prefixing the value with \u, as follows:

```
char letterN = '\u004E'; // The letter 'N'
```

Remember, characters are just 16-bit unsigned integers under the hood. That means you can assign a number literal, assuming it will fit into the unsigned 16-bit range (0 to 65535). For example, the following are all legal:

```
char a = 0x892;          // hexadecimal literal
char b = 982;            // int literal
char c = (char)70000;    // The cast is required; 70000 is
                         // out of char range
char d = (char) -98;     // Ridiculous, but legal
```

And the following are not legal and produce compiler errors:

```
char e = -29;    // Possible loss of precision; needs a cast
char f = 70000;  // Possible loss of precision; needs a cast
```

You can also use an escape code (the backslash) if you want to represent a character that can't be typed in as a literal, including the characters for linefeed, newline, horizontal tab, backspace, and quotes:

```
char c = '\"';    // A double quote
char d = '\n';    // A newline
char tab = '\t';  // A tab
```

Literal Values for Strings

A string literal is a source code representation of a value of a `String` object. The following is an example of two ways to represent a string literal:

```
String s = "Bill Joy";
System.out.println("Bill" + " Joy");
```

Although strings are not primitives, they're included in this section because they can be represented as literals—in other words, they can be typed directly into code. The only other nonprimitive type that has a literal representation is an array, which we'll look at later in the chapter.

```
Thread t = ???  // what literal value could possibly go here?
```

Assignment Operators

Assigning a value to a variable seems straightforward enough; you simply assign the stuff on the right side of the = to the variable on the left. Well, sure, but don't expect to be tested on something like this:

```
x = 6;
```

No, you won't be tested on the no-brainer (technical term) assignments. You will, however, be tested on the trickier assignments involving complex expressions and casting. We'll look at both primitive and reference variable assignments. But before we begin, let's back up and peek inside a variable. What is a variable? How are the variable and its value related?

Variables are just bit holders with a designated type. You can have an `int` holder, a `double` holder, a `Button` holder, and even a `String[]` holder. Within that holder is a bunch of bits representing the value. For primitives, the bits represent a numeric value (although we don't know what that bit pattern looks like for `boolean`, luckily, we don't care). A `byte` with a value of 6, for example, means that the bit pattern in the variable (the `byte` holder) is 00000110, representing the 8 bits.

So the value of a primitive variable is clear, but what's inside an object holder? If you say,

```
Button b = new Button();
```

what's inside the `Button` holder `b`? Is it the `Button` object? No! A variable referring to an object is just that—a *reference* variable. A reference variable bit holder contains bits representing a *way to get to the object*. We don't know what the format is. The way in which object references are stored is virtual-machine specific (it's a pointer to something, we just don't know what that something really is). All we can say for sure is that the variable's value is *not* the object, but rather a value representing a specific object on the heap. Or `null`. If the reference variable has not been assigned a value or has been explicitly assigned a value of `null`, the variable holds bits representing—you guessed it—`null`. You can read

```
Button b = null;
```

as "The `Button` variable `b` is not referring to any object."

So now that we know a variable is just a little box o' bits, we can get on with the work of changing those bits. We'll look first at assigning values to primitives and then finish with assignments to reference variables.

Primitive Assignments

The equal (=) sign is used for assigning a value to a variable, and it's cleverly named the assignment operator. There are actually 12 assignment operators, but only the 5 most commonly used assignment operators are on the exam, and they are covered in Chapter 4.

You can assign a primitive variable using a literal or the result of an expression.

Take a look at the following:

```
int x = 7;      // literal assignment
int y = x + 2; // assignment with an expression
                // (including a literal)
int z = x * y; // assignment with an expression
```

The most important point to remember is that a literal integer (such as 7) is always implicitly an `int`. Thinking back to Chapter 1, you'll recall that an `int` is a 32-bit value. No big deal if you're assigning a value to an `int` or a `long` variable, but what if you're assigning to a `byte` variable? After all, a `byte`-sized holder can't hold as many bits as an `int`-sized holder. Here's where it gets weird. The following is legal,

```
byte b = 27;
```

but only because the compiler automatically narrows the literal value to a `byte`. In other words, the compiler puts in the *cast*. The preceding code is identical to the following:

```
byte b = (byte) 27; // Explicitly cast the int literal to a byte
```

It looks as though the compiler gives you a break and lets you take a shortcut with assignments to integer variables smaller than an `int`. (Everything we're saying about `byte` applies equally to `char` and `short`, both of which are smaller than an `int`.) We're not actually at the weird part yet, by the way.

We know that a literal integer is always an `int`, but more importantly, the result of an expression involving anything `int`-sized or smaller is always an `int`. In other words, add two `byte`s together and you'll get an `int`—even if those two `byte`s are tiny. Multiply an `int` and a `short` and you'll get an `int`. Divide a `short` by a `byte` and you'll get...an `int`. Okay, now we're at the weird part. Check this out:

```
byte a = 3;      // No problem, 3 fits in a byte
byte b = 8;      // No problem, 8 fits in a byte
byte c = a + b; // Should be no problem, sum of the two bytes
                 // fits in a byte
```

The last line won't compile! You'll get an error something like what your grandfather used to get:

```
TestBytes.java:5: possible loss of precision
found   : int
required: byte
    byte c = a + b;
               ^
```

We tried to assign the sum of two `bytes` to a `byte` variable, the result of which (11) was definitely small enough to fit into a `byte`, but the compiler didn't care. It knew the rule about `int`-or-smaller expressions always resulting in an `int`. It would have compiled if we'd done the *explicit* cast:

```
byte c = (byte) (a + b);
```

exam watch

We were struggling to find a good way to teach this topic, and our friend, co–JavaRanch* moderator and repeat technical reviewer Marc Peabody, came up with the following. We think he did a great job: It's perfectly legal to declare multiple variables of the same type with a single line by placing a comma between each variable:

```
int a, b, c;
```

You also have the option to initialize any number of those variables right in place:

```
int j, k=1, l, m=3;
```

And these variables are each evaluated in the order that you read them, left to right. It's just as if you were to declare each one on a separate line:

```
int j;
int k=1;
int l;
int m=3;
```

But the order is important. This is legal:

```
int j, k=1, l, m=k+3; // legal: k is initialized before m uses it
```

But these are not:

```
int j, k=m+3, l, m=1; // illegal: m is not declared and initialized
                      // before k uses it
int x, y=x+1, z;      // illegal: x is not initialized before y uses it
```

****I know, I know, but it'll always be JavaRanch in our hearts.***

Primitive Casting

Casting lets you convert primitive values from one type to another. We mentioned primitive casting in the previous section, but now we're going to take a deeper look. (Object casting was covered in Chapter 2.)

Casts can be implicit or explicit. An implicit cast means you don't have to write code for the cast; the conversion happens automatically. Typically, an implicit cast happens when you're doing a widening conversion—in other words, putting a smaller thing (say, a `byte`) into a bigger container (such as an `int`). Remember those "`possible loss of precision`" compiler errors we saw in the assignments section? Those happened when we tried to put a larger thing (say, a `long`) into a smaller container (such as a `short`). The large-value-into-small-container conversion is referred to as *narrowing* and requires an explicit cast, where you tell the compiler that you're aware of the danger and accept full responsibility.

First we'll look at an implicit cast:

```
int a = 100;
long b = a;      // Implicit cast, an int value always fits in a long
```

An explicit cast looks like this:

```
float a = 100.001f;
int b = (int)a; // explicit cast, the int might lose some of float's info!
```

Integer values may be assigned to a `double` variable without explicit casting, because any integer value can fit in a 64-bit `double`. The following line demonstrates this:

```
double d = 100L; // Implicit cast
```

In the preceding statement, a `double` is initialized with a `long` value (as denoted by the `L` after the numeric value). No cast is needed in this case because a `double` can hold every piece of information that a `long` can store. If, however, we want to assign a `double` value to an integer type, we're attempting a narrowing conversion and the compiler knows it:

```
class Casting {
  public static void main(String [] args) {
    int x = 3957.229; // illegal
  }
}
```

If we try to compile the preceding code, we get an error something like this:

```
%javac Casting.java
Casting.java:3: Incompatible type for declaration. Explicit cast
needed to convert double to int.
      int x = 3957.229; // illegal
1 error
```

In the preceding code, a floating-point value is being assigned to an integer variable. Because an integer is not capable of storing decimal places, an error occurs. To make this work, we'll cast the floating-point number to an `int`:

```
class Casting {
  public static void main(String [] args) {
    int x = (int)3957.229; // legal cast
    System.out.println("int x = " + x);
  }
}
```

When you cast a floating-point number to an integer type, the value loses all the digits after the decimal. The preceding code will produce the following output:

```
int x = 3957
```

We can also cast a larger number type, such as a `long`, into a smaller number type, such as a `byte`. Look at the following:

```
class Casting {
  public static void main(String [] args) {
    long l = 56L;
    byte b = (byte)l;
    System.out.println("The byte is " + b);
  }
}
```

The preceding code will compile and run fine. But what happens if the `long` value is larger than 127 (the largest number a `byte` can store)? Let's modify the code:

```
class Casting {
  public static void main(String [] args) {
    long l = 130L;
    byte b = (byte)l;
    System.out.println("The byte is " + b);
  }
}
```

The code compiles fine, and when we run it we get the following:

```
%java Casting
The byte is -126
```

We don't get a runtime error, even when the value being narrowed is too large for the type. The bits to the left of the lower 8 just...go away. If the leftmost bit (the sign bit) in the `byte` (or any integer primitive) now happens to be a 1, the primitive will have a negative value.

EXERCISE 3-1

Casting Primitives

Create a `float` number type of any value, and assign it to a `short` using casting.

1. Declare a `float` variable: `float f = 234.56F;`
2. Assign the `float` to a `short`: `short s = (short)f;`

Assigning Floating-point Numbers

Floating-point numbers have a slightly different assignment behavior than integer types. First, you must know that every floating-point literal is implicitly a `double` (64 bits), not a `float`. So the literal `32.3`, for example, is considered a `double`. If you try to assign a `double` to a `float`, the compiler knows you don't have enough room in a 32-bit `float` container to hold the precision of a 64-bit `double`, and it lets you know. The following code looks good, but it won't compile:

```
float f = 32.3;
```

You can see that `32.3` should fit just fine into a float-sized variable, but the compiler won't allow it. In order to assign a floating-point literal to a `float` variable, you must either cast the value or append an `f` to the end of the literal. The following assignments will compile:

```
float f = (float) 32.3;
float g = 32.3f;
float h = 32.3F;
```

Assigning a Literal That Is Too Large for the Variable

We'll also get a compiler error if we try to assign a literal value that the compiler knows is too big to fit into the variable.

```
byte a = 128; // byte can only hold up to 127
```

The preceding code gives us an error something like this:

```
TestBytes.java:5: possible loss of precision
found   : int
required: byte
byte a = 128;
```

We can fix it with a cast:

```
byte a = (byte) 128;
```

But then what's the result? When you narrow a primitive, Java simply truncates the higher-order bits that won't fit. In other words, it loses all the bits to the left of the bits you're narrowing to.

Let's take a look at what happens in the preceding code. There, 128 is the bit pattern 10000000. It takes a full 8 bits to represent 128. But because the literal 128 is an `int`, we actually get 32 bits, with the 128 living in the rightmost (lower order) 8 bits. So a literal 128 is actually

00000000000000000000000010000000

Take our word for it; there are 32 bits there.

To narrow the 32 bits representing 128, Java simply lops off the leftmost (higher order) 24 bits. What remains is just the 10000000. But remember that a byte is signed, with the leftmost bit representing the sign (and not part of the value of the variable). So we end up with a negative number (the 1 that used to represent 128 now represents the negative sign bit). Remember, to find out the value of a negative number using 2's complement notation, you flip all of the bits and then add 1. Flipping the 8 bits gives us 01111111, and adding 1 to that gives us 10000000, or back to 128! And when we apply the sign bit, we end up with –128.

You must use an explicit cast to assign 128 to a byte, and the assignment leaves you with the value –128. A cast is nothing more than your way of saying to the compiler, "Trust me. I'm a professional. I take full responsibility for anything weird that happens when those top bits are chopped off."

That brings us to the compound assignment operators. This will compile:

```
byte b = 3;
b += 7;                 // No problem - adds 7 to b (result is 10)
```

and it is equivalent to this:

```
byte b = 3;
b = (byte) (b + 7);  // Won't compile without the
                     // cast, since b + 7 results in an int
```

The compound assignment operator += lets you add to the value of `b`, without putting in an explicit cast. In fact, +=, -=, *=, and /= will all put in an implicit cast.

Assigning One Primitive Variable to Another Primitive Variable

When you assign one primitive variable to another, the contents of the right-hand variable are copied. For example:

```
int a = 6;
int b = a;
```

This code can be read as, "Assign the bit pattern for the number 6 to the `int` variable `a`. Then copy the bit pattern in `a`, and place the copy into variable `b`."

So both variables now hold a bit pattern for 6, but the two variables have no other relationship. We used the variable `a` *only* to copy its contents. At this point, `a` and `b` have identical contents (in other words, identical values), but if we change the contents of *either* `a` or `b`, the other variable won't be affected.

Take a look at the following example:

```
class ValueTest {
  public static void main (String [] args) {
    int a = 10;  // Assign a value to a
    System.out.println("a = " + a);
    int b = a;
    b = 30;
    System.out.println("a = " + a + " after change to b");
  }
}
```

The output from this program is

```
%java ValueTest
a = 10
a = 10 after change to b
```

Notice the value of `a` stayed at 10. The key point to remember is that even after you assign `a` to `b`, `a` and `b` are not referring to the same place in memory. The `a` and `b` variables do not share a single value; they have identical copies.

Reference Variable Assignments

You can assign a newly created object to an object reference variable as follows:

```
Button b = new Button();
```

The preceding line does three key things:

- Makes a reference variable named `b`, of type `Button`
- Creates a new `Button` object on the heap
- Assigns the newly created `Button` object to the reference variable `b`

You can also assign `null` to an object reference variable, which simply means the variable is not referring to any object:

```
Button c = null;
```

The preceding line creates space for the `Button` reference variable (the bit holder for a reference value), but it doesn't create an actual `Button` object.

As we discussed in the last chapter, you can also use a reference variable to refer to any object that is a subclass of the declared reference variable type, as follows:

```
public class Foo {
  public void doFooStuff() { }
}
public class Bar extends Foo {
  public void doBarStuff() { }
}
class Test {
  public static void main (String [] args) {
     Foo reallyABar = new Bar();  // Legal because Bar is a
                                  // subclass of Foo
     Bar reallyAFoo = new Foo();  // Illegal! Foo is not a
                                  // subclass of Bar
  }
}
```

The rule is that you can assign a subclass of the declared type but not a superclass of the declared type. Remember, a `Bar` object is guaranteed to be able to do anything a `Foo` can do, so anyone with a `Foo` reference can invoke `Foo` methods even though the object is actually a `Bar`.

In the preceding code, we see that `Foo` has a method `doFooStuff()` that someone with a `Foo` reference might try to invoke. If the object referenced by the `Foo` variable is really a `Foo`, no problem. But it's also no problem if the object is a `Bar` because `Bar` inherited the `doFooStuff()` method. You can't make it work in reverse, however. If somebody has a `Bar` reference, they're going to invoke `doBarStuff()`, but if the object is a `Foo`, it won't know how to respond.

exam watch

The OCA 8 exam covers wrapper classes. We could have discussed wrapper classes in this chapter, but we felt it made more sense to discuss them in the context of ArrayLists (which we will cover in Chapter 6). So until you get to Chapter 6, all you'll need to know about wrappers follows:

A wrapper object is an object that holds the value of a primitive. Every kind of primitive has an associated wrapper class: `Boolean`, `Byte`, `Character`, `Double`, `Float`, `Integer`, `Long`, and `Short`. The following code creates two wrapper objects and then prints their values:

```
Long x = new Long(42);        // create an instance of Long with a value of 42
Short s = new Short("57");    // create an instance of Short with a value of 57

System.out.println(x + " " + s);
```

produces the following output:

```
42 57
```

We'll be diving much more deeply into wrappers in Chapter 5.

CERTIFICATION OBJECTIVE

Scope (OCA Objective 1.1)

1.1 Determine the scope of variables.

Variable Scope

Once you've declared and initialized a variable, a natural question is, "How long will this variable be around?" This is a question regarding the scope of variables. And not only is scope an important thing to understand in general, it also plays a big part in the exam. Let's start by looking at a class file:

```
class Layout {                          // class
  static int s = 343;                   // static variable
  int x;                                // instance variable
  { x = 7; int x2 = 5; }                // initialization block
  Layout() { x += 8; int x3 = 6;}       // constructor

  void doStuff() {                      // method
    int y = 0;                          // local variable
    for(int z = 0; z < 4; z++) {        // 'for' code block
      y += z + x;
    }
  }
}
```

As with variables in all Java programs, the variables in this program (s, x, x2, x3, y, and z) all have a scope:

- s is a static variable.
- x is an instance variable.
- y is a local variable (sometimes called a "method local" variable).
- z is a block variable.
- x2 is an init block variable, a flavor of local variable.
- x3 is a constructor variable, a flavor of local variable.

For the purposes of discussing the scope of variables, we can say that there are four basic scopes:

1. Static variables have the longest scope; they are created when the class is loaded, and they survive as long as the class stays loaded in the Java Virtual Machine (JVM).
2. Instance variables are the next most long-lived; they are created when a new instance is created, and they live until the instance is removed.
3. Local variables are next; they live as long as their method remains on the stack. As we'll soon see, however, local variables can be alive and still be "out of scope."
4. Block variables live only as long as the code block is executing.

Scoping errors come in many sizes and shapes. One common mistake happens when a variable is *shadowed* and two scopes overlap. We'll take a detailed look at shadowing in a few pages. The most common reason for scoping errors is an attempt to access a variable that is not in scope. Let's look at three common examples of this type of error:

- Attempting to access an instance variable from a static context (typically from `main()`):

```
class ScopeErrors {
  int x = 5;
  public static void main(String[] args) {
    x++;   // won't compile, x is an 'instance' variable
  }
}
```

- Attempting to access a local variable of the method that invoked you. When a method, say `go()`, invokes another method, say `go2()`, `go2()` won't have access to `go()`'s local variables. While `go2()` is executing, `go()`'s local variables are still *alive*, but they are *out of scope*. When `go2()` completes, it is removed from the stack, and `go()` resumes execution. At this point, all of `go()`'s previously declared variables are back in scope. For example:

```
class ScopeErrors {
  public static void main(String [] args) {
    ScopeErrors s = new ScopeErrors();
    s.go();
  }
  void go() {
    int y = 5;
    go2();
    y++;         // once go2() completes, y is back in scope
  }
  void go2() {
    y++;         // won't compile, y is local to go()
  }
}
```

- Attempting to use a block variable after the code block has completed. It's very common to declare and use a variable within a code block, but be careful not to try to use the variable once the block has completed:

```
void go3() {
  for(int z = 0; z < 5; z++) {
    boolean test = false;
    if(z == 3) {
      test = true;
      break;
```

```
        }
      }
      System.out.print(test);    // 'test' is an ex-variable,
                                 // it has ceased to be...
    }
```

In the last two examples, the compiler will say something like this:

```
cannot find symbol
```

This is the compiler's way of saying, "That variable you just tried to use? Well, it might have been valid in the distant past (like one line of code ago), but this is Internet time, baby, I have no memory of such a variable."

exam watch

Pay extra attention to code-block scoping errors. You might see them in switches, try-catches, `for`, `do`, and `while` loops, which we'll cover in later chapters.

CERTIFICATION OBJECTIVE

Variable Initialization (OCA Objectives 2.1, 4.1, and 4.2)

2.1 *Declare and initialize variables (including casting of primitive datatypes).*
4.1 *Declare, instantiate, initialize and use a one-dimensional array*
4.2 *Declare, instantiate, initialize and use multi-dimensional array (sic)*

Using a Variable or Array Element That Is Uninitialized and Unassigned

Java gives us the option of initializing a declared variable or leaving it uninitialized. When we attempt to use the uninitialized variable, we can get different behavior depending on what type of variable or array we are dealing with (primitives or objects). The behavior also depends on the level (scope) at which we are declaring our variable. An instance variable is declared within the class but outside any method or constructor, whereas a local variable is declared within a method (or in the argument list of the method).

Local variables are sometimes called stack, temporary, automatic, or method variables, but the rules for these variables are the same regardless of what you call them. Although you can leave a local variable uninitialized, the compiler complains if you try to use a local variable before initializing it with a value, as we shall see.

Primitive and Object Type Instance Variables

Instance variables (also called *member* variables) are variables defined at the class level. That means the variable declaration is not made within a method, constructor, or any other initializer block. Instance variables are initialized to a default value each time a new instance is created, although they may be given an explicit value after the object's superconstructors have completed. Table 3-1 lists the default values for primitive and object types.

TABLE 3-1 Default Values for Primitives and Reference Types

Variable Type	Default Value
Object reference	`null` (not referencing any object)
`byte, short, int, long`	`0`
`float, double`	`0.0`
`boolean`	`false`
`char`	`'\u0000'`

Primitive Instance Variables

In the following example, the integer `year` is defined as a class member because it is within the initial curly braces of the class and not within a method's curly braces:

```
public class BirthDate {
  int year;                              // Instance variable
  public static void main(String [] args) {
    BirthDate bd = new BirthDate();
    bd.showYear();
  }
  public void showYear() {
    System.out.println("The year is " + year);
  }
}
```

When the program is started, it gives the variable `year` a value of zero, the default value for primitive number instance variables.

on the job

It's a good idea to initialize all your variables, even if you're assigning them with the default value. Your code will be easier to read; programmers who have to maintain your code (after you win the lottery and move to Tahiti) will be grateful.

Object Reference Instance Variables

When compared with uninitialized primitive variables, object references that aren't initialized are a completely different story. Let's look at the following code:

```
public class Book {
  private String title;          // instance reference variable
  public String getTitle() {
    return title;
  }
  public static void main(String [] args) {
    Book b = new Book();
    System.out.println("The title is " + b.getTitle());
  }
}
```

This code will compile fine. When we run it, the output is

```
The title is null
```

The `title` variable has not been explicitly initialized with a `String` assignment, so the instance variable value is `null`. Remember that `null` is not the same as an empty String (`""`). A `null` value means the reference variable is not referring to any object on the heap. The following modification to the `Book` code runs into trouble:

```
public class Book {
  private String title;          // instance reference variable
  public String getTitle() {
    return title;
  }
  public static void main(String [] args) {
    Book b = new Book();
    String s = b.getTitle();     // Compiles and runs
    String t = s.toLowerCase();  // Runtime Exception!
  }
}
```

When we try to run the Book class, the JVM will produce something like this:

```
Exception in thread "main" java.lang.NullPointerException
    at Book.main(Book.java:9)
```

We get this error because the reference variable `title` does not point (refer) to an object. We can check to see whether an object has been instantiated by using the keyword `null`, as the following revised code shows:

```
public class Book {
  private String title;          // instance reference variable
  public String getTitle() {
    return title;
  }
  public static void main(String [] args) {
    Book b = new Book();
    String s = b.getTitle();     // Compiles and runs
    if (s != null) {
      String t = s.toLowerCase();
    }
  }
}
```

The preceding code checks to make sure the object referenced by the variable `s` is not `null` before trying to use it. Watch out for scenarios on the exam where you might have to trace back through the code to find out whether an object reference will have a value of `null`. In the preceding code, for example, you look at the instance variable declaration for title, see that there's no explicit initialization, recognize that the `title` variable will be given the default value of `null`, and then realize that the variable `s` will also have a value of `null`. Remember, the value of `s` is a copy of the value of `title` (as returned by the `getTitle()` method), so if `title` is a `null` reference, `s` will be, too.

Array Instance Variables

In Chapter 5 we'll be taking a very detailed look at declaring, constructing, and initializing arrays and multidimensional arrays. For now, we're just going to look at the rule for an array element's default values.

An array is an object; thus, an array instance variable that's declared but not explicitly initialized will have a value of `null`, just as any other object reference instance variable. But...if the array is initialized, what happens to the elements contained *in* the array? All array elements are given their default values—the same default values that elements of that type get when they're instance variables.

The bottom line: Array elements are always, always, always given default values, regardless of where the array itself is instantiated.

If we initialize an array, object reference elements will equal null if they are not initialized individually with values. If primitives are contained in an array, they will be given their respective default values. For example, in the following code, the array `year` will contain 100 integers that all equal to 0 (zero) by default:

```
public class BirthDays {
  static int [] year = new int[100];
  public static void main(String [] args) {
    for(int i=0;i<100;i++)
      System.out.println("year[" + i + "] = " + year[i]);
  }
}
```

When the preceding code runs, the output indicates that all 100 integers in the array have a value of 0.

Local (Stack, Automatic) Primitives and Objects

Local variables are defined within a method, and they include a method's parameters.

exam watch

Automatic *is just another term for* local variable. *It does not mean the automatic variable is automatically assigned a value! In fact, the opposite is true. An automatic variable must be assigned a value in the code or the compiler will complain.*

Local Primitives

In the following time-travel simulator, the integer `year` is defined as an automatic variable because it is within the curly braces of a method:

```
public class TimeTravel {
  public static void main(String [] args) {
    int year = 2050;
    System.out.println("The year is " + year);
  }
}
```

Local variables, including primitives, always, always, always must be initialized *before* you attempt to use them (though not necessarily on the same line of code). Java does not give local variables a default value; you must explicitly initialize them with a value, as in the preceding example. If you try to use an uninitialized primitive in your code, you'll get a compiler error:

```
public class TimeTravel {
  public static void main(String [] args) {
    int year; // Local variable (declared but not initialized)
    System.out.println("The year is " + year); // Compiler error
  }
}
```

Compiling produces output something like this:

```
%javac TimeTravel.java
TimeTravel.java:4: Variable year may not have been initialized.
           System.out.println("The year is " + year);
1 error
```

To correct our code, we must give the integer `year` a value. In this updated example, we declare it on a separate line, which is perfectly valid:

```
public class TimeTravel {
  public static void main(String [] args) {
    int year;              // Declared but not initialized
    int day;               // Declared but not initialized
    System.out.println("You step into the portal.");
    year = 2050;           // Initialize (assign an explicit value)
    System.out.println("Welcome to the year " + year);
  }
}
```

Notice in the preceding example we declared an integer called `day` that never gets initialized, yet the code compiles and runs fine. Legally, you can declare a local variable without initializing it as long as you don't use the variable—but, let's face it, if you declared it, you probably had a reason (although we have heard of programmers declaring random local variables just for sport, to see if they can figure out how and why they're being used).

on the job

The compiler can't always tell whether a local variable has been initialized before use. For example, if you initialize within a logically conditional block (in other words, a code block that may not run, such as an if block or for loop without a literal value of true or false in the test), the compiler knows that the initialization might not happen and can produce an error. The following code upsets the compiler:

```
public class TestLocal {
  public static void main(String [] args) {
    int x;
    if (args[0] != null) { // assume you know this is true
      x = 7;                // compiler can't tell that this
                            // statement will run
    }
    int y = x;              // the compiler will choke here
}}
```

The compiler will produce an error something like this:

```
TestLocal.java:9: variable x might not have been initialized
```

Because of the compiler-can't-tell-for-certain problem, you will sometimes need to initialize your variable outside the conditional block, just to make the compiler happy. You know why that's important if you've seen the bumper sticker, "When the compiler's not happy, ain't nobody happy."

Local Object References

Objects references, too, behave differently when declared within a method rather than as instance variables. With instance variable object references, you can get away with leaving an object reference uninitialized, as long as the code checks to make sure the reference isn't `null` before using it. Remember, to the compiler, `null` is a value. You can't use the dot operator on a `null` reference, because *there is no object at the other end of it*, but a `null` reference is not the same as an *uninitialized* reference. Locally declared references can't get away with checking for `null` before use, unless you explicitly initialize the local variable to `null`. The compiler will complain about the following code:

```
import java.util.Date;
public class TimeTravel {
  public static void main(String [] args) {
    Date date;
    if (date == null)
      System.out.println("date is null");
}}
```

Compiling the code results in an error similar to the following:

```
%javac TimeTravel.java
TimeTravel.java:5: Variable date may not have been initialized.
        if (date == null)
1 error
```

Instance variable references are always given a default value of `null`, until they are explicitly initialized to something else. But local references are not given a default value; in other words, *they aren't* `null`. If you don't initialize a local reference variable, then, by default, its value is—well that's the whole point: it doesn't have any value at all! So we'll make this simple: Just set the darn thing to `null` explicitly until you're ready to initialize it to something else. The following local variable will compile properly:

```
Date date = null; // Explicitly set the local reference
                  // variable to null
```

Local Arrays

Just like any other object reference, array references declared within a method must be assigned a value before use. That just means you must declare and construct the array. You do not, however, need to explicitly initialize the elements of an array. We've said it before, but it's important enough to repeat: Array elements are given their default values (`0`, `false`, `null`, `'\u0000'`, and so on) regardless of whether the array is declared as an instance or local variable. The array object itself, however, will not be initialized if it's declared locally. In other words, you must explicitly initialize an array reference if it's declared and used within a method, but at the moment you construct an array object, all of its elements are assigned their default values.

Assigning One Reference Variable to Another

With primitive variables, an assignment of one variable to another means the contents (bit pattern) of one variable are *copied* into another. Object reference variables work exactly the same way. The contents of a reference variable are a bit pattern, so if you assign reference variable `a1` to reference variable `b1`, the bit pattern in `a1` is *copied* and the new *copy* is placed into `b1`. (Some people have created a game around counting how many times we use the word *copy* in this chapter...this copy concept is a biggie!) If we assign an existing instance of an object to a new reference variable, then two reference variables will hold the same bit pattern—a bit pattern referring to a specific object on the heap. Look at the following code:

```
import java.awt.Dimension;
class ReferenceTest {
  public static void main (String [] args) {
    Dimension a1 = new Dimension(5,10);
    System.out.println("a1.height = " + a1.height);
    Dimension b1 = a1;
    b1.height = 30;
    System.out.println("a1.height = " + a1.height +
                       " after change to b1");
  }
}
```

In the preceding example, a `Dimension` object `a1` is declared and initialized with a width of 5 and a height of 10. Next, `Dimension b1` is declared and assigned the value of `a1`. At this point, both variables (`a1` and `b1`) hold identical values because the contents of `a1` were copied into `b1`. There is still only one `Dimension` object—the one that both `a1` and `b1` refer to. Finally, the `height` property is changed using the `b1` reference. Now think for a minute: is this going to change the `height` property of `a1` as well? Let's see what the output will be:

```
%java ReferenceTest
a1.height = 10
a1.height = 30 after change to b1
```

From this output, we can conclude that both variables refer to the same instance of the `Dimension` object. When we made a change to `b1`, the `height` property was also changed for `a1`.

One exception to the way object references are assigned is `String`. In Java, `String` objects are given special treatment. For one thing, `String` objects are immutable; you can't change the value of a `String` object (lots more on this concept in Chapter 6). But it sure looks as though you can. Examine the following code:

```
class StringTest {
  public static void main(String [] args) {
    String x = "Java";  // Assign a value to x
    String y = x;       // Now y and x refer to the same
                        // String object

    System.out.println("y string = " + y);
    x = x + " Bean";    // Now modify the object using
                        // the x reference
    System.out.println("y string = " + y);
  }
}
```

Because `String`s are objects, you might think `String y` will contain the characters `Java Bean` after the variable `x` is changed. Let's see what the output is:

```
%java StringTest
y string = Java
y string = Java
```

As you can see, even though `y` is a reference variable to the same object that `x` refers to, when we change `x`, it doesn't change `y`! For any other object type, where two references refer to the same object, if either reference is used to modify the object, both references will see the change because there is still only a single object. *But any time we make any changes at all to a `String`, the VM will update the reference variable to refer to a different object.* The different object might be a new object, or it might not be, but it will definitely be a different object. The reason we can't say for sure whether a new object is created is because of the `String` constant pool, which we'll cover in Chapter 6.

You need to understand what happens when you use a `String` reference variable to modify a string:

- A new string is created (or a matching `String` is found in the `String` pool), leaving the original `String` object untouched.
- The reference used to modify the `String` (or rather, make a new `String` by modifying a copy of the original) is then assigned the brand-new `String` object.

So when you say,

```
1. String s = "Fred";
2. String t = s;      // Now t and s refer to the same
                      // String object
3. t.toUpperCase();   // Invoke a String method that changes
                      // the String
```

you haven't changed the original `String` object created on line 1. When line 2 completes, both `t` and `s` reference the same `String` object. But when line 3 runs, rather than modifying the object referred to by `t` and `s` (which is the one and only `String` object up to this point), a brand new `String` object is created. And then it's abandoned. Because the new `String` isn't assigned to a `String` variable, the newly created `String` (which holds the string `"FRED"`) is toast. So although two `String` objects were created in the preceding code, only one is actually referenced, and both `t` and `s` refer to it. The behavior of `String`s is extremely important in the exam, so we'll cover it in much more detail in Chapter 6.

CERTIFICATION OBJECTIVE

Passing Variables into Methods (OCA Objective 6.6)

6.8 Determine the effect upon object references and primitive values when they are passed into methods that change the values.

Methods can be declared to take primitives and/or object references. You need to know how (or if) the caller's variable can be affected by the called method. The difference between object reference and primitive variables, when passed into methods, is huge and important. To understand this section, you'll need to be comfortable with the information covered in the "Literals, Assignments, and Variables" section in the early part of this chapter.

Passing Object Reference Variables

When you pass an object variable into a method, you must keep in mind that you're passing the object *reference*, not the actual object itself. Remember that a reference variable holds bits that represent (to the underlying VM) a way to get to a specific object in memory (on the heap). More importantly, you must remember that you aren't even passing the actual reference variable, but rather a *copy* of the reference variable. A copy of a variable means you get a copy of the bits in that variable, so when you pass a reference variable, you're passing a copy of the bits representing how to get to a specific object. In other words, both the caller and the called method will now have identical copies of the reference; thus, both will refer to the same exact (*not* a copy) object on the heap.

For this example, we'll use the `Dimension` class from the java.awt package:

```
import java.awt.Dimension;
class ReferenceTest {
  public static void main (String [] args) {
    Dimension d = new Dimension(5,10);
    ReferenceTest rt = new ReferenceTest();
    System.out.println("Before, d.height: " + d.height);
    rt.modify(d);
    System.out.println("After, d.height: " + d.height);
  }
  void modify(Dimension dim) {
    dim.height = dim.height + 1;
    System.out.println("dim = " + dim.height);
} }
```

When we run this class, we can see the `modify()` method was, indeed, able to modify the original (and only) `Dimension` object created on line 4.

```
C:\Java Projects\Reference>java ReferenceTest
Before, d.height: 10
dim = 11
After, d.height: 11
```

Notice when the `Dimension` object on line 4 is passed to the `modify()` method, any changes to the object that occur inside the method are being made to the object whose reference was passed. In the preceding example, reference variables `d` and `dim` both point to the same object.

Does Java Use Pass-By-Value Semantics?

If Java passes objects by passing the reference variable instead, does that mean Java uses pass-by-reference for objects? Not exactly, although you'll often hear and read that it does. Java is actually pass-by-value for all variables running within a single VM. Pass-by-value means pass-by-variable-value. And that means pass-by-copy-of-the-variable! (There's that word *copy* again!)

It makes no difference if you're passing primitive or reference variables; you are always passing a copy of the bits in the variable. So for a primitive variable, you're passing a copy of the bits representing the value. For example, if you pass an `int` variable with the value of `3`, you're passing a copy of the bits representing `3`. The called method then gets its own copy of the value to do with it what it likes.

And if you're passing an object reference variable, you're passing a copy of the bits representing the reference to an object. The called method then gets its own copy of the reference variable to do with it what it likes. But because two identical reference variables refer to the exact same object, if the called method modifies the object (by invoking setter methods, for example), the caller will see that the object the caller's original variable refers to has also been changed. In the next section, we'll look at how the picture changes when we're talking about primitives.

The bottom line on pass-by-value: The called method can't change the caller's variable, although for object reference variables, the called method can change the object the variable referred to. What's the difference between changing the variable and changing the object? For object references, it means the called method can't reassign the caller's original reference variable and make it refer to a different object or `null`. For example, in the following code fragment,

```
void bar() {
  Foo f = new Foo();
  doStuff(f);
}
void doStuff(Foo g) {
  g.setName("Boo");
  g = new Foo();
}
```

reassigning `g` does not reassign `f`! At the end of the `bar()` method, two `Foo` objects have been created: one referenced by the local variable `f` and one referenced by the local (argument) variable `g`. Because the `doStuff()` method has a copy of the reference variable, it has a way to get to the original `Foo` object, for instance to call the `setName()` method. But the `doStuff()` method does *not* have a way to get to the `f` reference variable. So `doStuff()` can change values within the object `f` refers to, but `doStuff()` can't change the actual contents (bit pattern) of `f`. In other words, `doStuff()` can change the state of the object that `f` refers to, but it can't make `f` refer to a different object!

Passing Primitive Variables

Let's look at what happens when a primitive variable is passed to a method:

```
class ReferenceTest {
  public static void main (String [] args) {
    int a = 1;
    ReferenceTest rt = new ReferenceTest();
    System.out.println("Before modify() a = " + a);
    rt.modify(a);
    System.out.println("After modify() a = " + a);
  }
  void modify(int number) {
    number = number + 1;
    System.out.println("number = " + number);
  }
}
```

In this simple program, the variable `a` is passed to a method called `modify()`, which increments the variable by 1. The resulting output looks like this:

```
Before modify() a = 1
number = 2
After modify() a = 1
```

Notice that a did not change after it was passed to the method. Remember, it was a copy of a that was passed to the method. When a primitive variable is passed to a method, it is passed by value, which means pass-by-copy-of-the-bits-in-the-variable.

FROM THE CLASSROOM

The Shadowy World of Variables

Just when you think you've got it all figured out, you see a piece of code with variables not behaving the way you think they should. You might have stumbled into code with a shadowed variable. You can shadow a variable in several ways. We'll look at one way that might trip you up: hiding a static variable by shadowing it with a local variable.

Shadowing involves reusing a variable name that's already been declared somewhere else. The effect of shadowing is to hide the previously declared variable in such a way that it may look as though you're using the hidden variable, but you're actually using the shadowing variable. You might find reasons to shadow a variable intentionally, but typically it happens by accident and causes hard-to-find bugs. On the exam, you can expect to see questions where shadowing plays a role.

You can shadow a variable by declaring a local variable of the same name, either directly or as part of an argument:

```
class Foo {
  static int size = 7;
  static void changeIt(int size) {
    size = size + 200;
    System.out.println("size in changeIt is " + size);
  }
  public static void main (String [] args) {
    Foo f = new Foo();
    System.out.println("size = " + size);
    changeIt(size);
    System.out.println("size after changeIt is " + size);
  }
}
```

The preceding code appears to change the static `size` variable in the `changeIt()` method, but because `changeIt()` has a parameter named `size`, the local `size` variable is modified while the static `size` variable is untouched.

FROM THE CLASSROOM

Running class `Foo` prints this:

```
%java Foo
size = 7
size in changeIt is 207
size after changeIt is 7
```

Things become more interesting when the shadowed variable is an object reference, rather than a primitive:

```
class Bar {
  int barNum = 28;
}

class Foo {
  Bar myBar = new Bar();
  void changeIt(Bar myBar) {
    myBar.barNum = 99;
    System.out.println("myBar.barNum in changeIt is " + myBar.barNum);
    myBar = new Bar();
    myBar.barNum = 420;
    System.out.println("myBar.barNum in changeIt is now " + myBar.barNum);
  }
  public static void main (String [] args) {
    Foo f = new Foo();
    System.out.println("f.myBar.barNum is " + f.myBar.barNum);
    f.changeIt(f.myBar);
    System.out.println("f.myBar.barNum after changeIt is "
                       + f.myBar.barNum);
  }
}
```

The preceding code prints out this:

```
f.myBar.barNum is 28
myBar.barNum in changeIt is 99
myBar.barNum in changeIt is now 420
f.myBar.barNum after changeIt is 99
```

You can see that the shadowing variable (the local parameter `myBar` in `changeIt()`) can still affect the `myBar` instance variable, because the `myBar` parameter receives a reference to the same `Bar` object. But when the local `myBar` is reassigned a new `Bar` object, which we then modify by changing its `barNum` value, `Foo`'s original `myBar` instance variable is untouched.

CERTIFICATION OBJECTIVE

Garbage Collection (OCA Objective 2.4)

2.4 Explain an object's lifecycle (creation, "dereference by reassignment," and garbage collection)

The phrase *garbage collection* seems to come and go from the exam objectives. As of the OCA 8 exam, it's back, and we're happy. Garbage collection is a well-known idea and a universal phrase in computer science.

Overview of Memory Management and Garbage Collection

This is the section you've been waiting for! It's finally time to dig into the wonderful world of memory management and garbage collection.

Memory management is a crucial element in many types of applications. Consider a program that reads in large amounts of data, say from somewhere else on a network, and then writes that data into a database on a hard drive. A typical design would be to read the data into some sort of collection in memory, perform some operations on the data, and then write the data into the database. After the data is written into the database, the collection that stored the data temporarily must be emptied of old data or deleted and re-created before processing the next batch. This operation might be performed thousands of times, and in languages like C or C++ that do not offer automatic garbage collection, a small flaw in the logic that manually empties or deletes the collection data structures can allow small amounts of memory to be improperly reclaimed or lost. Forever. These small losses are called memory leaks, and over many thousands of iterations they can make enough memory inaccessible that programs will eventually crash. Creating code that performs manual memory management cleanly and thoroughly is a nontrivial and complex task, and while estimates vary, it is arguable that manual memory management can double the development effort for a complex program.

Java's garbage collector provides an automatic solution to memory management. In most cases it frees you from having to add any memory management logic to your application. The downside to automatic garbage collection is that you can't completely control when it runs and when it doesn't.

Overview of Java's Garbage Collector

Let's look at what we mean when we talk about garbage collection in the land of Java. From the 30,000-foot level, garbage collection is the phrase used to describe automatic memory management in Java. Whenever a software program executes (in Java, C, C++, Lisp, Ruby, and so on), it uses memory in several different ways. We're not going to get into Computer Science 101 here, but it's typical for memory to be used to create a stack, a heap, in Java's case constant pools and method areas. **The heap is that part of memory where Java objects live, and it's the one and only part of memory that is in any way involved in the garbage collection process.**

A heap is a heap is a heap. For the exam, it's important that you know that you can call it the heap, you can call it the garbage collectible heap, or you can call it Johnson, but there is one and only one heap.

So all garbage collection revolves around making sure the heap has as much free space as possible. For the purpose of the exam, what this boils down to is deleting any objects that are no longer reachable by the Java program running. We'll talk more about what "reachable" means in a minute, but let's drill this point in. When the garbage collector runs, its purpose is to find and delete objects that cannot be reached. If you think of a Java program as being in a constant cycle of creating the objects it needs (which occupy space on the heap) and then discarding them when they're no longer needed, creating new objects, discarding them, and so on, the missing piece of the puzzle is the garbage collector. When it runs, it looks for those discarded objects and deletes them from memory, so that the cycle of using memory and releasing it can continue. Ah, the great circle of life.

When Does the Garbage Collector Run?

The garbage collector is under the control of the JVM; the JVM decides when to run the garbage collector. From within your Java program, you can ask the JVM to run the garbage collector; but there are no guarantees, under any circumstances, that the JVM will comply. Left to its own devices, the JVM will typically run the garbage collector when it senses that memory is running low. Experience indicates that when your Java program makes a request for garbage collection, the JVM will usually grant your request in short order, but there are no guarantees. Just when you think you can count on it, the JVM will decide to ignore your request.

How Does the Garbage Collector Work?

You just can't be sure. You might hear that the garbage collector uses a mark and sweep algorithm, and for any given Java implementation that might be true, but the Java specification doesn't guarantee any particular implementation. You might hear that the garbage collector uses reference counting; once again, maybe yes, maybe no. The important concept for you to understand for the exam is: When does an object become eligible for garbage collection?

In a nutshell, every Java program has from one to many threads. Each thread has its own little execution stack. Normally, you (the programmer) cause at least one thread to run in a Java program, the one with the `main()` method at the bottom of the stack. However, there are many really cool reasons to launch additional threads from your initial thread (which you'll get into if you prepare for the OCP 8 exam). In addition to having its own little execution stack, each thread has its own lifecycle. For now, all you need to know is that threads can be alive or dead.

With this background information, we can now say with stunning clarity and resolve that *an object is eligible for garbage collection when no live thread can access it.* (Note: Due to the vagaries of the `String` constant pool, the exam focuses its garbage collection questions on non-`String` objects, and so our garbage collection discussions apply to only non-`String` objects too.)

Based on that definition, the garbage collector performs some magical, unknown operations; and when it discovers an object that can't be reached by any live thread, it will consider that object as eligible for deletion, and it might even delete it at some point. (You guessed it: it also might never delete it.) When we talk about reaching an object, we're really talking about having a reachable reference variable that refers to the object in question. If our Java program has a reference variable that refers to an object and that reference variable is available to a live thread, then that object is considered reachable. We'll talk more about how objects can become unreachable in the following section.

Can a Java application run out of memory? Yes. The garbage collection system attempts to remove objects from memory when they are not used. However, if you maintain too many live objects (objects referenced from other live objects), the system can run out of memory. Garbage collection cannot ensure that there is enough memory, only that the memory that is available will be managed as efficiently as possible.

Writing Code That Explicitly Makes Objects Eligible for Collection

In the preceding section, you learned the theories behind Java garbage collection. In this section, we show how to make objects eligible for garbage collection using actual code. We also discuss how to attempt to force garbage collection if it is necessary and how you can perform additional cleanup on objects before they are removed from memory.

Nulling a Reference

As we discussed earlier, an object becomes eligible for garbage collection when there are no more reachable references to it. Obviously, if there are no reachable references, it doesn't matter what happens to the object. For our purposes it is just floating in space, unused, inaccessible, and no longer needed.

The first way to remove a reference to an object is to set the reference variable that refers to the object to `null`. Examine the following code:

```
1. public class GarbageTruck {
2.   public static void main(String [] args) {
3.     StringBuffer sb = new StringBuffer("hello");
4.     System.out.println(sb);
5.     // The StringBuffer object is not eligible for collection
6.     sb = null;
7.     // Now the StringBuffer object is eligible for collection
8.   }
9. }
```

The `StringBuffer` object with the value `hello` is assigned to the reference variable `sb` in the third line. To make the object eligible (for garbage collection), we set the reference variable `sb` to `null`, which removes the single reference that existed to the `StringBuffer` object. Once line 6 has run, our happy little `hello` `StringBuffer` object is doomed, eligible for garbage collection.

Reassigning a Reference Variable

We can also decouple a reference variable from an object by setting the reference variable to refer to another object. Examine the following code:

```
class GarbageTruck {
  public static void main(String [] args) {
    StringBuffer s1 = new StringBuffer("hello");
    StringBuffer s2 = new StringBuffer("goodbye");
    System.out.println(s1);
    // At this point the StringBuffer "hello" is not eligible
    s1 = s2; // Redirects s1 to refer to the "goodbye" object
    // Now the StringBuffer "hello" is eligible for collection
  }}
```

Objects that are created in a method also need to be considered. When a method is invoked, any local variables created exist only for the duration of the method. Once the method has returned, the objects created in the method are eligible for garbage collection. There is an obvious exception, however. If an object is returned from the method, its reference might be assigned to a reference variable in the method that called it; hence, it will not be eligible for collection. Examine the following code:

```
import java.util.Date;
public class GarbageFactory {
  public static void main(String [] args) {
    Date d = getDate();
    doComplicatedStuff();
    System.out.println("d = " + d);
  }

  public static Date getDate() {
    Date d2 = new Date();
    StringBuffer now = new StringBuffer(d2.toString());
    System.out.println(now);
    return d2;
  }
}
```

In the preceding example, we created a method called `getDate()` that returns a `Date` object. This method creates two objects: a `Date` and a `StringBuffer` containing the date information. Since the method returns a reference to the `Date` object and this reference is assigned to a local variable, it will not be eligible for collection even after the `getDate()` method has completed. The `StringBuffer` object, though, will be eligible, even though we didn't explicitly set the now variable to `null`.

Isolating a Reference

There is another way in which objects can become eligible for garbage collection, even if they still have valid references! We call this scenario "islands of isolation."

A simple example is a class that has an instance variable that is a reference variable to another instance of the same class. Now imagine that two such instances exist and that they refer to each other. If all other references to these two objects are removed, then even though each object still has a valid reference, there will be no way for any live thread to access either object. When the garbage collector runs, it can *usually* discover any such islands of objects and remove them. As you can imagine, such islands can become quite large, theoretically containing hundreds of objects. Examine the following code:

```
public class Island {
  Island i;
  public static void main(String [] args) {

    Island i2 = new Island();
    Island i3 = new Island();
    Island i4 = new Island();

    i2.i = i3;    // i2 refers to i3
    i3.i = i4;    // i3 refers to i4
    i4.i = i2;    // i4 refers to i2

    i2 = null;
    i3 = null;
    i4 = null;

    // do complicated, memory intensive stuff
  }
}
```

When the code reaches `// do complicated`, the three `Island` objects (previously known as `i2`, `i3`, and `i4`) have instance variables so that they refer to each other, but their links to the outside world (`i2`, `i3`, and `i4`) have been nulled. These three objects are eligible for garbage collection.

This covers everything you will need to know about making objects eligible for garbage collection. Study Figure 3-2 to reinforce the concepts of objects without references and islands of isolation.

Forcing Garbage Collection

The first thing that we should mention here is that, contrary to this section's title, garbage collection cannot be forced. However, Java provides some methods that allow you to *request* that the JVM perform garbage collection.

Note: The Java garbage collector has evolved to such an advanced state that it's recommended that you never invoke `System.gc()` in your code—leave it to the JVM.

In reality, it is possible only to suggest to the JVM that it perform garbage collection. However, there are no guarantees the JVM will actually remove all of the

FIGURE 3-2 Island objects eligible for garbage collection

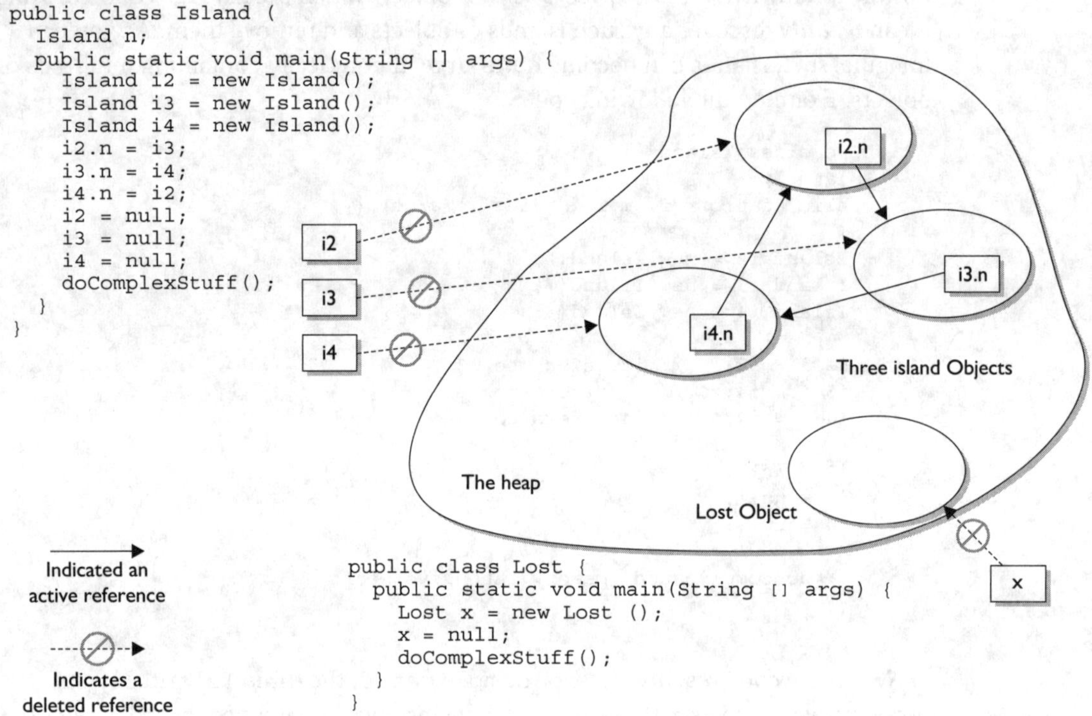

unused objects from memory (even if garbage collection is run). It is essential that you understand this concept for the exam.

The garbage collection routines that Java provides are members of the `Runtime` class. The `Runtime` class is a special class that has a single object (a `Singleton`) for each main program. The `Runtime` object provides a mechanism for communicating directly with the virtual machine. To get the `Runtime` instance, you can use the method `Runtime.getRuntime()`, which returns the `Singleton`. Once you have the `Singleton`, you can invoke the garbage collector using the `gc()` method. Alternatively, you can call the same method on the `System` class, which has static methods that can do the work of obtaining the `Singleton` for you. The simplest way to ask for garbage collection (remember—just a request) is

```
System.gc();
```

Theoretically, after calling `System.gc()`, you will have as much free memory as possible. We say "theoretically" because this routine does not always work that way. First, your JVM may not have implemented this routine; the language specification allows this routine to do nothing at all. Second, another thread might grab lots of memory right after you run the garbage collector.

This is not to say that `System.gc()` is a useless method—it's much better than nothing. You just can't rely on `System.gc()` to free up enough memory so that you don't have to worry about running out of memory. The Certification Exam is interested in guaranteed behavior, not probable behavior.

Now that you are somewhat familiar with how this works, let's do a little experiment to see the effects of garbage collection. The following program lets us know how much total memory the JVM has available to it and how much free memory it has. It then creates 10,000 `Date` objects. After this, it tells us how much memory is left and then calls the garbage collector (which, if it decides to run, should halt the program until all unused objects are removed). The final free memory result should indicate whether it has run. Let's look at the program:

```
import java.util.Date;
public class CheckGC {
  public static void main(String [] args) {
    Runtime rt = Runtime.getRuntime();
    System.out.println("Total JVM memory: "
                       + rt.totalMemory());
    System.out.println("Before Memory = "
                       + rt.freeMemory());
    Date d = null;
    for(int i = 0;i<10000;i++) {
      d = new Date();
      d = null;
    }
    System.out.println("After Memory = "
                       + rt.freeMemory());
    rt.gc();   // an alternate to System.gc()
    System.out.println("After GC Memory = "
                       + rt.freeMemory());
  }
}
```

Now, let's run the program and check the results:

```
Total JVM memory: 1048568
Before Memory = 703008
After Memory = 458048
After GC Memory = 818272
```

As you can see, the JVM actually did decide to garbage collect (that is, delete) the eligible objects. In the preceding example, we suggested that the JVM perform garbage collection with 458,048 bytes of memory remaining, and it honored our request. This program has only one user thread running, so there was nothing else going on when we called `rt.gc()`. Keep in mind that the behavior when `gc()` is called may be different for different JVMs; hence, there is no guarantee that the unused objects will be removed from memory. About the only thing you can guarantee is that if you are running very low on memory, the garbage collector will run before it throws an `OutOfMemoryException`.

EXERCISE 3-2

Garbage Collection Experiment

Try changing the CheckGC program by putting lines 13 and 14 inside a loop. You might see that not all memory is released on any given run of the GC.

Cleaning Up Before Garbage Collection—the finalize() Method

Java provides a mechanism that lets you run some code just before your object is deleted by the garbage collector. This code is located in a method named `finalize()` that all classes inherit from class `Object`. On the surface, this sounds like a great idea; maybe your object opened up some resources, and you'd like to close them before your object is deleted. The problem is that, as you may have gathered by now, you can never count on the garbage collector to delete an object. So, any code that you put into your class's overridden `finalize()` method is not guaranteed to run. Because the `finalize()` method for any given object might run, but you can't count on it, don't put any essential code into your `finalize()` method. In fact, we recommend that, in general, you don't override `finalize()` at all.

Tricky Little finalize() Gotchas

There are a couple of concepts concerning `finalize()` that you need to remember:

- For any given object, `finalize()` will be called only once (at most) by the garbage collector.
- Calling `finalize()` can actually result in saving an object from deletion.

Let's examine these statements a little further. First of all, remember that any code you can put into a normal method you can put into `finalize()`. For example, in the `finalize()` method you could write code that passes a reference to the object in question back to another object, effectively *ineligible-izing* the object for garbage collection. If at some later point this same object becomes eligible for garbage collection again, the garbage collector can still process the object and delete it. The garbage collector, however, will remember that, for this object, `finalize()` already ran, and it will not run `finalize()` again.

CERTIFICATION SUMMARY

This chapter covered a wide range of topics. Don't worry if you have to review some of these topics as you get into later chapters. This chapter includes a lot of foundational stuff that will come into play later.

We started the chapter by reviewing the stack and the heap; remember that local variables live on the stack and instance variables live with their objects on the heap.

We reviewed legal literals for primitives and `Strings`, and then we discussed the basics of assigning values to primitives and reference variables and the rules for casting primitives.

Next we discussed the concept of scope, or "How long will this variable live?" Remember the four basic scopes in order of lessening life span: static, instance, local, and block.

We covered the implications of using uninitialized variables and the importance of the fact that local variables MUST be assigned a value explicitly. We talked about some of the tricky aspects of assigning one reference variable to another and some of the finer points of passing variables into methods, including a discussion of "shadowing."

Finally, we dove into garbage collection, Java's automatic memory management feature. We learned that the heap is where objects live and where all the cool garbage collection activity takes place. We learned that in the end, the JVM will perform garbage collection whenever it wants to. You (the programmer) can request a garbage collection run, but you can't force it. We talked about garbage collection only applying to objects that are eligible, and that eligible means "inaccessible from any live thread." Finally, we discussed the rarely useful `finalize()` method and what you'll have to know about it for the exam. All in all, this was one fascinating chapter.

✓ TWO-MINUTE DRILL

Here are some of the key points from this chapter.

Stack and Heap

- ☐ Local variables (method variables) live on the stack.
- ☐ Objects and their instance variables live on the heap.

Literals and Primitive Casting (OCA Objective 2.1)

- ☐ Integer literals can be binary, decimal, octal (such as `013`), or hexadecimal (such as `0x3d`).
- ☐ Literals for `long`s end in `L` or `l`. (For the sake of readability, we recommend "`L`".)
- ☐ Float literals end in `F` or `f`, and `double` literals end in a digit or `D` or `d`.
- ☐ The `boolean` literals are `true` and `false`.
- ☐ Literals for `char`s are a single character inside single quotes: `'d'`.

Scope (OCA Objective 1.1)

- ☐ Scope refers to the lifetime of a variable.
- ☐ There are four basic scopes:
  - ☐ Static variables live basically as long as their class lives.
  - ☐ Instance variables live as long as their object lives.
  - ☐ Local variables live as long as their method is on the stack; however, if their method invokes another method, they are temporarily unavailable.
  - ☐ Block variables (for example, in a `for` or an `if`) live until the block completes.

Basic Assignments (OCA Objectives 2.1, 2.2, and 2.3)

- ☐ Literal integers are implicitly `int`s.
- ☐ Integer expressions always result in an `int`-sized result, never smaller.
- ☐ Floating-point numbers are implicitly doubles (64 bits).

- ☐ Narrowing a primitive truncates the *high order* bits.
- ☐ Compound assignments (such as +=) perform an automatic cast.
- ☐ A reference variable holds the bits that are used to refer to an object.
- ☐ Reference variables can refer to subclasses of the declared type but not to superclasses.
- ☐ When you create a new object, such as `Button b = new Button();`, the JVM does three things:
  - ☐ Makes a reference variable named `b`, of type `Button`.
  - ☐ Creates a new `Button` object.
  - ☐ Assigns the `Button` object to the reference variable `b`.

Using a Variable or Array Element That Is Uninitialized and Unassigned (OCA Objectives 4.1 and 4.2)

- ☐ When an array of objects is instantiated, objects within the array are not instantiated automatically, but all the references get the default value of `null`.
- ☐ When an array of primitives is instantiated, elements get default values.
- ☐ Instance variables are always initialized with a default value.
- ☐ Local/automatic/method variables are never given a default value. If you attempt to use one before initializing it, you'll get a compiler error.

Passing Variables into Methods (OCA Objective 6.6)

- ☐ Methods can take primitives and/or object references as arguments.
- ☐ Method arguments are always copies.
- ☐ Method arguments are never actual objects (they can be references to objects).
- ☐ A primitive argument is an unattached copy of the original primitive.
- ☐ A reference argument is another copy of a reference to the original object.
- ☐ Shadowing occurs when two variables with different scopes share the same name. This leads to hard-to-find bugs and hard-to-answer exam questions.

Garbage Collection (OCA Objective 2.4)

- ☐ In Java, garbage collection (GC) provides automated memory management.
- ☐ The purpose of GC is to delete objects that can't be reached.
- ☐ Only the JVM decides when to run the GC; you can only suggest it.
- ☐ You can't know the GC algorithm for sure.
- ☐ Objects must be considered eligible before they can be garbage collected.
- ☐ An object is eligible when no live thread can reach it.
- ☐ To reach an object, you must have a live, reachable reference to that object.
- ☐ Java applications can run out of memory.
- ☐ Islands of objects can be garbage collected, even though they refer to each other.
- ☐ Request garbage collection with `System.gc();`.
- ☐ The `Object` class has a `finalize()` method.
- ☐ The `finalize()` method is guaranteed to run once and only once before the garbage collector deletes an object.
- ☐ The garbage collector makes no guarantees; `finalize()` may never run.
- ☐ You can ineligible-ize an object for GC from within `finalize()`.

SELF TEST

1. Given:

```
class CardBoard {
  Short story = 200;
  CardBoard go(CardBoard cb) {
    cb = null;
    return cb;
  }
  public static void main(String[] args) {
    CardBoard c1 = new CardBoard();
    CardBoard c2 = new CardBoard();
    CardBoard c3 = c1.go(c2);
    c1 = null;
    // do Stuff
} }
```

When `// do Stuff` is reached, how many objects are eligible for garbage collection?

A. 0

B. 1

C. 2

D. Compilation fails

E. It is not possible to know

F. An exception is thrown at runtime

2. Given:

```
public class Fishing {
  byte b1 = 4;
  int i1 = 123456;
  long L1 = (long)i1;        // line A
  short s2 = (short)i1;      // line B
  byte b2 = (byte)i1;        // line C
  int i2 = (int)123.456;     // line D
  byte b3 = b1 + 7;          // line E
}
```

Which lines WILL NOT compile? (Choose all that apply.)

A. Line A

B. Line B

C. Line C

D. Line D

E. Line E

3. Given:

```
public class Literally {
  public static void main(String[] args) {
    int i1 = 1_000;         // line A
    int i2 = 10_00;         // line B
    int i3 = _10_000;       // line C
    int i4 = 0b101010;      // line D
    int i5 = 0B10_1010;     // line E
    int i6 = 0x2_a;         // line F
  }
}
```

Which lines WILL NOT compile? (Choose all that apply.)

A. Line A

B. Line B

C. Line C

D. Line D

E. Line E

F. Line F

4. Given:

```
class Mixer {
  Mixer() { }
  Mixer(Mixer m) { m1 = m; }
  Mixer m1;
  public static void main(String[] args) {
    Mixer m2 = new Mixer();
    Mixer m3 = new Mixer(m2);   m3.go();
    Mixer m4 = m3.m1;           m4.go();
    Mixer m5 = m2.m1;           m5.go();
  }
  void go() { System.out.print("hi "); }
}
```

What is the result?

A. `hi`

B. `hi hi`

C. `hi hi hi`

D. Compilation fails

E. `hi`, followed by an exception

F. `hi hi`, followed by an exception

5. Given:

```
class Fizz {
  int x = 5;
  public static void main(String[] args) {
    final Fizz f1 = new Fizz();
    Fizz f2 = new Fizz();
    Fizz f3 = FizzSwitch(f1,f2);
    System.out.println((f1 == f3) + " " + (f1.x == f3.x));
  }
  static Fizz FizzSwitch(Fizz x, Fizz y) {
    final Fizz z = x;
    z.x = 6;
    return z;
} }
```

What is the result?

A. `true true`

B. `false true`

C. `true false`

D. `false false`

E. Compilation fails

F. An exception is thrown at runtime

6. Given:

```
public class Mirror {
  int size = 7;
  public static void main(String[] args) {
    Mirror m1 = new Mirror();
    Mirror m2 = m1;
    int i1 = 10;
    int i2 = i1;
    go(m2, i2);
    System.out.println(m1.size + " " + i1);
  }
  static void go(Mirror m, int i) {
    m.size = 8;
    i = 12;
  }
}
```

What is the result?

A. `7 10`

B. `8 10`

C. `7 12`

D. `8 12`

E. Compilation fails

F. An exception is thrown at runtime

7. Given:

```
public class Wind {
  int id;
  Wind(int i) { id = i; }
  public static void main(String[] args) {
    new Wind(3).go();
    // commented line
  }
  void go() {
    Wind w1 = new Wind(1);
    Wind w2 = new Wind(2);
    System.out.println(w1.id + " " + w2.id);
  }
}
```

When execution reaches the commented line, which are true? (Choose all that apply.)

A. The output contains `1`

B. The output contains `2`

C. The output contains `3`

D. Zero `Wind` objects are eligible for garbage collection

E. One `Wind` object is eligible for garbage collection

F. Two `Wind` objects are eligible for garbage collection

G. Three `Wind` objects are eligible for garbage collection

8. Given:

```
public class Ouch {
  static int ouch = 7;
  public static void main(String[] args) {
    new Ouch().go(ouch);
    System.out.print(" " + ouch);
  }
```

```
  void go(int ouch) {
    ouch++;
    for(int ouch = 3; ouch < 6; ouch++)
      ;
    System.out.print(" " + ouch);
  }
}
```

What is the result?

A. 5 7

B. 5 8

C. 8 7

D. 8 8

E. Compilation fails

F. An exception is thrown at runtime

9. Given:

```
public class Happy {
  int id;
  Happy(int i) { id = i; }
  public static void main(String[] args) {
    Happy h1 = new Happy(1);
    Happy h2 = h1.go(h1);
    System.out.println(h2.id);
  }
  Happy go(Happy h) {
    Happy h3 = h;
    h3.id = 2;
    h1.id = 3;
    return h1;
  }
}
```

What is the result?

A. 1

B. 2

C. 3

D. Compilation fails

E. An exception is thrown at runtime

10. Given:

```
public class Network {
  Network(int x, Network n) {
    id = x;
    p = this;
    if(n != null) p = n;
  }
  int id;
  Network p;
  public static void main(String[] args) {
    Network n1 = new Network(1, null);
    n1.go(n1);
  }
  void go(Network n1) {
    Network n2 = new Network(2, n1);
    Network n3 = new Network(3, n2);
    System.out.println(n3.p.p.id);
  }
}
```

What is the result?

A. `1`

B. `2`

C. `3`

D. `null`

E. Compilation fails

11. Given:

```
class Beta { }
class Alpha {
  static Beta b1;
  Beta b2;
}
public class Tester {
  public static void main(String[] args) {
    Beta b1 = new Beta();      Beta b2 = new Beta();
    Alpha a1 = new Alpha();    Alpha a2 = new Alpha();
    a1.b1 = b1;
    a1.b2 = b1;
    a2.b2 = b2;
    a1 = null;  b1 = null;  b2 = null;
    // do stuff
  }
}
```

When line 16 is reached, how many objects will be eligible for garbage collection?

A. 0

B. 1

C. 2

D. 3

E. 4

F. 5

12. Given:

```
public class Telescope {
  static int magnify = 2;
  public static void main(String[] args) {
    go();
  }
  static void go() {
    int magnify = 3;
    zoomIn();
  }
  static void zoomIn() {
    magnify *= 5;
    zoomMore(magnify);
    System.out.println(magnify);
  }
  static void zoomMore(int magnify) {
    magnify *= 7;
  }
}
```

What is the result?

A. 2

B. 10

C. 15

D. 30

E. 70

F. 105

G. Compilation fails

13. Given:

```
public class Dark {
  int x = 3;
  public static void main(String[] args) {
    new Dark().go1();
  }
  void go1() {
    int x;
    go2(++x);
  }
  void go2(int y) {
    int x = ++y;
    System.out.println(x);
  }
}
```

What is the result?

A. 2

B. 3

C. 4

D. 5

E. Compilation fails

F. An exception is thrown at runtime

SELF TEST ANSWERS

1. ☑ **C** is correct. Only one `CardBoard object (c1)` is eligible, but it has an associated `Short` wrapper object that is also eligible.
   ☒ **A, B, D, E,** and **F** are incorrect based on the above. (OCA Objective 2.4)

2. ☑ **E** is correct; compilation of line E fails. When a mathematical operation is performed on any primitives smaller than `int`s, the result is automatically cast to an integer.
   ☒ **A, B, C,** and **D** are all legal primitive casts. (OCA Objective 2.1)

3. ☑ **C** is correct; line **C** will NOT compile. As of Java 7, underscores can be included in numeric literals, but not at the beginning or the end.
   ☒ **A, B, D, E,** and **F** are incorrect. **A** and **B** are legal numeric literals. **D** and **E** are examples of valid binary literals, which were new to Java 7, and **F** is a valid hexadecimal literal that uses an underscore. (OCA Objective 2.1)

4. ☑ **F** is correct. The `m2` object's `m1` instance variable is never initialized, so when `m5` tries to use it, a `NullPointerException` is thrown.
   ☒ **A, B, C, D,** and **E** are incorrect based on the above. (OCA Objectives 2.1 and 2.3)

5. ☑ **A** is correct. The references `f1`, `z`, and `f3` all refer to the same instance of `Fizz`. The `final` modifier assures that a reference variable cannot be referred to a different object, but `final` doesn't keep the object's state from changing.
   ☒ **B, C, D, E,** and **F** are incorrect based on the above. (OCA Objective 2.2)

6. ☑ **B** is correct. In the `go()` method, `m` refers to the single `Mirror` instance, but the `int i` is a new `int` variable, a detached copy of `i2`.
   ☒ **A, C, D, E,** and **F** are incorrect based on the above. (OCA Objectives 2.2 and 2.3)

7. ☑ **A, B,** and **G** are correct. The constructor sets the value of `id` for `w1` and `w2`. When the commented line is reached, none of the three `Wind` objects can be accessed, so they are eligible to be garbage collected.
   ☒ **C, D, E,** and **F** are incorrect based on the above. (OCA Objectives 1.1, 2.3, and 2.4)

8. ☑ **E** is correct. The parameter declared on line 9 is valid (although ugly), but the variable name `ouch` cannot be declared again on line 11 in the same scope as the declaration on line 9.
   ☒ **A, B, C, D,** and **F** are incorrect based on the above. (OCA Objectives 1.1 and 2.1)

9. ☑ **D** is correct. Inside the `go()` method, `h1` is out of scope.
   ☒ **A, B, C,** and **E** are incorrect based on the above. (OCA Objectives 1.1 and 6.1)

10. ☑ **A** is correct. Three `Network` objects are created. The `n2` object has a reference to the `n1` object, and the `n3` object has a reference to the `n2` object. The S.O.P. can be read as, "Use the `n3` object's `Network` reference (the first `p`), to find that object's reference (`n2`), and use that object's reference (the second `p`) to find that object's (`n1`'s) `id`, and print that `id`."
☒ **B, C, D,** and **E** are incorrect based on the above. (OCA Objectives, 2.2, 2.3, and 6.4)

11. ☑ **B** is correct. It should be clear that there is still a reference to the object referred to by `a2`, and that there is still a reference to the object referred to by `a2.b2`. What might be less clear is that you can still access the other `Beta` object through the static variable `a2.b1`—because it's static.
☒ **A, C, D, E,** and **F** are incorrect based on the above. (OCA Objective 2.4)

12. ☑ **B** is correct. In the `Telescope` class, there are three different variables named `magnify`. The `go()` method's version and the `zoomMore()` method's version are not used in the `zoomIn()` method. The `zoomIn()` method multiplies the class variable `* 5`. The result (`10`) is sent to `zoomMore()`, but what happens in `zoomMore()` stays in `zoomMore()`. The S.O.P. prints the value of `zoomIn()`'s `magnify`.
☒ **A, C, D, E, F,** and **G** are incorrect based on the above. (OCA Objectives 1.1 and 6.6)

13. ☑ **E** is correct. In `go1()` the local variable `x` is not initialized.
☒ **A, B, C, D,** and **F** are incorrect based on the above. (OCA Objectives 2.1 and 2.3)

4 Operators

CERTIFICATION OBJECTIVES

- Using Java Operators
- Use Parentheses to Override Operator Precedence
- Test Equality Between Strings and Other Objects Using == and equals( )

✓ Two-Minute Drill

Q&A Self Test

If you've got variables, you're going to modify them. (Unless you're one of those new-fangled "FP" programmers.) You'll increment them, add them together, and compare one to another (in about a dozen different ways). In this chapter, you'll learn how to do all that in Java. As an added bonus, you'll learn how to do things that you'll probably never use in the real world, but that will almost certainly be on the exam.

CERTIFICATION OBJECTIVE

Java Operators (OCA Objectives 3.1, 3.2, and 3.3)

3.1 *Use Java operators; including parentheses to override operator precedence.*
3.2 *Test equality between Strings and other objects using == and equals().*
3.3 *Create if and if/else and ternary constructs*

Java operators produce new values from one or more operands. (Just so we're all clear, remember that operands are the things on the right or left side of the operator.) The result of most operations is either a `boolean` or numeric value. Because you know by now that Java is not C++, you won't be surprised that Java operators aren't typically overloaded. There are, however, a few exceptional operators that come overloaded:

- The + operator can be used to add two numeric primitives together or to perform a concatenation operation if either operand is a `String`.
- The `&`, `|`, and `^` operators can all be used in two different ways, although on this version of the exam, their bit-twiddling capabilities won't be tested.

Stay awake. Operators are often the section of the exam where candidates see their lowest scores. Additionally, operators and assignments are a part of many questions dealing with other topics—it would be a shame to nail a really tricky lambdas question only to blow it on a pre-increment statement.

Assignment Operators

We covered most of the functionality of the equal (=) assignment operator in Chapter 3. To summarize:

- When assigning a value to a primitive, *size* matters. Be sure you know when implicit casting will occur, when explicit casting is necessary, and when truncation might occur.
- Remember that a reference variable isn't an object; it's a way to *get* to an object. (We know all you C++ programmers are just dying for us to say, "it's a pointer," but we're not going to.)
- When assigning a value to a reference variable, *type* matters. Remember the rules for supertypes, subtypes, and arrays.

Next we'll cover a few more details about the assignment operators that are on the exam, and when we get to the next chapter, we'll take a look at how the assignment operator = works with `Strings` (which are immutable).

exam watch

Don't spend time preparing for topics that are no longer on the exam! The following topics have NOT been on the exam since Java 1.4:

- ***Bit-shifting operators***
- ***Bitwise operators***
- ***Two's complement***
- ***Divide-by-zero stuff***

It's not that these aren't important topics; it's just that they're not on the exam anymore, and we're really focused on the exam. (Note: The reason we bring this up at all is because you might encounter mock exam questions on these topics—you can ignore those questions!)

Compound Assignment Operators

There are actually 11 or so compound assignment operators, but only the 4 most commonly used (+=, -=, *=, and /=) are on the exam. The compound assignment operators let lazy typists shave a few keystrokes off their workload.

Here are several example assignments, first without using a compound operator:

```
y = y - 6;
x = x + 2 * 5;
```

Now, with compound operators:

```
y -= 6;
x += 2 * 5;
```

The last two assignments give the same result as the first two.

Relational Operators

The exam covers six relational operators (<, <=, >, >=, ==, and !=). Relational operators always result in a `boolean` (`true` or `false`) value. This `boolean` value is most often used in an `if` test, as follows:

```
int x = 8;
if (x < 9) {
  // do something
}
```

But the resulting value can also be assigned directly to a `boolean` primitive:

```
class CompareTest {
  public static void main(String [] args) {
    boolean b = 100 > 99;
    System.out.println("The value of b is " + b);
  }
}
```

Java has four relational operators that can be used to compare any combination of integers, floating-point numbers, or characters:

- **>** Greater than
- **>=** Greater than or equal to

- `<` Less than
- `<=` Less than or equal to

Let's look at some legal comparisons:

```
class GuessAnimal {
  public static void main(String[] args) {
    String animal = "unknown";
    int weight = 700;
    char sex = 'm';
    double colorWaveLength = 1.630;
    if (weight >= 500) { animal = "elephant"; }
    if (colorWaveLength > 1.621) { animal = "gray " + animal; }
    if (sex <= 'f') { animal = "female " + animal; }
    System.out.println("The animal is a " + animal);
  }
}
```

In the preceding code, we are using a comparison between characters. It's also legal to compare a character primitive with any number (although it isn't great programming style). Running the preceding class will output the following:

```
The animal is a gray elephant
```

We mentioned that characters can be used in comparison operators. When comparing a character with a character or a character with a number, Java will use the Unicode value of the character as the numerical value for comparison.

"Equality" Operators

Java also has two relational operators (sometimes called "equality operators") that compare two similar "things" and return a `boolean` (`true` or `false`) that represents what's true about the two "things" being equal. These operators are

- `==` Equal (also known as equal to)
- `!=` Not equal (also known as not equal to)

Each individual comparison can involve two numbers (including `char`), two `boolean` values, or two object reference variables. You can't compare incompatible types, however. What would it mean to ask if a `boolean` is equal to a `char`? Or if a `Button` is equal to a `String` array? (This is nonsense, which is why you can't do it.) There are four different types of things that can be tested:

- Numbers
- Characters
- Boolean primitives
- Object reference variables

So what does == look at? The value in the variable—in other words, the bit pattern.

Equality for Primitives

Most programmers are familiar with comparing primitive values. The following code shows some equality tests on primitive variables:

```
class ComparePrimitives {
  public static void main(String[] args) {
    System.out.println("char 'a' == 'a'? " + ('a' == 'a'));
    System.out.println("char 'a' == 'b'? " + ('a' == 'b'));
    System.out.println("5 != 6? " + (5 != 6));
    System.out.println("5.0 == 5L? " + (5.0 == 5L));
    System.out.println("true == false? " + (true == false));
  }
}
```

This program produces the following output:

```
char 'a' == 'a'? true
char 'a' == 'b'? false
5 != 6? true
5.0 == 5L? true
true == false? false
```

As you can see, if a floating-point number is compared with an integer and the values are the same, the == operator usually returns `true` as expected.

Equality for Reference Variables

As you saw earlier, two reference variables can refer to the same object, as the following code snippet demonstrates:

```
JButton a = new JButton("Exit");
JButton b = a;
```

exam watch

Don't mistake = for == in a `boolean` expression. The following is legal:

```
11. boolean b = false;
12. if (b = true) { System.out.println("b is true");
13. } else { System.out.println("b is false");  }
```

Look carefully! You might be tempted to think the output is `b is false`, but look at the `boolean` test in line 12. The `boolean` variable `b` is not being compared to `true`; it's being set to `true`. Once `b` is set to `true`, the `println` executes and we get `b is true`. The result of any assignment expression is the value of the variable following the assignment. This substitution of = for == works only with `boolean` variables because the `if` test can be done only on `boolean` expressions. Thus, this does not compile:

```
7. int x = 1;
8. if (x = 0) { }
```

Because `x` is an integer (and not a `boolean`), the result of `(x = 0)` is 0 (the result of the assignment). Primitive `ints` cannot be used where a `boolean` value is expected, so the code in line 8 won't work unless it's changed from an assignment (=) to an equality test (==) as follows:

```
8. if (x == 0) { }
```

After running this code, both variable `a` and variable `b` will refer to the same object (a `JButton` with the label `Exit`). Reference variables can be tested to see if they refer to the same object by using the == operator. Remember, the == operator is looking at the bits in the variable, so for reference variables, this means that if the bits in both reference variables are identical, then both refer to the same object. Look at the following code:

```
import javax.swing.JButton;
class CompareReference {
  public static void main(String[] args) {
    JButton a = new JButton("Exit");
    JButton b = new JButton("Exit");
    JButton c = a;
    System.out.println("Is reference a == b? " + (a == b));
    System.out.println("Is reference a == c? " + (a == c));
  }
}
```

This code creates three reference variables. The first two, a and b, are separate JButton objects that happen to have the same label. The third reference variable, c, is initialized to refer to the same object that a refers to. When this program runs, the following output is produced:

```
Is reference a == b? false
Is reference a == c? true
```

This shows us that a and c reference the same instance of a JButton. The == operator will not test whether two objects are "meaningfully equivalent," a concept we'll cover in much more detail in Chapter 6, when we look at the equals() *method* (as opposed to the equals *operator* we're looking at here).

Equality for Strings and java.lang.Object.equals()

We just used == to determine whether two reference variables refer to the same object. Because objects are so central to Java, every class in Java inherits a method from class Object that tests to see if two objects of the class are "equal." Not surprisingly, this method is called equals(). In this case of the equals() method, the phrase "meaningfully equivalent" should be used instead of the word "equal." So the equals() method is used to determine if two objects of the same class are "meaningfully equivalent." For classes that you create, you have the option of overriding the equals() method that your class inherited from class Object and creating your own definition of "meaningfully equivalent" for instances of your class.

In terms of understanding the equals() method for the OCA exam, you need to understand two aspects of the equals() method:

- What equals() means in class Object
- What equals() means in class String

The equals() Method in Class Object The equals() method in class Object works the same way that the == operator works. If two references point to the same object, the equals() method will return true. If two references point to different objects, even if they have the same values, the method will return false.

The equals() Method in Class String The equals() method in class String has been overridden. When the equals() method is used to compare two strings, it will return true if the strings have the same value, and it will return false if the strings have different values. For String's equals() method, values ARE case sensitive.

Let's take a look at how the `equals()` method works in action (notice that the `Budgie` class did NOT override `Object.equals()`):

```
class Budgie {
  public static void main(String[] args) {
    Budgie b1 = new Budgie();
    Budgie b2 = new Budgie();
    Budgie b3 = b1;

    String s1 = "Bob";
    String s2 = "Bob";
    String s3 = "bob";                   // lower case "b"

    System.out.println(b1.equals(b2));   // false, different objects
    System.out.println(b1.equals(b3));   // true, same objects
    System.out.println(s1.equals(s2));   // true, same values
    System.out.println(s1.equals(s3));   // false, values are case sensitive
  }
}
```

which produces the output:

```
false
true
true
false
```

Equality for enums

Once you've declared an `enum`, it's not expandable. At runtime, there's no way to make additional `enum` constants. Of course, you can have as many variables as you'd like refer to a given `enum` constant, so it's important to be able to compare two `enum` reference variables to see if they're "equal"—that is, do they refer to the same `enum` constant? You can use either the `==` operator or the `equals()` method to determine whether two variables are referring to the same `enum` constant:

```
class EnumEqual {
  enum Color {RED, BLUE}                    // ; is optional
  public static void main(String[] args) {
    Color c1 = Color.RED;  Color c2 = Color.RED;
    if(c1 == c2) { System.out.println("=="); }
    if(c1.equals(c2)) { System.out.println("dot equals"); }
} }
```

(We know } } is ugly; we're prepping you.) This produces the output:

```
==
dot equals
```

instanceof Comparison

The `instanceof` operator is used for object reference variables only, and you can use it to check whether an object is of a particular type. By "type," we mean class or interface type—in other words, whether the object referred to by the variable on the left side of the operator passes the IS-A test for the class or interface type on the right side. (Chapter 2 covered IS-A relationships in detail.) The following simple example,

```
public static void main(String[] args) {
  String s = new String("foo");
  if (s instanceof String) {
    System.out.print("s is a String");
  }
}
```

prints this:

```
s is a String
```

Even if the object being tested is not an actual instantiation of the class type on the right side of the operator, `instanceof` will still return `true` if the object being compared is *assignment compatible* with the type on the right.

The following example demonstrates a common use for `instanceof`: testing an object to see if it's an instance of one of its subtypes before attempting a downcast:

```
class A { }
class B extends A {
  public static void main (String [] args) {
    A myA = new B();
    m2(myA);
  }
  public static void m2(A a) {
    if (a instanceof B)
      ((B)a).doBstuff();       // downcasting an A reference
                               // to a B reference
  }
  public static void doBstuff() {
    System.out.println("'a' refers to a B");
  }
}
```

The code compiles and produces this output:

```
'a' refers to a B
```

In examples like this, the use of the `instanceof` operator protects the program from attempting an illegal downcast.

You can test an object reference against its own class type or any of its superclasses. This means that *any* object reference will evaluate to `true` if you use the `instanceof` operator against type `Object`, as follows:

```
B b = new B();
if (b instanceof Object) {
   System.out.print("b is definitely an Object");
}
```

This prints

```
b is definitely an Object
```

exam Watch

Look for `instanceof` questions that test whether an object is an instance of an interface when the object's class implements the interface indirectly. An indirect implementation occurs when one of an object's superclasses implements an interface, but the actual class of the instance does not. In this example,

```
interface Foo { }
class A implements Foo { }
class B extends A { }
...
A a = new A();
B b = new B();
```

the following are true:

```
a instanceof Foo
b instanceof A
b instanceof Foo  // implemented indirectly
```

An object is said to be of a particular interface type (meaning it will pass the `instanceof` test) if any of the object's superclasses implement the interface.

In addition, it is legal to test whether the `null` reference is an instance of a class. This will always result in `false`, of course. This example,

```
class InstanceTest {
   public static void main(String [] args) {
      String a = null;
      boolean b = null instanceof String;
      boolean c = a instanceof String;
      System.out.println(b + " " + c);
   }}
```

prints this:

```
false false
```

instanceof Compiler Error

You can't use the `instanceof` operator to test across two different class hierarchies. For instance, the following will NOT compile:

```
class Cat { }
class Dog {
  public static void main(String [] args) {
    Dog d = new Dog();
    System.out.println(d instanceof Cat);
  }
}
```

Compilation fails—there's no way `d` could ever refer to a `Cat` or a subtype of `Cat`.

exam Watch

Remember that arrays are objects, even if the array is an array of primitives. Watch for questions that look something like this:

```
int [] nums = new int[3];
if (nums instanceof Object) { } // result is true
```

An array is always an instance of `Object`. Any array.

Table 4-1 summarizes the use of the `instanceof` operator given the following:

```
interface Face { }
class Bar implements Face{ }
class Foo extends Bar { }
```

Arithmetic Operators

We're sure you're familiar with the basic arithmetic operators:

- + addition
- – subtraction
- * multiplication
- / division

TABLE 4-1 Operands and Results Using `instanceof` Operator

First Operand (Reference Being Tested)	instanceof Operand (Type We're Comparing the Reference Against)	Result
null	Any class or interface type	false
Foo instance	Foo, Bar, Face, Object	true
Bar instance	Bar, Face, Object	true
Bar instance	Foo	false
Foo [ ]	Foo, Bar, Face	compiler error
Foo [ ]	Object	true
Foo [1]	Foo, Bar, Face, Object	true

These can be used in the standard way:

```
int x = 5 * 3;
int y = x - 4;
System.out.println("x - 4 is " +  y);   // Prints 11
```

The Remainder (%) Operator (a.k.a. the Modulus Operator)

One operator you might not be as familiar with is the remainder operator: %. The remainder operator divides the left operand by the right operand, and the result is the remainder, as the following code demonstrates:

```
class MathTest {
  public static void main (String [] args) {
    int x = 15;
    int y = x % 4;
    System.out.println("The result of 15 % 4 is the "
      + "remainder of 15 divided by 4. The remainder is " + y);
  }
}
```

Running class `MathTest` prints the following:

```
The result of 15 % 4 is the remainder of 15 divided by 4. The remainder
is 3
```

(Remember: Expressions are evaluated from left to right by default. You can change this sequence, or *precedence,* by adding parentheses. Also remember that the *, /, and % operators have a higher precedence than the + and - operators.)

exam Watch

When working with `ints`, the remainder operator (a.k.a. the modulus operator) and the division operator relate to each other in an interesting way:

- ***The modulus operator throws out*** *everything but* ***the remainder.***
- ***The division operator throws out the remainder.***

String Concatenation Operator

The plus sign can also be used to concatenate two strings together, as we saw earlier (and as we'll definitely see again):

```
String animal = "Gray " + "elephant";
```

String concatenation gets interesting when you combine numbers with `Strings`. Check out the following:

```
String a = "String";
int b = 3;
int c = 7;
System.out.println(a + b + c);
```

Will the + operator act as a plus sign when adding the `int` variables `b` and `c`? Or will the + operator treat `3` and `7` as characters and concatenate them individually? Will the result be `String10` or `String37`? Okay, you've had long enough to think about it.

The `int` values were simply treated as characters and glued on to the right side of the `String`, giving the result:

```
String37
```

So we could read the previous code as

"Start with the value `String`, and concatenate the character `3` (the value of `b`) to it, to produce a new string `String3`, and then concatenate the character `7` (the value of `c`) to that, to produce a new string `String37`. Then print it out."

However, if you put parentheses around the two `int` variables, as follows,

```
System.out.println(a + (b + c));
```

you'll get this:

```
String10
```

Using parentheses causes the `(b + c)` to evaluate first, so the rightmost + operator functions as the addition operator, given that both operands are `int` values. The key point here is that within the parentheses, the left-hand operand is not a `String`. If it were, then the + operator would perform `String` concatenation. The previous code can be read as

"Add the values of `b and c` together, and then take the sum and convert it to a `String` and concatenate it with the `String` from variable `a`."

The rule to remember is this:

If either operand is a `String`, the + operator becomes a `String` concatenation operator. If both operands are numbers, the + operator is the addition operator.

You'll find that sometimes you might have trouble deciding whether, say, the left-hand operator is a `String` or not. On the exam, don't expect it always to be obvious. (Actually, now that we think about it, don't expect it *ever* to be obvious.) Look at the following code:

```
System.out.println(x.foo() + 7);
```

You can't know how the + operator is being used until you find out what the `foo()` method returns! If `foo()` returns a `String`, then `7` is concatenated to the returned `String`. But if `foo()` returns a number, then the + operator is used to add `7` to the return value of `foo()`.

Finally, you need to know that it's legal to mush together the compound additive operator (+=) and `Strings`, like so:

```
String s = "123";
s += "45";
s += 67;
System.out.println(s);
```

Since both times the += operator was used and the left operand was a `String`, both operations were concatenations, resulting in

```
1234567
```

exam watch

If you don't understand how `String` concatenation works, especially within a `print` statement, you could actually fail the exam even if you know the rest of the answers to the questions! Because so many questions ask "What is the result?", you need to know not only the result of the code running but also how that result is printed. Although at least a few questions will directly test your `String` knowledge, `String` concatenation shows up in other questions on virtually every objective. Experiment! For example, you might see a line such as this:

```
int b = 2;
System.out.println("" + b + 3);
```

It prints this:

```
23
```

But if the `print` statement changes to this:

```
System.out.println(b + 3);
```

The printed result becomes

```
5
```

Increment and Decrement Operators

Java has two operators that will increment or decrement a variable by exactly one. These operators are either two plus signs (++) or two minus signs (--):

- **++** Increment (prefix and postfix)
- **--** Decrement (prefix and postfix)

The operator is placed either before (prefix) or after (postfix) a variable to change its value. Whether the operator comes before or after the operand can change the outcome of an expression. Examine the following:

```
1. class MathTest {
2.   static int players = 0;
3.     public static void main (String [] args) {
4.       System.out.println("players online: " + players++);
5.       System.out.println("The value of players is "
                                    + players);
```

```
6.         System.out.println("The value of players is now "
                                   + ++players);
7.     }
8. }
```

Notice that in the fourth line of the program the increment operator is *after* the variable `players`. That means we're using the postfix increment operator, which causes `players` to be incremented by one but only *after* the value of `players` is used in the expression. When we run this program, it outputs the following:

```
%java MathTest
players online: 0
The value of players is 1
The value of players is now 2
```

Notice that when the variable is written to the screen, at first it says the value is `0`. Because we used the postfix increment operator, the increment doesn't happen until after the `players` variable is used in the `print` statement. Get it? The "post" in postfix means *after*. Line 5 doesn't increment `players`; it just outputs its value to the screen, so the newly incremented value displayed is 1. Line 6 applies the prefix increment operator to `players`, which means the increment happens *before* the value of the variable is used, so the output is `2`.

Expect to see questions mixing the increment and decrement operators with other operators, as in the following example:

```
int x = 2;  int y = 3;
if ((y == x++) | (x < ++y)) {
  System.out.println("x = " + x + " y = " + y);
}
```

The preceding code prints this:

```
x = 3 y = 4
```

You can read the code as follows: "If 3 is equal to 2 OR 3 < 4"

The first expression compares `x` and `y`, and the result is `false`, because the increment on `x` doesn't happen until *after* the == test is made. Next, we increment `x`, so now `x` is `3`. Then we check to see if `x` is less than `y`, but we increment `y` *before* comparing it with `x`! So the second logical test is `(3 < 4)`. The result is `true`, so the `print` statement runs.

As with `String` concatenation, the increment and decrement operators are used throughout the exam, even on questions that aren't trying to test your knowledge of how those operators work. You might see them in questions on `for` loops, exceptions, or even threads. Be ready.

exam watch

Look out for questions that use the increment or decrement operators on a `final` variable. Because `final` variables can't be changed, the increment and decrement operators can't be used with them, and any attempt to do so will result in a compiler error. The following code won't compile:

```
final int x = 5;
int y = x++;
```

It produces this error:

```
Test.java:4: cannot assign a value to final variable x
int y = x++;
        ^
```

You can expect a violation like this to be buried deep in a complex piece of code. If you spot it, you know the code won't compile, and you can move on without working through the rest of the code.

This question might seem to be testing you on some complex arithmetic operator trivia, when, in fact, it's testing you on your knowledge of the `final` modifier.

Conditional Operator

The conditional operator is a *ternary* operator (it has *three* operands) and is used to evaluate `boolean` expressions—much like an `if` statement, except instead of executing a block of code if the test is `true`, a conditional operator will assign a value to a variable. In other words, the goal of the conditional operator is to decide which of two values to assign to a variable. This operator is constructed using a `?` (question mark) and a `:` (colon). The parentheses are optional. Here is its structure:

```
x = (boolean expression) ? value to assign if true : value to assign if false
```

Let's take a look at a conditional operator in code:

```
class Salary {
  public static void main(String [] args) {
    int numOfPets = 3;
    String status = (numOfPets<4) ? "Pet limit not exceeded"
                    : "too many pets";
    System.out.println("This pet status is " + status);
  }
}
```

You can read the preceding code as "Set `numOfPets` equal to `3`".

Next we're going to assign a `String` to the status variable. If `numOfPets` is less than `4`, assign `"Pet limit not exceeded"` to the `status` variable; otherwise, assign `"too many pets"` to the `status` variable.

A conditional operator starts with a `boolean` operation, followed by two possible values for the variable to the left of the assignment (=) operator. The first value (the one to the left of the colon) is assigned if the conditional (`boolean`) test is `true`, and the second value is assigned if the conditional test is `false`. You can even nest conditional operators into one statement:

```
class AssignmentOps {
  public static void main(String [] args) {
    int sizeOfYard = 10;
    int numOfPets = 3;
    String status = (numOfPets<4)?"Pet count OK"
        :(sizeOfYard > 8)? "Pet limit on the edge"
          :"too many pets";
     System.out.println("Pet status is " + status);
  }
}
```

Don't expect many questions using conditional operators, but you might get one.

Logical Operators

The exam objectives specify six "logical" operators (`&`, `|`, `^`, `!`, `&&`, and `||`). Some Oracle documentation uses other terminology for these operators, but for our purposes and in the exam objectives, these six are the logical operators.

Bitwise Operators (Not an Exam Topic!)

Okay, this is going to be confusing. Of the six logical operators just listed, three of them (`&`, `|`, and `^`) can also be used as "bitwise" operators. Bitwise operators were included in previous versions of the exam, but they're NOT on the Java 6, Java 7, or Java 8 exam. We bring them up here just so you have a more complete picture of the logical operators.

Here are several legal statements that use bitwise operators:

```
byte b1 = 6 & 8;
byte b2 = 7 | 9;
byte b3 = 5 ^ 4;
System.out.println(b1 + " " + b2 + " " + b3);
```

Bitwise operators compare two variables bit by bit and return a variable whose bits have been set based on whether the two variables being compared had respective bits that were either both "on" (&), one or the other "on" (|), or exactly one "on" (^). By the way, when we run the preceding code, we get

```
0 15 1
```

exam watch

Having said all this about bitwise operators, the key thing to remember is this:

BITWISE OPERATORS ARE NOT ON THE Java 6, Java 7, or Java 8 EXAM!

Short-Circuit Logical Operators

Five logical operators on the exam are used to evaluate statements that contain more than one `boolean` expression. The most commonly used of the five are the two *short-circuit* logical operators:

- `&&` Short-circuit AND
- `||` Short-circuit OR

They are used to link little `boolean` expressions together to form bigger `boolean` expressions. The `&&` and `||` operators evaluate only `boolean` values. For an AND (`&&`) expression to be `true`, both operands must be `true`. For example:

```
if ((2 < 3) && (3 < 4)) { }
```

The preceding expression evaluates to `true` because *both* operand one `(2 < 3)` and operand two `(3 < 4)` evaluate to `true`.

The short-circuit feature of the `&&` *operator is so named because it doesn't waste its time on pointless evaluations.* A short-circuit `&&` evaluates the left side of the operation first (operand one), and if it resolves to `false`, the `&&` operator doesn't bother looking at the right side of the expression (operand two) since the `&&` operator already *knows* that the complete expression can't possibly be `true`.

```
class Logical {
  public static void main(String [] args) {
    boolean b1 = false, b2 = false;
    boolean b3 = (b1 == true) && (b2 = true);  // will b2 be set to true?
    System.out.println(b3 + " " + b2);
  }
}
```

When we run the preceding code, the **assignment** `(b2 = true)` never runs because of the short-circuit operator, so the output is

```
%java Logical
false false
```

The `||` operator is similar to the `&&` operator, except that it evaluates to `true` if EITHER of the operands is true. If the first operand in an OR operation is `true`, the result will be `true`, so the short-circuit `||` doesn't waste time looking at the right side of the equation. If the first operand is `false`, however, the short-circuit `||` has to evaluate the second operand to see if the result of the OR operation will be `true` or `false`. Pay close attention to the following example; you'll see quite a few questions like this on the exam:

```
class TestOR {
  public static void main(String[] args) {
    if ((isItSmall(3)) || (isItSmall(7))) {
      System.out.println("Result is true");
    }
    if ((isItSmall(6)) || (isItSmall(9))) {
      System.out.println("Result is true");
    }
  }

  public static boolean isItSmall(int i) {
    if (i < 5) {
      System.out.println("i < 5");
      return true;
    } else {
      System.out.println("i >= 5");
      return false;
    }
  }
}
```

What is the result?

```
% java TestOR
i < 5
Result is true
i >= 5
i >= 5
```

Here's what happened when the `main()` method ran:

1. When we hit line 3, the first operand in the `||` expression (in other words, the *left* side of the `||` operation) is evaluated.
2. The `isItSmall(3)` method is invoked, prints `"i < 5"`, and returns `true`.
3. Because the *first* operand in the `||` expression on line 3 is `true`, the `||` operator doesn't bother evaluating the second operand. So we never see the `"i >= 5"` that would have printed had the *second* operand been evaluated (which would have invoked `isItSmall(7)`).
4. Line 6 is evaluated, beginning with the *first* operand in the `||` expression.
5. The `isItSmall(6)` method is called, prints `"i >= 5"`, and returns `false`.
6. Because the *first* operand in the `||` expression on line 6 is `false`, the `||` operator can't skip the *second* operand; there's still a chance the expression can be `true`, if the *second* operand evaluates to `true`.
7. The `isItSmall(9)` method is invoked and prints `"i >= 5"`.
8. The `isItSmall(9)` method returns `false`, so the expression on line 6 is `false`, and thus line 7 never executes.

exam watch

The `||` and `&&` operators work only with boolean operands. The exam may try to fool you by using integers with these operators:

```
if (5 && 6) { }
```

It looks as though we're trying to do a bitwise AND on the bits representing the integers 5 and 6, but the code won't even compile.

Logical Operators (not Short-Circuit)

There are two *non-short-circuit* logical operators:

- `&` Non-short-circuit AND
- `|` Non-short-circuit OR

These operators are used in logical expressions just like the `&&` and `||` operators are used, but because they aren't the short-circuit operators, they evaluate both sides of the expression—always! They're inefficient. For example, even if the *first* operand (left side) in an `&` expression is `false`, the *second* operand will still be evaluated—even though it's now impossible for the result to be `true`! And the `|` is just as inefficient: if the *first* operand is `true`, the Java Virtual Machine (JVM) still plows ahead and evaluates the *second* operand even when it knows the expression will be `true` regardless.

You'll find a lot of questions on the exam that use both the short-circuit and non-short-circuit logical operators. You'll have to know exactly which operands are evaluated and which are not, because the result will vary depending on whether the second operand in the expression is evaluated. Consider this,

```
int z = 5;
if(++z > 5 || ++z > 6) z++;     // z = 7 after this code
```

versus this:

```
int z = 5;
if(++z > 5 | ++z > 6) z++;     // z = 8 after this code
```

Logical Operators ^ and !

The last two logical operators on the exam are

- `^` Exclusive-OR (XOR)
- `!` Boolean invert

The `^` (exclusive-OR) operator evaluates only `boolean` values. The `^` operator is related to the non-short-circuit operators we just reviewed, in that it always evaluates *both* the left and right operands in an expression. For an exclusive-OR (`^`) expression to be `true`, EXACTLY one operand must be `true`. This example,

```
System.out.println("xor " + ((2 < 3) ^ (4 > 3)));
```

produces this output:

```
xor false
```

The preceding expression evaluates to `false` because BOTH operand one `(2 < 3)` and operand two `(4 > 3)` evaluate to `true`.

The ! (boolean invert) operator returns the opposite of a boolean's current value. The following statement,

```
if(!(7 == 5)) { System.out.println("not equal"); }
```

can be read "If it's not true that 7 == 5," and the statement produces this output:

```
not equal
```

Here's another example using booleans:

```
boolean t = true;
boolean f = false;
System.out.println("! " + (t & !f) + " " + f);
```

It produces this output:

```
! true false
```

In the preceding example, notice that the & test succeeded (printing `true`) and that the value of the `boolean` variable `f` did not change, so it printed `false`.

Operator Precedence

The OCA 8 exam has reintroduced the topic of operator precedence. As you probably already know but will definitely see demonstrated in this section, when several operators are used in combination, the order in which they are evaluated can alter the result of the expression.

Operator Precedence Rant

Allow us to rant for a minute here. Memorizing operator precedence was on the old SCJP 1.2 exam about 15 years ago. Starting with the SCJP 1.4 exam, and for all the exams until the OCA 8, operator precedence has not been on the exam. For a glorious 15 years, candidates didn't have to do this bit of memorization. Sadly, this topic snuck its way back into the exam for OCA 8. Why do we care so much about this? Take a look at this code:

```
System.out.println(true & false == false | true);
```

What result would you expect? Imagine a more realistic version, evaluating some booleans:

```
System.out.println(b1 & b2 == b3 | b4);
```

What would you guess the programmer's intention was here? There are two likely scenarios:

Scenario 1: (b1 & b2) == (b3 | b4) If this was the programmer's intention, then he just created a bug.

Scenario 2: b1 & (b2 == b3) | b4 If this was the programmer's intention, then the code will work as intended, but his boss and fellow workers will want to strangle him.

This is a long-winded way to say that when you're writing code, you shouldn't rely on everyone's memory of operator precedence. You should just use parentheses like civilized people do.

The Actual Beginning of the Operator Precedence Section

Table 4-2 lists the most commonly used operators and their relative precedence, starting at the top with the highest precedence operators and ending at the bottom with the lowest. (Note, not all of Java's operators are in this table!)

TABLE 4-2 Precedence Hierarchy of Common Operators (from Highest to Lowest)

<table>
<tr><th>Types of Operators</th><th>Symbols</th><th>Example Uses</th></tr>
<tr><td>Unary operators</td><td>-, !, ++, --</td><td>-7 * 4,   !myBoolean</td></tr>
<tr><td>Multiplication, division, modulus</td><td>*, /, %</td><td>7 % 4</td></tr>
<tr><td>Addition, subtraction</td><td>+, -</td><td>7 + 4</td></tr>
<tr><td>Relational operators</td><td><, >, <=, >=</td><td>y > x</td></tr>
<tr><td>Equality operators</td><td>==, !=</td><td>y != x</td></tr>
<tr><td>Logical operators (& beats |)</td><td>&, |</td><td>myBool & yourBool</td></tr>
<tr><td>Short-circuit (&& beats ||)</td><td>&&, ||</td><td>myBool || yourBool</td></tr>
<tr><td>Assignment operators</td><td>=, +=, -=</td><td>X += 5;</td></tr>
</table>

JavaRanch (we know, we know, "Coderanch") moderator Fritz Walraven shared this tip with us. We like it, and we're passing it along to you: for the table above, you might make up a word like "UMARELSA," or a sentence using those first letters, to help you remember the precedence rules!

There are three important general rules for determining how Java will evaluate expressions with operators:

- When two operators of the same precedence are in the same expression, Java evaluates the expression from left to right.
- When parts of an expression are placed in parentheses, those parts are evaluated first.
- When parentheses are nested, the innermost parentheses are evaluated first.

A good way to burn these precedence rules into your brain is to—as always—write some test code and play around with it. We've added an example of some test code that demonstrates several of the precedence hierarchy rules listed here. As you can see, we often compared parentheses-free expressions with their parentheses-rich counterparts to prove the rules:

```
System.out.println((-7 - 4) + " " + (-(7 - 4)));          // unary (-7), beats minus
                                                          // output: -11 -3

System.out.println((2 + 3 * 4) + " " + ((2 + 3) * 4));    // * beats +
                                                          // output: 14 20

System.out.println(7 > 5 && 2 > 3);                       // > beats &&
                                                          // output: false

System.out.print((true & false == false | true) + " ");   // == beats & System.out.
print(((true & false) == (false | true)));     // output: true
```

And to repeat, the output is:

```
-11 -3
14 20
false
true false
```

We're so sorry that you need to memorize this stuff, but if you master what's in this short section, you should be able to handle whatever weird precedence-related questions the exam throws at you.

CERTIFICATION SUMMARY

If you've studied this chapter diligently, you should have a firm grasp on Java operators, and you should understand what equality means when tested with the == operator. Let's review the highlights of what you've learned in this chapter.

The logical operators (`&&`, `||`, `&`, `|`, and `^`) can be used only to evaluate two `boolean` expressions. The difference between `&&` and `&` is that the `&&` operator won't bother testing the right operand if the left evaluates to `false`, because the result of the `&&` expression can never be `true`. The difference between `||` and `|` is that the `||` operator won't bother testing the right operand if the left evaluates to `true` because the result is already known to be `true` at that point.

The == operator can be used to compare values of primitives, but it can also be used to determine whether two reference variables refer to the same object.

The `instanceof` operator is used to determine whether the object referred to by a reference variable passes the IS-A test for a specified type.

The + operator is overloaded to perform `String` concatenation tasks and can also concatenate `Strings` and primitives, but be careful—concatenation can be tricky.

The conditional operator (a.k.a. the "ternary operator") has an unusual, three-operand syntax—don't mistake it for a complex assert statement.

The ++ and `--` operators will be used throughout the exam, and you must pay attention to whether they are prefixed or postfixed to the variable being updated.

Even though you should use parentheses in real life, for the exam you should memorize Table 4-2 so you can determine how code that doesn't use parentheses for complex expressions will be evaluated, based on Java's operator-precedence hierarchy.

Be prepared for a lot of exam questions involving the topics from this chapter. Even within questions testing your knowledge of another objective, the code will frequently use operators, assignments, object and primitive passing, and so on.

TWO-MINUTE DRILL

Here are some of the key points from each section in this chapter.

Relational Operators (OCA Objectives 3.1 and 3.2)

- Relational operators always result in a `boolean` value (`true` or `false`).
- There are six relational operators: >, >=, <, <=, ==, and !=. The last two (== and !=) are sometimes referred to as *equality operators*.
- When comparing characters, Java uses the Unicode value of the character as the numerical value.
- Equality operators
  - There are two equality operators: == and !=.
  - Four types of things can be tested: numbers, characters, booleans, and reference variables.
- When comparing reference variables, == returns `true` only if both references refer to the same object.

instanceof Operator (OCA Objective 3.1)

- `instanceof` is for reference variables only; it checks whether the object is of a particular type.
- The `instanceof` operator can be used only to test objects (or `null`) against class types that are in the same class hierarchy.
- For interfaces, an object passes the `instanceof` test if any of its superclasses implement the interface on the right side of the `instanceof` operator.

Arithmetic Operators (OCA Objective 3.1)

- The four primary math operators are add (+), subtract (–), multiply (*), and divide (/).
- The remainder (a.k.a. modulus) operator (`%`) returns the remainder of a division.

- ☐ Expressions are evaluated from left to right, unless you add parentheses, or unless some operators in the expression have higher precedence than others.
- ☐ The `*`, `/`, and `%` operators have higher precedence than + and –.

String Concatenation Operator (OCA Objective 3.1)

- ☐ If either operand is a `String`, the + operator concatenates the operands.
- ☐ If both operands are numeric, the + operator adds the operands.

Increment/Decrement Operators (OCA Objective 3.1)

- ☐ Prefix operators (e.g. `--x`) run before the value is used in the expression.
- ☐ Postfix operators (e.g., `x++`) run after the value is used in the expression.
- ☐ In any expression, both operands are fully evaluated *before* the operator is applied.
- ☐ Variables marked `final` cannot be incremented or decremented.

Ternary (Conditional) Operator (OCA Objective 3.3)

- ☐ Returns one of two values based on the state of its `boolean` expression.
  - ☐ Returns the value after the `?` if the expression is `true`.
  - ☐ Returns the value after the `:` if the expression is `false`.

Logical Operators (OCA Objective 3.1)

- ☐ The exam covers six "logical" operators: `&`, `|`, `^`, `!`, `&&`, and `||`.
- ☐ Work with two expressions (except for `!`) that must resolve to boolean values.
- ☐ The `&&` and `&` operators return `true` only if both operands are `true`.
- ☐ The `||` and `|` operators return `true` if either or both operands are `true`.
- ☐ The `&&` and `||` operators are known as short-circuit operators.
- ☐ The `&&` operator does not evaluate the right operand if the left operand is `false`.
- ☐ The `||` does not evaluate the right operand if the left operand is `true`.
- ☐ The `&` and `|` operators always evaluate both operands.

- ☐ The ^ operator (called the "logical XOR") returns `true` if exactly one operand is `true`.
- ☐ The `!` operator (called the "inversion" operator) returns the opposite value of the boolean operand it precedes.

Parentheses and Operator Precedence (OCA Objective 3.1)

- ☐ In real life, use parentheses to clarify your code, and force Java to evaluate expressions as intended.
- ☐ For the exam, memorize Table 4-2 to determine how parentheses-free code will be evaluated.

SELF TEST

1. Given:

```
class Hexy {
  public static void main(String[] args) {
    int i = 42;
    String s = (i<40)?"life":(i>50)?"universe":"everything";
    System.out.println(s);
  }
}
```

What is the result?

A. `null`

B. `life`

C. `universe`

D. `everything`

E. Compilation fails

F. An exception is thrown at runtime

2. Given:

```
public class Dog {
  String name;
  Dog(String s) { name = s; }
  public static void main(String[] args) {
    Dog d1 = new Dog("Boi");
    Dog d2 = new Dog("Tyri");
    System.out.print((d1 == d2) + " ");
    Dog d3 = new Dog("Boi");
    d2 = d1;
    System.out.print((d1 == d2) + " ");
    System.out.print((d1 == d3) + " ");
  }
}
```

What is the result?

A. `true true true`

B. `true true false`

C. `false true false`

D. `false true true`

E. `false false false`

F. An exception will be thrown at runtime

3. Given:

```
class Fork {
  public static void main(String[] args) {
    if(args.length == 1 | args[1].equals("test")) {
      System.out.println("test case");
    } else {
      System.out.println("production " + args[0]);
    }
  }
}
```

And the command-line invocation:

```
java Fork live2
```

What is the result?

A. `test case`

B. `production live2`

C. `test case live2`

D. Compilation fails

E. An exception is thrown at runtime

4. Given:

```
class Feline {
  public static void main(String[] args) {
    long x = 42L;
    long y = 44L;
    System.out.print(" " + 7 + 2 + " ");
    System.out.print(foo() + x + 5 + " ");
    System.out.println(x + y + foo());
  }
  static String foo() { return "foo"; }
}
```

What is the result?

A. `9 foo47 86foo`

B. `9 foo47 4244foo`

C. `9 foo425 86foo`

D. `9 foo425 4244foo`

E. `72 foo47 86foo`

F. `72 foo47 4244foo`

G. `72 foo425 86foo`

H. `72 foo425 4244foo`

I. Compilation fails

5. **Note**: Here's another old-style drag-and-drop question...just in case.

   Place the fragments into the code to produce the output `33`. Note that you must use each fragment exactly once.

```
CODE:
class Incr {
  public static void main(String[] args) {
    Integer x = 7;
    int y = 2;

    x    ___  ___;
    ___  ___  ___;
    ___  ___  ___;
    ___  ___  ___;

    System.out.println(x);
  }
}
```

FRAGMENTS:

```
    y    y    y    y

    y    x    x

    -=   *=   *=   *=
```

6. Given:

```
public class Cowboys {
  public static void main(String[] args) {
    int x = 12;
    int a = 5;
    int b = 7;
    System.out.println(x/a + " " + x/b);
  }
}
```

What is the result? (Choose all that apply.)

A. `2 1`

B. `2 2`

C. `3 1`

D. `3 2`

E. An exception is thrown at runtime

7. Given:

```
 3. public class McGee {
 4.   public static void main(String[] args) {
 5.     Days d1 = Days.TH;
 6.     Days d2 = Days.M;
 7.     for(Days d: Days.values()) {
 8.       if(d.equals(Days.F)) break;
 9.       d2 = d;
10.     }
11.     System.out.println((d1 == d2)?"same old" : "newly new");
12.   }
13.   enum Days {M, T, W, TH, F, SA, SU};
14. }
```

What is the result?

A. `same old`

B. `newly new`

C. Compilation fails due to multiple errors

D. Compilation fails due only to an error on line 7

E. Compilation fails due only to an error on line 8

F. Compilation fails due only to an error on line 11

G. Compilation fails due only to an error on line 13

8. Given:

```
public class SpecialOps {
  public static void main(String[] args) {
    String s = "";
    boolean b1 = true;
    boolean b2 = false;
    if((b2 = false) | (21%5) > 2) s += "x";
    if(b1 || (b2 = true))         s += "y";
    if(b2 == true)                s += "z";
    System.out.println(s);
  }
}
```

Which are true? (Choose all that apply.)

A. Compilation fails

B. x will be included in the output

C. y will be included in the output

D. z will be included in the output

E. An exception is thrown at runtime

9. Given:

```
 3. public class Spock {
 4.   public static void main(String[] args) {
 5.     int mask = 0;
 6.     int count = 0;
 7.     if( ((5<7) || (++count < 10)) | mask++ < 10 )    mask = mask + 1;
 8.     if(  (6 > 8) ^ false)                            mask = mask + 10;
 9.     if( !(mask > 1) && ++count > 1)                  mask = mask + 100;
10.     System.out.println(mask + " " + count);
11.   }
12. }
```

Which two are true about the value of mask and the value of count at line 10? (Choose two.)

A. mask is 0

B. mask is 1

C. mask is 2

D. mask is 10

E. mask is greater than 10

F. count is 0

G. count is greater than 0

10. Given:

```
interface Vessel { }
interface Toy { }
class Boat implements Vessel { }
class Speedboat extends Boat implements Toy { }
public class Tree {
  public static void main(String[] args) {
    String s = "0";
    Boat b = new Boat();
    Boat b2 = new Speedboat();
    Speedboat s2 = new Speedboat();
    if((b instanceof Vessel) && (b2 instanceof Toy))  s += "1";
    if((s2 instanceof Vessel) && (s2 instanceof Toy)) s += "2";
    System.out.println(s);
  }
}
```

What is the result?

A. `0`

B. `01`

C. `02`

D. `012`

E. Compilation fails

F. An exception is thrown at runtime

11. Given:

```
boolean b1 = false;
boolean b2;
int x = 2, y = 5;
b1 = 2-12/4 > 5+-7 && b1 != y++>5 == 7%4 > ++x | b1 == true;
b2 = (2-12/4 > 5+-7) && (b1 != y++>5) == (7%4 > ++x) | (b1 == true);
System.out.println(b1 + " " + b2);
```

What is the result? (This is a tricky one. If you want a hint, go take another look at the operator precedence rant in the chapter.)

A. `true true`

B. `false true`

C. `true false`

D. `false false`

E. Compilation fails

F. An exception is thrown at runtime

SELF TEST ANSWERS

1. ☑ **D** is correct. This is a ternary nested in a ternary. Both ternary expressions are false.
   ☒ **A, B, C, E,** and **F** are incorrect based on the above. (OCA Objective 3.1 and 3.3)

2. ☑ **C** is correct. The == operator tests for reference variable equality, not object equality.
   ☒ **A, B, D, E,** and **F** are incorrect based on the above. (OCA Objectives 3.1 and 3.2)

3. ☑ **E** is correct. Because the short-circuit (||) is not used, both operands are evaluated. Since `args[1]` is past the `args` array bounds, an `ArrayIndexOutOfBoundsException` is thrown.
   ☒ **A, B, C,** and **D** are incorrect based on the above. (OCA Objectives 3.1 and 3.2)

4. ☑ **G** is correct. Concatenation runs from left to right, and if either operand is a `String`, the operands are concatenated. If both operands are numbers, they are added together.
   ☒ **A, B, C, D, E, F, H,** and **I** are incorrect based on the above. (OCA Objective 3.1)

5. Answer:

```
class Incr {
  public static void main(String[] args) {
    Integer x = 7;
    int y = 2;

    x *= x;
    y *= y;
    y *= y;
    x -= y;

    System.out.println(x);
  }
}
```

   Yeah, we know it's kind of puzzle-y, but you might encounter something like it on the real exam if Oracle reinstates this type of question. (OCA Objective 3.1)

6. ☑ **A** is correct. When dividing `int`s, remainders are always rounded down.
   ☒ **B, C, D,** and **E** are incorrect based on the above. (OCA Objective 3.1)

7. ☑ **A** is correct. All this syntax is correct. The for-each iterates through the `enum` using the `values()` method to return an array. An `enum` can be compared using either `equals()` or `==`. An `enum` can be used in a ternary operator's boolean test.
   ☒ **B, C, D, E, F,** and **G** are incorrect based on the above. (OCA Objectives 3.1, 3.2, and 3.3)

8. ☑ **C** is correct. Line 9 uses the modulus operator, which returns the remainder of the division, which in this case is `1`. Also, line 9 sets `b2` to `false`, and it doesn't test `b2`'s value. Line 10 would set `b2` to `true`; however, the short-circuit operator keeps the expression `b2 = true` from being executed.

☒ **A, B, D,** and **E** are incorrect based on the above. (OCA Objectives 3.1, and 3.2)

9. ☑ **C** and **F** are correct. At line 7 the `||` keeps `count` from being incremented, but the `|` allows `mask` to be incremented. At line 8 the `^` returns true only if exactly one operand is true. At line 9 `mask` is `2` and the `&&` keeps `count` from being incremented.

☒ **A, B, D, E,** and **G** are incorrect based on the above. (OCA Objective 3.1)

10. ☑ **D** is correct. First, remember that `instanceof` can look up through multiple levels of an inheritance tree. Also remember that `instanceof` is commonly used before attempting a downcast; so in this case, after line 15, it would be possible to say `Speedboat s3 = (Speedboat)b2;`.

☒ **A, B, C, E,** and **F** are incorrect based on the above. (OCA Objective 3.1)

11. ☑ **A** is correct. We're pretty sure you won't encounter anything as horrible as this on the real exam. But if you got this one correct, pat yourself on the back! The way to tackle a problem like this is to evaluate the expression in stages. In this case you might solve it like so:

Stage 1: resolve any use of unary operators

Stage 2: resolve any use of multiplication-related operators

Stage 3: handle addition and subtraction

Stage 4: handle any relationship operators

Stage 5: deal with the equality operators

Stage 6: deal with the logical operators

Stage 7: do the short-circuit operators

Stage 8: finally, do the assignment operators

☒ **B, C, D, E,** and **F** are incorrect based on the above. (OCA Objective 3.1)

5

Flow Control and Exceptions

CERTIFICATION OBJECTIVES

- Use if and switch Statements
- Develop for, do, and while Loops
- Use break and continue Statements
- Use try, catch, and finally Statements
- State the Effects of Exceptions
- Recognize Common Exceptions

✓ Two-Minute Drill

Q&A Self Test

Can you imagine trying to write code using a language that didn't give you a way to execute statements conditionally? Flow control is a key part of most any useful programming language, and Java offers several ways to accomplish it. Some statements, such as `if` statements and `for` loops, are common to most languages. But Java also throws in a couple of flow control features you might not have used before—exceptions and assertions. (We'll discuss assertions in the next chapter.)

The `if` statement and the `switch` statement are types of conditional/decision controls that allow your program to behave differently at a "fork in the road," depending on the result of a logical test. Java also provides three different looping constructs—`for`, `while`, and `do`—so you can execute the same code over and over again depending on some condition being true. Exceptions give you a clean, simple way to organize code that deals with problems that might crop up at runtime.

With these tools, you can build a robust program that can handle any logical situation with grace. Expect to see a wide range of questions on the exam that include flow control as part of the question code, even on questions that aren't testing your knowledge of flow control.

CERTIFICATION OBJECTIVE

Using if and switch Statements (OCA Objectives 3.3 and 3.4)

3.3 Create if and if-else and ternary constructs.
3.5 Use a switch statement.

The `if` and `switch` statements are commonly referred to as decision statements. When you use decision statements in your program, you're asking the program to evaluate a given expression to determine which course of action to take. We'll look at the `if` statement first.

if-else Branching

The basic format of an `if` statement is as follows:

```
if (booleanExpression) {
  System.out.println("Inside if statement");
}
```

The expression in parentheses must evaluate to (a `boolean`) `true` or `false`. Typically, you're testing something to see if it's true and then running a code block (one or more statements) if it is true and (optionally) another block of code if it isn't. The following code demonstrates a legal `if-else` statement:

```
if (x > 3) {
  System.out.println("x is greater than 3");
} else {
  System.out.println("x is not greater than 3");
}
```

The `else` block is optional, so you can also use the following:

```
if (x > 3) {
  y = 2;
}
z += 8;
a = y + x;
```

The preceding code will assign 2 to `y` if the test succeeds (meaning `x` really is greater than 3), but the other two lines will execute regardless. Even the curly braces are optional if you have only one statement to execute within the body of the conditional block. The following code example is legal (although not recommended for readability):

```
if (x > 3)     // bad practice, but seen on the exam
  y = 2;
z += 8;
a = y + x;
```

Most developers consider it good practice to enclose blocks within curly braces, even if there's only one statement in the block. Be careful with code like the preceding, because you might think it should read as

"If `x` is greater than 3, then set `y` to 2, `z` to `z` + 8, and `a` to `y` + `x`."

But the last two lines are going to execute no matter what! They aren't part of the conditional flow. You might find it even more misleading if the code were indented as follows:

```
if (x > 3)
  y = 2;
  z += 8;
  a = y + x;
```

You might have a need to nest `if-else` statements (although, again, it's not recommended for readability, so nested `if` tests should be kept to a minimum). You can set up an `if-else` statement to test for multiple conditions. The following example uses two conditions, so if the first test fails, we want to perform a second test before deciding what to do:

```
if (price < 300) {
  buyProduct();
} else {
  if (price < 400) {
    getApproval();
  }
  else {
    dontBuyProduct();
  }
}
```

This brings up the other `if-else` construct, the `if, else if, else`. The preceding code could (and should) be rewritten like this:

```
if (price < 300) {
  buyProduct();
} else if (price < 400) {
    getApproval();
} else {
    dontBuyProduct();
}
```

There are a couple of rules for using `else` and `else if`:

- You can have zero or one `else` for a given `if`, and it must come after any `else ifs`.
- You can have zero to many `else ifs` for a given `if`, and they must come before the (optional) `else`.
- Once an `else if` succeeds, none of the remaining `else ifs` nor the `else` will be tested.

The following example shows code that is horribly formatted for the real world. As you've probably guessed, it's fairly likely that you'll encounter formatting like this on the exam. In any case, the code demonstrates the use of multiple `else ifs`:

```
int x = 1;
if ( x == 3 ) { }
else if (x < 4) {System.out.println("<4"); }
else if (x < 2) {System.out.println("<2"); }
else { System.out.println("else"); }
```

It produces this output:

```
<4
```

(Notice that even though the second `else if` is true, it is never reached.)

Sometimes you can have a problem figuring out which `if` your `else` should pair with, as follows:

```
if (exam.done())
if (exam.getScore() < 0.61)
System.out.println("Try again.");
// Which if does this belong to?
else System.out.println("Java master!");
```

We intentionally left out the indenting in this piece of code so it doesn't give clues as to which `if` statement the `else` belongs to. Did you figure it out? Java law decrees that an `else` clause belongs to the innermost `if` statement to which it might possibly belong (in other words, the closest preceding `if` that doesn't have an `else`). In the case of the preceding example, the `else` belongs to the second `if` statement in the listing. With proper indenting, it would look like this:

```
if (exam.done())
  if (exam.getScore() < 0.61)
    System.out.println("Try again.");
  // Which if does this belong to?
  else
    System.out.println("Java master!");
```

Following our coding conventions by using curly braces, it would be even easier to read:

```
if (exam.done()) {
  if (exam.getScore() < 0.61) {
    System.out.println("Try again.");
  // Which if does this belong to?
  } else {
    System.out.println("Java master!");
  }
}
```

Don't get your hopes up about the exam questions being all nice and indented properly. Some exam takers even have a slogan for the way questions are presented on the exam: Anything that can be made more confusing will be.

Be prepared for questions that not only fail to indent nicely but also intentionally indent in a misleading way. Pay close attention for misdirection like the following:

```
if (exam.done())
  if (exam.getScore() < 0.61)
    System.out.println("Try again.");
else
  System.out.println("Java master!"); // Hmmmmm... now where does
                                      // it belong?
```

Of course, the preceding code is exactly the same as the previous two examples, except for the way it looks.

Legal Expressions for if Statements

The expression in an `if` statement must be a `boolean` expression. Any expression that resolves to a `boolean` is fine, and some of the expressions can be complex. Assume `doStuff()` returns `true`,

```
int y = 5;
int x = 2;
if (((x > 3) && (y < 2)) | doStuff()) {
  System.out.println("true");
}
```

which prints

```
true
```

You can read the preceding code as, "If both (`x > 3`) and (`y < 2`) are `true`, or if the result of `doStuff()` is `true`, then print `true`." So, basically, if just `doStuff()` alone is `true`, we'll still get `true`. If `doStuff()` is `false`, though, then both (`x > 3`) and (`y < 2`) will have to be `true` in order to print `true`. The preceding code is even more complex if you leave off one set of parentheses as follows:

```
int y = 5;
int x = 2;
if ((x > 3) && (y < 2) | doStuff()) {
  System.out.println("true");
}
```

This now prints...nothing! Because the preceding code (with one less set of parentheses) evaluates as though you were saying, "If (`x > 3`) is `true`, and either (`y < 2`) or the result of `doStuff()` is `true`, then print `true`. So if (`x > 3`) is not `true`, no point in looking at the rest of the expression." Because of the short-circuit

`&&`, the expression is evaluated as though there were parentheses around `(y < 2) | doStuff()`. In other words, it is evaluated as a single expression before the `&&` and a single expression after the `&&`.

Remember that the only legal expression in an `if` test is a `boolean`. In some languages, 0 == false and 1 == true. Not so in Java! The following code shows `if` statements that might look tempting but are illegal, followed by legal substitutions:

```
int trueInt = 1;
int falseInt = 0;
if (trueInt)              // illegal
if (trueInt == true)      // illegal
if (1)                    // illegal
if (falseInt == false)    // illegal
if (trueInt == 1)         // legal
if (falseInt == 0)        // legal
```

exam watch

One common mistake programmers make (and that can be difficult to spot) is assigning a `boolean` variable when you meant to test a `boolean` variable. Look out for code like the following:

```
boolean boo = false;
if (boo = true) { }
```

You might think one of three things:

1. ***The code compiles and runs fine, and the `if` test fails because `boo` is `false`.***
2. ***The code won't compile because you're using an assignment (=) rather than an equality test (==).***
3. ***The code compiles and runs fine, and the `if` test succeeds because `boo` is SET to `true` (rather than TESTED for `true`) in the `if` argument!***

Well, number 3 is correct—pointless, but correct. Given that the result of any assignment is the value of the variable after the assignment, the expression `(boo = true)` has a result of `true`. Hence, the `if` test succeeds. But the only variables that can be assigned (rather than tested against something else) are a `boolean` or a `Boolean`; all other assignments will result in something non-`boolean`, so they're not legal, as in the following:

```
int x = 3;
if (x = 5) { }  // Won't compile because x is not a boolean!
```

Because `if` tests require `boolean` expressions, you need to be really solid on both logical operators and `if` test syntax and semantics.

switch Statements

You've seen how `if` and `else-if` statements can be used to support both simple and complex decision logic. In many cases, the `switch` statement provides a cleaner way to handle complex decision logic. Let's compare the following `if-else if` statement to the equivalently performing `switch` statement:

```
int x = 3;
if(x == 1) {
  System.out.println("x equals 1");
}
else if(x == 2) {
  System.out.println("x equals 2");
}
else {
  System.out.println("No idea what x is");
}
```

Now let's see the same functionality represented in a `switch` construct:

```
int x = 3;
switch (x) {
  case 1:
    System.out.println("x equals 1");
    break;
  case 2:
    System.out.println("x equals 2");
    break;
  default:
    System.out.println("No idea what x is");
}
```

Note: The reason this `switch` statement emulates the `if` is because of the `break` statements that were placed inside of the `switch`. In general, `break` statements are optional, and as you will see in a few pages, their inclusion or exclusion causes huge changes in how a `switch` statement will execute.

Legal Expressions for switch and case

The general form of the `switch` statement is

```
switch (expression) {
  case constant1: code block
  case constant2: code block
  default: code block
}
```

A `switch`'s expression must evaluate to a `char`, `byte`, `short`, `int`, an enum (as of Java 5), and a `String` (as of Java 7). That means if you're not using an enum or a `String`, only variables and values that can be automatically promoted (in other words, implicitly cast) to an `int` are acceptable. You won't be able to compile if you use anything else, including the remaining numeric types of `long`, `float`, and `double`.

A `case` constant must evaluate to the same type that the `switch` expression can use, with one additional—and big—constraint: the `case` constant must be a compile-time constant! Since the `case` argument has to be resolved at compile time, you can use only a constant or `final` variable that is immediately initialized with a literal value. It is not enough to be `final`; it must be a compile-time *constant*. Here's an example:

```
final int a = 1;
final int b;
b = 2;
int x = 0;
switch (x) {
  case a:      // ok
  case b:      // compiler error
```

Also, the `switch` can only check for equality. This means the other relational operators such as greater than are rendered unusable in a `case`. The following is an example of a valid expression using a method invocation in a `switch` statement. Note that for this code to be legal, the method being invoked on the object reference must return a value compatible with an `int`.

```
String s = "xyz";
switch (s.length()) {
  case 1:
    System.out.println("length is one");
    break;
  case 2:
    System.out.println("length is two");
    break;
  case 3:
    System.out.println("length is three");
    break;
  default:
    System.out.println("no match");
}
```

One other rule you might not expect involves the question, "What happens if I `switch` on a variable smaller than an `int`?" Look at the following `switch`:

```
byte g = 2;
switch(g) {
  case 23:
  case 128:
}
```

This code won't compile. Although the `switch` argument is legal—a byte is implicitly cast to an `int`—the second `case` argument (128) is too large for a `byte`, and the compiler knows it! Attempting to compile the preceding example gives you an error something like this:

```
Test.java:6: possible loss of precision
found   : int
required: byte
    case 128:
         ^
```

It's also illegal to have more than one `case` label using the same value. For example, the following block of code won't compile because it uses two `case`s with the same value of 80:

```
int temp = 90;
switch(temp) {
  case 80 :  System.out.println("80");
  case 80 :  System.out.println("80");    // won't compile!
  case 90 :  System.out.println("90");
  default :  System.out.println("default");
}
```

It *is* legal to leverage the power of boxing in a `switch` expression. For instance, the following is legal:

```
switch(new Integer(4)) {
  case 4: System.out.println("boxing is OK");
}
```

exam watch

Look for any violation of the rules for `switch` and `case` arguments. For example, you might find illegal examples like the following snippets:

```
switch(x) {
  case 0 {
    y = 7;
  }
}

switch(x) {
  0: { }
  1: { }
}
```

In the first example, the `case` omits the colon. The second example omits the keyword `case`.

An Intro to String "equality"

As we've been discussing, the operation of `switch` statements depends on the expression "matching" or being "equal" to one of the cases. We've talked about how we know when primitives are equal, but what does it mean for objects to be equal? This is another one of those surprisingly tricky topics, and for those of you who intend to take the OCP exam, you'll spend a lot of time studying "object equality." For you OCA candidates, all you have to know is that for a `switch` statement, two `Strings` will be considered "equal" if they have the same case-sensitive sequence of characters. For example, in the following partial `switch` statement, the expression would match the case:

```
String s = "Monday";
switch(s) {
  case "Monday":   // matches!
```

But the following would NOT match:

```
String s = "MONDAY";
switch(s) {
  case "Monday":   // Strings are case-sensitive, DOES NOT match
```

Break and Fall-Through in switch Blocks

We're finally ready to discuss the `break` statement and offer more details about flow control within a `switch` statement. The most important thing to remember about the flow of execution through a `switch` statement is this:

> `case` constants are evaluated from the top down, and the first `case` constant that matches the `switch`'s expression is the execution *entry point*.

In other words, once a `case` constant is matched, the Java Virtual Machine (JVM) will execute the associated code block and ALL subsequent code blocks (barring a `break` statement), too! The following example uses a `String` in a `case` statement:

```
class SwitchString {
  public static void main(String [] args) {
    String s = "green";
    switch(s) {
      case "red": System.out.print("red ");
      case "green": System.out.print("green ");
      case "blue": System.out.print("blue ");
      default: System.out.println("done");
    }
  }
}
```

In this example `case "green":` matched, so the JVM executed that code block and all subsequent code blocks to produce the output:

```
green blue done
```

Again, when the program encounters the keyword `break` during the execution of a `switch` statement, execution will immediately move out of the `switch` block to the next statement after the `switch`. If `break` is omitted, the program just keeps executing the remaining `case` blocks until either a `break` is found or the `switch` statement ends. Examine the following code:

```
int x = 1;
switch(x) {
  case 1:  System.out.println("x is one");
  case 2:  System.out.println("x is two");
  case 3:  System.out.println("x is three");
}
System.out.println("out of the switch");
```

The code will print the following:

```
x is one
x is two
x is three
out of the switch
```

This combination occurs because the code didn't hit a `break` statement; execution just kept dropping down through each `case` until the end. This dropping down is actually called "fall-through," because of the way execution falls from one `case` to the next. Remember, the matching `case` is simply your entry point into the `switch` block! In other words, you must *not* think of it as, "Find the matching `case`, execute just that code, and get out." That's *not* how it works. If you do want that "just the matching code" behavior, you'll insert a `break` into each `case` as follows:

```
int x = 1;
switch(x) {
  case 1:  {
    System.out.println("x is one");  break;
  }
  case 2:  {
    System.out.println("x is two");  break;
  }
  case 3:  {
    System.out.println("x is two");  break;
  }
}
System.out.println("out of the switch");
```

Running the preceding code, now that we've added the `break` statements, prints:

```
x is one
out of the switch
```

And that's it. We entered into the `switch` block at `case 1`. Because it matched the `switch()` argument, we got the `println` statement and then hit the `break` and jumped to the end of the `switch`.

An interesting example of this fall-through logic is shown in the following code:

```
int x = someNumberBetweenOneAndTen;
switch (x) {
  case 2:
  case 4:
  case 6:
  case 8:
  case 10: {
    System.out.println("x is an even number");  break;
  }}
```

This `switch` statement will print `x is an even number` or nothing, depending on whether the number is between one and ten and is odd or even. For example, if `x` is 4, execution will begin at `case 4`, but then fall down through `6`, `8`, and `10`, where it prints and then breaks. The `break` at `case 10`, by the way, is not needed; we're already at the end of the `switch` anyway.

Note: Because fall-through is less than intuitive, Oracle recommends that you add a comment such as `// fall through` when you use fall-through logic.

The Default Case

What if, using the preceding code, you wanted to print `x is an odd number` if none of the `cases` (the even numbers) matched? You couldn't put it after the `switch` statement, or even as the last `case` in the `switch`, because in both of those situations it would always print `x is an odd number`. To get this behavior, you'd use the `default` keyword. (By the way, if you've wondered why there is a `default` keyword even though we don't use a modifier for default access control, now you'll see that the `default` keyword is used for a completely different purpose.) The only change we need to make is to add the `default` case to the preceding code:

```
int x = someNumberBetweenOneAndTen;
switch (x) {
  case 2:
  case 4:
  case 6:
  case 8:
  case 10: { System.out.println("x is even"); break; }
  default: System.out.println("x is an odd number");
}
```

exam watch

The `default case` doesn't have to come at the end of the `switch`. Look for it in strange places such as the following:

```
int x = 2;
switch (x) {
  case 2:  System.out.println("2");
  default: System.out.println("default");
  case 3: System.out.println("3");
  case 4: System.out.println("4");
}
```

Running the preceding code prints this:

```
2
default
3
4
```

And if we modify it so the only match is the `default case`, like this,

```
int x = 7;
switch (x) {
  case 2:  System.out.println("2");
  default: System.out.println("default");
  case 3: System.out.println("3");
  case 4: System.out.println("4");
}
```

then running the preceding code prints this:

```
default
3
4
```

The rule to remember is that `default` works just like any other `case` for fall-through!

EXERCISE 5-1

Creating a switch-case Statement

Try creating a `switch` statement using a `char` value as the `case`. Include a default behavior if none of the `char` values match.

- Make sure a `char` variable is declared before the `switch` statement.
- Each `case` statement should be followed by a `break`.
- The `default case` can be located at the end, middle, or top.

CERTIFICATION OBJECTIVE

Creating Loops Constructs (OCA Objectives 5.1, 5.2, 5.3, 5.4, and 5.5)

5.1 *Create and use while loops.*
5.2 *Create and use for loops including the enhanced for loop.*
5.3 *Create and use do/while loops.*
5.4 *Compare loop constructs.*
5.5 *Use break and continue.*

Java loops come in three flavors: `while`, `do`, and `for` (and as of Java 5, the `for` loop has two variations). All three let you repeat a block of code as long as some condition is true or for a specific number of iterations. You're probably familiar with loops from other languages, so even if you're somewhat new to Java, these won't be a problem to learn.

Using while Loops

The `while` loop is good when you don't know how many times a block or statement should repeat but you want to continue looping as long as some condition is true. A `while` statement looks like this:

```
while (expression) {
  // do stuff
}
```

Or this:

```
int x = 2;
while(x == 2) {
  System.out.println(x);
  ++x;
}
```

In this case, as in all loops, the expression (test) must evaluate to a `boolean` result. The body of the `while` loop will execute only if the expression (sometimes called the "condition") results in a value of `true`. Once inside the loop, the loop body will repeat until the condition is no longer met because it evaluates to `false`. In the previous example, program control will enter the loop body because `x` is equal to 2. However, `x` is incremented in the loop, so when the condition is checked again it will evaluate to `false` and exit the loop.

Any variables used in the expression of a `while` loop must be declared before the expression is evaluated. In other words, you can't say this:

```
while (int x = 2) { }   // not legal
```

Then again, why would you? Instead of testing the variable, you'd be declaring and initializing it, so it would always have the exact same value. Not much of a test condition!

The key point to remember about a `while` loop is that it might not ever run. If the test expression is `false` the first time the `while` expression is checked, the loop body will be skipped and the program will begin executing at the first statement *after* the `while` loop. Look at the following example:

```
int x = 8;
while (x > 8) {
  System.out.println("in the loop");
  x = 10;
}
System.out.println("past the loop");
```

Running this code produces

```
past the loop
```

Because the expression `(x > 8)` evaluates to `false`, none of the code within the `while` loop ever executes.

Using do Loops

The do loop is similar to the `while` loop, except the expression is not evaluated until after the do loop's code is executed. Therefore, the code in a do loop is guaranteed to execute at least once. The following shows a do loop in action:

```
do {
  System.out.println("Inside loop");
} while(false);
```

The `System.out.println()` statement will print once, even though the expression evaluates to `false`. Remember, the do loop will always run the code in the loop body at least once. Be sure to note the use of the semicolon at the end of the `while` expression.

exam watch

As with `if` tests, look for `while` loops (and the `while` test in a `do` loop) with an expression that does not resolve to a `boolean`. Take a look at the following examples of legal and illegal `while` expressions:

```
int x = 1;
while (x) { }          // Won't compile; x is not a boolean
while (x = 5) { }      // Won't compile; resolves to 5
                       // (as the result of assignment)
while (x == 5) { }     // Legal, equality test
while (true) { }       // Legal
```

Using for Loops

As of Java 5, the `for` loop took on a second structure. We'll call the old style of `for` loop the "basic `for` loop," and we'll call the new style of `for` loop the "enhanced `for` loop" (it's also sometimes called the `for-each`). Depending on what documentation you use, you'll see both terms, along with `for-in`. The terms `for-in`, `for-each`, and "enhanced `for`" all refer to the same Java construct.

The basic `for` loop is more flexible than the enhanced `for` loop, but the enhanced `for` loop was designed to make iterating through arrays and collections easier to code.

The Basic for Loop

The `for` loop is especially useful for flow control when you already know how many times you need to execute the statements in the loop's block. The `for` loop declaration has three main parts besides the body of the loop:

- Declaration and initialization of variables
- The `boolean` expression (conditional test)
- The iteration expression

The three `for` declaration parts are separated by semicolons. The following two examples demonstrate the `for` loop. The first example shows the parts of a `for` loop in a pseudocode form, and the second shows a typical example of a `for` loop:

```
for (/*Initialization*/ ; /*Condition*/ ;  /* Iteration */) {
  /* loop body */
}

for (int i = 0; i<10; i++) {
  System.out.println("i is " + i);
}
```

The Basic for Loop: Declaration and Initialization

The first part of the `for` statement lets you declare and initialize zero, one, or multiple variables of the same type inside the parentheses after the `for` keyword. If you declare more than one variable of the same type, you'll need to separate them with commas as follows:

```
for (int x = 10, y = 3; y > 3; y++) { }
```

The declaration and initialization happen before anything else in a `for` loop. And whereas the other two parts—the `boolean` test and the iteration expression—will run with each iteration of the loop, the declaration and initialization happen just once, at the very beginning. You also must know that the scope of variables declared in the `for` loop ends with the `for` loop! The following demonstrates this:

```
for (int x = 1; x < 2; x++) {
  System.out.println(x);   // Legal
}
System.out.println(x);     // Not Legal! x is now out of scope
                           // and can't be accessed.
```

If you try to compile this, you'll get something like this:

```
Test.java:19: cannot resolve symbol
symbol   : variable x
location: class Test
  System.out.println(x);
                     ^
```

Basic for Loop: Conditional (boolean) Expression

The next section that executes is the conditional expression, which (like all other conditional tests) must evaluate to a `boolean` value. You can have only one logical expression, but it can be very complex. Look out for code that uses logical expressions like this:

```
for (int x = 0; ((((x < 10) && (y-- > 2)) | x == 3)); x++) { }
```

The preceding code is legal, but the following is not:

```
for (int x = 0; (x > 5), (y < 2); x++) { } // too many
                                           // expressions
```

The compiler will let you know the problem:

```
TestLong.java:20: ';' expected
for (int x = 0; (x > 5), (y < 2); x++) { }
                       ^
```

The rule to remember is this: *You can have only one test expression.*

In other words, you can't use multiple tests separated by commas, even though, the other two parts of a `for` statement can have multiple parts.

Basic for Loop: Iteration Expression

After each execution of the body of the `for` loop, the iteration expression is executed. This is where you get to say what you want to happen with each iteration of the loop. Remember that it always happens after the loop body runs! Look at the following:

```
for (int x = 0; x < 1; x++) {
  // body code that doesn't change the value of x
}
```

This loop executes just once. The first time into the loop, `x` is set to 0, then `x` is tested to see if it's less than 1 (which it is), and then the body of the loop executes.

After the body of the loop runs, the iteration expression runs, incrementing `x` by 1. Next, the conditional test is checked, and since the result is now `false`, execution jumps to below the `for` loop and continues.

Keep in mind that barring a forced exit, evaluating the iteration expression and then evaluating the conditional expression are always the last two things that happen in a `for` loop!

Examples of forced exits include a `break`, a return, a `System.exit()`, and an exception, which will all cause a loop to terminate abruptly, without running the iteration expression. Look at the following code:

```
static boolean doStuff() {
  for (int x = 0; x < 3; x++) {
    System.out.println("in for loop");
    return true;
  }
  return true;
}
```

Running this code produces

```
in for loop
```

The statement prints only once because a `return` causes execution to leave not just the current iteration of a loop, but the entire method. So the iteration expression never runs in that case. Table 5-1 lists the causes and results of abrupt loop termination.

Basic for Loop: for Loop Issues

None of the three sections of the `for` declaration are required! The following example is perfectly legal (although not necessarily good practice):

```
for( ; ; ) {
  System.out.println("Inside an endless loop");
}
```

TABLE 5-1 Causes of Early Loop Termination

Code in Loop	What Happens
`break`	Execution jumps immediately to the first statement after the `for` loop.
`return`	Execution jumps immediately back to the calling method.
`System.exit()`	All program execution stops; the VM shuts down.

In this example, all the declaration parts are left out, so the `for` loop will act like an endless loop.

For the exam, it's important to know that with the absence of the initialization and increment sections, the loop will act like a `while` loop. The following example demonstrates how this is accomplished:

```
int i = 0;

for (;i<10;) {
  i++;
  // do some other work
}
```

The next example demonstrates a `for` loop with multiple variables in play. A comma separates the variables, and they must be of the same type. Remember that the variables declared in the `for` statement are all local to the `for` loop and can't be used outside the scope of the loop.

```
for (int i = 0,j = 0; (i<10) && (j<10); i++, j++) {
  System.out.println("i is " + i + " j is " +j);
}
```

exam watch

Variable scope plays a large role in the exam. You need to know that a variable declared in the `for` loop can't be used beyond the `for` loop. But a variable only initialized in the `for` statement (but declared earlier) can be used beyond the loop. For example, the following is legal:

```
int x = 3;
for (x = 12; x < 20; x++) { }
System.out.println(x);
```

But this is not:

```
for (int x = 3; x < 20; x++) { } System.out.println(x);
```

The last thing to note is that all three sections of the `for` loop are independent of each other. The three expressions in the `for` statement don't need to operate on the same variables, although they typically do. But even the iterator expression, which many mistakenly call the "increment expression," doesn't need to increment or set anything; you can put in virtually any arbitrary code statements that you want to happen with each iteration of the loop. Look at the following:

```
int b = 3;
for (int a = 1;  b != 1; System.out.println("iterate")) {
  b = b - a;
}
```

The preceding code prints

```
iterate
iterate
```

exam watch

Many questions in the Java 8 exams list "Compilation fails" and "An exception occurs at runtime" as possible answers, making them more difficult because you can't simply work through the behavior of the code. You must first make sure the code isn't violating any fundamental rules that will lead to a compiler error and then look for possible exceptions. Only after you've satisfied those two should you dig into the logic and flow of the code in the question.

The Enhanced for Loop (for Arrays)

The enhanced `for` loop, new as of Java 5, is a specialized `for` loop that simplifies looping through an array or a collection. In this chapter we're going to focus on using the enhanced `for` to loop through arrays. In Chapter 6 we'll revisit the enhanced `for`, when we discuss the ArrayList collection class—where the enhanced `for` really comes into its own.

Instead of having *three* components, the enhanced `for` has *two*. Let's loop through an array the basic (old) way and then using the enhanced `for`:

```
int [] a = {1,2,3,4};
for(int x = 0; x < a.length; x++)    // basic for loop
  System.out.print(a[x]);
for(int n : a)                       // enhanced for loop
  System.out.print(n);
```

This produces the following output:

```
12341234
```

More formally, let's describe the enhanced `for` as follows:

```
for(declaration : expression)
```

The two pieces of the `for` statement are

- **`declaration`** The *newly declared* block variable of a type compatible with the elements of the array you are accessing. This variable will be available within the `for` block, and its value will be the same as the current array element.
- **`expression`** This must evaluate to the array you want to loop through. This could be an array variable or a method call that returns an array. The array can be any type: primitives, objects, or even arrays of arrays.

Using the preceding definitions, let's look at some legal and illegal enhanced `for` declarations:

```
int x;
long x2;
long [] la = {7L, 8L, 9L};
int [][] twoDee = {{1,2,3}, {4,5,6}, {7,8,9}};
String [] sNums = {"one", "two", "three"};
Animal [] animals = {new Dog(), new Cat()};

// legal 'for' declarations
for(long y : la ) ;          // loop thru an array of longs
for(int[] n : twoDee) ;      // loop thru the array of arrays
for(int n2 : twoDee[2]) ;    // loop thru the 3rd sub-array
for(String s : sNums) ;      // loop thru the array of Strings
for(Object o : sNums) ;      // set an Object reference to
                             // each String
for(Animal a : animals) ;    // set an Animal reference to each
                             // element

// ILLEGAL 'for' declarations
for(x2 : la) ;               // x2 is already declared
for(int x4 : twoDee) ;       // can't stuff an array into an int
for(int x3 : la) ;           // can't stuff a long into an int
for(Dog d : animals) ;       // you might get a Cat!
```

The enhanced `for` loop assumes that, barring an early exit from the loop, you'll always loop through every element of the array. The following discussions of `break` and `continue` apply to both the basic and enhanced `for` loops.

Using break and continue

The `break` and `continue` keywords are used to stop either the entire loop (`break`) or just the current iteration (`continue`). Typically, if you're using `break` or `continue`, you'll do an `if` test within the loop, and if some condition becomes `true` (or `false` depending on the program), you want to get out immediately. The difference between them is whether or not you continue with a new iteration or jump to the first statement below the loop and continue from there.

exam watch

Remember, `continue` statements must be inside a loop; otherwise, you'll get a compiler error. `break` statements must be used inside either a loop or a `switch` statement.

The `break` statement causes the program to stop execution of the innermost loop and start processing the next line of code after the block.

The `continue` statement causes only the current iteration of the innermost loop to cease and the next iteration of the same loop to start if the condition of the loop is met. When using a `continue` statement with a `for` loop, you need to consider the effects that `continue` has on the loop iteration. Examine the following code:

```
for (int i = 0; i < 10; i++) {
  System.out.println("Inside loop");
  continue;
}
```

The question is, is this an endless loop? The answer is no. When the `continue` statement is hit, the iteration expression still runs! It runs just as though the current iteration ended "in the natural way." So in the preceding example, `i` will still increment before the condition `(i < 10)` is checked again.

Most of the time, a `continue` is used within an `if` test as follows:

```
for (int i = 0; i < 10; i++) {
  System.out.println("Inside loop");
  if (foo.doStuff() == 5) {
    continue;
  }
  // more loop code, that won't be reached when the above if
  // test is true
}
```

Unlabeled Statements

Both the `break` statement and the `continue` statement can be unlabeled or labeled. Although it's far more common to use `break` and `continue` unlabeled, the exam expects you to know how labeled `break` and `continue` statements work. As stated before, a `break` statement (unlabeled) will exit out of the innermost looping construct and proceed with the next line of code beyond the loop block. The following example demonstrates a `break` statement:

```
boolean problem = true;
while (true) {
  if (problem) {
    System.out.println("There was a problem");
    break;
  }
}
// next line of code
```

In the previous example, the `break` statement is unlabeled. The following is an example of an unlabeled `continue` statement:

```
while (!EOF) {
                          // read a field from a file
  if (wrongField) {
    continue;             // move to the next field in the file
  }
                          // otherwise do other stuff with the field
}
```

In this example, a file is being read one field at a time. When an error is encountered, the program moves to the next field in the file and uses the `continue` statement to go back into the loop (if it is not at the end of the file) and keeps reading the various fields. If the `break` command were used instead, the code would stop reading the file once the error occurred and move on to the next line of code after the loop. The `continue` statement gives you a way to say, "This particular iteration of the loop needs to stop, but not the whole loop itself. I just don't want the rest of the code in this iteration to finish, so do the iteration expression and then start over with the test, and don't worry about what was below the `continue` statement."

Labeled Statements

Although many statements in a Java program can be labeled, it's most common to use labels with loop statements like `for` or `while`, in conjunction with `break` and `continue` statements. A label statement must be placed just before the statement being labeled, and it consists of a valid identifier that ends with a colon (`:`).

You need to understand the difference between labeled and unlabeled break and continue. The labeled varieties are needed only in situations where you have a nested loop, and they need to indicate which of the nested loops you want to break from, or from which of the nested loops you want to continue with the next iteration. A break statement will exit out of the labeled loop, as opposed to the innermost loop, if the break keyword is combined with a label.

Here's an example of what a label looks like:

```
foo:
  for (int x = 3; x < 20; x++) {
    while(y > 7) {
      y--;
    }
  }
```

The label must adhere to the rules for a valid variable name and should adhere to the Java naming convention. The syntax for the use of a label name in conjunction with a break statement is the break keyword, then the label name, followed by a semicolon. A more complete example of the use of a labeled break statement is as follows:

```
boolean isTrue = true;
outer:
  for(int i=0; i<5; i++) {
    while (isTrue) {
      System.out.println("Hello");
      break outer;
    }    // end of inner while loop
    System.out.println("Outer loop."); // Won't print
  }      // end of outer for loop
System.out.println("Good-Bye");
```

Running this code produces

```
Hello
Good-Bye
```

In this example, the word Hello will be printed one time. Then, the labeled break statement will be executed, and the flow will exit out of the loop labeled outer. The next line of code will then print Good-Bye.

Let's see what will happen if the continue statement is used instead of the break statement. The following code example is similar to the preceding one, with the exception of substituting continue for break:

```
outer:
  for (int i=0; i<5; i++) {
    for (int j=0; j<5; j++) {
```

```
            System.out.println("Hello");
            continue outer;
        }    // end of inner loop
        System.out.println("outer"); // Never prints
    }
    System.out.println("Good-Bye");
```

Running this code produces

```
Hello
Hello
Hello
Hello
Hello
Good-Bye
```

In this example, `Hello` will be printed five times. After the `continue` statement is executed, the flow continues with the next iteration of the loop identified with the label. Finally, when the condition in the outer loop evaluates to `false`, this loop will finish and `Good-Bye` will be printed.

EXERCISE 5-2

Creating a Labeled while Loop

Try creating a labeled `while` loop. Make the label `outer` and provide a condition to check whether a variable `age` is less than or equal to 21. Within the loop, increment `age` by 1. Every time the program goes through the loop, check whether `age` is 16. If it is, print the message "get your driver's license" and continue to the outer loop. If not, print "Another year."

- The `outer` label should appear just before the `while` loop begins.
- Make sure `age` is declared outside of the `while` loop.

exam watch

Labeled `continue` and `break` statements must be inside the loop that has the same label name; otherwise, the code will not compile.

CERTIFICATION OBJECTIVE

Handling Exceptions (OCA Objectives 8.1, 8.2, 8.3, 8.4, and 8.5)

8.1 Differentiate among checked exceptions, unchecked exceptions, and errors.
8.2 Create a try-catch block and determine how exceptions alter normal program flow.
8.3 Describe the advantages of Exception handling.
8.4 Create and invoke a method that throws an exception.
8.5 Recognize common exception classes (such as NullPointerException, ArithmeticException, ArrayIndexOutOfBoundsException, ClassCastException) (sic)

An old maxim in software development says that 80 percent of the work is used 20 percent of the time. The 80 percent refers to the effort required to check and handle errors. In many languages, writing program code that checks for and deals with errors is tedious and bloats the application source into confusing spaghetti. Still, error detection and handling may be the most important ingredient of any robust application. Here are some of the benefits of Java's exception-handling features:

- It arms developers with an elegant mechanism for handling errors that produces efficient and organized error-handling code.
- It allows developers to detect errors easily without writing special code to test return values.
- It lets us keep exception-*handling* code cleanly separated from exception-*generating* code.
- It also lets us use the same exception-handling code to deal with a range of possible exceptions.

Java 7 added several new exception-handling capabilities to the language. For our purposes, Oracle split the various exception-handling topics into two main parts:

1. The OCA exam covers the Java 6 version of exception handling.
2. The OCP exam adds the new exception features added in Java 7.

In order to mirror Oracle's OCA 8 objectives versus the OCP 8 objectives, this chapter will give you only the basics of exception handling—but plenty to handle the OCA 8 exam.

Catching an Exception Using try and catch

Before we begin, let's introduce some terminology. The term *exception* means "exceptional condition" and is an occurrence that alters the normal program flow. A bunch of things can lead to exceptions, including hardware failures, resource exhaustion, and good old bugs. When an exceptional event occurs in Java, an exception is said to be "thrown." The code that's responsible for doing something about the exception is called an "exception handler," and it "catches" the thrown exception.

Exception handling works by transferring the execution of a program to an appropriate exception handler when an exception occurs. For example, if you call a method that opens a file but the file cannot be opened, execution of that method will stop, and code that you wrote to deal with this situation will be run. Therefore, we need a way to tell the JVM what code to execute when a certain exception happens. To do this, we use the `try` and `catch` keywords. The `try` is used to define a block of code in which exceptions may occur. This block of code is called a "guarded region" (which really means "risky code goes here"). One or more `catch` clauses match a specific exception (or group of exceptions—more on that later) to a block of code that handles it. Here's how it looks in pseudocode:

```
1. try {
2.   // This is the first line of the "guarded region"
3.   // that is governed by the try keyword.
4.   // Put code here that might cause some kind of exception.
5.   // We may have many code lines here or just one.
6. }
7. catch(MyFirstException) {
8.   // Put code here that handles this exception.
9.   // This is the next line of the exception handler.
10.  // This is the last line of the exception handler.
11. }
12. catch(MySecondException) {
13.   // Put code here that handles this exception
14. }
15.
16.   // Some other unguarded (normal, non-risky) code begins here
```

In this pseudocode example, lines 2 through 5 constitute the guarded region that is governed by the `try` clause. Line 7 is an exception handler for an exception of type `MyFirstException`. Line 12 is an exception handler for an exception of type `MySecondException`. Notice that the `catch` blocks immediately follow the `try` block. This is a requirement; if you have one or more `catch` blocks, they must immediately follow the `try` block. Additionally, the `catch` blocks must all follow each other, without any other statements or blocks in between. Also, the order in which the `catch` blocks appear matters, as we'll see a little later.

Execution of the guarded region starts at line 2. If the program executes all the way past line 5 with no exceptions being thrown, execution will transfer to line 15 and continue downward. However, if at any time in lines 2 through 5 (the `try` block) an exception of type `MyFirstException` is thrown, execution will immediately transfer to line 7. Lines 8 through 10 will then be executed so that the entire `catch` block runs, and then execution will transfer to line 15 and continue.

Note that if an exception occurred on, say, line 3 of the `try` block, the remaining lines in the `try` block (4 and 5) would never be executed. Once control jumps to the `catch` block, it never returns to complete the balance of the `try` block. This is exactly what you want, though. Imagine that your code looks something like this pseudocode:

```
try {
  getTheFileFromOverNetwork
  readFromTheFileAndPopulateTable
}
catch(CantGetFileFromNetwork) {
  displayNetworkErrorMessage
}
```

This pseudocode demonstrates how you typically work with exceptions. Code that's dependent on a risky operation (as populating a table with file data is dependent on getting the file from the network) is grouped into a `try` block in such a way that if, say, the first operation fails, you won't continue trying to run other code that's also guaranteed to fail. In the pseudocode example, you won't be able to read from the file if you can't get the file off the network in the first place.

One of the benefits of using exception handling is that code to handle any particular exception that may occur in the governed region needs to be written only once. Returning to our earlier code example, there may be three different places in our `try` block that can generate a `MyFirstException`, but wherever it occurs it will be handled by the same `catch` block (on line 7). We'll discuss more benefits of exception handling near the end of this chapter.

Using finally

Although try and catch provide a terrific mechanism for trapping and handling exceptions, we are left with the problem of how to clean up after ourselves if an exception occurs. Because execution transfers out of the try block as soon as an exception is thrown, we can't put our cleanup code at the bottom of the try block and expect it to be executed if an exception occurs. Almost as bad an idea would be placing our cleanup code in each of the catch blocks—let's see why.

Exception handlers are a poor place to clean up after the code in the try block because each handler then requires its own copy of the cleanup code. If, for example, you allocated a network socket or opened a file somewhere in the guarded region, each exception handler would have to close the file or release the socket. That would make it too easy to forget to do cleanup and also lead to a lot of redundant code. To address this problem, Java offers the finally block.

A finally block encloses code that is always executed at some point after the try block, whether an exception was thrown or not. Even if there is a return statement in the try block, the finally block executes right after the return statement is encountered and before the return executes!

This is the right place to close your files, release your network sockets, and perform any other cleanup your code requires. If the try block executes with no exceptions, the finally block is executed immediately after the try block completes. If there was an exception thrown, the finally block executes immediately after the proper catch block completes. Let's look at another pseudocode example:

```
try {
  // This is the first line of the "guarded region".
}
catch(MyFirstException) {
  // Put code here that handles this exception
}
catch(MySecondException) {
  // Put code here that handles this exception
}
finally {
  // Put code here to release any resource we
  // allocated in the try clause
}

  // More code here
```

As before, execution starts at the first line of the `try` block, line 2. If there are no exceptions thrown in the `try` block, execution transfers to line 11, the first line of the `finally` block. On the other hand, if a `MySecondException` is thrown while the code in the `try` block is executing, execution transfers to the first line of that exception handler, line 8 in the `catch` clause. After all the code in the `catch` clause is executed, the program moves to line 11, the first line of the `finally` clause. Repeat after me: `finally` always runs! Okay, we'll have to refine that a little, but for now, start burning in the idea that `finally` always runs. If an exception is thrown, `finally` runs. If an exception is not thrown, `finally` runs. If the exception is caught, `finally` runs. If the exception is not caught, `finally` runs. Later we'll look at the few scenarios in which `finally` might not run or complete.

Remember, `finally` clauses are not required. If you don't write one, your code will compile and run just fine. In fact, if you have no resources to clean up after your `try` block completes, you probably don't need a `finally` clause. Also, because the compiler doesn't even require `catch` clauses, sometimes you'll run across code that has a `try` block immediately followed by a `finally` block. Such code is useful when the exception is going to be passed back to the calling method, as explained in the next section. Using a `finally` block allows the cleanup code to execute even when there isn't a `catch` clause.

The following legal code demonstrates a `try` with a `finally` but no `catch`:

```
try {
  // do stuff
} finally {
  // clean up
}
```

The following legal code demonstrates a `try`, `catch`, and `finally`:

```
try {
  // do stuff
} catch (SomeException ex) {
  // do exception handling
} finally {
  // clean up
}
```

The following ILLEGAL code demonstrates a `try` without a `catch` or `finally`:

```
try {
  // do stuff
}
```

```
  // need a catch or finally here
System.out.println("out of try block");
```

The following ILLEGAL code demonstrates a misplaced `catch` block:

```
try {
  // do stuff
}
  // can't have code between try/catch
System.out.println("out of try block");
catch(Exception ex) { }
```

exam watch

It is illegal to use a `try` clause without either a `catch` clause or a `finally` clause. A `try` clause by itself will result in a compiler error. Any `catch` clauses must immediately follow the `try` block. Any `finally` clause must immediately follow the last `catch` clause (or it must immediately follow the `try` block if there is no `catch`). It is legal to omit either the `catch` clause or the `finally` clause, but not both.

Propagating Uncaught Exceptions

Why aren't `catch` clauses required? What happens to an exception that's thrown in a `try` block when there is no `catch` clause waiting for it? Actually, there's no requirement that you code a `catch` clause for every possible exception that could be thrown from the corresponding `try` block. In fact, it's doubtful that you could accomplish such a feat! If a method doesn't provide a `catch` clause for a particular exception, that method is said to be "ducking" the exception (or "passing the buck").

So what happens to a ducked exception? Before we discuss that, we need to briefly review the concept of the call stack. Most languages have the concept of a method stack or a call stack. Simply put, the call stack is the chain of methods that your program executes to get to the current method. If your program starts in method `main()` and `main()` calls method `a()`, which calls method `b()`, which in turn calls method `c()`, the call stack consists of the following:

```
c
b
a
main
```

We will represent the stack as growing upward (although it can also be visualized as growing downward). As you can see, the last method called is at the top of the stack, while the first calling method is at the bottom. The method at the very top of the stack trace would be the method you were currently executing. If we move back down the call stack, we're moving from the current method to the previously called method. Figure 5-1 illustrates a way to think about how the call stack in Java works.

FIGURE 5-1

The Java method call stack

1) The call stack while `method3()` is running.

4	`method3()`	`method2` invokes `method3`
3	`method2()`	`method1` invokes `method2`
2	`method1()`	`main` invokes `method1`
1	`main()`	`main` begins

The order in which methods are put on the call stack

2) The call stack after `method3()` completes
Execution returns to `method2()`

1	`method2()`	`method2()` will complete
2	`method1()`	`method1()` will complete
3	`main()`	`main()` will complete and the JVM will exit

The order in which methods complete

Now let's examine what happens to ducked exceptions. Imagine a building, say, five stories high, and at each floor there is a deck or balcony. Now imagine that on each deck, one person is standing holding a baseball mitt. Exceptions are like balls dropped from person to person, starting from the roof. An exception is first thrown from the top of the stack (in other words, the person on the roof); and if it isn't caught by the same person who threw it (the person on the roof), it drops down the call stack to the previous method, which is the person standing on the deck one floor down. If not caught there by the person one floor down, the exception/ball again drops down to the previous method (person on the next floor down), and so on, until it is caught or until it reaches the very bottom of the call stack. This is called "exception propagation."

If an exception reaches the bottom of the call stack, it's like reaching the bottom of a very long drop; the ball explodes, and so does your program. An exception that's never caught will cause your application to stop running. A description (if one is available) of the exception will be displayed, and the call stack will be "dumped." This helps you debug your application by telling you what exception was thrown, from what method it was thrown, and what the stack looked like at the time.

exam watch

You can keep throwing an exception down through the methods on the stack. But what happens when you get to the `main()` method at the bottom? You can throw the exception out of `main()` as well. This results in the JVM halting, and the stack trace will be printed to the output. The following code throws an exception:

```
class TestEx {
  public static void main (String [] args) {
    doStuff();
  }
  static void doStuff() {
    doMoreStuff();
  }
  static void doMoreStuff() {
    int x = 5/0;  // Can't divide by zero!
                  // ArithmeticException is thrown here
  }
}
```

It prints out a stack trace something like this:

```
 %java TestEx
Exception in thread "main" java.lang.ArithmeticException: / by zero
at TestEx.doMoreStuff(TestEx.java:10)
at TestEx.doStuff(TestEx.java:7)
at TestEx.main(TestEx.java:3)
```

EXERCISE 5-3

Propagating and Catching an Exception

In this exercise, you're going to create two methods that deal with exceptions. One of the methods is the `main()` method, which will call another method. If an exception is thrown in the other method, `main()` must deal with it. A `finally` statement will be included to indicate that the program has completed. The method that `main()` will call will be named `reverse`, and it will reverse the order of the characters in a `String`. If the `String` contains no characters, `reverse` will propagate an exception up to the `main()` method.

1. Create a class called `Propagate` and a `main()` method, which will remain empty for now.
2. Create a method called `reverse`. It takes an argument of a `String` and returns a `String`.
3. In `reverse`, check whether the `String` has a length of 0 by using the `String.length()` method. If the length is 0, the `reverse` method will throw an exception.
4. Now include the code to reverse the order of the `String`. Because this isn't the main topic of this chapter, the reversal code has been provided, but feel free to try it on your own.

```
String reverseStr = "";
for(int i=s.length()-1;i>=0;--i) {
  reverseStr += s.charAt(i);
}
return reverseStr;
```

5. Now in the `main()` method you will attempt to call this method and deal with any potential exceptions. Additionally, you will include a `finally` statement that displays when `main()` has finished.

Defining Exceptions

We have been discussing exceptions as a concept. We know that they are thrown when a problem of some type happens, and we know what effect they have on the flow of our program. In this section, we will develop the concepts further and use exceptions in functional Java code.

Earlier we said that an exception is an occurrence that alters the normal program flow. But because this is Java, anything that's not a primitive must be...an object. Exceptions are no different. Every exception is an instance of a class that has class `Exception` in its inheritance hierarchy. In other words, exceptions are always some subclass of `java.lang.Exception`.

When an exception is thrown, an object of a particular `Exception` subtype is instantiated and handed to the exception handler as an argument to the `catch` clause. An actual `catch` clause looks like this:

```
try {
  // some code here
}
catch (ArrayIndexOutOfBoundsException e) {
  e.printStackTrace();
}
```

In this example, e is an instance of the ArrayIndexOutOfBoundsException class. As with any other object, you can call its methods.

Exception Hierarchy

All exception classes are subtypes of class Exception. This class derives from the class Throwable (which derives from the class Object). Figure 5-2 shows the hierarchy for the exception classes.

As you can see, there are two subclasses that derive from Throwable: Exception and Error. Classes that derive from Error represent unusual situations that are not caused by program errors and indicate things that would not normally happen during program execution, such as the JVM running out of memory. Generally, your application won't be able to recover from an Error, so you're not required to handle them. If your code does not handle them (and it usually won't), it will still compile with no trouble. Although often thought of as exceptional conditions, Errors are technically not exceptions because they do not derive from class Exception.

In general, an exception represents something that happens not as a result of a programming error, but rather because some resource is not available or some other condition required for correct execution is not present. For example, if your application is supposed to communicate with another application or computer that is not answering, this is an exception that is not caused by a bug. Figure 5-2 also

FIGURE 5-2

Exception class hierarchy

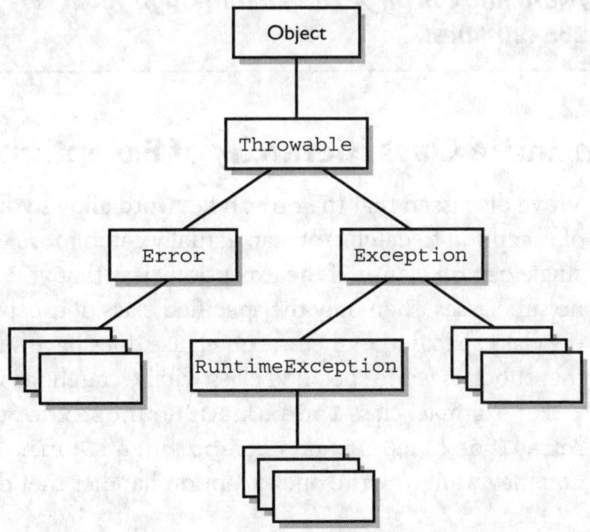

shows a subtype of `Exception` called `RuntimeException`. These exceptions are a special case because they sometimes do indicate program errors. They can also represent rare, difficult-to-handle exceptional conditions. Runtime exceptions are discussed in greater detail later in this chapter.

Java provides many exception classes, most of which have quite descriptive names. There are two ways to get information about an exception. The first is from the type of the exception itself. The next is from information that you can get from the exception object. Class `Throwable` (at the top of the inheritance tree for exceptions) provides its descendants with some methods that are useful in exception handlers. One of these is `printStackTrace()`. As you would expect, if you call an exception object's `printStackTrace()` method, as in the earlier example, a stack trace from where the exception occurred will be printed.

We discussed that a call stack builds upward with the most recently called method at the top. You will notice that the `printStackTrace()` method prints the most recently entered method first and continues down, printing the name of each method as it works its way down the call stack (this is called "unwinding the stack") from the top.

exam watch

For the exam, you don't need to know any of the methods contained in the `Throwable` classes, including `Exception` and `Error`. You are expected to know that `Exception`, `Error`, `RuntimeException`, and `Throwable` types can all be thrown using the `throw` keyword and can all be caught (although you rarely will catch anything other than `Exception` subtypes).

Handling an Entire Class Hierarchy of Exceptions

We've discussed that the `catch` keyword allows you to specify a particular type of exception to catch. You can actually catch more than one type of exception in a single `catch` clause. If the exception class that you specify in the `catch` clause has no subclasses, then only the specified class of exception will be caught. However, if the class specified in the `catch` clause does have subclasses, any exception object that subclasses the specified class will be caught as well.

For example, class `IndexOutOfBoundsException` has two subclasses, `ArrayIndexOutOfBoundsException` and `StringIndexOutOfBoundsException`. You may want to write one exception handler that deals with exceptions produced by either type of boundary error, but you might not be concerned with which exception you actually have. In this case, you could write a `catch` clause like the following:

```
try {
  // Some code here that can throw a boundary exception
}
catch (IndexOutOfBoundsException e) {
  e.printStackTrace();
}
```

If any code in the `try` block throws `ArrayIndexOutOfBoundsException` or `StringIndexOutOfBoundsException`, the exception will be caught and handled. This can be convenient, but it should be used sparingly. By specifying an exception class's superclass in your `catch` clause, you're discarding valuable information about the exception. You can, of course, find out exactly what exception class you have, but if you're going to do that, you're better off writing a separate `catch` clause for each exception type of interest.

on the job

Resist the temptation to write a single catchall exception handler such as the following:

```
try {
  // some code
}
catch (Exception e) {
  e.printStackTrace();
}
```

This code will catch every exception generated. Of course, no single exception handler can properly handle every exception, and programming in this way defeats the design objective. Exception handlers that trap many errors at once will probably reduce the reliability of your program, because it's likely that an exception will be caught that the handler does not know how to handle.

Exception Matching

If you have an exception hierarchy composed of a superclass exception and a number of subtypes, and you're interested in handling one of the subtypes in a special way but want to handle all the rest together, you need write only two `catch` clauses.

When an exception is thrown, Java will try to find (by looking at the available `catch` clauses from the top down) a `catch` clause for the exception type. If it doesn't find one, it will search for a handler for a supertype of the exception. If it does not find a `catch` clause that matches a supertype for the exception, then the exception is propagated down the call stack. This process is called "exception matching." Let's look at an example.

```
 1: import java.io.*;
 2: public class ReadData {
 3:   public static void main(String args[]) {
 4:     try {
 5:       RandomAccessFile raf =
 6:         new RandomAccessFile("myfile.txt", "r");
 7:       byte b[] = new byte[1000];
 8:       raf.readFully(b, 0, 1000);
 9:     }
10:     catch(FileNotFoundException e) {
11:       System.err.println("File not found");
12:       System.err.println(e.getMessage());
13:       e.printStackTrace();
14:     }
15:     catch(IOException e) {
16:       System.err.println("IO Error");
17:       System.err.println(e.toString());
18:       e.printStackTrace();
19:     }
20:   }
21: }
```

This short program attempts to open a file and to read some data from it. Opening and reading files can generate many exceptions, most of which are some type of `IOException`. Imagine that in this program we're interested in knowing only whether the exact exception is a `FileNotFoundException`. Otherwise, we don't care exactly what the problem is.

`FileNotFoundException` is a subclass of `IOException`. Therefore, we could handle it in the `catch` clause that catches all subtypes of `IOException`, but then we would have to test the exception to determine whether it was a `FileNotFoundException`. Instead, we coded a special exception handler for the `FileNotFoundException` and a separate exception handler for all other `IOException` subtypes.

If this code generates a `FileNotFoundException`, it will be handled by the `catch` clause that begins at line 10. If it generates another `IOException`—

perhaps EOFException, which is a subclass of IOException—it will be handled by the catch clause that begins at line 15. If some other exception is generated, such as a runtime exception of some type, neither catch clause will be executed and the exception will be propagated down the call stack.

Notice that the catch clause for the FileNotFoundException was placed above the handler for the IOException. This is really important! If we do it the opposite way, the program will not compile. The handlers for the most specific exceptions must always be placed above those for more general exceptions. The following will not compile:

```
try {
  // do risky IO things
} catch (IOException e) {
  // handle general IOExceptions
} catch (FileNotFoundException ex) {
  // handle just FileNotFoundException
}
```

You'll get a compiler error something like this:

```
TestEx.java:15: exception java.io.FileNotFoundException has
 already been caught
} catch (FileNotFoundException ex) {
  ^
```

If you think back to the people with baseball mitts (in the section "Propagating Uncaught Exceptions"), imagine that the most general mitts are the largest and can thus catch many kinds of balls. An IOException mitt is large enough and flexible enough to catch any type of IOException. So if the person on the fifth floor (say, Fred) has a big ol' IOException mitt, he can't help but catch a FileNotFoundException ball with it. And if the guy (say, Jimmy) on the second floor is holding a FileNotFoundException mitt, that FileNotFoundException ball will never get to him because it will always be stopped by Fred on the fifth floor, standing there with his big-enough-for-any-IOException mitt.

So what do you do with exceptions that are siblings in the class hierarchy? If one Exception class is not a subtype or supertype of the other, then the order in which the catch clauses are placed doesn't matter.

Exception Declaration and the Public Interface

So, how do we know that some method throws an exception that we have to catch? Just as a method must specify what type and how many arguments it accepts and what is returned, the exceptions that a method can throw must be *declared* (unless the exceptions are subclasses of `RuntimeException`). The list of thrown exceptions is part of a method's public interface. The `throws` keyword is used as follows to list the exceptions that a method can throw:

```
void myFunction() throws MyException1, MyException2 {
  // code for the method here
}
```

This method has a `void` return type, accepts no arguments, and declares that it can throw one of two types of exceptions: either type `MyException1` or type `MyException2`. (Just because the method declares that it throws an exception doesn't mean it always will. It just tells the world that it might.)

Suppose your method doesn't directly throw an exception but calls a method that does. You can choose not to handle the exception yourself and instead just declare it, as though it were your method that actually throws the exception. If you do declare the exception that your method might get from another method and you don't provide a `try/catch` for it, then the method will propagate back to the method that called your method and will either be caught there or continue on to be handled by a method further down the stack.

Any method that might throw an exception (unless it's a subclass of `RuntimeException`) must declare the exception. That includes methods that aren't actually throwing it directly, but are "ducking" and letting the exception pass down to the next method in the stack. If you "duck" an exception, it is just as if you were the one actually throwing the exception. `RuntimeException` subclasses are exempt, so the compiler won't check to see if you've declared them. But all non-`RuntimeExceptions` are considered "checked" exceptions because the compiler checks to be certain you've acknowledged that "bad things could happen here."

Remember this:

> Each method must either handle all checked exceptions by supplying a `catch` clause or list each unhandled checked exception as a thrown exception.

This rule is referred to as Java's "handle or declare" requirement (sometimes called "catch or declare").

exam watch

Look for code that invokes a method declaring an exception, where the calling method doesn't handle or declare the checked exception. The following code (which uses the `throw` keyword to throw an exception manually—more on this next) has two big problems that the compiler will prevent:

```
void doStuff() {
  doMore();
}
void doMore() {
  throw new IOException();
}
```

First, the `doMore()` method throws a checked exception but does not declare it! But suppose we fix the `doMore()` method as follows:

```
void doMore() throws IOException { … }
```

The `doStuff()` method is still in trouble because it, too, must declare the `IOException`, unless it handles it by providing a `try/catch`, with a `catch` clause that can take an `IOException`.

Again, some exceptions are exempt from this rule. An object of type `RuntimeException` may be thrown from any method without being specified as part of the method's public interface (and a handler need not be present). And even if a method does declare a `RuntimeException`, the calling method is under no obligation to handle or declare it. `RuntimeException`, `Error`, and all their subtypes are unchecked exceptions, and unchecked exceptions do not have to be specified or handled. Here is an example:

```
import java.io.*;
class Test {
  public int myMethod1() throws EOFException {
    return myMethod2();
  }
  public int myMethod2() throws EOFException {
    // code that actually could throw the exception goes here
    return 1;
  }
}
```

Let's look at myMethod1(). Because EOFException subclasses IOException and IOException subclasses Exception, it is a checked exception and must be declared as an exception that may be thrown by this method. But where will the exception actually come from? The public interface for method myMethod2() called here declares that an exception of this type can be thrown. Whether that method actually throws the exception itself or calls another method that throws it is unimportant to us; we simply know that we either have to catch the exception or declare that we threw it. The method myMethod1() does not catch the exception, so it declares that it throws it. Now let's look at another legal example, myMethod3():

```
public void myMethod3() {
  // code that could throw a NullPointerException goes here
}
```

According to the comment, this method can throw a NullPointerException. Because RuntimeException is the superclass of NullPointerException, it is an unchecked exception and need not be declared. We can see that myMethod3() does not declare any exceptions.

Runtime exceptions are referred to as *unchecked* exceptions. All other exceptions are *checked* exceptions, and they don't derive from java.lang.RuntimeException. A checked exception must be caught somewhere in your code. If you invoke a method that throws a checked exception but you don't catch the checked exception somewhere, your code will not compile. That's why they're called checked exceptions: the compiler checks to make sure they're handled or declared. A number of the methods in the Java API throw checked exceptions, so you will often write exception handlers to cope with exceptions generated by methods you didn't write.

You can also throw an exception yourself, and that exception can be either an existing exception from the Java API or one of your own. To create your own exception, you simply subclass Exception (or one of its subclasses) as follows:

```
class MyException extends Exception { }
```

And if you throw the exception, the compiler will guarantee that you declare it as follows:

```
class TestEx {
  void doStuff() {
    throw new MyException();  // Throw a checked exception
  }
}
```

The preceding code upsets the compiler:

```
TestEx.java:6: unreported exception MyException; must be caught or
declared to be thrown
  throw new MyException();
  ^
```

exam watch

When an object of a subtype of `Exception` is thrown, it must be handled or declared. These objects are called "checked exceptions" and include all exceptions except those that are subtypes of `RuntimeException`, which are unchecked exceptions. Be ready to spot methods that don't follow the "handle or declare" rule, such as this:

```
class MyException extends Exception {
  void someMethod () {
    doStuff();
  }
  void doStuff() throws MyException {
    try {
      throw new MyException();
    }
    catch(MyException me) {
      throw me;
    }
  }
}
```

You need to recognize that this code won't compile. If you try, you'll get this:

```
MyException.java:3: unreported exception MyException;
must be caught or declared to be thrown
doStuff();
       ^
```

Notice that `someMethod()` fails either to handle or declare the exception that can be thrown by `doStuff()`. In the next pages, we'll discuss several ways to deal with this sort of situation.

You need to know how an `Error` compares with checked and unchecked exceptions. Objects of type `Error` are not `Exception` objects, although they do represent exceptional conditions. Both `Exception` and `Error` share a common superclass, `Throwable`; thus, both can be thrown using the `throw` keyword. When an `Error` or a subclass of `Error` (like `StackOverflowError`) is thrown, it's unchecked. You are not required to catch Error objects or Error subtypes. You can also throw an Error yourself (although, other than AssertionError, you probably won't ever want to), and you can catch one, but again, you probably won't. What, for example, would you actually do if you got an OutOfMemoryError? It's not like you can tell the garbage collector to run; you can bet the JVM fought desperately to save itself (and reclaimed all the memory it could) by the time you got the error. In other words, don't expect the JVM at that point to say, "Run the garbage collector? Oh, thanks so much for telling me. That just never occurred to me. Sure, I'll get right on it." Even better, what would you do if a VirtualMachineError arose? Your program is toast by the time you'd catch the error, so there's really no point in trying to catch one of these babies. Just remember, though, that you can! The following compiles just fine:

```
class TestEx {
  public static void main (String [] args) {
    badMethod();
  }
  static void badMethod() {  // No need to declare an Error
    doStuff();
  }
  static void doStuff() {    // No need to declare an Error
    try {
      throw new Error();
    }
    catch(Error me) {
      throw me;              // We catch it, but then rethrow it
    }
  }
}
```

If we were throwing a checked exception rather than Error, then the doStuff() method would need to declare the exception. But remember, since Error is not a subtype of Exception, it doesn't need to be declared. You're free to declare it if you like, but the compiler just doesn't care one way or another when or how the Error is thrown or by whom.

on the job

Because Java has checked exceptions, it's commonly said that Java forces developers to handle exceptions. Yes, Java forces us to write exception handlers for each exception that can occur during normal operation, but it's up to us to make the exception handlers actually do something useful. We know software managers who melt down when they see a programmer write something like this:

```
try {
  callBadMethod();
} catch (Exception ex) { }
```

Notice anything missing? Don't "eat" the exception by catching it without actually handling it. You won't even be able to tell that the exception occurred because you'll never see the stack trace.

Rethrowing the Same Exception

Just as you can throw a new exception from a `catch` clause, you can also throw the same exception you just caught. Here's a `catch` clause that does this:

```
catch(IOException e) {
  // Do things, then if you decide you can't handle it…
  throw e;
}
```

All other `catch` clauses associated with the same `try` are ignored; if a `finally` block exists, it runs, and the exception is thrown back to the calling method (the next method down the call stack). If you throw a checked exception from a `catch` clause, you must also declare that exception! In other words, you must handle *and* declare, as opposed to handle *or* declare. The following example is illegal:

```
public void doStuff() {
  try {
    // risky IO things
  } catch(IOException ex) {
    // can't handle it
     throw ex;  // Can't throw it unless you declare it
  }
}
```

In the preceding code, the `doStuff()` method is clearly able to throw a checked exception—in this case an `IOException`—so the compiler says, "Well, that's just peachy that you have a `try/catch` in there, but it's not good enough. If you might rethrow the `IOException` you catch, then you must declare it (in the method signature)!"

EXERCISE 5-4

Creating an Exception

In this exercise, we attempt to create a custom exception. We won't put in any new methods (it will have only those inherited from `Exception`); and because it extends `Exception`, the compiler considers it a checked exception. The goal of the program is to determine whether a command-line argument representing a particular food (as a string) is considered bad or okay.

1. Let's first create our exception. We will call it `BadFoodException`. This exception will be thrown when a bad food is encountered.
2. Create an enclosing class called `MyException` and a `main()` method, which will remain empty for now.
3. Create a method called `checkFood()`. It takes a `String` argument and throws our exception if it doesn't like the food it was given. Otherwise, it tells us it likes the food. You can add any foods you aren't particularly fond of to the list.
4. Now in the `main()` method, you'll get the command-line argument out of the `String` array and then pass that `String` on to the `checkFood()` method. Because it's a checked exception, the `checkFood()` method must declare it, and the `main()` method must handle it (using a `try/catch`). Do not have `main()` declare the exception, because if `main()` ducks the exception, who else is back there to catch it? (Actually, `main()` can legally declare exceptions, but don't do that in this exercise.)

As nifty as exception handling is, it's still up to the developer to make proper use of it. Exception handling makes organizing code and signaling problems easy, but the exception handlers still have to be written. You'll find that even the most complex situations can be handled, and your code will be reusable, readable, and maintainable.

CERTIFICATION OBJECTIVE

Common Exceptions and Errors (OCA Objective 8.5)

8.5 Recognize common exception classes (such as NullPointerException, ArithmeticException, ArrayIndexOutOfBoundsException, ClassCastException) (sic)

The intention of this objective is to make sure that you are familiar with some of the most common exceptions and errors you'll encounter as a Java programmer.

exam watch

The questions from this section are likely to be along the lines of, "Here's some code that just did something bad, which exception will be thrown?" Throughout the exam, questions will present some code and ask you to determine whether the code will run or whether an exception will be thrown. Since these questions are so common, understanding the causes for these exceptions is critical to your success.

This is another one of those objectives that will turn up all through the real exam (does "An exception is thrown at runtime" ring a bell?), so make sure this section gets a lot of your attention.

Where Exceptions Come From

Jump back a page and take a look at the last sentence. It's important that you understand what causes exceptions and errors and where they come from. For the purposes of exam preparation, let's define two broad categories of exceptions and errors:

- **JVM exceptions** Those exceptions or errors that are either exclusively or most logically thrown by the JVM
- **Programmatic exceptions** Those exceptions that are thrown explicitly by application and/or API programmers

JVM-Thrown Exceptions

Let's start with a very common exception, the `NullPointerException`. As we saw in earlier chapters, this exception occurs when you attempt to access an object using a reference variable with a current value of `null`. There's no way that the compiler can hope to find these problems before runtime. Take a look at the following:

```
class NPE {
  static String s;
  public static void main(String [] args) {
    System.out.println(s.length());
  }
}
```

Surely, the compiler can find the problem with that tiny little program! Nope, you're on your own. The code will compile just fine, and the JVM will throw a `NullPointerException` when it tries to invoke the `length()` method.

Earlier in this chapter we discussed the call stack. As you recall, we used the convention that `main()` would be at the bottom of the call stack, and that as `main()` invokes another method, and that method invokes another, and so on, the stack grows upward. Of course, the stack resides in memory, and even if your OS gives you a gigabyte of RAM for your program, it's still a finite amount. It's possible to grow the stack so large that the OS runs out of space to store the call stack. When this happens, you get (wait for it...) a `StackOverflowError`. The most common way for this to occur is to create a recursive method. A recursive method invokes itself in the method body. Although that may sound weird, it's a very common and useful technique for such things as searching and sorting algorithms. Take a look at this code:

```
void go() {     // recursion gone bad
   go();
}
```

As you can see, if you ever make the mistake of invoking the `go()` method, your program will fall into a black hole—`go()` invoking `go()` invoking `go()`, until, no matter how much memory you have, you'll get a `StackOverflowError`. Again, only the JVM knows when this moment occurs, and the JVM will be the source of this error.

Programmatically Thrown Exceptions

Now let's look at programmatically thrown exceptions. Remember we defined *programmatically* as meaning something like this:

Created by an application and/or API developer

For instance, many classes in the Java API have methods that take `String` arguments and convert these `Strings` into numeric primitives. A good example of these classes is the so-called "wrapper classes" that we will study in Chapter 6. Even though we haven't talked much about wrapper classes yet, the following example should make sense.

At some point long ago, some programmer wrote the java.lang.Integer class and created methods like parseInt() and valueOf(). That programmer wisely decided that if one of these methods was passed a String that could not be converted into a number, the method should throw a NumberFormatException. The partially implemented code might look something like this:

```
int parseInt(String s) throws NumberFormatException {
  boolean parseSuccess = false;
  int result = 0;
  // do complicated parsing
  if (!parseSuccess)    // if the parsing failed
    throw new NumberFormatException();
  return result;
}
```

Other examples of programmatic exceptions include an AssertionError (okay, it's not an exception, but it IS thrown programmatically) and throwing an IllegalArgumentException. In fact, our mythical API developer could have used IllegalArgumentException for her parseInt() method. But it turns out that NumberFormatException extends IllegalArgumentException and is a little more precise, so in this case, using NumberFormatException supports the notion we discussed earlier: that when you have an exception hierarchy, you should use the most precise exception that you can.

Of course, as we discussed earlier, you can also make up your very own special custom exceptions and throw them whenever you want to. These homemade exceptions also fall into the category of "programmatically thrown exceptions."

A Summary of the Exam's Exceptions and Errors

OCA 8 Objective 8.5 lists a few specific exceptions and errors; it says "Recognize common exception classes (such as....."). Table 5-2 summarizes the ten exceptions and errors that are most likely a part of the OCA 8 exam.

TABLE 5-2 Descriptions and Sources of Common Exceptions

Exception	Description	Typically Thrown
`ArrayIndexOutOfBoundsException` (this chapter)	Thrown when attempting to access an array with an invalid index value (either negative or beyond the length of the array).	By the JVM
`ClassCastException` (Chapter 2)	Thrown when attempting to cast a reference variable to a type that fails the IS-A test.	By the JVM
`IllegalArgumentException`	Thrown when a method receives an argument formatted differently than the method expects.	Programmatically
`IllegalStateException`	Thrown when the state of the environment doesn't match the operation being attempted—for example, using a scanner that's been closed.	Programmatically
`NullPointerException` (Chapter 3)	Thrown when attempting to invoke a method on, or access a property from, a reference variable whose current value is `null`.	By the JVM
`NumberFormatException` (this chapter)	Thrown when a method that converts a `String` to a number receives a `String` that it cannot convert.	Programmatically
`ArithmeticException`	Thrown when an illegal math operation (such as dividing by zero) is attempted.	By the JVM
`ExceptionInInitializerError` (Chapter 2)	Thrown when attempting to initialize a static variable or an initialization block.	By the JVM
`StackOverflowError` (this chapter)	Typically thrown when a method recurses too deeply. (Each invocation is added to the stack.)	By the JVM
`NoClassDefFoundError`	Thrown when the JVM can't find a class it needs, because of a command-line error, a classpath issue, or a missing `.class` file.	By the JVM

CERTIFICATION SUMMARY

This chapter covered a lot of ground, all of which involved ways of controlling your program flow based on a conditional test. First, you learned about `if` and `switch` statements. The `if` statement evaluates one or more expressions to a `boolean` result. If the result is `true`, the program will execute the code in the block that is encompassed by the `if`. If an `else` statement is used and the `if` expression evaluates to `false`, then the code following the `else` will be performed. If no `else` block is defined, then none of the code associated with the `if` statement will execute.

You also learned that the `switch` statement can be used to replace multiple `if-else` statements. The `switch` statement can evaluate integer primitive types that can be implicitly cast to an `int` (those types are `byte`, `short`, `int`, and `char`); or it can evaluate `enums`; and as of Java 7, it can evaluate `Strings`. At runtime, the JVM will try to find a match between the expression in the `switch` statement and a constant in a corresponding `case` statement. If a match is found, execution will begin at the matching case and continue on from there, executing code in all the remaining `case` statements until a `break` statement is found or the end of the `switch` statement occurs. If there is no match, then the `default` case will execute, if there is one.

You've learned about the three looping constructs available in the Java language. These constructs are the `for` loop (including the basic `for` and the enhanced `for`, which was new to Java 5), the `while` loop, and the `do` loop. In general, the `for` loop is used when you know how many times you need to go through the loop. The `while` loop is used when you do not know how many times you want to go through, whereas the `do` loop is used when you need to go through at least once. In the `for` loop and the `while` loop, the expression has to evaluate to `true` to get inside the block and will check after every iteration of the loop. The `do` loop does not check the condition until after it has gone through the loop once. The major benefit of the `for` loop is the ability to initialize one or more variables and increment or decrement those variables in the `for` loop definition.

The `break` and `continue` statements can be used in either a labeled or unlabeled fashion. When unlabeled, the `break` statement will force the program to stop processing the innermost looping construct and start with the line of code following the loop. Using an unlabeled `continue` command will cause the program to stop execution of the current iteration of the innermost loop and proceed with the next iteration. When a `break` or a `continue` statement is used in a labeled manner, it will perform in the same way, with one exception: the statement will not apply to the innermost loop; instead, it will apply to the loop with the label. The `break` statement is used most often in conjunction with the `switch` statement. When there is a match between the `switch` expression and the `case` constant, the code following the `case` constant will be performed. To stop execution, a `break` is needed.

You've seen how Java provides an elegant mechanism in exception handling. Exception handling allows you to isolate your error-correction code into separate blocks so the main code doesn't become cluttered by error-checking code. Another elegant feature allows you to handle similar errors with a single error-handling block, without code duplication. Also, the error handling can be deferred to methods further back on the call stack.

You learned that Java's `try` keyword is used to specify a guarded region—a block of code in which problems might be detected. An exception handler is the code that is executed when an exception occurs. The handler is defined by using Java's `catch` keyword. All `catch` clauses must immediately follow the related `try` block.

Java also provides the `finally` keyword. This is used to define a block of code that is always executed, either immediately after a `catch` clause completes or immediately after the associated `try` block in the case that no exception was thrown (or there was a `try` but no `catch`). Use `finally` blocks to release system resources and to perform any cleanup required by the code in the `try` block. A `finally` block is not required, but if there is one, it must immediately follow the last `catch`. (If there is no `catch` block, the `finally` block must immediately follow the `try` block.) It's guaranteed to be called except when the `try` or `catch` issues a `System.exit()`.

An exception object is an instance of class `Exception` or one of its subclasses. The `catch` clause takes, as a parameter, an instance of an object of a type derived from the `Exception` class. Java requires that each method either catches any checked exception it can throw or else declares that it throws the exception. The exception declaration is part of the method's signature. To declare that an exception may be thrown, the `throws` keyword is used in a method definition, along with a list of all checked exceptions that might be thrown.

Runtime exceptions are of type `RuntimeException` (or one of its subclasses). These exceptions are a special case because they do not need to be handled or declared, and thus are known as "unchecked" exceptions. Errors are of type `java.lang.Error` or its subclasses, and like runtime exceptions, they do not need to be handled or declared. Checked exceptions include any exception types that are not of type `RuntimeException` or `Error`. If your code fails either to handle a checked exception or declare that it is thrown, your code won't compile. But with unchecked exceptions or objects of type `Error`, it doesn't matter to the compiler whether you declare them or handle them, do nothing about them, or do some combination of declaring and handling. In other words, you're free to declare them and handle them, but the compiler won't care one way or the other. It's not good practice to handle an `Error`, though, because you can rarely recover from one.

Finally, remember that exceptions can be generated by the JVM or by a programmer.

✓ TWO-MINUTE DRILL

Here are some of the key points from each certification objective in this chapter. You might want to loop through them several times.

Writing Code Using if and switch Statements (OCA Objectives 3.3 and 3.4)

- ☐ The only legal expression in an `if` statement is a `boolean` expression—in other words, an expression that resolves to a `boolean` or a `Boolean` reference.
- ☐ Watch out for `boolean` assignments (=) that can be mistaken for `boolean` equality (==) tests:

```
boolean x = false;
if (x = true) { } // an assignment, so x will always be true!
```

- ☐ Curly braces are optional for `if` blocks that have only one conditional statement. But watch out for misleading indentations.
- ☐ `switch` statements can evaluate only to enums or the `byte`, `short`, `int`, `char`, and, as of Java 7, `String` data types. You can't say this:

```
long s = 30;
switch(s) { }
```

- ☐ The `case` constant must be a literal or a compile-time constant, including an enum or a `String`. You cannot have a case that includes a nonfinal variable or a range of values.
- ☐ If the condition in a `switch` statement matches a `case` constant, execution will run through all code in the `switch` following the matching `case` statement until a `break` statement or the end of the `switch` statement is encountered. In other words, the matching `case` is just the entry point into the `case` block, but unless there's a `break` statement, the matching `case` is not the only `case` code that runs.
- ☐ The `default` keyword should be used in a `switch` statement if you want to run some code when none of the `case` values match the conditional value.

- ☐ The `default` block can be located anywhere in the `switch` block, so if no preceding `case` matches, the `default` block will be entered; if the `default` does not contain a `break`, then code will continue to execute (fall-through) to the end of the `switch` or until the `break` statement is encountered.

Writing Code Using Loops (OCA Objectives 5.1, 5.2, 5.3, and 5.4)

- ☐ A basic `for` statement has three parts: declaration and/or initialization, boolean evaluation, and the iteration expression.
- ☐ If a variable is incremented or evaluated within a basic `for` loop, it must be declared before the loop or within the `for` loop declaration.
- ☐ A variable declared (not just initialized) within the basic `for` loop declaration cannot be accessed outside the `for` loop—in other words, code below the `for` loop won't be able to use the variable.
- ☐ You can initialize more than one variable of the same type in the first part of the basic `for` loop declaration; each initialization must be comma separated.
- ☐ An enhanced `for` statement (new as of Java 5) has two parts: the *declaration* and the *expression*. It is used only to loop through arrays or collections.
- ☐ With an enhanced `for`, the *expression* is the array or collection through which you want to loop.
- ☐ With an enhanced `for`, the *declaration* is the block variable, whose type is compatible with the elements of the array or collection, and that variable contains the value of the element for the given iteration.
- ☐ Unlike with C, you cannot use a number or anything that does not evaluate to a `boolean` value as a condition for an `if` statement or looping construct. You can't, for example, say `if (x)`, unless `x` is a `boolean` variable.
- ☐ The do loop will **always** enter the body of the loop at least once.

Using break and continue (OCA Objective 5.5)

- ☐ An unlabeled `break` statement will cause the current iteration of the innermost loop to stop and the line of code following the loop to run.
- ☐ An unlabeled `continue` statement will cause the current iteration of the innermost loop to stop, the condition of that loop to be checked, and if the condition is met, the loop to run again.
- ☐ If the `break` statement or the `continue` statement is labeled, it will cause a similar action to occur on the labeled loop, not the innermost loop.

Handling Exceptions (OCA Objectives 8.1, 8.2, 8.3, 8.4, and 8.5)

- ☐ Some of the benefits of Java's exception-handling features include organized error-handling code, easy error detection, keeping exception-handling code separate from other code, and the ability to reuse exception-handling code for a range of issues.
- ☐ Exceptions come in two flavors: checked and unchecked.
- ☐ Checked exceptions include all subtypes of `Exception`, excluding classes that extend `RuntimeException`.
- ☐ Checked exceptions are subject to the handle or declare rule; any method that might throw a checked exception (including methods that invoke methods that can throw a checked exception) must either declare the exception using `throws` or handle the exception with an appropriate `try/catch`.
- ☐ Subtypes of `Error` or `RuntimeException` are unchecked, so the compiler doesn't enforce the handle or declare rule. You're free to handle them or to declare them, but the compiler doesn't care one way or the other.
- ☐ A `finally` block will always be invoked, regardless of whether an exception is thrown or caught in its `try/catch`.
- ☐ The only exception to the `finally`-will-always-be-called rule is that a `finally` will not be invoked if the JVM shuts down. That could happen if code from the `try` or `catch` blocks calls `System.exit()`.
- ☐ Just because `finally` is invoked does not mean it will complete. Code in the `finally` block could itself raise an exception or issue a `System.exit()`.
- ☐ Uncaught exceptions propagate back through the call stack, starting from the method where the exception is thrown and ending with either the first method that has a corresponding catch for that exception type or a JVM shutdown (which happens if the exception gets to `main()` and `main()` is "ducking" the exception by declaring it).
- ☐ You can almost always create your own exceptions by extending `Exception` or one of its checked exception subtypes. Such an exception will then be considered a checked exception by the compiler. (In other words, it's rare to extend `RuntimeException`.)
- ☐ All `catch` blocks must be ordered from most specific to most general. If you have a `catch` clause for both `IOException` and `Exception`, you must put the `catch` for `IOException` first in your code. Otherwise, the `IOException` would be caught by `catch(Exception e)`, because a `catch` argument can catch the specified exception or any of its subtypes!
- ☐ Some exceptions are created by programmers and some by the JVM.

SELF TEST

1. Given that `toLowerCase()` is an aptly named `String` method that returns a `String`, and given the code:

```
public class Flipper {
  public static void main(String[] args) {
    String o = "-";
    switch("RED".toLowerCase()) {
      case "yellow":
        o += "y";
      case "red":
        o += "r";
      case "green":
        o += "g";
    }
    System.out.println(o);
  }
}
```

What is the result?

A. -

B. -r

C. -rg

D. Compilation fails

E. An exception is thrown at runtime

2. Given:

```
class Plane {
  static String s = "-";
  public static void main(String[] args) {
    new Plane().s1();
    System.out.println(s);
  }
  void s1() {
    try { s2(); }
    catch (Exception e) { s += "c"; }
  }
  void s2() throws Exception  {
    s3();  s += "2";
    s3();  s += "2b";
  }
  void s3() throws Exception {
    throw new Exception();
  }
}
```

What is the result?

A. `-`

B. `-c`

C. `-c2`

D. `-2c`

E. `-c22b`

F. `-2c2b`

G. `-2c2bc`

H. Compilation fails

3. Given:

```
try { int x = Integer.parseInt("two"); }
```

Which could be used to create an appropriate `catch` block? (Choose all that apply.)

A. `ClassCastException`

B. `IllegalStateException`

C. `NumberFormatException`

D. `IllegalArgumentException`

E. `ExceptionInInitializerError`

F. `ArrayIndexOutOfBoundsException`

4. Given:

```
public class Flip2 {
  public static void main(String[] args) {
    String o = "-";
    String[] sa = new String[4];
    for(int i = 0; i < args.length; i++)
      sa[i] = args[i];
    for(String n: sa) {
      switch(n.toLowerCase()) {
        case "yellow": o += "y";
        case "red":    o += "r";
        case "green":  o += "g";
      }
    }
    System.out.print(o);
  }
}
```

And given the command-line invocation:

```
Java Flip2 RED Green YeLLow
```

Which are true? (Choose all that apply.)

A. The string `rgy` will appear somewhere in the output

B. The string `rgg` will appear somewhere in the output

C. The string `gyr` will appear somewhere in the output

D. Compilation fails

E. An exception is thrown at runtime

5. Given:

```
1. class Loopy {
2.   public static void main(String[] args) {
3.     int[] x = {7,6,5,4,3,2,1};
4.     // insert code here
5.       System.out.print(y + " ");
6.     }
7.   }
8. }
```

Which, inserted independently at line 4, compiles? (Choose all that apply.)

A. `for(int y : x) {`

B. `for(x : int y) {`

C. `int y = 0; for(y : x) {`

D. `for(int y=0, z=0; z<x.length; z++) { y = x[z];`

E. `for(int y=0, int z=0; z<x.length; z++) { y = x[z];`

F. `int y = 0; for(int z=0; z<x.length; z++) { y = x[z];`

6. Given:

```
class Emu {
  static String s = "-";
  public static void main(String[] args) {
    try {
      throw new Exception();
    } catch (Exception e) {
      try {
        try { throw new Exception();
        } catch (Exception ex) { s += "ic "; }
        throw new Exception(); }
      catch (Exception x) { s += "mc "; }
      finally { s += "mf "; }
    } finally { s += "of "; }
    System.out.println(s);
} }
```

What is the result?

A. `-ic of`

B. `-mf of`

C. `-mc mf`

D. `-ic mf of`

E. `-ic mc mf of`

F. `-ic mc of mf`

G. Compilation fails

7. Given:

```
3. class SubException extends Exception { }
4. class SubSubException extends SubException { }
5.
6. public class CC { void doStuff() throws SubException { } }
7.
8. class CC2 extends CC { void doStuff() throws SubSubException { } }
9.
10. class CC3 extends CC { void doStuff() throws Exception { } }
11.
12. class CC4 extends CC { void doStuff(int x) throws Exception { } }
13.
14. class CC5 extends CC {  void doStuff()  { } }
```

What is the result? (Choose all that apply.)

A. Compilation succeeds

B. Compilation fails due to an error on line 8

C. Compilation fails due to an error on line 10

D. Compilation fails due to an error on line 12

E. Compilation fails due to an error on line 14

8. Given:

```
public class Ebb {
  static int x = 7;
  public static void main(String[] args) {
    String s = "";
    for(int y = 0; y < 3; y++) {
      x++;
      switch(x) {
        case 8: s += "8 ";
        case 9: s += "9 ";
        case 10: { s+= "10 "; break; }
        default: s += "d ";
```

```
            case 13: s+= "13 ";
          }
        }
        System.out.println(s);
    }
    static { x++; }
}
```

What is the result?

A. `9 10 d`

B. `8 9 10 d`

C. `9 10 10 d`

D. `9 10 10 d 13`

E. `8 9 10 10 d 13`

F. `8 9 10 9 10 10 d 13`

G. Compilation fails

9. Given:

```
 3. class Infinity { }
 4. public class Beyond extends Infinity {
 5.   static Integer i;
 6.   public static void main(String[] args) {
 7.     int sw = (int)(Math.random() * 3);
 8.     switch(sw) {
 9.       case 0: {  for(int x = 10; x > 5; x++)
10.                    if(x > 10000000) x = 10;
11.                  break; }
12.       case 1: {  int y = 7 * i;  break;  }
13.       case 2: {  Infinity inf = new Beyond();
14.                  Beyond b = (Beyond)inf;  }
15.     }
16.   }
17. }
```

And given that line 7 will assign the value 0, 1, or 2 to `sw`, which are true? (Choose all that apply.)

A. Compilation fails

B. A `ClassCastException` might be thrown

C. A `StackOverflowError` might be thrown

D. A `NullPointerException` might be thrown

E. An `IllegalStateException` might be thrown

F. The program might hang without ever completing

G. The program will always complete without exception

10. Given:

```
public class Circles {
  public static void main(String[] args) {
    int[] ia = {1,3,5,7,9};
    for(int x : ia) {
      for(int j = 0; j < 3; j++) {
        if(x > 4 && x < 8) continue;
        System.out.print(" " + x);
        if(j == 1) break;
        continue;
      }
      continue;
    }
  }
}
```

What is the result?

A. `1 3 9`

B. `5 5 7 7`

C. `1 3 3 9 9`

D. `1 1 3 3 9 9`

E. `1 1 1 3 3 3 9 9 9`

F. Compilation fails

11. Given:

```
public class OverAndOver {
  static String s = "";
  public static void main(String[] args) {
    try {
      s += "1";
      throw new Exception();
    } catch (Exception e) { s += "2";
    } finally { s += "3"; doStuff(); s += "4";
    }
    System.out.println(s);
  }
  static void doStuff() { int x = 0; int y = 7/x; }
}
```

What is the result?

A. `12`

B. `13`

C. `123`

D. `1234`

E. Compilation fails
F. `123` followed by an exception
G. `1234` followed by an exception
H. An exception is thrown with no other output

12. Given:

```
public class Wind {
  public static void main(String[] args) {
    foreach:
    for(int j=0; j<5; j++) {
      for(int k=0; k< 3; k++) {
        System.out.print(" " + j);
        if(j==3 && k==1) break foreach;
        if(j==0 || j==2) break;
      }
    }
  }
}
```

What is the result?

A. `0 1 2 3`
B. `1 1 1 3 3`
C. `0 1 1 1 2 3 3`
D. `1 1 1 3 3 4 4 4`
E. `0 1 1 1 2 3 3 4 4 4`
F. Compilation fails

13. Given:

```
public class Gotcha {
  public static void main(String[] args) {
    // insert code here

  }
  void go() {
    go();
  }
}
```

And given the following three code fragments:

```
I.   new Gotcha().go();

II.  try { new Gotcha().go(); }
     catch (Error e) { System.out.println("ouch"); }

III. try { new Gotcha().go(); }
     catch (Exception e) { System.out.println("ouch"); }
```

When fragments I–III are added, independently, at line 5, which are true? (Choose all that apply.)

A. Some will not compile
B. They will all compile
C. All will complete normally
D. None will complete normally
E. Only one will complete normally
F. Two of them will complete normally

14. Given the code snippet:

```
String s = "bob";
String[] sa = {"a", "bob"};
final String s2 = "bob";
StringBuilder sb = new StringBuilder("bob");

// switch(sa[1]) {              // line 1
// switch("b" + "ob") {         // line 2
// switch(sb.toString()) {      // line 3

// case "ann":    ;             // line 4
// case s:        ;             // line 5
// case s2:       ;             // line 6
}
```

And given that the numbered lines will all be tested by uncommenting one `switch` statement and one `case` statement together, which line(s) will FAIL to compile? (Choose all that apply.)

A. line 1
B. line 2
C. line 3
D. line 4
E. line 5
F. line 6
G. All six lines of code will compile

15. Given that `IOException` is in the `java.io` package and given:

```
public class Frisbee {
  // insert code here
    int x = 0;
    System.out.println(7/x);
  }
}
```

And given the following four code fragments:

```
I.   public static void main(String[] args) {
II.  public static void main(String[] args) throws Exception {
III. public static void main(String[] args) throws IOException {
IV.  public static void main(String[] args) throws RuntimeException {
```

If the four fragments are inserted independently at line 2, which are true? (Choose all that apply.)

A. All four will compile and execute without exception
B. All four will compile and execute and throw an exception
C. Some, but not all, will compile and execute without exception
D. Some, but not all, will compile and execute and throw an exception
E. When considering fragments II, III, and IV, of those that will compile, adding a `try/catch` block around line 4 will cause compilation to fail

16. Given:

```
 2. class MyException extends Exception { }
 3. class Tire {
 4.   void doStuff() { }
 5. }
 6. public class Retread extends Tire {
 7.   public static void main(String[] args) {
 8.     new Retread().doStuff();
 9.   }
10.   // insert code here
11.     System.out.println(7/0);
12.   }
13. }
```

And given the following four code fragments:

```
I.   void doStuff() {
II.  void doStuff() throws MyException {
III. void doStuff() throws RuntimeException {
IV.  void doStuff() throws ArithmeticException {
```

When fragments I–IV are added, independently, at line 10, which are true? (Choose all that apply.)

A. None will compile
B. They will all compile
C. Some, but not all, will compile
D. All those that compile will throw an exception at runtime
E. None of those that compile will throw an exception at runtime
F. Only some of those that compile will throw an exception at runtime

SELF TEST ANSWERS

1. ☑ **C** is correct. As of Java 7 it's legal to switch on a String, and remember that switches use "entry point" logic.

☒ **A, B, D,** and **E** are incorrect based on the above. (OCA Objective 3.4)

2. ☑ **B** is correct. Once `s3()` throws the exception to `s2()`, `s2()` throws it to `s1()`, and no more of `s2()`'s code will be executed.

☒ **A, C, D, E, F, G,** and **H** are incorrect based on the above. (OCA Objectives 8.2 and 8.4)

3. ☑ **C** and **D** are correct. `Integer.parseInt` can throw a `NumberFormatException`, and `IllegalArgumentException` is its superclass (that is, a broader exception).

☒ **A, B, E,** and **F** are not in `NumberFormatException`'s class hierarchy. (OCA Objective 8.5)

4. ☑ **E** is correct. As of Java 7 the syntax is legal. The `sa[]` array receives only three arguments from the command line, so on the last iteration through `sa[]`, a `NullPointerException` is thrown.

☒ **A, B, C,** and **D** are incorrect based on the above. (OCA Objectives 1.3, 5.2, and 8.5)

5. ☑ **A, D,** and **F** are correct. **A** is an example of the enhanced `for` loop. **D** and **F** are examples of the basic `for` loop.

☒ **B, C,** and **E** are incorrect. **B** is incorrect because its operands are swapped. **C** is incorrect because the enhanced `for` must declare its first operand. **E** is incorrect syntax to declare two variables in a `for` statement. (OCA Objective 5.2)

6. ☑ **E** is correct. There is no problem nesting `try/catch` blocks. As is normal, when an exception is thrown, the code in the `catch` block runs, and then the code in the `finally` block runs.

☒ **A, B, C, D,** and **F** are incorrect based on the above. (OCA Objectives 8.2 and 8.4)

7. ☑ **C** is correct. An overriding method cannot throw a broader exception than the method it's overriding. Class CC4's method is an overload, not an override.

☒ **A, B, D,** and **E** are incorrect based on the above. (OCA Objectives 8.2 and 8.4)

8. ☑ **D** is correct. Did you catch the static initializer block? Remember that switches work on "fall-through" logic and that fall-through logic also applies to the default case, which is used when no other case matches.

☒ **A, B, C, E, F,** and **G** are incorrect based on the above. (OCA Objective 3.4)

9. ☑ **D** and **F** are correct. Because `i` was not initialized, case 1 will throw a `NullPointerException`. Case 0 will initiate an endless loop, not a stack overflow. Case 2's downcast will *not* cause an exception.

☒ **A, B, C, E,** and **G** are incorrect based on the above. (OCA Objectives 3.4 and 8.5)

10. ☑ **D** is correct. The basic rule for unlabeled `continue` statements is that the current iteration stops early and execution jumps to the next iteration. The last two `continue` statements are redundant!
☒ **A, B, C, E,** and **F** are incorrect based on the above. (OCA Objectives 5.2 and 5.5)

11. ☑ **H** is correct. It's true that the value of `String s` is `123` at the time that the divide-by-zero exception is thrown, but `finally()` is *not* guaranteed to complete, and in this case `finally()` never completes, so the `System.out.println` (S.O.P) never executes.
☒ **A, B, C, D, E, F,** and **G** are incorrect based on the above. (OCA Objectives 8.2 and 8.5)

12. ☑ **C** is correct. A `break` breaks out of the current innermost loop and carries on. A labeled `break` breaks out of and terminates the labeled loops.
☒ **A, B, D, E,** and **F** are incorrect based on the above. (OCA Objectives 5.2 and 5.5)

13. ☑ **B** and **E** are correct. First off, `go()` is a badly designed recursive method, guaranteed to cause a `StackOverflowError`. Since `Exception` is not a superclass of `Error`, catching an `Exception` will not help handle an `Error`, so fragment III will not complete normally. Only fragment II will catch the `Error`.
☒ **A, C, D,** and **F** are incorrect based on the above. (OCA Objectives 8.1, 8.2, and 8.4)

14. ☑ **E** is correct. A `switch's cases` must be compile-time constants or `enum` values.
☒ **A, B, C, D, F,** and **G** are incorrect based on the above. (OCA Objective 3.4)

15. ☑ **D** is correct. This is kind of sneaky, but remember that we're trying to toughen you up for the real exam. If you're going to throw an `IOException`, you have to import the java.io package or declare the exception with a fully qualified name.
☒ **A, B, C,** and **E** are incorrect. **A, B,** and **C** are incorrect based on the above. **E** is incorrect because it's okay both to handle and declare an exception. (OCA Objectives 8.2 and 8.5)

16. ☑ **C** and **D** are correct. An overriding method cannot throw checked exceptions that are broader than those thrown by the overridden method. However, an overriding method *can* throw `RuntimeExceptions` not thrown by the overridden method.
☒ **A, B, E,** and **F** are incorrect based on the above. (OCA Objective 8.1)

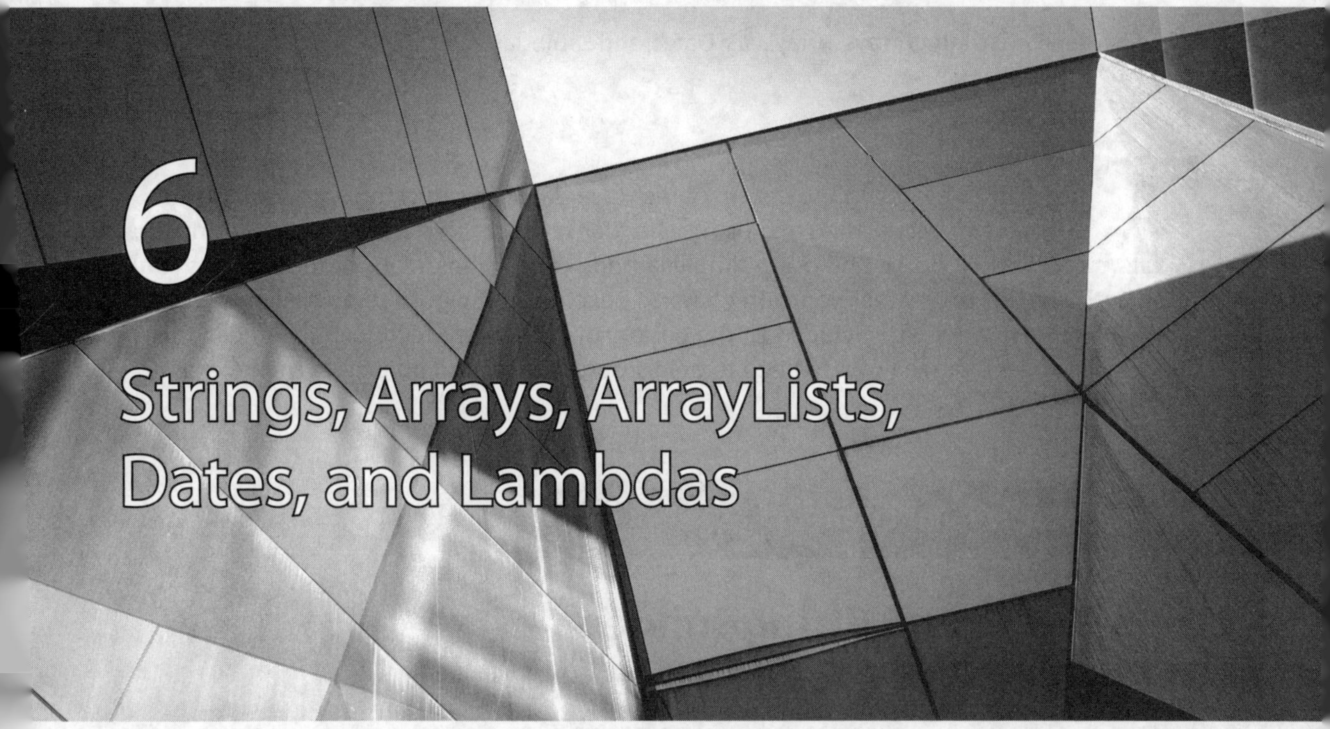

6 Strings, Arrays, ArrayLists, Dates, and Lambdas

CERTIFICATION OBJECTIVES

- Create and Manipulate Strings
- Manipulate Data Using the StringBuilder Class and Its Methods
- Create and Use Calendar Data
- Declare, Instantiate, Initialize, and Use a One-Dimensional Array
- Declare, Instantiate, Initialize, and Use a Multidimensional Array
- Declare and Use an ArrayList
- Use Wrapper Classes
- Use Encapsulation for Reference Variables
- Use Simple Lambda Expressions

✓ Two-Minute Drill

Q&A Self Test

This chapter focuses on the exam objectives related to searching, formatting, and parsing strings; creating and using calendar-related objects; creating and using arrays and `ArrayLists`; and using simple lambda expressions. Many of these topics could fill an entire book. Fortunately, you won't have to become a total guru to do well on the exam. The exam team intended to include just the basic aspects of these technologies, and in this chapter, we cover *more* than you'll need to get through the related objectives on the exam.

CERTIFICATION OBJECTIVE

Using String and StringBuilder (OCA Objectives 9.2 and 9.1)

9.2 Creating and manipulating Strings.

9.1 Manipulate data using the `StringBuilder` class and its methods.

Everything you needed to know about strings in the older OCJP exams you'll need to know for the OCA 8 exam. Closely related to the `String` class are the `StringBuilder` class and the almost identical `StringBuffer` class. (For the exam, the only thing you need to know about the `StringBuffer` class is that it has exactly the same methods as the `StringBuilder` class, but `StringBuilder` is faster because its methods aren't synchronized.) Both classes, `StringBuilder` and `StringBuffer`, give you `String`-like objects and ways to manipulate them, with the important difference being that these objects are mutable.

The String Class

This section covers the `String` class, and the key concept for you to understand is that once a `String` object is created, it can never be changed. So, then, what is happening when a `String` object seems to be changing? Let's find out.

Strings Are Immutable Objects

We'll start with a little background information about strings. You may not need this for the test, but a little context will help. Handling "strings" of characters is a fundamental aspect of most programming languages. In Java, each character in a string is a 16-bit Unicode character. Because Unicode characters are 16 bits (not the skimpy 7 or 8 bits that ASCII provides), a rich, international set of characters is easily represented in Unicode.

In Java, strings are objects. As with other objects, you can create an instance of a string with the `new` keyword, as follows:

```
String s = new String();
```

This line of code creates a new object of class `String` and assigns it to the reference variable `s`.

So far, `String` objects seem just like other objects. Now, let's give the string a value:

```
s = "abcdef";
```

(As you'll find out shortly, these two lines of code aren't quite what they seem, so stay tuned.)

It turns out the `String` class has about a zillion constructors, so you can use a more efficient shortcut:

```
String s = new String("abcdef");
```

And this is even more concise:

```
String s = "abcdef";
```

There are some subtle differences between these options that we'll discuss later, but what they have in common is that they all create a new `String` object, with a value of `"abcdef"`, and assign it to a reference variable `s`. Now let's say you want a second reference to the `String` object referred to by `s`:

```
String s2 = s;   //  refer s2 to the same String as s
```

So far so good. `String` objects seem to be behaving just like other objects, so what's all the fuss about? Immutability! (What the heck is immutability?) Once you have assigned a `String` a value, that value can never change—it's immutable, frozen solid, won't budge, *fini*, done. (We'll talk about why later; don't let us forget.) The good news is that although the `String` object is immutable, its reference variable is not, so to continue with our previous example, consider this:

```
s = s.concat(" more stuff");  // the concat() method 'appends'
                              // a literal to the end
```

Now, wait just a minute, didn't we just say that `String` objects were immutable? So what's all this "appending to the end of the string" talk? Excellent question: let's look at what really happened.

The Java Virtual Machine (JVM) took the value of string `s` (which was `"abcdef"`) and tacked `" more stuff"` onto the end, giving us the value `"abcdef more stuff"`. Since strings are immutable, the JVM couldn't stuff this new value into the old `String` referenced by `s`, so it created a new `String` object, gave it the value `"abcdef more stuff"`, and made `s` refer to it. At this point in our example, we have two `String` objects: the first one we created, with the value `"abcdef"`, and the second one with the value `"abcdef more stuff"`. Technically there are now three `String` objects, because the literal argument to `concat`, `" more stuff"`, is itself a new `String` object. But we have references only to `"abcdef"` (referenced by `s2`) and `"abcdef more stuff"` (referenced by `s`).

What if we didn't have the foresight or luck to create a second reference variable for the `"abcdef"` string before we called `s = s.concat(" more stuff");`? In that case, the original, unchanged string containing `"abcdef"` would still exist in memory, but it would be considered "lost." No code in our program has any way to reference it—it is lost to us. Note, however, that the original `"abcdef"` string didn't change (it can't, remember; it's immutable); only the reference variable `s` was changed so that it would refer to a different string.

Figure 6-1 shows what happens on the heap when you reassign a reference variable. Note that the dashed line indicates a deleted reference.

To review our first example:

```
String s = "abcdef";    // create a new String object, with
                        // value "abcdef", refer s to it
String s2 = s;          // create a 2nd reference variable
                        // referring to the same String

// create a new String object, with value "abcdef more stuff",
// refer s to it. (Change s's reference from the old String
// to the new String.) (Remember s2 is still referring to
// the original "abcdef" String.)

s = s.concat(" more stuff");
```

Let's look at another example:

```
String x = "Java";
x.concat(" Rules!");
System.out.println("x = " + x);  // the output is "x = Java"
```

FIGURE 6-1

`String` objects and their reference variables

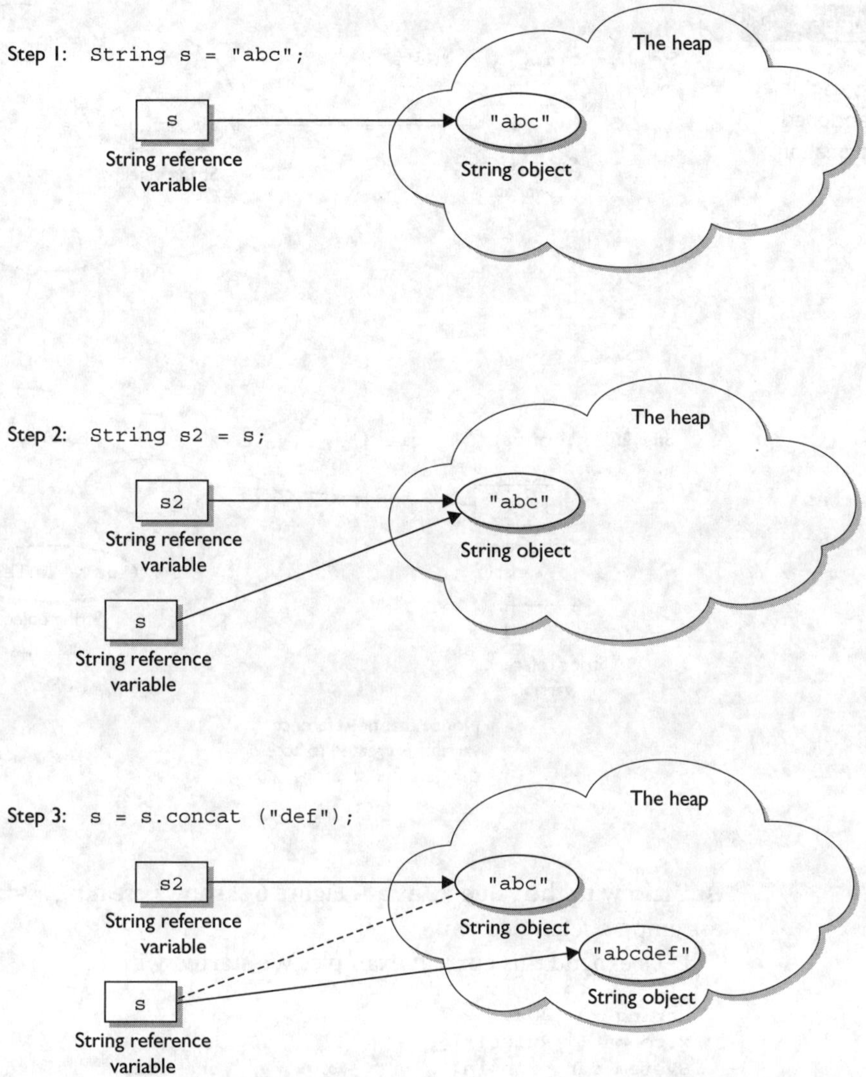

The first line is straightforward: Create a new `String` object, give it the value `"Java"`, and refer `x` to it. Next the JVM creates a second `String` object with the value `"Java Rules!"` but nothing refers to it. The second `String` object is instantly lost; you can't get to it. The reference variable `x` still refers to the original

FIGURE 6-2

A `String` object is abandoned upon creation.

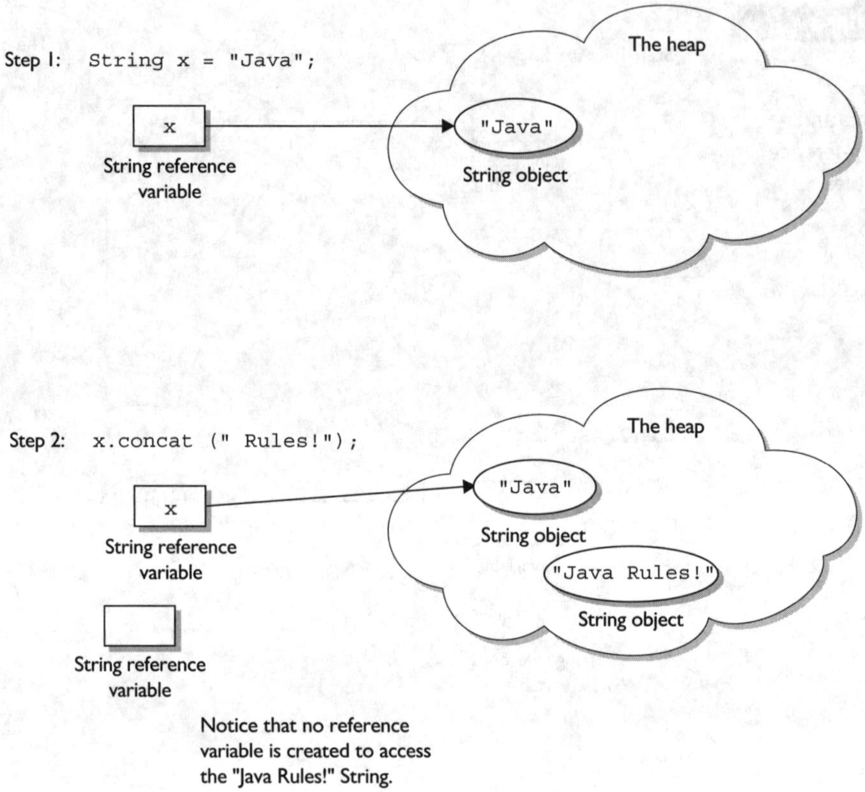

`String` with the value `"Java"`. Figure 6-2 shows creating a `String` without assigning a reference to it.

Let's expand this current example. We started with

```
String x = "Java";
x.concat(" Rules!");
System.out.println("x = " + x);   // the output is: x = Java
```

Now let's add

```
x.toUpperCase();
System.out.println("x = " + x);   // the output is still:
                                  // x = Java
```

(We actually did just create a new `String` object with the value `"JAVA"`, but it was lost, and `x` still refers to the original unchanged string `"Java"`.) How about adding this:

```
x.replace('a', 'X');
System.out.println("x = " + x);    // the output is still: x = Java
```

Can you determine what happened? The JVM created yet another new `String` object, with the value `"JXvX"`, (replacing the a's with X's), but once again this new `String` was lost, leaving `x` to refer to the original unchanged and unchangeable `String` object, with the value `"Java"`. In all these cases, we called various string methods to create a new `String` by altering an existing `String`, but we never assigned the newly created `String` to a reference variable.

But we can put a small spin on the previous example:

```
String x = "Java";
x = x.concat(" Rules!");           // assign new string to x
System.out.println("x = " + x);    // output: x = Java Rules!
```

This time, when the JVM runs the second line, a new `String` object is created with the value `"Java Rules!"`, and `x` is set to reference it. But wait…there's more—now the original `String` object, `"Java"`, has been lost, and no one is referring to it. So in both examples, we created two `String` objects and only one reference variable, so one of the two `String` objects was left out in the cold. (See Figure 6-3 for a graphic depiction of this sad story.)

Let's take this example a little further:

```
String x = "Java";
x = x.concat(" Rules!");
System.out.println("x = " + x);    // output: x = Java Rules!

x.toLowerCase();                   // no assignment, create a
                                   // new, abandoned String

System.out.println("x = " + x);    // no assignment, the output
                                   // is still: x = Java Rules!

x = x.toLowerCase();               // create a new String,
                                   // assigned to x
System.out.println("x = " + x);    // the assignment causes the
                                   // output: x = java rules!
```

FIGURE 6-3

An old `String` object being abandoned. The dashed line indicates a deleted reference.

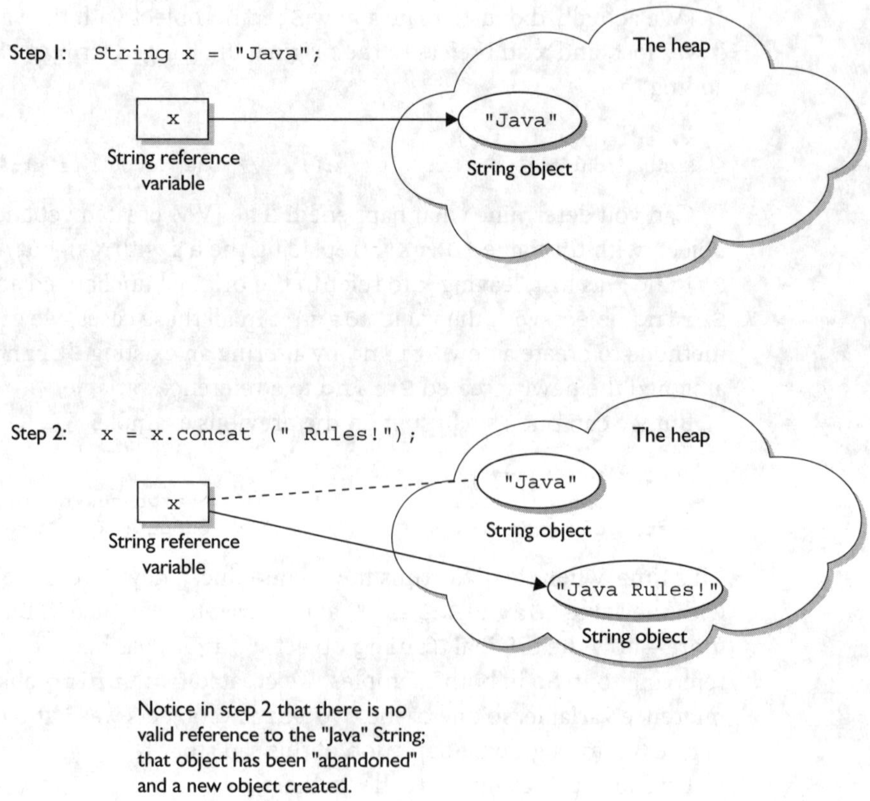

The preceding discussion contains the keys to understanding Java string immutability. If you really, really get the examples and diagrams, backward and forward, you should get 80 percent of the `String` questions on the exam correct.

We will cover more details about strings next, but make no mistake—in terms of bang for your buck, what we've already covered is by far the most important part of understanding how `String` objects work in Java.

We'll finish this section by presenting an example of the kind of devilish `String` question you might expect to see on the exam. Take the time to work it out on paper. (Hint: try to keep track of how many objects and reference variables there are, and which ones refer to which.)

```
String s1 = "spring ";
String s2 = s1 + "summer ";
s1.concat("fall ");
s2.concat(s1);
s1 += "winter ";
System.out.println(s1 + " " + s2);
```

What is the output? For extra credit, how many `String` objects and how many reference variables were created prior to the `println` statement?

Answer: The result of this code fragment is `spring winter spring summer`. There are two reference variables: `s1` and `s2`. A total of eight `String` objects were created as follows: `"spring "`, `"summer "` (lost), `"spring summer "`, `"fall "` (lost), `"spring fall "` (lost), `"spring summer spring "` (lost), `"winter "` (lost), `"spring winter "` (at this point `"spring "` is lost). Only two of the eight `String` objects are not lost in this process.

Important Facts About Strings and Memory

In this section, we'll discuss how Java handles `String` objects in memory and some of the reasons behind these behaviors.

One of the key goals of any good programming language is to make efficient use of memory. As an application grows, it's very common for string literals to occupy large amounts of a program's memory, and there is often a lot of redundancy within the universe of `String` literals for a program. To make Java more memory efficient, the JVM sets aside a special area of memory called the *String constant pool.* When the compiler encounters a `String` literal, it checks the pool to see if an identical `String` already exists. If a match is found, the reference to the new literal is directed to the existing `String`, and no new `String` literal object is created. (The existing `String` simply has an additional reference.) Now you can start to see why making `String` objects immutable is such a good idea. If several reference variables refer to the same `String` without even knowing it, it would be very bad if any of them could change the `String`'s value.

You might say, "Well that's all well and good, but what if someone overrides the `String` class functionality; couldn't that cause problems in the pool?" That's one of the main reasons that the `String` class is marked `final`. Nobody can override the behaviors of any of the `String` methods, so you can rest assured that the `String` objects you are counting on to be immutable will, in fact, be immutable.

Creating New Strings

Earlier we promised to talk more about the subtle differences between the various methods of creating a `String`. Let's look at a couple of examples of how a `String` might be created, and let's further assume that no other `String` objects exist in the pool. In this simple case, `"abc"` will go in the pool, and `s` will refer to it:

```
String s = "abc";     //  creates one String object and one
                      //  reference variable
```

In the next case, because we used the new keyword, Java will create a new `String` object in normal (nonpool) memory, and `s` will refer to it. In addition, the literal `"abc"` will be placed in the pool:

```
String s = new String("abc");  // creates two objects,
                               // and one reference variable
```

Important Methods in the String Class

The following methods are some of the more commonly used methods in the `String` class, and they are also the ones you're most likely to encounter on the exam.

- **`charAt()`** Returns the character located at the specified index
- **`concat()`** Appends one string to the end of another (+ also works)
- **`equalsIgnoreCase()`** Determines the equality of two strings, ignoring case
- **`length()`** Returns the number of characters in a string
- **`replace()`** Replaces occurrences of a character with a new character
- **`substring()`** Returns a part of a string
- **`toLowerCase()`** Returns a string, with uppercase characters converted to lowercase
- **`toString()`** Returns the value of a string
- **`toUpperCase()`** Returns a string, with lowercase characters converted to uppercase
- **`trim()`** Removes whitespace from both ends of a string

Let's look at these methods in more detail.

public char charAt(int index)

This method returns the character located at the String's specified index. Remember, String indexes are zero-based—here's an example:

```
String x = "airplane";
System.out.println( x.charAt(2) );       //  output is 'r'
```

public String concat(String s)

This method returns a string with the value of the String passed in to the method appended to the end of the String used to invoke the method—here's an example:

```
String x = "taxi";
System.out.println( x.concat(" cab") ); // output is "taxi cab"
```

The overloaded + and += operators perform functions similar to the concat() method—here's an example:

```
String x = "library";
System.out.println( x + " card");  // output is "library card"

String x = "Atlantic";
x+= " ocean";
System.out.println( x );           // output is "Atlantic ocean"
```

In the preceding "Atlantic ocean" example, notice that the value of x really did change! Remember the += operator is an assignment operator, so line 2 is really creating a new string, "Atlantic ocean", and assigning it to the x variable. After line 2 executes, the original string x was referring to, "Atlantic", is abandoned.

public boolean equalsIgnoreCase(String s)

This method returns a boolean value (true or false) depending on whether the value of the String in the argument is the same as the value of the String used to invoke the method. This method will return true even when characters in the String objects being compared have differing cases—here's an example:

```
String x = "Exit";
System.out.println( x.equalsIgnoreCase("EXIT"));   // is "true"
System.out.println( x.equalsIgnoreCase("tixe"));   // is "false"
```

public int length()

This method returns the length of the `String` used to invoke the method—here's an example:

```
String x = "01234567";
System.out.println( x.length() );      // returns "8"
```

exam watch

Arrays have an attribute (not a method) called `length`. You may encounter questions in the exam that attempt to use the `length()` method on an array or that attempt to use the `length` attribute on a `String`. Both cause compiler errors—consider these, for example:

```
String x = "test";
System.out.println( x.length );      // compiler error
```

and

```
String[] x = new String[3];
System.out.println( x.length() );    // compiler error
```

public String replace(char old, char new)

This method returns a `String` whose value is that of the `String` used to invoke the method, but updated so that any occurrence of the char in the first argument is replaced by the char in the second argument—here's an example:

```
String x = "oxoxoxox";
System.out.println( x.replace('x', 'X') );    // output is "oXoXoXoX"
```

public String substring(int begin) and public String substring(int begin, int end)

The `substring()` method is used to return a part (or substring) of the `String` used to invoke the method. The first argument represents the starting location (zero-based) of the substring. If the call has only one argument, the substring returned will include the characters at the end of the original `String`. If the call has two arguments, the substring returned will end with the character located in the *n*th position of the original `String` where *n* is the second argument. Unfortunately, the ending argument is not zero-based, so if the second argument is 7, the last character in the returned `String` will be in the original `String`'s 7 position, which is index 6 (ouch). Let's look at some examples:

```
String x = "0123456789";                    // as if by magic, the value of
each
                                            // char is the same as its
index!
System.out.println( x.substring(5) );       // output is  "56789"
System.out.println( x.substring(5, 8));     // output is "567"
```

The first example should be easy: start at index 5 and return the rest of the `String`. The second example should be read as follows: start at index 5 and return the characters up to and including the 8th position (index 7).

public String toLowerCase()

Converts all characters of a `String` to lowercase—here's an example:

```
String x = "A New Moon";
System.out.println( x.toLowerCase() );    // output is "a new moon"
```

public String toString()

This method returns the value of the `String` used to invoke the method. What? Why would you need such a seemingly "do nothing" method? All objects in Java must have a `toString()` method, which typically returns a `String` that in some meaningful way describes the object in question. In the case of a `String` object, what's a more meaningful way than the `String`'s value? For the sake of consistency, here's an example:

```
String x = "big surprise";
System.out.println( x.toString() );    // output? [reader's exercise :-) ]
```

public String toUpperCase()

Converts all characters of a `String` to uppercase—here's an example:

```
String x = "A New Moon";
System.out.println( x.toUpperCase() );  // output is "A NEW MOON"
```

public String trim()

This method returns a `String` whose value is the `String` used to invoke the method, but with any leading or trailing whitespace removed—here's an example:

```
String x = "  hi  ";
System.out.println( x + "t" );          // output is "  hi  t"
System.out.println( x.trim() + "t");    // output is "hit"
```

The StringBuilder Class

The `java.lang.StringBuilder` class should be used when you have to make a lot of modifications to strings of characters. As discussed in the previous section, `String` objects are immutable, so if you choose to do a lot of manipulations with `String` objects, you will end up with a lot of abandoned `String` objects in the `String` pool. (Even in these days of gigabytes of RAM, it's not a good idea to waste precious memory on discarded `String` pool objects.) On the other hand, objects of type `StringBuilder` can be modified over and over again without leaving behind a great effluence of discarded `String` objects.

on the job

A common use for `StringBuilders` is file I/O when large, ever-changing streams of input are being handled by the program. In these cases, large blocks of characters are handled as units, and `StringBuilder` objects are the ideal way to handle a block of data, pass it on, and then reuse the same memory to handle the next block of data.

Prefer StringBuilder to StringBuffer

The `StringBuilder` class was added in Java 5. It has exactly the same API as the `StringBuffer` class, except `StringBuilder` is not thread-safe. In other words, its methods are not synchronized. Oracle recommends that you use `StringBuilder` instead of `StringBuffer` whenever possible, because `StringBuilder` will run faster (and perhaps jump higher). So apart from synchronization, anything we say about `StringBuilder`'s methods holds true for `StringBuffer`'s methods, and vice versa. That said, for the OCA 8 exam, `StringBuffer` is not tested.

Using StringBuilder (and This Is the Last Time We'll Say This: StringBuffer)

In the previous section, you saw how the exam might test your understanding of `String` immutability with code fragments like this:

```
String x = "abc";
x.concat("def");
System.out.println("x = " + x);      //  output is "x = abc"
```

Because no new assignment was made, the new `String` object created with the `concat()` method was abandoned instantly. You also saw examples like this:

```
String x = "abc";
x = x.concat("def");
System.out.println("x = " + x);    // output is "x = abcdef"
```

We got a nice new `String` out of the deal, but the downside is that the old `String` `"abc"` has been lost in the `String` pool, thus wasting memory. If we were using a `StringBuilder` instead of a `String`, the code would look like this:

```
StringBuilder sb = new StringBuilder("abc");
sb.append("def");
System.out.println("sb = " + sb);     // output is "sb = abcdef"
```

All of the `StringBuilder` methods we will discuss operate on the value of the `StringBuilder` object invoking the method. So a call to `sb.append("def");` is actually appending `"def"` to itself (`StringBuilder sb`). In fact, these method calls can be chained to each other—here's an example:

```
StringBuilder sb = new StringBuilder("abc");
sb.append("def").reverse().insert(3, "---");
System.out.println( sb );                   // output is  "fed---cba"
```

Notice that in each of the previous two examples, there was a single call to `new`, so in each example we weren't creating any extra objects. Each example needed only a single `StringBuilder` object to execute.

exam watch

So far we've seen `StringBuilders` being built with an argument specifying an initial value. `StringBuilders` can also be built empty, and they can also be constructed with a specific size or, more formally, a "capacity." For the exam, there are three ways to create a new `StringBuilder`:

```
1. new StringBuilder();          // default cap. = 16 chars
2. new StringBuilder("ab");    // cap. = 16 + arg's length
3. new StringBuilder(x);        // capacity = x (an integer)
```

(continued)

The two most common ways to work with `StringBuilders` is via an `append()` method or an `insert()` method. In terms of a `StringBuilder`'s capacity, there are three rules to keep in mind when appending and inserting:

- ***If an `append()` grows a `StringBuilder` past its capacity, the capacity is updated automatically.***
- ***If an `insert()` starts within a `StringBuilder`'s capacity but ends after the current capacity, the capacity is updated automatically.***
- ***If an `insert()` attempts to start at an index after the `StringBuilder`'s current length, an exception will be thrown.***

Important Methods in the StringBuilder Class

The `StringBuilder` class has a zillion methods. Following are the methods you're most likely to use in the real world and, happily, the ones you're most likely to find on the exam.

public StringBuilder append(String s)

As you've seen earlier, this method will update the value of the object that invoked the method, whether or not the returned value is assigned to a variable. Versions of this heavily overloaded method will take many different arguments, including `boolean`, `char`, `double`, `float`, `int`, `long`, and others, but the one most likely used on the exam will be a `String` argument—for example,

```
StringBuilder sb = new StringBuilder("set ");
sb.append("point");
System.out.println(sb);        // output is "set point"
StringBuilder sb2 = new StringBuilder("pi = ");
sb2.append(3.14159f);
System.out.println(sb2);       // output is  "pi = 3.14159"
```

public StringBuilder delete(int start, int end)

This method modifies the value of the `StringBuilder` object used to invoke it. The starting index of the substring to be removed is defined by the first argument (which is zero-based), and the ending index of the substring to be removed is defined by the second argument (but it is one-based)! Study the following example carefully:

```
StringBuilder sb = new StringBuilder("0123456789");
System.out.println(sb.delete(4,6));       // output is "01236789"
```

exam watch

The exam will probably test your knowledge of the difference between `String` and `StringBuilder` objects. Because `StringBuilder` objects are changeable, the following code fragment will behave differently than a similar code fragment that uses `String` objects:

```
StringBuilder sb = new StringBuilder("abc");
sb.append("def");
System.out.println( sb );
```

In this case, the output will be: `"abcdef"`

public StringBuilder insert(int offset, String s)

This method updates the value of the `StringBuilder` object that invoked the method call. The `String` passed in to the second argument is inserted into the `StringBuilder` starting at the offset location represented by the first argument (the offset is zero-based). Again, other types of data can be passed in through the second argument (**`boolean`**, **`char`**, **`double`**, **`float`**, **`int`**, **`long`**, and so on), but the `String` argument is the one you're most likely to see:

```
StringBuilder sb = new StringBuilder("01234567");
sb.insert(4, "---");
System.out.println( sb );          //  output is  "0123---4567"
```

public StringBuilder reverse()

This method updates the value of the `StringBuilder` object that invoked the method call. When invoked, the characters in the `StringBuilder` are reversed—the first character becoming the last, the second becoming the second to the last, and so on:

```
StringBuilder sb = new StringBuilder("A man a plan a canal Panama");
sb.reverse();
System.out.println(sb); // output: "amanaP lanac a nalp a nam A"
```

public String toString()

This method returns the value of the `StringBuilder` object that invoked the method call as a `String`:

```
StringBuilder sb = new StringBuilder("test string");
System.out.println( sb.toString() );  // output is "test string"
```

That's it for `StringBuilders`. If you take only one thing away from this section, it's that unlike `String` objects, `StringBuilder` objects can be changed.

exam watch

Many of the exam questions covering this chapter's topics use a tricky bit of Java syntax known as "chained methods." A statement with chained methods has this general form:

```
result = method1().method2().method3();
```

In theory, any number of methods can be chained in this fashion, although typically you won't see more than three. Here's how to decipher these "handy Java shortcuts" when you encounter them:

1. ***Determine what the leftmost method call will return (let's call it x).***
2. ***Use x as the object invoking the second (from the left) method. If there are only two chained methods, the result of the second method call is the expression's result.***
3. ***If there is a third method, the result of the second method call is used to invoke the third method, whose result is the expression's result—for example,***

```
String x = "abc";
String y = x.concat("def").toUpperCase().replace('C','x');   //chained methods
System.out.println("y = " + y); // result is "y = ABxDEF"
```

Let's look at what happened. The literal `def` was concatenated to `abc`, creating a temporary, intermediate `String` (soon to be lost), with the value `abcdef`. The `toUpperCase()` method was called on this `String`, which created a new (soon to be lost) temporary `String` with the value `ABCDEF`. The `replace()` method was then called on this second `String` object, which created a final `String` with the value `ABxDEF` and referred `y` to it.

CERTIFICATION OBJECTIVE

Working with Calendar Data (OCA Objective 9.3)

9.3 Create and manipulate calendar data using the following classes: java.time .LocalDateTime, java.time.LocalDate, java.time.LocalTime, java.time.format .DateTimeFormatter, java.time.Period

Java 8 introduced a large collection (argh) of new packages related to working with calendars, dates, and times. The OCA 8 creators chose to include knowledge of a subset of these packages and classes as an exam objective. If you understand the classes included in the exam objective, you'll have a good introduction to the entire calendar/date/time topic. As we work through this section, we'll use the phrase "calendar object," which we use to refer to objects of one of the several types of calendar-related classes we're covering. So "calendar object" is a made-up umbrella term. Here's a summary of the five calendar-related classes we'll study, plus an interface that looms large:

- **`java.time.LocalDateTime`** This class is used to create immutable objects, each of which represents a specific date and time. Additionally, this class provides methods that can manipulate the values of the date/time objects created and assign them to new immutable objects. `LocalDateTime` objects contain BOTH information about days, months, and years, AND about hours, minutes, seconds, and fractions of seconds.
- **`java.time.LocalDate`** This class is used to create immutable objects, each of which represents a specific date. Additionally, this class provides methods that can manipulate the values of the date objects created and assign them to new immutable objects. `LocalDate` objects are accurate only to days. Hours, minutes, and seconds are **not** part of a `LocalDate` object.
- **`java.time.LocalTime`** This class is used to create immutable objects, each of which represents a specific time. Additionally, this class provides methods that can manipulate the values of the time objects created and assign them to new immutable objects. `LocalTime` objects refer only to hours, minutes, seconds, and fractions of seconds. Days, months, and years are **not** a part of `LocalTime` objects.

- **`java.time.format.DateTimeFormatter`** This class is used by the classes just described to format date/time objects for output and to parse input strings and convert them to date/time objects. `DateTimeFormatter` objects are also immutable.
- **`java.time.Period`** This class is used to create immutable objects that represent a period of time, for example, "one year, two months, and three days." This class works in years, months, and days. If you want to represent chunks of time in increments finer than a day (e.g., hours and minutes), you can use the `java.time.Duration` class, but `Duration` is not on the exam.
- **`java.time.temporal.TemporalAmount`** This interface is implemented by the `Period` class. When you use `Period` objects to manipulate (see the following section), calendar objects, you'll often use methods that take objects that implement `TemporalAmount`. In general, as you use the Java API more and more, it's a good idea to learn which classes implement which interfaces; this is a key way to learn how the classes in complex packages interact with each other.

Immutability

There are a couple of recurring themes in the previous definitions. First, notice that most of the calendar-related objects you'll create are **immutable**. Just like `String` objects! So when we say we're going to "manipulate" a calendar object, what we "really" mean is that we'll invoke a method on a calendar object, and we'll return a new calendar object that represents the result of **manipulating the value** of the original calendar object. But the original calendar object's value is not, and cannot, be changed. Just like `Strings`! Let's see an example:

```
LocalDate date1 = LocalDate.of(2017, 1, 31);
    Period period1 = Period.ofMonths(1);
    System.out.println(date1);
    date1.plus(period1);                    // new value is lost
    System.out.println(date1);
    LocalDate date2 = date1.plus(period1);  // new value is captured
    System.out.println(date2);
```

which produces:

```
2017-01-31
2017-01-31
2017-02-28
```

Notice that invoking the plus method on date1 doesn't change its value, but assigning the result of the plus method to date2 captures a new value. Expect exam questions that test your understanding of the immutability of calendar objects.

Factory Classes

The next thing to notice in the previous code listing is that we never used the keyword new in the code. We didn't directly invoke a constructor. None of the five classes listed in OCA 8 objective 9.3 have public constructors. Instead, for all these classes, you invoke a public static method in the class to create a new object. As you go further into your studies of OO design, you'll come across the phrases "factory pattern," "factory methods," and "factory classes." Usually, when a class has no public constructors and provides at least one public static method that can create new instances of the class, that class is called a *factory class,* and any method that is invoked to get a new instance of the class is called a *factory method.* There are many good reasons to create factory classes, most of which are beyond the scope of this book, but one of them we will discuss now. If we use the LocalDate class as an example, we find the following static methods that create and return a new instance:

```
from()
now()          // three overloaded methods exist
of()           // two overloaded methods exist
ofEpochDay()
ofYearDay()
parse()        // two overloaded methods exist
```

So we have what, about ten different ways to create a new LocalDate object? By using methods with different names (instead of using overloaded constructors), the method names themselves make the code more readable. It's clearer what variation of LocalDate we're making. As you use more and more classes from the Java API, you'll discover that the API creators use factory classes a lot.

exam watch

Whenever you see an exam question relating to dates or times, be on the lookout for the new keyword. This is your tipoff that the code won't compile:

```
LocalDateTime d1 = new LocalDateTime();  // won't compile
```

Remember the exam's date and time classes use factory methods to create new objects.

Using and Manipulating Dates and Times

Now that we know how to create new calendar-related objects, let's turn to using and manipulating them. (And you know what we mean when we say "manipulate.") The following code demonstrates some common uses and powerful features of the new Java 8 calendar-related classes:

```
import java.time.*;
import java.time.format.*;
import java.time.temporal.ChronoUnit;                    // not on the exam
                                                         // but VERY useful
public class DrWho {
  public static void main(String[] args) {
    DateTimeFormatter f =
              DateTimeFormatter.ofPattern("MMddyyyy");    // describe a format
    LocalDate bday = null;
    try {
      bday = LocalDate.parse(args[0], f);                 // verify input date
                                                          // often parse() methods
                                                          // throw exceptions!
    } catch (java.time.DateTimeException e) {
      System.out.println("bad dates Indy");
      System.exit(0);
    }
    System.out.println("your birthday is: " + bday);
    System.out.println("a " + bday.getDayOfWeek());       // useful

    Period p1 = Period.between(bday, LocalDate.now());    // very useful!

    System.out.println("you've lived for: ");
    System.out.print(p1.getDays() + " days, ");           // split up a Period
    System.out.print(p1.getMonths() + " months, ");
    System.out.println(p1.getYears() + " years");

    int yearsOld = p1.getYears();
    if(yearsOld < 0 || yearsOld > 119)
      System.out.println("Wow, are you a time lord?");

    long tDays = bday.until(LocalDate.now(),              // handy method +
                            ChronoUnit.DAYS);             // handy enum
                                                          // = powerful date math
    System.out.println("you've lived for " + tDays
                       + " days, so far");

    System.out.println("you'll reach 30,000 days on "
                       + bday.plusDays(30_000));          // date math

    LocalDate d2000 = LocalDate.of(2_000, 1, 1);          // of() is a
                                                          // commonly used
                                                          // 'factory' method
    Period p2 = Period.between(d2000, LocalDate.now());
    System.out.println("period since Y2K: " + p2);
  }
}
```

Invoking the program with a relevant birthday:

```
java 01201934
```

produces the output (when run on January 13, 2017):

```
your birthday is: 1934-01-20
a SATURDAY
you've lived for:
24 days, 11 months, 82 years
 you've lived for 30309 days, so far
 you'll reach 30000 days on 2016-03-10
 period since Y2K: P17Y12D
```

There's a lot going on here, so let's do a walk-through. First, we want users to enter their birthday in the form of *mmddyyyy*. We use a `DateTimeFormatter` object to parse the user's first argument and verify that it's a valid date of the form we're hoping for. Usually in the Java API, `parse()` methods can throw exceptions, so we have to do our parsing in a `try/catch` block.

Next, we print out the verified date and show off a bit by printing out what day of the week that date occurred on. This calculation would be quite tricky to do by hand!

Next, we create a `Period` object that represents the amount of time between the user's birthday and today, and we use various `getX()` methods to list the details of the `Period` object.

After making sure we're not dealing with a time lord, we then use the very powerful `until()` method and "day" as the unit of time to determine how many days the user has been alive. We cheated a bit here and used the `ChronoUnit` enum from the `java.time.temporal` package. (Even though `ChronoUnit` isn't on the exam, we think if you do a lot of calendar calculations, you'll end up using this enum a lot.)

Next, we add 30,000 days to the user's birthday so we can calculate on which date our user will have lived for 30,000 days. It's a short jump to seeing how these sorts of calendar calculations will be very powerful for scheduling applications, project management applications, travel planning, and so on.

Finally, we use a common factory method, `of()`, to create another date object (representing today's date), and we use that in conjunction with the very powerful `between()` method to see how long it's been since January 1, 2000, Y2K.

Formatting Dates and Times

Now let's turn to formatting dates and times using the `DateTimeFormatter` class, so your calendar objects will look all shiny when you want to include them in your program's output. For the exam, you should know the following two-step process for creating `Strings` that represent well-formatted calendar objects:

1. Use formatters and patterns from the HUGE lists provided in the `DateTimeFormatter` class to create a `DataTimeFormatter` object.
2. In the `LocalDate`, `LocalDateTime`, and `LocalTime` classes, use the `format()` method with the `DateTimeFormatter` object as the argument to create a well-formed `String`—or use the `DateTimeFormatter.format()` method with a calendar argument to create a well-formed `String`. Let's look at a few examples:

```
import java.time.*;
import java.time.format.*;
public class NiceDates {
  public static void main(String[] args) {
    DateTimeFormatter f1 =
              DateTimeFormatter.ofPattern("MMM dd, yyyy");
    DateTimeFormatter f2 =
              DateTimeFormatter.ofPattern("E MMM dd, yyyy G");
    DateTimeFormatter tf1 =
              DateTimeFormatter.ofPattern("k:m:s A a");

    LocalDate d = LocalDate.now();
    String s = d.format(f1);            // thus proving that the format()
                                        // method makes String objects
    System.out.println(s);
    System.out.println(d.format(f2));

    LocalTime t = LocalTime.now();
    System.out.println(t.format(tf1));
  }
}
```

which, when we ran this code, produced the following (your output will vary):

```
Jan 14, 2017
Sat Jan 14, 2017 AD
14:17:9 51429958 PM
```

Some of the pattern codes we used are self-evident (e.g. MMM dd yyyy), and some are fairly arbitrary like "E" for day of week or "k" for military hours. All of the codes can be found in the `DateTimeFormatter` API.

That's enough about calendars; on to arrays!

CERTIFICATION OBJECTIVE

Using Arrays (OCA Objectives 4.1 and 4.2)

4.1 Declare, instantiate, initialize, and use a one-dimensional array.
4.2 Declare, instantiate, initialize, and use a multi-dimensional array.

Arrays are objects in Java that store multiple variables of the same type. Arrays can hold either primitives or object references, but the array itself will always be an object on the heap, even if the array is declared to hold primitive elements. In other words, there is no such thing as a primitive array, but you can make an array of primitives. For this objective, you need to know three things:

- How to make an array reference variable (declare)
- How to make an array object (construct)
- How to populate the array with elements (initialize)

There are several different ways to do each of these, and you need to know about all of them for the exam.

on the job

Arrays are efficient, but most of the time you'll want to use one of the Collection types from java.util (including `HashMap`, `ArrayList`, and `TreeSet`). Collection classes offer more flexible ways to access an object (for insertion, deletion, and so on), and unlike arrays, they can expand or contract dynamically as you add or remove elements (they're really managed arrays, since they use arrays behind the scenes). There's a Collection type for a wide range of needs. Do you need a fast sort? A group of objects with no duplicates? A way to access a name/value pair? A linked list? The OCP 8 exam covers collections in more detail.

Declaring an Array

Arrays are declared by stating the type of element the array will hold, which can be an object or a primitive, followed by square brackets to the left or right of the identifier.

Declaring an array of primitives:

```
int[] key;          // brackets before name (recommended)
int key [];         // brackets after name (legal but less readable)
                    // spaces between the name and [] legal, but bad
```

Declaring an array of object references:

```
Thread[] threads;  // Recommended
Thread threads[];  // Legal but less readable
```

When declaring an array reference, you should always put the array brackets immediately after the declared type rather than after the identifier (variable name). That way, anyone reading the code can easily tell that, for example, `key` is a reference to an `int` array object and not an `int` primitive.

We can also declare multidimensional arrays, which are, in fact, arrays of arrays. This can be done in the following manner:

```
String[][][] occupantName;   // recommended
String[] managerName [];     // yucky, but legal
```

The first example is a three-dimensional array (an array of arrays of arrays) and the second is a two-dimensional array. Notice in the second example we have one square bracket before the variable name and one after. This is perfectly legal to the compiler, proving once again that just because it's legal doesn't mean it's right.

It is never legal to include the size of the array in your declaration. Yes, we know you can do that in some other languages, which is why you might see a question or two in the exam that include code similar to the following:

```
int[5] scores;    // will NOT compile
```

The preceding code won't make it past the compiler. Remember, the JVM doesn't allocate space until you actually instantiate the array object. That's when size matters.

Constructing an Array

Constructing an array means creating the array object on the heap (where all objects live)—that is, doing a `new` on the array type. To create an array object, Java must know how much space to allocate on the heap, so you must specify the size of the array at creation time. The size of the array is the number of elements the array will hold.

Constructing One-Dimensional Arrays

The most straightforward way to construct an array is to use the keyword `new` followed by the array type, with a bracket specifying how many elements of that type the array will hold. The following is an example of constructing an array of type `int`:

```
int[] testScores;           // Declares the array of ints
testScores = new int[4]; // constructs an array and assigns it
                            // to the testScores variable
```

The preceding code puts one new object on the heap—an array object holding four elements—with each element containing an `int` with a default value of 0. Think of this code as saying to the compiler, "Create an array object that will hold four `ints`, and assign it to the reference variable named `testScores`. Also, go ahead and set each `int` element to zero. Thanks." (The compiler appreciates good manners.)

Figure 6-4 shows the `testScores` array on the heap, after construction.

FIGURE 6-4

A one-dimensional array on the heap

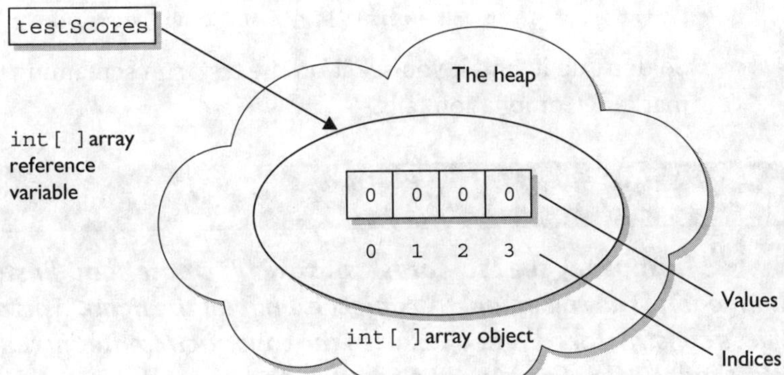

You can also declare and construct an array in one statement, as follows:

```
int[] testScores = new int[4];
```

This single statement produces the same result as the two previous statements.

Arrays of object types can be constructed in the same way:

```
Thread[] threads = new Thread[5];     // no Thread objects created!
                                      // one Thread array created
```

Remember that, despite how the code appears, the `Thread` constructor is not being invoked. We're not creating a `Thread` instance, but rather a single `Thread` array object. After the preceding statement, there are still no actual `Thread` objects!

exam watch

Think carefully about how many objects are on the heap after a code statement or block executes. The exam will expect you to know, for example, that the preceding code produces just one object (the array assigned to the reference variable named `threads`). The single object referenced by `threads` holds five `Thread` reference variables, but no `Thread` objects have been created or assigned to those references.

Remember, arrays must always be given a size at the time they are constructed. The JVM needs the size to allocate the appropriate space on the heap for the new array object. It is never legal, for example, to do the following:

```
int[] carList = new int[]; // Will not compile; needs a size
```

So don't do it, and if you see it on the test, run screaming toward the nearest answer marked "Compilation fails."

exam watch

You may see the words "construct," "create," and "instantiate" used interchangeably. They all mean, "An object is built on the heap." This also implies that the object's constructor runs as a result of the construct/create/instantiate code. You can say with certainty, for example, that any code that uses the keyword `new` will (if it runs successfully) cause the class constructor and all superclass constructors to run.

In addition to being constructed with `new`, arrays can be created using a kind of syntax shorthand that creates the array while simultaneously initializing the array elements to values supplied in code (as opposed to default values). We'll look at that in the next section. For now, understand that because of these syntax shortcuts, objects can still be created even without you ever using or seeing the keyword `new`.

Constructing Multidimensional Arrays

Multidimensional arrays, remember, are simply arrays of arrays. So a two-dimensional array of type `int` is really an object of type `int` array (`int []`), with each element in that array holding a reference to another `int` array. The second dimension holds the actual `int` primitives.

The following code declares and constructs a two-dimensional array of type `int`:

```
int[][] myArray = new int[3][];
```

Notice that only the first brackets are given a size. That's acceptable in Java because the JVM needs to know only the size of the object assigned to the variable `myArray`.

Figure 6-5 shows how a two-dimensional `int` array works on the heap.

FIGURE 6-5

A two-dimensional array on the heap

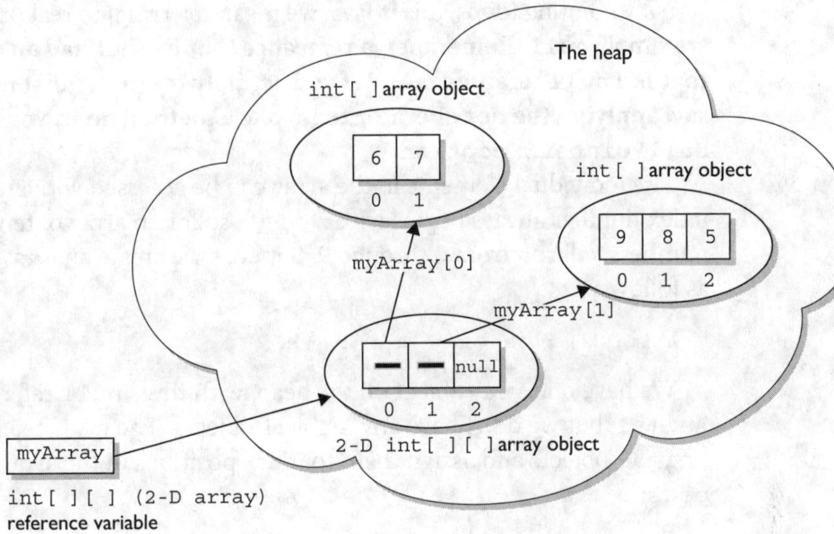

Picture demonstrates the result of the following code:

```
int[ ][ ] myArray = new int[3][ ];
myArray[0] = new int[2];
myArray[0][0] = 6;
myArray[0][1] = 7;
myArray[1] = new int[3];
myArray[1][0] = 9;
myArray[1][1] = 8;
myArray[1][2] = 5;
```

Initializing an Array

Initializing an array means putting things into it. The "things" in the array are the array's elements, and they're either primitive values (2, x, `false`, and so on) or objects referred to by the reference variables in the array. If you have an array of objects (as opposed to primitives), the array doesn't actually hold the objects—just as any other nonprimitive variable never actually holds the object—but instead holds a *reference* to the object. But we talk about arrays as, for example, "an array of five strings," even though what we really mean is "an array of five references to `String` objects." Then the big question becomes whether those references are actually pointing (oops, this is Java, we mean referring) to real `String` objects or are simply `null`. **Remember, a reference that has not had an object assigned to it is a `null` reference. And if you actually try to use that `null` reference by, say, applying the dot operator to invoke a method on it, you'll get the infamous `NullPointerException`.**

The individual elements in the array can be accessed with an index number. The index number always begins with zero (0), so for an array of ten objects, the index numbers will run from 0 through 9. Suppose we create an array of three `Animals` as follows:

```
Animal [] pets = new Animal[3];
```

We have one array object on the heap, with three `null` references of type `Animal`, but we don't have any `Animal` objects. The next step is to create some `Animal` objects and assign them to index positions in the array referenced by `pets`:

```
pets[0] = new Animal();
pets[1] = new Animal();
pets[2] = new Animal();
```

This code puts three new `Animal` objects on the heap and assigns them to the three index positions (elements) in the `pets` array.

exam watch

Look for code that tries to access an out-of-range array index. For example, if an array has three elements, trying to access the element `[3]` will raise an `ArrayIndexOutOfBoundsException`, because in an array of three elements, the legal index values are 0, 1, and 2. You also might see an attempt to use a negative number as an array index. The following are examples of legal and illegal array access attempts. Be sure to recognize that these cause runtime exceptions and not compiler errors!

Nearly all the exam questions list both runtime exception and compiler error as possible answers:

```
int[] x = new int[5];
x[4] = 2;     // OK, the last element is at index 4
x[5] = 3;     // Runtime  exception. There is no element at index 5!

int[] z = new int[2];
int y = -3;
z[y] = 4;     // Runtime exception. y is a negative number
```

These can be hard to spot in a complex loop, but that's where you're most likely to see array index problems in exam questions.

A two-dimensional array (an array of arrays) can be initialized as follows:

```
int[][] scores = new int[3][];
// Declare and create an array (scores) holding three references
// to int arrays

scores[0] = new int[4];
// the first element in the scores array is an int array
// of four int elements

scores[1] = new int[6];
// the second element is an int array of six int elements

scores[2] = new int[1];
// the third element is an int array of one int element
```

Initializing Elements in a Loop

Array objects have a single public variable, `length`, that gives you the number of elements in the array. The last index value, then, is always one less than the `length`. For example, if the `length` of an array is 4, the index values are from 0 through 3. Often, you'll see array elements initialized in a loop, as follows:

```
Dog[] myDogs = new Dog[6]; // creates an array of 6 Dog references
for(int x = 0; x < myDogs.length; x++) {
    myDogs[x] = new Dog(); // assign a new Dog to index position x
}
```

The `length` variable tells us how many elements the array holds, but it does not tell us whether those elements have been initialized.

Declaring, Constructing, and Initializing on One Line

You can use two different array-specific syntax shortcuts both to initialize (put explicit values into an array's elements) and construct (instantiate the array object itself) in a single statement. The first is used to declare, create, and initialize in one statement, as follows:

```
1.  int x = 9;
2.  int[] dots = {6,x,8};
```

Line 2 in the preceding code does four things:

- Declares an `int` array reference variable named `dots`.
- Creates an `int` array with a length of three (three elements).
- Populates the array's elements with the values 6, 9, and 8.
- Assigns the new array object to the reference variable `dots`.

The size (length of the array) is determined by the number of comma-separated items between the curly braces. The code is functionally equivalent to the following longer code:

```
int[] dots;
dots = new int[3];
int x = 9;
dots[0] = 6;
dots[1] = x;
dots[2] = 8;
```

This begs the question, "Why would anyone use the longer way?" One reason comes to mind. You might not know—at the time you create the array—the values that will be assigned to the array's elements.

With object references rather than primitives, it works exactly the same way:

```
Dog puppy = new Dog("Frodo");
Dog[] myDogs = {puppy, new Dog("Clover"), new Dog("Aiko")};
```

The preceding code creates one Dog array, referenced by the variable myDogs, with a length of three elements. It assigns a previously created Dog object (assigned to the reference variable puppy) to the first element in the array. It also creates two new Dog objects (Clover and Aiko) and adds them to the last two Dog reference variable elements in the myDogs array. This array shortcut alone (combined with the stimulating prose) is worth the price of this book. Figure 6-6 shows the result.

FIGURE 6-6

Declaring, constructing, and initializing an array of objects

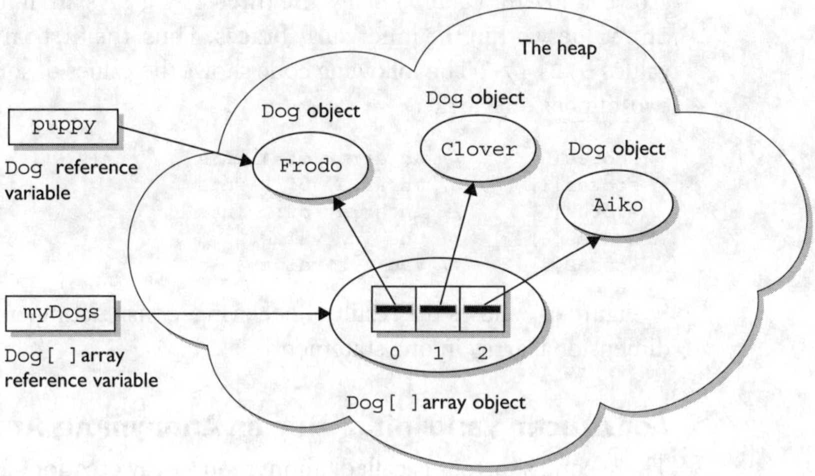

Picture demonstrates the result of the following code:

```
Dog puppy = new Dog ("Frodo");
Dog[ ] myDogs = {puppy, new Dog("Clover"), new Dog("Aiko")};
```

Four objects are created:
1 Dog object referenced by puppy and by myDogs[0]
1 Dog[ ] array referenced by myDogs
2 Dog object referenced by myDogs[1] and myDogs[2]

You can also use the shortcut syntax with multidimensional arrays, as follows:

```
int[][] scores = {{5,2,4,7}, {9,2}, {3,4}};
```

This code creates a total of four objects on the heap. First, an array of `int` arrays is constructed (the object that will be assigned to the `scores` reference variable). The `scores` array has a length of three, derived from the number of comma-separated items between the outer curly braces. Each of the three elements in the `scores` array is a reference variable to an `int` array, so the three `int` arrays are constructed and assigned to the three elements in the `scores` array.

The size of each of the three `int` arrays is derived from the number of items within the corresponding inner curly braces. For example, the first array has a length of four, the second array has a length of two, and the third array has a length of two. So far, we have four objects: one array of `int` arrays (each element is a reference to an `int` array), and three `int` arrays (each element in the three `int` arrays is an `int` value). Finally, the three `int` arrays are initialized with the actual `int` values within the inner curly braces. Thus, the first `int` array contains the values `5,2,4,7`. The following code shows the values of some of the elements in this two-dimensional array:

```
scores[0]      // an array of 4 ints
scores[1]      // an array of 2 ints
scores[2]      // an array of 2 ints
scores[0][1]   // the int value 2
scores[2][1]   // the int value 4
```

Figure 6-7 shows the result of declaring, constructing, and initializing a two-dimensional array in one statement.

Constructing and Initializing an Anonymous Array

The second shortcut is called "anonymous array creation" and can be used to construct and initialize an array and then assign the array to a previously declared array reference variable:

```
int[] testScores;
testScores = new int[] {4,7,2};
```

The preceding code creates a new `int` array with three elements; initializes the three elements with the values `4`, `7`, and `2`; and then assigns the new array to the previously declared `int` array reference variable `testScores`.

FIGURE 6-7 Declaring, constructing, and initializing a two-dimensional array

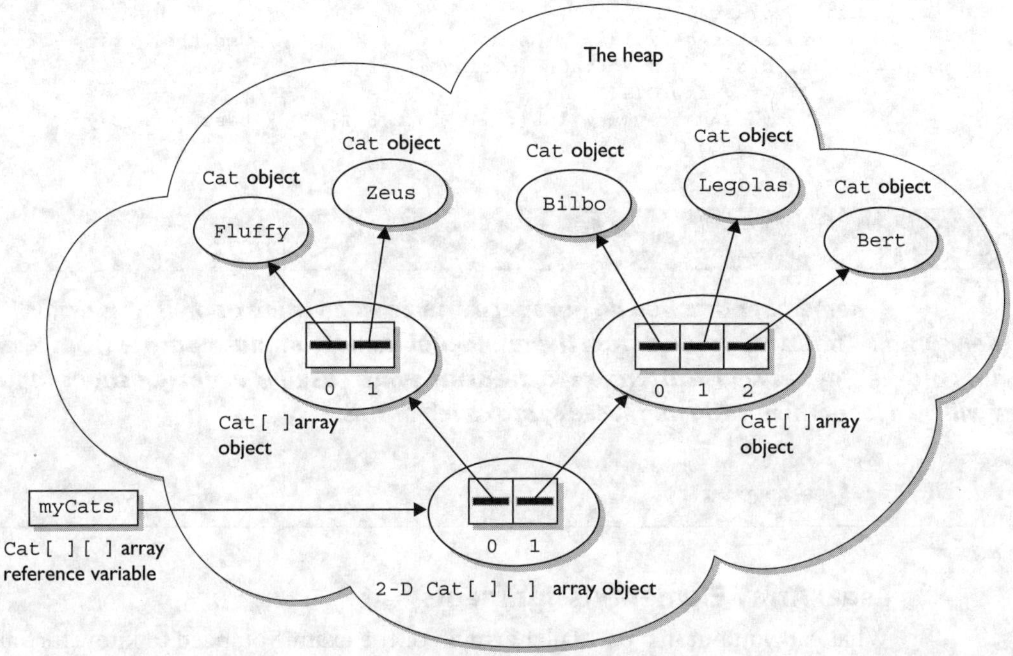

Picture demonstrates the result of the following code:

```
Cat[ ][ ] myCats = {{new Cat("Fluffy"), new Cat("Zeus")},
{new Cat("Bilbo"), new Cat("Legolas"), new Cat("Bert")}};
```

Eight objects are created:
1 2-D Cat[ ][ ] array object
2 Cat[ ] array object
5 Cat object

We call this anonymous array creation because with this syntax, you don't even need to assign the new array to anything. Maybe you're wondering, "What good is an array if you don't assign it to a reference variable?" You can use it to create a just-in-time array to use, for example, as an argument to a method that takes an array parameter.

The following code demonstrates a just-in-time array argument:

```
public class JIT {
  void takesAnArray(int[] someArray) {        // use the array
  public static void main (String [] args) {
    JIT j = new JIT();
    j.takesAnArray(new int[] {7,7,8,2,5});    // pass an array
}}
```

exam Watch

Remember that you do not specify a size when using anonymous array creation syntax. The size is derived from the number of items (comma-separated) between the curly braces. Pay very close attention to the array syntax used in exam questions (and there will be a lot of them). You might see syntax such as this:

```
new Object[3] {null, new Object(), new Object()};
  // not legal; size must not be specified
```

Legal Array Element Assignments

What can you put in a particular array? For the exam, you need to know that arrays can have only one declared type (`int[]`, `Dog[]`, `String[]`, and so on), but that doesn't necessarily mean that only objects or primitives of the declared type can be assigned to the array elements. And what about the array reference itself? What kind of array object can be assigned to a particular array reference? For the exam, you'll need to know the answers to all of these questions. And, as if by magic, we're actually covering those very same topics in the following sections. Pay attention.

Arrays of Primitives Primitive arrays can accept any value that can be promoted implicitly to the declared type of the array. For example, an `int` array can hold any value that can fit into a 32-bit `int` variable. Thus, the following code is legal:

```
int[] weightList = new int[5];
byte b = 4;
char c = 'c';
short s = 7;
weightList[0] = b;  // OK, byte is smaller than int
weightList[1] = c;  // OK, char is smaller than int
weightList[2] = s;  // OK, short is smaller than int
```

Arrays of Object References If the declared array type is a class, you can put objects of any subclass of the declared type into the array. For example, if `Subaru` is a subclass of `Car`, you can put both `Subaru` objects and `Car` objects into an array of type `Car` as follows:

```
class Car {}
class Subaru extends Car {}
class Ferrari extends Car {}
...
Car [] myCars = {new Subaru(), new Car(), new Ferrari()};
```

It helps to remember that the elements in a `Car` array are nothing more than `Car` reference variables. So anything that can be assigned to a `Car` reference variable can be legally assigned to a `Car` array element.

If the array is declared as an interface type, the array elements can refer to any instance of any class that implements the declared interface. The following code demonstrates the use of an interface as an array type:

```
interface Sporty {
  void beSporty();
}
class Ferrari extends Car implements Sporty {
  public void beSporty() {
    // implement cool sporty method in a Ferrari-specific way
  }}
class RacingFlats extends AthleticShoe implements Sporty {
  public void beSporty() {
    // implement cool sporty method in a RacingFlat-specific way
  }}
class GolfClub { }
class TestSportyThings {
  public static void main (String [] args) {
    Sporty[] sportyThings = new Sporty [3];
    sportyThings[0] = new Ferrari();      // OK, Ferrari
                                          // implements Sporty
    sportyThings[1] = new RacingFlats();  // OK, RacingFlats
                                          // implements Sporty
    sportyThings[2] = new GolfClub();     // NOT ok..

        // Not OK; GolfClub does not implement Sporty
        // I don't care what anyone says
  }}
```

The bottom line is this: any object that passes the IS-A test for the declared array type can be assigned to an element of that array.

Array Reference Assignments for One-Dimensional Arrays For the exam, you need to recognize legal and illegal assignments for array reference variables. We're not talking about references in the array (in other words, array elements), but rather references to the array object. For example, if you declare an `int` array, the reference variable you declared can be reassigned to any `int` array (of any size), but the variable cannot be reassigned to anything that is not an `int` array, including an `int` value. Remember, all arrays are objects, so an `int` array reference cannot refer to an `int` primitive. The following code demonstrates legal and illegal assignments for primitive arrays:

```
int[] splats;
int[] dats = new int[4];
char[] letters = new char[5];
splats = dats;    // OK, dats refers to an int array
splats = letters; // NOT OK, letters refers to a char array
```

It's tempting to assume that because a variable of type `byte`, `short`, or `char` can be explicitly promoted and assigned to an `int`, an array of any of those types could be assigned to an `int` array. You can't do that in Java, but it would be just like those cruel, heartless (but otherwise attractive) exam developers to put tricky array assignment questions in the exam.

Arrays that hold object references, as opposed to primitives, aren't as restrictive. Just as you can put a `Honda` object in a `Car` array (because `Honda` extends `Car`), you can assign an array of type `Honda` to a `Car` array reference variable as follows:

```
Car[] cars;
Honda[] cuteCars = new Honda[5];
cars = cuteCars;    // OK because Honda is a type of Car
Beer[] beers = new Beer [99];
cars = beers;       // NOT OK, Beer is not a type of Car
```

Apply the IS-A test to help sort the legal from the illegal. Honda IS-A Car, so a `Honda` array can be assigned to a `Car` array. Beer IS-A Car is not true; `Beer` does not extend `Car` (plus it doesn't make sense, unless you've already had too much of it).

The rules for array assignment apply to interfaces as well as classes. An array declared as an interface type can reference an array of any type that implements the interface. Remember, any object from a class implementing a particular interface will pass the IS-A (`instanceof`) test for that interface. For example, if `Box` implements `Foldable`, the following is legal:

```
Foldable[]  foldingThings;
Box[] boxThings = new Box[3];
foldingThings = boxThings;
// OK, Box implements Foldable, so Box IS-A Foldable
```

exam watch

You cannot reverse the legal assignments. A `Car` array cannot be assigned to a `Honda` array. A `Car` is not necessarily a `Honda`, so if you've declared a `Honda` array, it might blow up if you assigned a `Car` array to the `Honda` reference variable. Think about it: a `Car` array could hold a reference to a `Ferrari`, so someone who thinks they have an array of `Honda`s could suddenly find themselves with a `Ferrari`. Remember that the IS-A test can be checked in code using the `instanceof` operator.

Array Reference Assignments for Multidimensional Arrays When you assign an array to a previously declared array reference, the array you're assigning must be in the same dimension as the reference you're assigning it to. For example, a two-dimensional array of `int` arrays cannot be assigned to a regular `int` array reference, as follows:

```
int[] blots;
int[][] squeegees = new int[3][];
blots = squeegees;          // NOT OK, squeegees is a
                            // two-d array of int arrays
int[] blocks = new int[6];
blots = blocks;             // OK, blocks is an int array
```

Pay particular attention to array assignments using different dimensions. You might, for example, be asked if it's legal to assign an `int` array to the first element in an array of `int` arrays, as follows:

```
int[][]  books = new int[3][];
int[] numbers = new int[6];
int aNumber = 7;
books[0] = aNumber;      // NO, expecting an int array not an int
books[0] = numbers;      // OK, numbers is an int array
```

Figure 6-8 shows an example of legal and illegal assignments for references to an array.

FIGURE 6-8 Legal and illegal array assignments

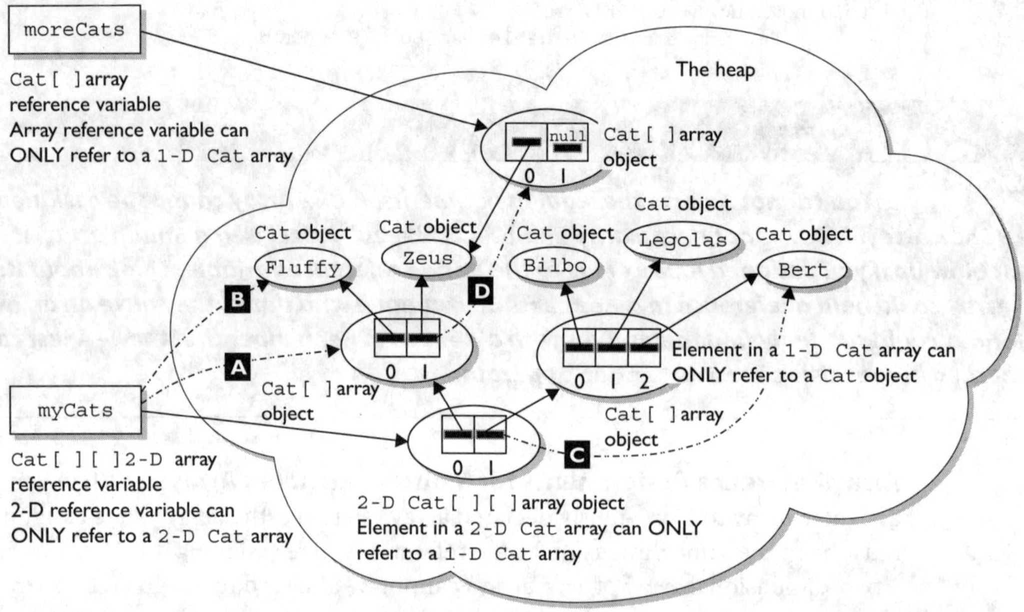

Illegal Array Reference Assignments

A `myCats = myCats[0];`
`// Can't assign a 1-D array to a 2-D array reference`

B `myCats = myCats[0][0];`
`// Can't assign a nonarray object to a 2-D array reference`

C `myCats[1] = myCats[1][2];`
`// Can't assign a nonarray object to a 1-D array reference`

D `myCats[0][1] = moreCats;`
`// Can't assign an array object to a nonarray reference`
`// myCats[0][1] can only refer to a Cat object`

KEY

→ Legal

⇢ Illegal

CERTIFICATION OBJECTIVE

Using ArrayLists and Wrappers (OCA Objectives 9.4 and 2.5)

9.3 Declare and use an ArrayList of a given type.
2.5 Develop code that uses wrapper classes such as Boolean, Double, and Integer.

Data structures are a part of almost every application you'll ever work on. The Java API provides an extensive range of classes that support common data structures such as `Lists`, `Sets`, `Maps`, *and* `Queues`. For the purpose of the OCA exam, you should remember that the classes that support these common data structures are a part of what is known as "The Collection API" (one of its many aliases). (The OCP exam covers the most common implementations of all these structures.)

When to Use ArrayLists

We've already talked about arrays. Arrays seem useful and pretty darned flexible. So why do we need more functionality than arrays provide? Consider these two situations:

- You need to be able to increase and decrease the size of your list of things.
- The order of things in your list is important and might change.

Both situations can be handled with arrays, but it's not easy....

Suppose you want to plan a vacation to Europe. You have several destinations in mind (Paris, Oslo, Rome), but you're not yet sure in what order you want to visit these cities, and as your planning progresses, you might want to add or subtract cities from your list. Let's say your first idea is to travel from north to south, so your list looks like this:
Oslo, Paris, Rome.

If we were using an array, we could start with this:

```
String[] cities = {"Oslo", "Paris", "Rome"};
```

But now imagine that you remember that you REALLY want to go to London, too! You've got two problems:

- Your cities array is already full.
- If you're going from north to south, you need to insert London before Paris.

Of course, you can figure out a way to do this. Maybe you create a second array, and you copy cities from one array to the other, and at the correct moment you add London to the second array. Doable, but difficult.

Now let's see how you could do the same thing with an `ArrayList`:

```
import java.util.*;                           // ArrayList lives in .util
public class Cities {
  public static void main(String[] args) {

    List<String> c = new ArrayList<String>(); // create an ArrayList, c
    c.add("Oslo");                            // add original cities
    c.add("Paris");
    c.add("Rome");
    int index = c.indexOf("Paris");           // find Paris' index
    System.out.println(c + " " + index);
    c.add(index, "London");                   // add London before Paris
    System.out.println(c);                    // show the contents of c
  }
}
```

The output will be something like this:

```
[Oslo, Paris, Rome] 1
[Oslo, London, Paris, Rome]
```

By reviewing the code, we can learn some important facts about `ArrayLists`:

- The `ArrayList` class is in the `java.util` package.
- Similar to arrays, when you build an `ArrayList`, you have to declare what kind of objects it can contain. In this case, we're building an `ArrayList` of `String` objects. (We'll look at the line of code that creates the `ArrayList` in a lot more detail in a minute.)
- `ArrayList` implements the List interface.
- We work with the `ArrayList` through methods. In this case we used a couple of versions of `add()`; we used `indexOf()`; and, indirectly, we used `toString()` to display the `ArrayList`'s contents. (More on `toString()` in a minute.)

- Like arrays, indexes for `ArrayLists` are zero-based.
- We didn't declare how big the `ArrayList` was when we built it.
- We were able to add a new element to the `ArrayList` on the fly.
- We were able to add the new element in the middle of the list.
- The `ArrayList` maintained its order.

As promised, we need to look at the following line of code more closely:

```
List<String> c = new ArrayList<String>();
```

First off, we see that this is a polymorphic declaration. As we said earlier, `ArrayList` implements the `List` interface (also in `java.util`). If you plan to take the OCP 8 exam after you've aced the OCA 8, you'll learn a lot more about why we might want to do a polymorphic declaration. For now, imagine that someday you might want to create a `List` of your `ArrayLists`.

Next, we have this weird-looking syntax with the < and > characters. This syntax was added to the language in Java 5, and it has to do with "generics." Generics aren't really included in the OCA exam, so we don't want to spend a lot of time on them here, but what's important to know is that this is how you tell the compiler and the JVM that for this particular `ArrayList` you want only `Strings` to be allowed. What this means is if the compiler can tell that you're trying to add a "not-a-`String`" object to this `ArrayList`, your code won't compile. This is a good thing!

Also as promised, let's look at THIS line of code:

```
System.out.println(c);
```

Remember that all classes ultimately inherit from class `Object`. Class `Object` contains a method called `toString()`. Again, `toString()` isn't "officially" on the OCA exam (of course, it IS in the OCP exam!), but you need to understand it a bit for now. When you pass an object reference to either `System.out.print()` or `System.out.println()`, you're telling them to invoke that object's `toString()` method. (Whenever you make a new class, you can optionally override the `toString()` method your class inherited from `Object` to show useful information about your class's objects.) The API developers were nice enough to override `ArrayList`'s `toString()` method for you to show the contents of the `ArrayList`, as you saw in the program's output. Hooray!

ArrayLists and Duplicates

As you're planning your trip to Europe, you realize that halfway through your stay in Rome, there's going to be a fantastic music festival in Naples! Naples is just down the coast from Rome! You've got to add that side trip to your itinerary. The question is, can an `ArrayList` have duplicate entries? Is it legal to say this:

```
c.add("Rome");
c.add("Naples");
c.add("Rome");
```

And the short answer is: **Yes, ArrayLists can have duplicates**. Now if you stop and think about it, the notion of "duplicate Java objects" is actually a bit tricky. Relax, because you won't have to get into that trickiness until you study for the OCP 8.

exam watch

Technically speaking, `ArrayLists` hold only object references, not actual objects and not primitives. If you see code like this,

```
myArrayList.add(7);
```

what's really happening is the `int` is being autoboxed (converted) into an `Integer` object and then added to the `ArrayList`. We'll talk more about autoboxing in a few pages.

ArrayList Methods in Action

Let's look at another piece of code that shows off most of the `ArrayList` methods you need to know for the exam:

```
import java.util.*;
public class TweakLists {
  public static void main(String[] args) {

    List<String> myList = new ArrayList<String>();

    myList.add("z");
    myList.add("x");
    myList.add(1, "y");             // zero based
    myList.add(0, "w");             //  "     "
    System.out.println(myList);     // [w, z, y, x]
```

```
    myList.clear();                    // remove everything
    myList.add("b");
    myList.add("a");
    myList.add("c");
    System.out.println(myList);      // [b, a, c]
    System.out.println(myList.contains("a") + " " + myList.contains("x"));

    System.out.println("get 1: " + myList.get(1));
    System.out.println("index of c: " + myList.indexOf("c"));

    myList.remove(1);                  // remove "a"
    System.out.println("size: " + myList.size() + " contents: " + myList);
  }
}
```

which should produce something like this:

```
[w, z, y, x]
[b, a, c]
true false
get 1: a
index of c: 2
size: 2 contents: [b, c]
```

A couple of quick notes about this code: First off, notice that `contains()` returns a boolean. This makes `contains()` great to use in "if" tests. Second, notice that `ArrayList` has a `size()` method. It's important to remember that arrays have a length attribute and `ArrayLists` have a `size()` method.

Important Methods in the ArrayList Class

The following methods are some of the more commonly used methods in the `ArrayList` class and also those that you're most likely to encounter on the exam:

- **`add(element)`** Adds this element to the **end** of the `ArrayList`
- **`add(index, element)`** Adds this element at the index point and shifts the remaining elements back (for example, what was at `index` is now at `index + 1`)
- **`clear()`** Removes all the elements from the `ArrayList`
- **`boolean contains(element)`** Returns whether the `element` is in the list
- **`Object get(index)`** Returns the `Object` located at `index`
- **`int indexOf(Object)`** Returns the (`int`) location of the element or `-1` if the `Object` is not found

- **`remove(index)`** Removes the element at that `index` and shifts later elements toward the beginning one space
- **`remove(Object)`** Removes the **first** occurrence of the `Object` and shifts later elements toward the beginning one space
- **`int size()`** Returns the number of elements in the `ArrayList`

To summarize, the OCA 8 exam tests only for very basic knowledge of `ArrayLists`. If you go on to take the OCP 8 exam, you'll learn a lot more about `ArrayLists` and other common collections-oriented classes.

Autoboxing with ArrayLists

In general, collections like `ArrayList` can hold objects but not primitives. Prior to Java 5, a common use for the so-called wrapper classes (e.g., `Integer`, `Float`, `Boolean`, and so on) was to provide a way to get primitives into and out of collections. Prior to Java 5, you had to "wrap" a primitive manually before you could put it into a collection. As of Java 5, primitives still have to be wrapped before they can be added to ArrayLists, but autoboxing takes care of it for you.

```
List myInts = new ArrayList();    // pre Java 5 declaration
myInts.add(new Integer(42));      // Use Integer class to "wrap" an int
```

In the previous example, we create an instance of class `Integer` with a value of `42`. We've created an entire object to "wrap around" a primitive value. As of Java 5, we can say:

```
myInts.add(42);                   // autoboxing handles it!
```

In this last example, we are still adding an `Integer` object to `myInts` (not an `int` primitive); it's just that autoboxing handles the wrapping for us. There are some sneaky implications when we need to use wrapper objects; let's take a closer look...

In the old, pre–Java 5 days, if you wanted to make a wrapper, unwrap it, use it, and then rewrap it, you might do something like this:

```
Integer y = new Integer(567);    // make it
int x = y.intValue();            // unwrap it
x++;                             // use it
y = new Integer(x);              // rewrap it
System.out.println("y = " + y);  // print it
```

Now you can say:

```
Integer y = new Integer(567);     // make it
y++;                              // unwrap it, increment it,
                                  // rewrap it
System.out.println("y = " + y);   // print it
```

Both examples produce the following output:

```
y = 568
```

And yes, you read that correctly. The code appears to be using the postincrement operator on an object reference variable! But it's simply a convenience. Behind the scenes, the compiler does the unboxing and reassignment for you. Earlier, we mentioned that wrapper objects are immutable… this example appears to contradict that statement. It sure looks like y's value changed from `567` to `568`. What actually happened, however, is that a second wrapper object was created and its value was set to `568`. If only we could access that first wrapper object, we could prove it….

Let's try this:

```
Integer y = 567;                   // make a wrapper
Integer x = y;                     // assign a second ref
                                   // var to THE wrapper

System.out.println(y==x);          // verify that they refer
                                   // to the same object
y++;                               // unwrap, use, "rewrap"
System.out.println(x + " " + y);   // print values

System.out.println(y==x);          // verify that they refer
                                   // to different objects
```

which produces the output:

```
true
  567 568
  false
```

So, under the covers, when the compiler got to the line `y++;` it had to substitute something like this:

```
int x2 = y.intValue();             // unwrap it
x2++;                              // use it
y = new Integer(x2);               // rewrap it
```

Just as we suspected, there's gotta be a call to new in there somewhere.

exam watch

All the wrapper classes except `Character` provide two constructors: one takes a primitive of the type being constructed, and the other takes a `String` representation of the type being constructed. For example,

```
Integer i1 = new Integer(42);
Integer i2 = new Integer("42");
```

are both valid ways to construct a new `Integer` object (that "wraps" the value 42).

Boxing, ==, and equals()

We just used == to do a little exploration of wrappers. Let's take a more thorough look at how wrappers work with ==, !=, and `equals()`.The API developers decided that for all the wrapper classes, two objects are equal if they are of the same type and have the same value. It shouldn't be surprising that

```
Integer i1 = 1000;
Integer i2 = 1000;
if(i1 != i2) System.out.println("different objects");
if(i1.equals(i2)) System.out.println("meaningfully equal");
```

produces the output

```
different objects
meaningfully equal
```

It's just two wrapper objects happen to have the same value. Because they have the same `int` value, the `equals()` method considers them to be "meaningfully equivalent" and, therefore, returns `true`. How about this one?

```
Integer i3 = 10;
Integer i4 = 10;
if(i3 == i4) System.out.println("same object");
if(i3.equals(i4)) System.out.println("meaningfully equal");
```

This example produces the output:

```
same object
meaningfully equal
```

Yikes! The `equals()` method seems to be working, but what happened with == and !=? Why is != telling us that `i1` and `i2` are different objects, when == is saying that `i3` and `i4` are the same object? In order to save memory, two instances of the following wrapper objects (created through boxing) will always be == when their primitive values are the same:

- `Boolean`
- `Byte`
- `Character` from `\u0000` to `\u007f` (`7f` is `127` in decimal)
- `Short` and `Integer` from `-128` to `127`

When == is used to compare a primitive to a wrapper, the wrapper will be unwrapped and the comparison will be primitive to primitive.

Where Boxing Can Be Used

As we discussed earlier, it's common to use wrappers in conjunction with collections. Any time you want your collection to hold objects and primitives, you'll want to use wrappers to make those primitives collection-compatible. The general rule is that boxing and unboxing work wherever you can normally use a primitive or a wrapped object. The following code demonstrates some legal ways to use boxing:

```
class UseBoxing {
  public static void main(String [] args) {
    UseBoxing u = new UseBoxing();
    u.go(5);
  }
  boolean go(Integer i) {       // boxes the int it was passed
    Boolean ifSo = true;        // boxes the literal
    Short s = 300;              // boxes the primitive
    if(ifSo) {                  // unboxing
      System.out.println(++s);  // unboxes, increments, reboxes
    }
    return !ifSo;               // unboxes, returns the inverse
  }
}
```

exam watch

Remember, wrapper reference variables can be null. That means you have to watch out for code that appears to be doing safe primitive operations but that could throw a `NullPointerException`:

```
class Boxing2 {
  static Integer x;
  public static void main(String [] args) {
    doStuff(x);
  }
  static void doStuff(int z) {
    int z2 = 5;
    System.out.println(z2 + z);
} }
```

This code compiles fine, but the JVM throws a `NullPointerException` when it attempts to invoke `doStuff(x)` because `x` doesn't refer to an `Integer` object, so there's no value to unbox.

The Java 7 "Diamond" Syntax

Earlier in the book, we discussed several small additions/improvements to the language that were added under the name "Project Coin." The last Project Coin improvement we'll discuss is the "diamond syntax." We've already seen several examples of declaring type-safe `ArrayLists` like this:

```
ArrayList<String> stuff = new ArrayList<String>();
ArrayList<Dog> myDogs = new ArrayList<Dog>();
```

Notice that the type parameters are duplicated in these declarations. As of Java 7, these declarations could be simplified to:

```
ArrayList<String> stuff = new ArrayList<>();
ArrayList<Dog> myDogs = new ArrayList<>();
```

Notice that in the simpler Java 7 declarations, the right side of the declaration included the two characters "<>," which together make a diamond shape—doh!

You cannot swap these; for example, the following declaration is NOT legal:

```
ArrayList<> stuff = new ArrayList<String>();     // NOT a legal diamond syntax
```

For the purposes of the exam, that's all you'll need to know about the diamond operator. For the remainder of the book, we'll use the pre-diamond syntax and the Java 7 diamond syntax somewhat randomly—just like the real world!

CERTIFICATION OBJECTIVE

Advanced Encapsulation (OCA Objective 6.5)

6.5 *Apply encapsulation principles to a class.*

Encapsulation for Reference Variables

In Chapter 2 we began our discussion of the object-oriented concept of encapsulation. At that point, we limited our discussion to protecting a class's primitive fields and (immutable) `String` fields. Now that you've learned more about what it means to "pass-by-copy" and we've looked at nonprimitive ways of handling data such as arrays, `StringBuilders`, and `ArrayLists`, it's time to take a closer look at encapsulation.

Let's say we have some special data whose value we're saving in a `StringBuilder`. We're happy to share the value with other programmers, but we don't want them to change the value:

```
class Special {
  private StringBuilder s = new StringBuilder("bob");  // our special data
  StringBuilder getName() { return s; }
  void printName() { System.out.println(s); }          // verify our special
                                                       // data
}
public class TestSpecial {
  public static void main(String[] args) {
    Special sp = new Special();
    StringBuilder s2 = sp.getName();
    s2.append("fred");
    sp.printName();
  }
}
```

When we run the code, we get this:

```
bobfred
```

Uh oh! It looks like we practiced good encapsulation techniques by making our field private and providing a "getter" method, but based on the output, it's clear that we didn't do a very good job of protecting the data in the `Special` class. Can you figure out why? Take a minute....

Okay—just to verify your answer—when we invoke `getName()`, we do, in fact, return a copy, just like Java always does. But we're not returning a copy of the `StringBuilder` object; we're returning a copy of the reference variable that points to (I know) the one and only `StringBuilder` object we ever built. So at the point that `getName()` returns, we have one `StringBuilder` object and two reference variables pointing to it (`s` and `s2`).

For the purpose of the OCA exam, the key point is this: When encapsulating a mutable object like a `StringBuilder`, or an array, or an `ArrayList`, if you want to let outside classes have a copy of the object, you must actually copy the object and return a reference variable to the object that is a copy. If all you do is return a copy of the original object's reference variable, you **DO NOT** have encapsulation.

CERTIFICATION OBJECTIVE

Using Simple Lambdas (OCA Objective 9.5)

9.5 Write a simple Lambda expression that consumes a Lambda Predicate expression.

Java 8 is probably best known as the version of Java that finally added lambdas and streams. These two new features (lambdas and streams) give programmers tools to tackle some common and complex problems with easier-to-read, more concise, and, in many cases, faster-running code. The creators of the OCA 8 exam felt that, in general, lambdas and streams are topics more appropriate for the OCP 8 exam, but they wanted OCA 8 candidates to get an introduction, perhaps to whet their appetite...

In this section, we're going to do a really basic introduction to lambdas. We suspect this discussion will raise some questions in your mind, and we're sorry for that, but we're going to restrict ourselves to just the introduction that the exam creators had in mind.

exam watch

On the real exam, you should expect to see many questions that test for more than one objective. In the following pages, as we discuss lambdas, we'll be leaning heavily on `ArrayLists` and wrapper classes. You'll see that we combine `ArrayLists`, wrappers, AND lambdas into many of our code listings, and we also use this combination in the mock exam questions we provide. The real exam (and real-life programming) will do the same.

Suppose you're creating an application for a veterinary hospital. We want to focus on that part of the application that allows the vets to get summary information about all the dogs that they work with. Here's our `Dog` class:

```
class Dog {
  String name;
  int weight;
  int age;
  // constructor assigns a name, weight and age
  Dog(String name, int weight, int age) {
    this.name = name;
    this.weight = weight;
    this.age = age;
  }
  String getName() {return name;}
  int getWeight() { return weight;}
  int getAge() { return age;}
  public String toString() {
    return name;
  }
}
```

Now let's write some test code to create some sample Dogs, put them into an ArrayList as we go, and then run some "queries" against the ArrayList.

First here's the summary pseudo code:

```
// create and populate an ArrayList of Dog objects
// invoke a few "queries" on the ArrayList
// declare a couple of "query" methods
```

Here's the actual test code:

```
import java.util.*;
public class TestDogs {
  public static void main(String[] args) {
    ArrayList<Dog> dogs = new ArrayList<>();     // create and populate
    dogs.add(new Dog("boi", 30, 6));    dogs.add(new Dog("tyri", 40, 12));
    dogs.add(new Dog("charis", 120, 7));  dogs.add(new Dog("aiko", 50, 10));
    dogs.add(new Dog("clover", 35, 12));  dogs.add(new Dog("mia", 15, 4));
    dogs.add(new Dog("zooey", 45, 8));
                                                 // run a few "queries"
    System.out.println("all dogs  " + dogs);
    System.out.println("min age 7 " + minAge(dogs, 7).toString());
    System.out.println("max wght. " + maxWeight(dogs,40).toString());
  }
                                                 // declare "query" methods
  static ArrayList<Dog> minAge(ArrayList<Dog> dogList, int testFor) {
    ArrayList<Dog> result1 = new ArrayList<>(); // do a minimum age query
    for(Dog d: dogList)
      if(d.getAge() >= testFor)                  // the key moment!
        result1.add(d);
    return result1;
  }
  static ArrayList<Dog> maxWeight(ArrayList<Dog> dogList, int testFor) {
    ArrayList<Dog> result1 = new ArrayList<>(); // do a max weight query
    for(Dog d: dogList)
      if(d.getWeight() <= testFor)               // the key moment!
        result1.add(d);
    return result1;
  } }
```

which produces the following (predictable we hope) output:

```
all dogs  [boi, tyri, charis, aiko, clover, mia, zooey]
min age 7 [tyri, charis, aiko, clover, zooey]
max wght. [boi, tyri, clover, mia]
```

You're probably way ahead of us here, but notice how similar the `minAge()` and `maxWeight()` methods are. And it should be easy to imagine other similar methods with names like `maxAge()` or `namesStartingWithC()`. So the line of code we want to focus on is:

```
if( d.getAge() >= testFor )     // the query expression is in bold
```

What if—just sayin'—we could create a single `Dog`-querying method (instead of the many we've been contemplating) and pass it the query expression we wanted it to use? It would sort of look like this:

```
static ArrayList<Dog> dogQuerier(ArrayList<Dog> dogList, // query expression) {
  // do an "on the fly" query
  ArrayList<Dog> result1 = new ArrayList<>();
  for(Dog d: dogList)
    if( // query expression )                // the key moment!
      result1.add(d);
  return result1;
}
```

Now we're thinking about passing code as an argument? Lambdas let us do just that! Let's look at our `dogQuerier()` method a little more closely. First off, the code we're going to pass in is going to be used as the expression in an `if` statement. What do we know about `if` expressions? Right! They have to resolve to a `boolean` value. So when we declare our method, the second argument (the one that's going to hold the passed-in-code) has to be declared as a `boolean`. The folks who brought us Java 8 and lambdas and streams provided a bunch of new interfaces in the API, and one of the most useful of these is the `java.util.function.Predicate` interface. The `Predicate` interface has some of those new-fangled `static` and `default` interface methods, we discussed earlier in the book, and, most importantly for us, it has one nonconcrete method called `test()` that returns—you guessed it—a `boolean`.

Here's the multipurpose `dogQuerier()` method:

```
static ArrayList<Dog> dogQuerier(ArrayList<Dog> dogList, Predicate<Dog> expr) {
    // do an "on the fly" query
    ArrayList<Dog> result1 = new ArrayList<>();
    for(Dog d: dogList)
      if( expr.test(d) )              // the key moment!
        result1.add(d);
    return result1;
  }
```

So far this looks like good-old Java; it's when we invoke `dogQuerier()` that the syntax gets interesting:

```
dogQuerier(dogs, d -> d.getAge() < 9);
```

When we say **`d -> d.getAge() < 9`**—THAT is the lambda expression. The `d` represents the argument, and then the code must return a `boolean`. Let's put all of this together in a new version of `TestDogs`:

```
import java.util.*;
import java.util.function.Predicate;
public class TestDogs {
  public static void main(String[] args) {
    ArrayList<Dog> dogs = new ArrayList<>();    // create and populate
    dogs.add(new Dog("boi", 30, 6));  dogs.add(new Dog("tyri", 40, 12));
    dogs.add(new Dog("charis", 120, 7));  dogs.add(new Dog("aiko", 50, 10));
    dogs.add(new Dog("clover", 35, 12));   dogs.add(new Dog("mia", 15, 4));
    dogs.add(new Dog("zooey", 45, 8));
                                                 // run a few old "queries"
    System.out.println("all dogs   " + dogs);
    System.out.println("min age 7 " + minAge(dogs, 7).toString());
    System.out.println("max wght. " + maxWeight(dogs,40).toString());
                                                 // run a few lambda queries
    System.out.println("age < 9    " + dogQuery(dogs, d -> d.getAge() < 9));
    System.out.println("w > 100    " + dogQuery(dogs, d -> d.getWeight() > 100));
  }
  // declare old style "query" methods
  static ArrayList<Dog> minAge(ArrayList<Dog> dogList, int testFor) {
    // do a minimum age query
    ArrayList<Dog> result1 = new ArrayList<>();
    for(Dog d: dogList)
      if(d.getAge() >= testFor)                 // the key moment!
        result1.add(d);
    return result1;
  }
  static ArrayList<Dog> maxWeight(ArrayList<Dog> dogList, int testFor) {
// do a max weight query
    ArrayList<Dog> result1 = new ArrayList<>();
    for(Dog d: dogList)
      if(d.getWeight() <= testFor)              // the key moment!
        result1.add(d);
    return result1;
  }

  // declare a new lambda powered, generic, multi-purpose query method
  static ArrayList< >Dog> dogQuery(ArrayList< >Dog> dogList, Predicate< >Dog> expr) {
    // do an "on the fly" query
    ArrayList< >Dog> result1 = new ArrayList< >>();
    for(Dog d: dogList)
      if(expr.test(d))                  // the key moment, lambda powered!
        result1.add(d);
    return result1;
  }
}
```

which produces the following output (the last two lines generated using lambdas!):

```
all dogs   [boi, tyri, charis, aiko, clover, mia, zooey]
min age 7 [tyri, charis, aiko, clover, zooey]
max wght. [boi, tyri, clover, mia]
age < > 9    [boi, charis, mia, zooey]
w > 100    [charis]
```

Let's step back now and cover some syntax rules. The following rules are for the purposes of the OCA 8 exam only! If you decide to earn your OCP 8, you'll do a much deeper dive into lambdas, and there are lots of "cans of worms" you'll have to open, which we're purposely going to avoid. So what follows is an OCA 8 appropriate simplification.

The basic syntax for a `Predicate` lambda has three parts:

A Single Parameter	An Arrow-Token	A Body
`x`	->	7 < > 5

Other types of lambdas take zero or more parameters, but for the OCA 8, we're focused exclusively on the `Predicate`, which must take exactly one parameter. Here are some detailed syntax rules for `Predicate` lambdas:

- The parameter can be just a variable name, or it can be the type followed by a variable name all in parentheses.
- The body MUST (one way or another) return a `boolean`.
- The body can be a single expression, which cannot have a `return` statement.
- The body can be a code block surrounded by curly braces, containing one or more valid statements, each ending with a semicolon, and the block must end with a `return` statement.

Following is a code listing that shows examples of legal and then illegal examples of `Predicate` lambdas:

```
import java.util.function.Predicate;                // type of lambda
                                                    // we're learning

public class Lamb2 {
  public static void main(String[] args) {
    Lamb2 m1 = new Lamb2();
```

```
    // ==== LEGAL LAMBDAS ========================

      m1.go(x -> 7 < 5);                                    // extra terse
      m1.go(x -> { return adder(2, 1) > 5; });              // block
      m1.go((Lamb2 x) -> { int y = 5;
                           return adder(y, 7) > 8; }); // multi-stmt block
      m1.go(x -> { int y=5; return adder(y,6) > 8; }); // no arg type, block
      int a = 5; int b = 6;
      m1.go(x -> { return adder(a, b) > 8; });              // in scope vars
      m1.go((Lamb2 x) -> adder(a, b) > 13);                 // arg type, no block
    // ==== ILLEGAL LAMBDAS ======================

      // m1.go(x ->   return adder(2, 1) > 5;  );           // return w/o block
      // m1.go(Lamb2 x -> adder(2, 3) > 7);                 // type needs parens
      // m1.go(() -> adder(2, 3) > 7);                      // Predicate needs 1 arg
      // m1.go(x -> { adder(4, 2) > 9 });                   // blocks need statements
      // m1.go(x -> { int y = 5; adder(y, 7) > 8; });       // block needs return
    }
    void go(Predicate<Lamb2> e) {                           // go() takes a predicate
      Lamb2 m2 = new Lamb2();
      System.out.println(e.test(m2) ? "ternary true"        // ternary uses boolean expr
                                    : "ternary false");
    }
    static int adder(int x, int y) { return x + y; }        // complex calculation
  }
```

This code is mostly about valid and invalid syntax, but let's look a little more closely at the `go()` method. The test is mainly concerned with the code to be passed to a method, but it's useful to look (but not TOO closely) at a method that receives lambda code. In both the Dogs code and the code directly above, the receiving method took a `Predicate`. Inside the receiving methods, we created an object of the type we're working with, which we pass to the `Predicate.test()` method. The receiving method expects the `test()` method to return a `boolean`.

We have to admit that lambdas are a bit tricky to learn. Again, we expect we've left you with some unanswered questions, but we think Oracle did a reasonable job of slicing out a piece of the lambda puzzle to start with. If you understand the bits we've covered, you should be able to handle the lambda-related questions Oracle throws you.

CERTIFICATION SUMMARY

The most important thing to remember about `Strings` is that `String` objects are immutable, but references to `Strings` are not! You can make a new `String` by using an existing `String` as a starting point, but if you don't assign a reference variable to the new `String`, it will be lost to your program—you will have no way to access your new `String`. Review the important methods in the `String` class.

The StringBuilder class was added in Java 5. It has exactly the same methods as the old StringBuffer class, except StringBuilder's methods aren't thread-safe. Because StringBuilder's methods are not thread-safe, they tend to run faster than StringBuffer methods, so choose StringBuilder whenever threading is not an issue. Both StringBuffer and StringBuilder objects can have their value changed over and over without your having to create new objects. If you're doing a lot of string manipulation, these objects will be more efficient than immutable String objects, which are, more or less, "use once, remain in memory forever." Remember, these methods ALWAYS change the invoking object's value, even with no explicit assignment.

Next we discussed key classes and interfaces in the new Java 8 calendar and time-related packages. Similar to Strings, all of the calendar classes we studied create immutable objects. In addition, these classes use factory methods exclusively to create new objects. The keyword new cannot be used with these classes. We looked at some of the powerful features of these classes, like calculating the amount of time between two different dates or times. Then we took a look at how the DateTimeFormatter class is used to parse Strings into calendar objects and how it is used to beautify calendar objects.

The next topic was arrays. We talked about declaring, constructing, and initializing one-dimensional and multidimensional arrays. We talked about anonymous arrays and the fact that arrays of objects are actually arrays of references to objects.

Next, we discussed the basics of ArrayLists. ArrayLists are like arrays with superpowers that allow them to grow and shrink dynamically and to make it easy for you to insert and delete elements at locations of your choosing within the list. We discussed the idea that ArrayLists cannot hold primitives, and that if you want to make an ArrayList filled with a given type of primitive values, you use "wrapper" classes to turn a primitive value into an object that represents that value. Then we discussed how with autoboxing, turning primitives into wrapper objects, and vice versa, is done automatically.

Finally, we discussed a specific subset of the topic of lambdas, using the Predicate interface. The basic idea of lambdas is that you can pass a bit of code from one method to another. The Predicate interface is one of many "functional interfaces" provided in the Java 8 API. A functional interface is one that has only one method to be implemented. In the case of the Predicate interface, this method is called test(), and it takes a single argument and returns a boolean. To wrap up our discussion of lambdas, we covered some of the tricky syntax rules you need to know to write valid lambdas.

✓ TWO-MINUTE DRILL

Here are some of the key points from the certification objectives in this chapter.

Using String and StringBuilder (OCA Objectives 9.2 and 9.1)

- ☐ `String` objects are immutable, and `String` reference variables are not.
- ☐ If you create a new `String` without assigning it, it will be lost to your program.
- ☐ If you redirect a `String` reference to a new `String`, the old `String` can be lost.
- ☐ `String` methods use zero-based indexes, except for the second argument of `substring()`.
- ☐ The `String` class is `final`—it cannot be extended.
- ☐ When the JVM finds a `String` literal, it is added to the `String` literal pool.
- ☐ Strings have a *method* called `length()`—arrays have an *attribute* named `length`.
- ☐ `StringBuilder` objects are mutable—they can change without creating a new object.
- ☐ `StringBuilder` methods act on the invoking object, and objects can change without an explicit assignment in the statement.
- ☐ Remember that chained methods are evaluated from left to right.
- ☐ `String` methods to remember: `charAt()`, `concat()`, `equalsIgnoreCase()`, `length()`, `replace()`, `substring()`, `toLowerCase()`, `toString()`, `toUpperCase()`, and `trim()`.
- ☐ `StringBuilder` methods to remember: `append()`, `delete()`, `insert()`, `reverse()`, and `toString()`.

Manipulating Calendar Data (OCA Objective 9.3)

- ☐ On the exam all the objects created using the calendar classes are immutable, but their reference variables are not.
- ☐ If you create a new calendar object without assigning it, it will be lost to your program.

- ☐ If you redirect a calendar reference to a new calendar object, the old calendar object can be lost.
- ☐ All of the objects created using the exam's calendar classes must be created using factory methods (e.g., `from()`, `now()`, `of()`, `parse()`); the keyword new is not allowed.
- ☐ The `until()` and `between()` methods perform complex calculations that determine the amount of time between the values of two calendar objects.
- ☐ The `DateTimeFormatter` class uses the `parse()` method to parse input Strings into valid calendar objects.
- ☐ The `DateTimeFormatter` class uses the `format()` method to format calendar objects into beautifully formed Strings.

Using Arrays (OCA Objectives 4.1 and 4.2)

- ☐ Arrays can hold primitives or objects, but the array itself is always an object.
- ☐ When you declare an array, the brackets can be to the left or right of the name.
- ☐ It is never legal to include the size of an array in the declaration.
- ☐ You must include the size of an array when you construct it (using `new`) unless you are creating an anonymous array.
- ☐ Elements in an array of objects are not automatically created, although primitive array elements are given default values.
- ☐ You'll get a `NullPointerException` if you try to use an array element in an object array if that element does not refer to a real object.
- ☐ Arrays are indexed beginning with zero.
- ☐ An `ArrayIndexOutOfBoundsException` occurs if you use a bad index value.
- ☐ Arrays have a `length` attribute whose value is the number of array elements.
- ☐ The last index you can access is always one less than the length of the array.
- ☐ Multidimensional arrays are just arrays of arrays.
- ☐ The dimensions in a multidimensional array can have different lengths.

- ☐ An array of primitives can accept any value that can be promoted implicitly to the array's declared type—for example, a `byte` variable can go in an `int` array.
- ☐ An array of objects can hold any object that passes the IS-A (or `instanceof`) test for the declared type of the array. For example, if `Horse` extends `Animal`, then a `Horse` object can go into an `Animal` array.
- ☐ If you assign an array to a previously declared array reference, the array you're assigning must be the same dimension as the reference you're assigning it to.
- ☐ You can assign an array of one type to a previously declared array reference of one of its supertypes. For example, a `Honda` array can be assigned to an array declared as type `Car` (assuming `Honda` extends `Car`).

Using ArrayList (OCA Objective 9.4)

- ☐ `ArrayLists` allow you to resize your list and make insertions and deletions to your list far more easily than arrays.
- ☐ `ArrayLists` are ordered by default. When you use the `add()` method with no index argument, the new entry will be appended to the end of the `ArrayList`.
- ☐ For the OCA 8 exam, the only `ArrayList` declarations you need to know are of this form:

```
ArrayList<type> myList  = new ArrayList<type>();
List<type> myList2 = new ArrayList<type>();  // polymorphic
List<type> myList3 = new ArrayList<>();  // diamond operator, polymorphic
optional
```

- ☐ `ArrayLists` can hold only objects, not primitives, but remember that autoboxing can make it look like you're adding primitives to an `ArrayList` when, in fact, you're adding a wrapper object version of a primitive.
- ☐ An `ArrayList`'s index starts at 0.
- ☐ `ArrayLists` can have duplicate entries. Note: Determining whether two objects are duplicates is trickier than it seems and doesn't come up until the OCP 8 exam.
- ☐ `ArrayList` methods to remember: `add(element)`, `add(index, element)`, `clear()`, `contains(object)`, `get(index)`, `indexOf(object)`, `remove(index)`, `remove(object)`, and `size()`.

Encapsulating Reference Variables (OCA Objective 6.5)

- ☐ If you want to encapsulate mutable objects like `StringBuilders` or arrays or `ArrayLists`, you cannot return a reference to these objects; you must first make a copy of the object and return a reference to the copy.
- ☐ Any class that has a method that returns a reference to a mutable object is breaking encapsulation.

Using Predicate Lambda Expressions (OCA Objective 9.5)

- ☐ Lambdas allow you to pass bits of code from one method to another. And the receiving method can run whatever complying code it is sent.
- ☐ While there are many types of lambdas that Java 8 supports, for this exam, the only lambda type you need to know is the `Predicate`.
- ☐ The `Predicate` interface has a single method to implement that's called `test()`, and it takes one argument and returns a `boolean`.
- ☐ As the `Predicate.test()` method returns a boolean, it can be placed (mostly?) wherever a boolean expression can go, e.g., in `if`, `while`, `do`, and ternary statements.
- ☐ `Predicate` lambda expressions have three parts: a single argument, an arrow (`->`), and an expression or code block.
- ☐ A `Predicate` lambda expression's argument can be just a variable or a type and variable together in parentheses, e.g., `(MyClass m)`.
- ☐ A `Predicate` lambda expression's body can be an expression that resolves to a boolean, OR it can be a block of statements (surrounded by curly braces) that ends with a boolean-returning `return` statement.

SELF TEST

1. Given:

```
public class Mutant {
  public static void main(String[] args) {
    StringBuilder sb = new StringBuilder("abc");
    String s = "abc";
    sb.reverse().append("d");
    s.toUpperCase().concat("d");
    System.out.println("." + sb + ". ." + s + ".");
  }
}
```

Which two substrings will be included in the result? (Choose two.)

A. `.abc.`

B. `.ABCd.`

C. `.ABCD.`

D. `.cbad.`

E. `.dcba.`

2. Given:

```
public class Hilltop {
  public static void main(String[] args) {
    String[] horses = new String[5];
    horses[4] = null;
    for(int i = 0; i < horses.length; i++) {
      if(i < args.length)
        horses[i] = args[i];
      System.out.print(horses[i].toUpperCase() + " ");
    }
  }
}
```

And, if the code compiles, the command line:

```
java Hilltop eyra vafi draumur kara
```

What is the result?

A. `EYRA VAFI DRAUMUR KARA`

B. `EYRA VAFI DRAUMUR KARA null`

C. An exception is thrown with no other output

D. `EYRA VAFI DRAUMUR KARA`, and then a `NullPointerException`

E. `EYRA VAFI DRAUMUR KARA`, and then an `ArrayIndexOutOfBoundsException`

F. Compilation fails

3. Given:

```
public class Actors {
  public static void main(String[] args) {
    char[] ca = {0x4e, \u004e, 78};
    System.out.println((ca[0] == ca[1]) + " " + (ca[0] == ca[2]));
  }
}
```

What is the result?

A. `true true`

B. `true false`

C. `false true`

D. `false false`

E. Compilation fails

4. Given:

```
1. class Dims {
2.   public static void main(String[] args) {
3.     int[][] a = {{1,2}, {3,4}};
4.     int[] b = (int[]) a[1];
5.     Object o1 = a;
6.     int[][] a2 = (int[][]) o1;
7.     int[] b2 = (int[]) o1;
8.     System.out.println(b[1]);
9. } }
```

What is the result? (Choose all that apply.)

A. 2

B. 4

C. An exception is thrown at runtime

D. Compilation fails due to an error on line 4

E. Compilation fails due to an error on line 5

F. Compilation fails due to an error on line 6

G. Compilation fails due to an error on line 7

5. Given:

```
import java.util.*;
public class Sequence {
  public static void main(String[] args) {
    ArrayList<String> myList = new ArrayList<String>();
    myList.add("apple");
    myList.add("carrot");
    myList.add("banana");
    myList.add(1, "plum");
    System.out.print(myList);
  }
}
```

What is the result?

A. `[apple, banana, carrot, plum]`

B. `[apple, plum, carrot, banana]`

C. `[apple, plum, banana, carrot]`

D. `[plum, banana, carrot, apple]`

E. `[plum, apple, carrot, banana]`

F. `[banana, plum, carrot, apple]`

G. Compilation fails

6. Given:

```
 3. class Dozens {
 4.   int[] dz = {1,2,3,4,5,6,7,8,9,10,11,12};
 5. }
 6. public class Eggs {
 7.   public static void main(String[] args) {
 8.     Dozens [] da = new Dozens[3];
 9.     da[0] = new Dozens();
10.     Dozens d = new Dozens();
11.     da[1] = d;
12.     d = null;
13.     da[1] = null;
14.     // do stuff
15.   }
16. }
```

Which two are true about the objects created within `main()`, and which are eligible for garbage collection when line 14 is reached?

A. Three objects were created

B. Four objects were created

C. Five objects were created

D. Zero objects are eligible for GC

E. One object is eligible for GC

F. Two objects are eligible for GC

G. Three objects are eligible for GC

7. Given:

```
public class Tailor {
  public static void main(String[] args) {
    byte[][] ba = {{1,2,3,4}, {1,2,3}};
    System.out.println(ba[1].length + " " + ba.length);
  }
}
```

What is the result?

A. `2 4`

B. `2 7`

C. `3 2`

D. `3 7`

E. `4 2`

F. `4 7`

G. Compilation fails

8. Given:

```
public class Theory {
  public static void main(String[] args) {
    String s1 = "abc";
    String s2 = s1;
    s1 += "d";
    System.out.println(s1 + " " + s2 + " " + (s1==s2));

    StringBuilder sb1 = new StringBuilder("abc");
    StringBuilder sb2 = sb1;
    sb1.append("d");
    System.out.println(sb1 + " " + sb2 + " " + (sb1==sb2));
  }
}
```

Which are true? (Choose all that apply.)

A. Compilation fails

B. The first line of output is `abc abc true`

C. The first line of output is `abc abc false`

D. The first line of output is `abcd abc false`

E. The second line of output is `abcd abc false`

F. The second line of output is `abcd abcd true`

G. The second line of output is `abcd abcd false`

9. Given:

```
public class Mounds {
  public static void main(String[] args) {
    StringBuilder sb = new StringBuilder();
    String s = new String();
    for(int i = 0; i < 1000; i++) {
      s = " " + i;
      sb.append(s);
    }
    // done with loop
  }
}
```

If the garbage collector does NOT run while this code is executing, approximately how many objects will exist in memory when the loop is done?

A. Less than 10

B. About 1000

C. About 2000

D. About 3000

E. About 4000

10. Given:

```
class Box {
  int size;
  Box(int s) { size = s; }
}
public class Laser {
  public static void main(String[] args) {
    Box b1 = new Box(5);
    Box[] ba = go(b1, new Box(6));
    ba[0] = b1;
    for(Box b : ba) System.out.print(b.size + " ");
  }
```

```
   static Box[] go(Box b1, Box b2) {
      b1.size = 4;
      Box[] ma = {b2, b1};
      return ma;
   }
}
```

What is the result?

A. `4 4`

B. `5 4`

C. `6 4`

D. `4 5`

E. `5 5`

F. Compilation fails

11. Given:

```
public class Hedges {
  public static void main(String[] args) {
    String s = "JAVA";
    s = s + "rocks";
    s = s.substring(4,8);
    s.toUpperCase();
    System.out.println(s);
  }
}
```

What is the result?

A. `JAVA`

B. `JAVAROCKS`

C. `rocks`

D. `rock`

E. `ROCKS`

F. `ROCK`

G. Compilation fails

12. Given:

```
import java.util.*;
class Fortress {
  private String name;
  private ArrayList<Integer> list;
  Fortress() { list = new ArrayList<Integer>(); }

```

```
 7.   String getName() { return name; }
 8.   void addToList(int x) { list.add(x); }
 9.   ArrayList getList() { return list; }
10. }
```

Which lines of code (if any) break encapsulation? (Choose all that apply.)

A. Line 3
B. Line 4
C. Line 5
D. Line 7
E. Line 8
F. Line 9
G. The class is already well encapsulated

13. Given:

```
 import java.util.function.Predicate;
public class Sheep {
  public static void main(String[] args) {
    Sheep s = new Sheep();
    s.go(() -> adder(5, 1) < 7);     // line A
    s.go(x -> adder(6, 2) < 9);      // line B
    s.go(x, y -> adder(3, 2) < 4);   // line C
  }
  void go(Predicate<Sheep> e) {
    Sheep s2 = new Sheep();
    if(e.test(s2))
      System.out.print("true ");
    else
      System.out.print("false ");
  }
  static int adder(int x, int y) {
    return x + y;
  }
}
```

What is the result?

A. `true true false`
B. Compilation fails due only to an error at line A
C. Compilation fails due only to an error at line B
D. Compilation fails due only to an error at line C
E. Compilation fails due only to errors at lines A and B
F. Compilation fails due only to errors at lines A and C
G. Compilation fails due only to errors at lines A, B, and C
H. Compilation fails for reasons not listed

14. Given:

```
import java.time.*;
import java.time.format.*;
public class Shiny {
  public static void main(String[] args) {
    DateTimeFormatter f1 =
               DateTimeFormatter.ofPattern("MMM dd, yyyy");
    LocalDate d = LocalDate.of(2018, Month.JANUARY, 15);
    LocalDate d2 = d.plusDays(1);
    System.out.print(f1.format(d) + " ");
    System.out.println(d2.format(f1));
  }
}
```

What is the result?

A. `2018-01-15 2018-01-15`

B. `2018-01-15 2018-01-16`

C. `Jan 15, 2018 Jan 15, 2018`

D. `Jan 15, 2018 Jan 16, 2018`

E. Compilation fails

F. An exception is thrown at runtime

15. Given:

```
import java.util.*;
public class Jackets {
  public static void main(String[] args) {
    List<Integer> myList = new ArrayList<>();  // line 5
    myList.add(new Integer(5));
    myList.add(42);                            // line 7
    myList.add("113");                         // line 8
    myList.add(new Integer("7"));              // line 9
    System.out.println(myList);
  }
}
```

What is the result?

A. `[5, 42, 113, 7]`

B. Compilation fails due only to an error on line 5

C. Compilation fails due only to an error on line 8

D. Compilation fails due only to errors on lines 5 and 8

E. Compilation fails due only to errors on lines 7 and 8

F. Compilation fails due only to errors on lines 5, 7, and 8

G. Compilation fails due only to errors on lines 5, 7, 8, and 9

16. Given that `adder()` returns an `int`, which are valid `Predicate` lambdas? (Choose all that apply.)

A. `x, y -> 7 < 5`

B. `x -> { return adder(2, 1) > 5; }`

C. `x -> return adder(2, 1) > 5;`

D.
```
x -> { int y = 5;
       int z = 7;
       adder(y, z) > 8; }
```

E.
```
x -> { int y = 5;
       int z = 7;
       return adder(y, z) > 8; }
```

F. `(MyClass x) -> 7 > 13`

G. `(MyClass x) -> 5 + 4`

17. Given:

```
import java.util.*;
public class Baking {
  public static void main(String[] args) {
    ArrayList<String> steps = new ArrayList<String>();
    steps.add("knead");
    steps.add("oil pan");
    steps.add("turn on oven");
    steps.add("roll");
    steps.add("turn on oven");
    steps.add("bake");
    System.out.println(steps);
  }
}
```

What is the result?

A. `[knead, oil pan, roll, turn on oven, bake]`

B. `[knead, oil pan, turn on oven, roll, bake]`

C. `[knead, oil pan, turn on oven, roll, turn on oven, bake]`

D. The output is unpredictable

E. Compilation fails

F. An exception is thrown at runtime

18. Given:

```
import java.time.*;
public class Bachelor {
  public static void main(String[] args) {
    LocalDate d = LocalDate.of(2018, 8, 15);
    d = d.plusDays(1);
    LocalDate d2 = d.plusDays(1);
    LocalDate d3 = d2;
    d2 = d2.plusDays(1);
    System.out.println(d + " " + d2 + " " + d3);   // line X
  }
}
```

Which are true? (Choose all that apply.)

A. The output is: `2018-08-16 2018-08-17 2018-08-18`

B. The output is: `2018-08-16 2018-08-18 2018-08-17`

C. The output is: `2018-08-16 2018-08-17 2018-08-17`

D. At line X, zero `LocalDate` objects are eligible for garbage collection

E. At line X, one `LocalDate` object is eligible for garbage collection

F. At line X, two `LocalDate` objects are eligible for garbage collection

G. Compilation fails

19. Given that `e` refers to an object that implements `Predicate`, which could be valid code snippets or statements? (Choose all that apply.)

A. `if(e.test(m))`

B. `switch (e.test(m))`

C. `while(e.test(m))`

D. `e.test(m) ? "yes" : "no";`

E. `do {} while(e.test(m));`

F. `System.out.print(e.test(m));`

G. `boolean b = e.test(m));`

SELF TEST ANSWERS

1. ☑ **A** and **D** are correct. The `String` operations are working on a new (lost) `String` not `String s`. The `StringBuilder` operations work from left to right.
   ☒ **B, C,** and **E** are incorrect based on the above. (OCA Objectives 9.2 and 9.1)

2. ☑ **D** is correct. The `horses` array's first four elements contain `Strings`, but the fifth is null, so the `toUpperCase()` invocation for the fifth element throws a `NullPointerException`.
   ☒ **A, B, C, E,** and **F** are incorrect based on the above. (OCA Objectives 4.1 and 1.3)

3. ☑ **E** is correct. The Unicode declaration must be enclosed in single quotes: `'\u004e'`. If this were done, the answer would be **A**, but that equality isn't on the OCA exam.
   ☒ **A, B, C,** and **D** are incorrect based on the above. (OCA Objectives 2.1 and 4.1)

4. ☑ **C** is correct. A `ClassCastException` is thrown at line 7 because `o1` refers to an `int [][]`, not an `int []`. If line 7 were removed, the output would be 4.
   ☒ **A, B, D, E, F,** and **G** are incorrect based on the above. (OCA Objective 4.2)

5. ☑ **B** is correct. `ArrayList` elements are automatically inserted in the order of entry; they are not automatically sorted. `ArrayLists` use zero-based indexes, and the last `add()` inserts a new element and shifts the remaining elements back.
   ☒ **A, C, D, E, F,** and **G** are incorrect based on the above. (OCA Objective 9.4)

6. ☑ **C** and **F** are correct. da refers to an object of type "`Dozens` array," and each `Dozens` object that is created comes with its own "`int` array" object. When line 14 is reached, only the second `Dozens` object (and its "`int` array" object) are not reachable.
   ☒ **A, B, D, E,** and **G** are incorrect based on the above. (OCA Objectives 4.1 and 2.4)

7. ☑ **C** is correct. A two-dimensional array is an "array of arrays." The length of `ba` is 2 because it contains 2 one-dimensional arrays. Array indexes are zero-based, so `ba[1]` refers to `ba`'s second array.
   ☒ **A, B, D, E, F,** and **G** are incorrect based on the above. (OCA Objective 4.2)

8. ☑ **D** and **F** are correct. Although `String` objects are immutable, references to `Strings` are mutable. The code `s1 += "d";` creates a new `String` object. `StringBuilder` objects are mutable, so the `append()` is changing the single `StringBuilder` object to which both `StringBuilder` references refer.
   ☒ **A, B, C, E,** and **G** are incorrect based on the above. (OCA Objectives 9.2 and 9.1)

9. ☑ **B** is correct. `StringBuilders` are mutable, so all of the `append()` invocations are acting on the same `StringBuilder` object over and over. `Strings`, however, are immutable, so every `String` concatenation operation results in a new `String` object. Also, the string `" "` is created once and reused in every loop iteration.
   ☒ **A, C, D,** and **E** are incorrect based on the above. (OCA Objectives 9.2 and 9.1)

10. ☑ **A** is correct. Although `main()`'s `b1` is a different reference variable than `go()`'s `b1`, they refer to the same `Box` object.
☒ **B, C, D, E,** and **F** are incorrect based on the above. (OCA Objectives 4.1, 6.1, and 6.6)

11. ☑ **D** is correct. The `substring()` invocation uses a zero-based index and the second argument is exclusive, so the character at index 8 is NOT included. The `toUpperCase()` invocation makes a new `String` object that is instantly lost. The `toUpperCase()` invocation does NOT affect the `String` referred to by `s`.
☒ **A, B, C, E, F,** and **G** are incorrect based on the above. (OCA Objective 9.2)

12. ☑ **F** is correct. When encapsulating a mutable object like an `ArrayList`, your getter must return a reference to a copy of the object, not just the reference to the original object.
☒ **A, B, C, D, E,** and **G** are incorrect based on the above. (OCA Objective 6.5)

13. ☑ **F** is correct. Predicate lambdas take exactly one parameter; the rest of the code is correct.
☒ **A, B, C, D, E, G,** and **H** are incorrect based on the above. (OCA Objective 9.5)

14. ☑ **D** is correct. Invoking the `plusDays()` method creates a new object, and both `LocalDate` and `DateTimeFormatter` have `format()` methods.
☒ **A, B, C, E,** and **F** are incorrect based on the above. (OCA Objective 9.3)

15. ☑ **C** is correct. The only error in this code is attempting to add a `String` to an `ArrayList` of `Integer` wrapper objects. Line 7 uses autoboxing, and lines 6 and 9 demonstrate using a wrapper class's two constructors.
☒ **A, B, D, E, F,** and **G** are incorrect based on the above. (OCA Objectives 2.5 and 9.4)

16. ☑ **B, E** and **F** use correct syntax.
☒ **A, C, D,** and **G** are incorrect. **A** passes two parameters. **C**, a `return`, must be in a code block, and code blocks must be in curly braces. **D**, a block, must have a `return` statement. **G**, the result, is not a `boolean`. (OCA Objective 9.5)

17. ☑ **C** is correct. `ArrayLists` can have duplicate entries.
☒ **A, B, D, E,** and **F** are incorrect based on the above. (OCA Objective 9.4)

18. ☑ **B** and **E** are correct. A total of four `LocalDate` objects are created, but the one created using the `of()` method is abandoned on the next line of code when its reference variable is assigned to the new `LocalDate` object created via the first `plusDays()` invocation. The reference variables are swapped a bit, which accounts for the dates not printing in chronological order.
☒ **A, C, D, F,** and **G** are incorrect based on the above. (OCA Objectives 2.4 and 9.3)

19. ☑ **A, C, D, E, F,** and **G** are correct; they all require a `boolean`.
☒ **B** is incorrect. A `switch` doesn't take a `boolean`. (OCA Objective 9.5)

A

About the CD-ROM

The CD-ROM included with this book comes complete with Oracle Press Practice Exam Software that simulates the OCA 1Z0-808 exam and a secured PDF copy of the book. The software is easy to install on any Mac or Windows computer and must be installed to access the Practice Exam feature. You may, however, browse the PDF content directly from the CD without installation.

System Requirements

The software requires the following:

Windows

- 2.33GHz or faster x86-compatible processor, or Intel Atom™ 1.6GHz or faster processor for netbook class devices
- Microsoft® Windows Server 2008, Windows 7, Windows 8.1 Classic, or Windows 10
- 512MB of RAM (1GB recommended)

Mac OS

- Intel® Core™ Duo 1.83GHz or faster processor
- Mac OS X v10.7, and above
- 512MB of RAM (1GB recommended)

Installing the Practice Exam Software

Follow the instructions for Windows or Mac OS.

NOTE: If you do not have a CD-ROM drive you may download the CD-ROM material by going to the McGraw-Hill Professional Media Center at http://mhprofessional.com/mediacenter, entering the ISBN 1260011380, and providing your e-mail. You will then receive an e-mail message with a link to download the CD-ROM content along with a file with instructions for installing the software from download. If you do not receive the e-mail, be sure to check your spam folder.

Windows

Step 1 Insert the CD into your CD-ROM drive.

Step 2 After a few moments, the installer will open automatically. If the installer does not open automatically, check the following note.

NOTE: If the installer does not automatically open, from the Start menu, select Run and enter:

***X*:\Installer.exe**

(where "*X*" is the letter of your CD-ROM drive). Then click OK.

Step 3 Follow the onscreen instructions to install the application.

Mac OS

Step 1 Insert the CD into your external CD-ROM drive.

Step 2 After a few moments, the contents of the CD will be displayed.

Step 3 Double-click Installer to begin installation.

Step 4 Follow the onscreen instructions to install the application.

NOTE: If you get an error while installing the software, please ensure your antivirus or Internet security programs are disabled and try installing the software again. You may enable the antivirus or Internet security program again after installation is complete.

Running the Practice Exam Software

Follow the instructions after you have completed the software installation.

Windows

After installing, you can start the application using *either* of the two following methods:

1. Double-click the Oracle Press Java SE 8 Practice icon on your desktop *or*
2. Go to the Start menu and click Programs or All Programs. Click Oracle Press OCA Java SE 8 Practice to start the application.

Mac OS

Open the OCA Java SE 8 Practice folder inside your Mac's Application folder and double-click the OCA Java SE 8 Practice icon to run the application.

Practice Exam Software Features

The Practice Exam Software provides you with a simulation of the actual exam. The software also features a custom mode that can be used to generate quizzes by exam objective domain. Quiz mode is the default mode. To launch an exam simulation, select one of the OCA exam buttons at the top of the screen, or select the Exam Mode check box at the bottom of the screen and then select the OCA exam in the custom window.

The number of questions, types of questions, and the time allowed on the exam simulation are intended to be representative of the live exam. The custom exam mode includes hints and references, and in-depth answer explanations are provided through the Feedback feature.

When you launch the software, a digital clock display will appear in the upper-right corner of the question window. The clock will continue to count unless you choose to end the exam by selecting Grade the Exam.

Removing Installation

The Practice Exam Software is installed on your hard drive. For best results for removal of programs using a Windows PC, use the Control Panel | Uninstall a Program option and then choose OCA Java SE 8 Practice to uninstall.

For best results for removal of programs using a Mac, go to the OCA Java SE 8 Practice folder inside your Applications folder and drag the OCA Java SE 8 Practice icon to the Trash.

Help

A help file is provided through the Help button on the main page in the top-right corner. A readme file is also included in the Bonus Content folder that provides more information about the additional content available with the book.

Secured PDF Copy of the Book

The entire contents of the Exam Guide are provided in PDF format. Download Adobe Acrobat Reader from **www.adobe.com**.

Technical Support

Technical support information is provided in the following sections by feature.

Windows 8 Troubleshooting

The following known errors on Windows 8 have been reported. Please see the following for information on troubleshooting these known issues.

If you get an error while installing the software, such as "The application could not be installed because the installer file is damaged. Try obtaining the new installer from the application author," you may need to disable your antivirus or Internet security programs and try installing the software again. You may enable the antivirus or Internet security program again after installation is complete.

For more information on how to disable antivirus programs in Windows, please visit the website of the software provider of your antivirus program. For example, if you use Norton or MacAfee products, you may need to visit the Norton or MacAfee website and search for "how to disable antivirus in Windows 8." Antivirus programs are different from firewall technology, so be sure to disable the antivirus program, and be sure to reenable the program after you have installed the Practice Exam Software.

Although Windows doesn't include default antivirus software, it can often detect antivirus software installed by you or the manufacturer of your computer and typically displays the status of any such software in the Action Center, which is located in the Control Panel under System and Security (select Review Your Computer's Status). Windows' Help feature can also provide more information on how to detect your antivirus software. If the antivirus software is on, check the Help feature that came with that software for information on how to disable it.

Windows will not detect all antivirus software. If your antivirus software isn't displayed in the Action Center, you can try typing the name of the software or the publisher in the Start menu's search field.

McGraw-Hill Education Content Support

For questions regarding the secured PDF copy of the book, e-mail **techsolutions@mhedu.com** or visit **http://mhp.softwareassist.com**.

For questions regarding book content, e-mail **hep_customer.service@mheducation.com**. For customers outside the United States, e-mail **international_cs@mheducation.com**.

INDEX

A

E

F

P

Q

R

S

T

U

V

LICENSE AGREEMENT

THIS PRODUCT (THE "PRODUCT") CONTAINS PROPRIETARY SOFTWARE, DATA AND INFORMATION (INCLUDING DOCUMENTATION) OWNED BY McGRAW-HILL EDUCATION AND ITS LICENSORS. YOUR RIGHT TO USE THE PRODUCT IS GOVERNED BY THE TERMS AND CONDITIONS OF THIS AGREEMENT.

LICENSE: Throughout this License Agreement, "you" shall mean either the individual or the entity whose agent opens this package. You are granted a non-exclusive and non-transferable license to use the Product subject to the following terms:
(i) If you have licensed a single user version of the Product, the Product may only be used on a single computer (i.e., a single CPU). If you licensed and paid the fee applicable to a local area network or wide area network version of the Product, you are subject to the terms of the following subparagraph (ii).
(ii) If you have licensed a local area network version, you may use the Product on unlimited workstations located in one single building selected by you that is served by such local area network. If you have licensed a wide area network version, you may use the Product on unlimited workstations located in multiple buildings on the same site selected by you that is served by such wide area network; provided, however, that any building will not be considered located in the same site if it is more than five (5) miles away from any building included in such site. In addition, you may only use a local area or wide area network version of the Product on one single server. If you wish to use the Product on more than one server, you must obtain written authorization from McGraw-Hill Education and pay additional fees.
(iii) You may make one copy of the Product for back-up purposes only and you must maintain an accurate record as to the location of the back-up at all times.

COPYRIGHT; RESTRICTIONS ON USE AND TRANSFER: All rights (including copyright) in and to the Product are owned by McGraw-Hill Education and its licensors. You are the owner of the enclosed disc on which the Product is recorded. You may not use, copy, decompile, disassemble, reverse engineer, modify, reproduce, create derivative works, transmit, distribute, sublicense, store in a database or retrieval system of any kind, rent or transfer the Product, or any portion thereof, in any form or by any means (including electronically or otherwise) except as expressly provided for in this License Agreement. You must reproduce the copyright notices, trademark notices, legends and logos of McGraw-Hill Education and its licensors that appear on the Product on the back-up copy of the Product which you are permitted to make hereunder. All rights in the Product not expressly granted herein are reserved by McGraw-Hill Education and its licensors.

TERM: This License Agreement is effective until terminated. It will terminate if you fail to comply with any term or condition of this License Agreement. Upon termination, you are obligated to return to McGraw-Hill Education the Product together with all copies thereof and to purge all copies of the Product included in any and all servers and computer facilities.

DISCLAIMER OF WARRANTY: THE PRODUCT AND THE BACK-UP COPY ARE LICENSED "AS IS." McGRAW-HILL EDUCATION, ITS LICENSORS AND THE AUTHORS MAKE NO WARRANTIES, EXPRESS OR IMPLIED, AS TO THE RESULTS TO BE OBTAINED BY ANY PERSON OR ENTITY FROM USE OF THE PRODUCT, ANY INFORMATION OR DATA INCLUDED THEREIN AND/OR ANY TECHNICAL SUPPORT SERVICES PROVIDED HEREUNDER, IF ANY ("TECHNICAL SUPPORT SERVICES"). McGRAW-HILL EDUCATION, ITS LICENSORS AND THE AUTHORS MAKE NO EXPRESS OR IMPLIED WARRANTIES OF MERCHANTABILITY OR FITNESS FOR A PARTICULAR PURPOSE OR USE WITH RESPECT TO THE PRODUCT. McGRAW-HILL EDUCATION, ITS LICENSORS, AND THE AUTHORS MAKE NO GUARANTEE THAT YOU WILL PASS ANY CERTIFICATION EXAM WHATSOEVER BY USING THIS PRODUCT. NEITHER McGRAW-HILL EDUCATION, ANY OF ITS LICENSORS NOR THE AUTHORS WARRANT THAT THE FUNCTIONS CONTAINED IN THE PRODUCT WILL MEET YOUR REQUIREMENTS OR THAT THE OPERATION OF THE PRODUCT WILL BE UNINTERRUPTED OR ERROR FREE. YOU ASSUME THE ENTIRE RISK WITH RESPECT TO THE QUALITY AND PERFORMANCE OF THE PRODUCT.

LIMITED WARRANTY FOR DISC: To the original licensee only, McGraw-Hill Education warrants that the enclosed disc on which the Product is recorded is free from defects in materials and workmanship under normal use and service for a period of ninety (90) days from the date of purchase. In the event of a defect in the disc covered by the foregoing warranty, McGraw-Hill Education will replace the disc.

LIMITATION OF LIABILITY: NEITHER McGRAW-HILL EDUCATION, ITS LICENSORS NOR THE AUTHORS SHALL BE LIABLE FOR ANY INDIRECT, SPECIAL OR CONSEQUENTIAL DAMAGES, SUCH AS BUT NOT LIMITED TO, LOSS OF ANTICIPATED PROFITS OR BENEFITS, RESULTING FROM THE USE OR INABILITY TO USE THE PRODUCT EVEN IF ANY OF THEM HAS BEEN ADVISED OF THE POSSIBILITY OF SUCH DAMAGES. THIS LIMITATION OF LIABILITY SHALL APPLY TO ANY CLAIM OR CAUSE WHATSOEVER WHETHER SUCH CLAIM OR CAUSE ARISES IN CONTRACT, TORT, OR OTHERWISE. Some states do not allow the exclusion or limitation of indirect, special or consequential damages, so the above limitation may not apply to you.

U.S. GOVERNMENT RESTRICTED RIGHTS: Any software included in the Product is provided with restricted rights subject to subparagraphs (c), (1) and (2) of the Commercial Computer Software-Restricted Rights clause at 48 C.F.R. 52.227-19. The terms of this Agreement applicable to the use of the data in the Product are those under which the data are generally made available to the general public by McGraw-Hill Education. Except as provided herein, no reproduction, use, or disclosure rights are granted with respect to the dat included in the Product and no right to modify or create derivative works from any such data is hereby granted.

GENERAL: This License Agreement constitutes the entire agreement between the parties relating to the Product. The terms of any Purchase Order shall have no effect on the terms of this License Agreement. Failure of McGraw-Hill Education to insist at any time on strict compliance with this License Agreement shall not constitute a waiver of any rights under this License Agreement. This License Agreement shall be construed and governed in accordance with the laws of the State of New York. If any provision of this License Agreement is held to be contrary to law, that provision will be enforced to the maximum extent permissible and the remaining provisions will remain in full force and effect.